Structure and Process

Structure and Process

Readings in Introductory Sociology

Richard J. Peterson
Charlotte A. Vaughan
Cornell College

Wadsworth Publishing Company
Belmont, California
A Division of Wadsworth, Inc.

Sociology Editor: **Sheryl Fullerton**
Production Editor: **Vicki Friedberg**
Managing Designer: **MaryEllen Podgorski**
Print Buyer: **Karen Hunt**
Designer: **Emily Kissin**
Copy Editor: **Anne Draus**
Cover: **Merle Sanderson**

Printed in the United States of America
1 2 3 4 5 6 7 8 9 10—90 89 88 87 86

ISBN 0-534-05172-3

Library of Congress Cataloging-in-Publication Data
Main entry under title:

Structure and process.

Includes bibliographies.
1. Sociology—Addresses, essays, lectures.
2. Social structure—United States—Addresses, essays,
lectures, 3. Sociology—Research—Methodology—Addresses, essays,
lectures. I. Peterson, Richard J. II. Vaughan, Charlotte A.
HM24.S786 1986   301   85-9033
ISBN 0-534-05172-3

Contents

PART FOUR   Institutions and Their Interrelationships   185

PART FIVE   Social Deviance   243

Preface

This book grew out of frustration. In our several years of teaching introductory sociology, we became increasingly distressed at how difficult it was to find interesting and challenging reading materials that integrated the theoretical and research foundations of sociology. On the one hand, existing texts and readers seemed overly simple, with examples and illustrations so brief that students could not develop insight into the social world. They seemed to promote surface memorization rather than the development of useful, general understandings of social patterns and interaction processes. On the other hand, exclusive use of monographs also left something to be desired. As specific research treatments of particular problems they were useful, but they did not include the general coverage we wanted. We were looking for a single textbook that combined both breadth and depth, while integrating theoretical orientations and research methods. We couldn't find such a book, so we created our own.

Special Features

The book has five unique features:

1. An integrated combination of text material and illustrative readings
2. Emphasis on theory and research methods in every section of the book
3. Stress on social structure, interaction processes, and the relationships between them
4. Introductions that are reading guides, not summaries
5. Challenging material that is representative of the discipline

First, this book is organized as an *integrated combination text and reader*. The text chapters come from outstanding classic textbooks. The first five selections in the book, which together with an illustrative reading make up Part One, "Introduction to Social Analysis," and the first selection in each of the five following parts are drawn from these sources. These "keynote" readings, as we have called them, present an overview of a particular area of sociological concern. They serve to introduce the substantive areas, define important concepts, and show how these concepts direct attention to particular aspects of the social world. The illustrative readings that follow the keynotes both amplify important points and explore new areas. These selections tend to be considerably longer than those usually found in an introductory reader, allowing students to understand more fully the development of the author's ideas.

The book focuses on five core areas: socialization; social stratification; institutions and their interrelations; social deviance; and social change. Although we have selected these five as core concepts in sociology, the illustrative readings also explore the topics usually covered in the introductory course, including culture, work, gender roles, social movements, and industrialization.

The second unique feature of this book is its continuing emphasis on *major theoretical orientations* and *methods of social research*. Most introductory books pay little attention to the fact that sociologists are guided in their work by theoretical orientations and methods of social research. Too often these books include an early chapter on these important topics and then never mention them again. We take advantage of the fact that sociologists use theories and research methods in their work by giving examples *showing* how they do so. We systematically discuss and illustrate major theoretical orientations and research methods in every part of the book, continually bringing the student back to these important tools. (We also include a User's Guide on pages xiii–xiv, which identifies the various readings that illustrate each of the major theoretical orientations and methods of social research.)

A third important feature of this book is its explicit organization around the two broadest concepts in sociology: *structure* and *process*. We examine social structures and interactive processes in each part of the book and, whenever possible, demonstrate the reciprocal nature of these elements. For example, Joel Roache, in his article "Confessions of a Househusband," examines interaction patterns between a husband and wife. However, these social structures and interactive processes have broader implications that students may miss. The Editors' Introduction to the reading points out these implications and shows the reciprocal nature of structure and process. The introduction to Melvin Kohn's study of parental values for children helps students identify the effects of social structure on socialization processes. This concern with structure and process, and the emphasis on the interrelations between the readings, theoretical orientations, and methods of social research, provide the strands that integrate the book.

The fourth unique feature of this book is the *format of the introductions* written for each of the selections. Most introductory readers provide introductions that summarize the major findings in the articles. This book, however, provides no such summaries. Instead, the introductions raise issues, point out what to look for, and lead students to the crucial arguments. This is especially important for some of the more difficult readings: students often need help in locating the structure of the argument and following the flow of evidence. The questions provided in the introductions also can serve as study guides, because they "tip off" students to the important points in the reading, and as guides to class discussion. (With some modification, the points raised in the introductions might serve as examination questions.) Featured in the introductions are discussions of the major theoretical orientations and research

methods as they appear in the selections. It is here that students can observe clearly how these tools of social analysis are actually used.

The introductions also serve to integrate the various parts of the book. In the introduction, the central ideas of a reading often are tied to other readings in the book. Thus, although each part and each reading in a part may stand alone, the overall organization of the book is highly integrated, allowing the student to see the complex interrelations that exist in modern society.

One final feature—the book is made up of interesting materials that *challenge students* and represent the discipline of sociology. The readings come from a variety of sources: outstanding textbooks, professional journals, research monographs, and, in a couple of cases, popular media sources. You will find readable selections from the *American Sociological Review, Social Problems,* and *Society.* These readings give students the opportunity to sample this professional literature at a manageable level with the help provided by the introductions. You will also find selections from E. E. LeMasters's *Blue-Collar Aristocrats,* Gary Marx's *Protest and Prejudice,* Charles Silberman's *Criminal Violence, Criminal Justice,* and Bowles and Gintis's *Schooling in Capitalist America.* The reading level will challenge most college students but certainly not overwhelm them. During the last several years, we have very successfully used a wide sampling of these readings with our own students. Together, the keynote readings, the illustrative selections, and the integrative introductions, make up the unique core-text/reader approach.

Alternate Ways to Use the Readings

Obviously, many combinations of parts and of individual readings are pedagogically possible. In whatever way they are put together, the book's thrust toward theoretical orientations and methods of social research is not lost, since these topics appear regularly in the introductions to both keynote and illustrative readings.

Instructors can easily tailor the readings to their own tastes. For example, if an instructor wants to devote a section of the course to the family, he or she can pull together Kohn's "Social Class and Parental Values," LeMasters's "Battle of the Sexes," Roache's "Confessions of a Househusband," and Kanter's "Jobs and Families." A section on education can be constructed from Lever's "Sex Differences in the Complexity of Children's Play and Games," Gracey's "Learning the Student Role: Kindergarten as Academic Boot Camp," and Bowles and Gintis's "Beyond the Educational Frontier." Another arrangement of some of these same readings could produce a section on work, consisting of the selections by Kohn, Kanter, Bowles and Gintis, and adding Murray's "The Abolition of *El Cortito*, the Short-Handled Hoe."

A section on gender roles could be created by drawing on the Roache article about househusbands, the introduction to which includes some data about the current position of women in society. It could include LeMasters' "Battle of the Sexes," Lever's study of play and games characteristic of boys and of girls, and Freeman's study of the origins of the contemporary women's movement. Although we include Pearce's article on race (with an introduction including some data on the current situation of blacks) in Part Three, "Social Stratification," it could be put with Freman's material on the origins of the Civil Rights movement, Murray's study of *el cortito*, Wiley's "The Ethnic Mobility Trap and Stratification Theory," and Marx's "Religion: Opiate or Inspiration of Civil Rights Militancy?" in a section on race and ethnicity.

In one last example, Smelser's "The Processes of Social Change," Marx's "Religion: Opiate or Inspiration of Civil Rights Militancy?," Murray's "The Abolition of *El Cortito*, the Short-Handled Hoe," and Freeman's "On the Origins of Social Movements" could be combined to form a section on social movements. We could construct other examples (culture, industrialization, and so on), but we'll leave them up to the creativity of individual instructors.

If more illustrative readings are wanted for any particular part of the book, an instructor can find appropriate selections from other parts. For example, Silberman's "Poverty and Crime," in Part Five on social deviance, also is applicable to Parts Two, Three, and Four on socialization, social stratification, and institutions and their interrelations. The User's Guide that follows the Preface includes a convenient table cross-classifying the readings in each part with the other parts to which they may pertain.

Within Part One entitled "Introduction to Social Analysis," an instructor may want to start with the sections on "The Sociological Perspective," "Major Theoretical Orientations," and "Basic Concepts" (along with the LeMasters illustrative reading), waiting to introduce the full complexities of Rose's reading on "Methods of Sociological Study" until later in the course. An instructor may wish to take up the part on social change earlier in the course, using readings in other parts to illustrate it.

To help in finding the specific readings that illustrate the different theoretical orientations and the various methods of social research, we have provided two summary lists in the User's Guide (see pp. xii–xiv), one for each of these aspects. They accompany the cross-reference table. Together these should make the book easier to use—for the instructor in course planning and for the student in coming to grips with concrete examples of works that analyze the structure and process of human social behavior.

Ways to Use This Book

This book may be used in several combinations with other materials, or it may stand alone as the sole source of reading material in an introductory sociology course. When we assembled it, we had in mind combining it with a number of complete monographs, for example, Erikson's *Everything in Its Path* and Rubin's *Women of a Certain Age*. In this way, the book becomes the backbone of the course, laying out the important groundwork of the discipline and illustrating it with well-integrated readings. The two or three monographs can then supplement it carrying the students beyond this basic framework into more complex social analysis and giving them a more complete understanding of the workings of society.

However, not everyone teaches with monographs. For those who do not, this book can still serve a useful and important function. First, the book has been designed so that it can stand alone. All of the important areas of sociology are covered here and integrated in a way seldom found in *any* sociology text. The readings are thought- (and discussion-) provoking and are of sufficient length to cover several issues and points in each reading.

For those who have already found a textbook that serves their needs, this book is still an important addition to course materials. Because of the extended discussions of theoretical orientations and research methods and the efforts to integrate all of the material, this book complements most standard texts. By reinforcing the material in the text through the extensive introductions and keynote readings, and by taking the text material into specific settings through the use of the illustrative readings, this book takes the students beyond the usual "survey" course.

Some Final Considerations

Two special points must be made about the selections included in the book. First, we have concentrated on American society. Although strong arguments can be made for and against this concentration, we have opted for American pieces because we feel that students in introductory sociology often demonstrate a distressing lack of information about their own society, a deficiency that needs to be rectified. We see the need for comparative material but also realize that including enough of this material to represent it properly would make this book unmanageably long.

Second, we have made no effort to correct the "inappropriate" language used in some of the older readings. Although the jury is still out on the proper English usage of *man, he, his,* and so on, our own ideological position is that such words should not be used in the generic sense.

Man refers to one sex; *woman* to the other. However, if sexist language appears in a reading in its original, it appears in this book.

Acknowledgements

As with all works of extended length or effort, this book is not the result of the isolated labors of the two people named on the cover. We must thank several others for their contributions to the final product. First among these is Curt Peoples, who, during his tenure at Wadsworth, first signed us to this project and gave us our initial motivation. Sheryl Fullerton, our most recent Wadsworth editor, is responsible for seeing our ideas take concrete form. She managed to rescue a project that had been lost in the interstices of the publishing business. We are most grateful for and relieved to have had her expert guidance. Vicki Friedberg, our able production editor, has been a real joy to work with. Her efforts, too, have made this book a reality. Vicki is a master at saying "I want it yesterday!" We all need those people around. We would also like to thank the following reviewers: Janet Grigsby, Davidson College; Paul Kingston, University of Virginia; Reece McGee, Purdue University; Elizabeth Monk-Turner, University of Oklahoma; David Orenstein, Wright State University; Harold Osborne, Baylor University; Brian Pendleton, University of Akron; Joseph Sheley, Tulane University; Stephen Stack, Pennsylvania State University; Robert Stauffer, Kalamazoo College; Dennis Teitge, Valparaiso University; Thomas Van Valey, Western Michigan University; and Kristen Wenzel, College of New Rochelle. We did not always agree with them, but they did make us go back and think about what we had done.

Chris Carlson, our colleague, deserves special thanks. He steered us to some very worthwhile selections included in this book, and he critically read much of what we wrote. But most important, Chris was a constant source of moral support. We are lucky to have such a colleague.

User's Guide

I. Readings illustrating the use of basic theoretical orientations

A. Functional theoretical orientation

LeMasters, *Battle of the Sexes* (Part One, "Introduction to Social Analysis")

Mack and Bradford, *Social Organization and Survival* (Part Four, "Institutions and Their Interrelationships")

Marx, *Religion: Opiate or Inspiration of Civil Rights Militancy?* (Part Four, "Institutions and Their Interrelationships")

McGee, *Deviance as Variance from Norms* (Part Five, "Social Deviance")

Silberman, *Poverty and Crime* (Part Five, "Social Deviance")

Cottrell, *Death by Dieselization* (Part Six, "Social Change")

B. Conflict theoretical orientation

Gracey, *Learning the Student Role: Kindergarten as Academic Boot Camp* (Part Two, "Socialization")

Pearce, *Gatekeepers and Homeseekers* (Part Three, "Social Stratification")

Roache, *Confessions of a Househusband* (Part Three, "Social Stratification")

Murray, *The Abolition of* El Cortito, *the Short-Handled Hoe* (Part Three, "Social Stratification")

Dreier, *The Position of the Press in the U.S. Power Structure* (Part Four, "Institutions and Their Interrelationships")

Bowles and Gintis, *Beyond the Educational Frontier* (Part Four, "Institutions and Their Interrelationships)

Chambliss, *The Saints and the Roughnecks* (Part Five, "Social Deviance")

Cottrell, *Death by Dieselization* (Part Six, "Social Change")

C. Symbolic interactionist theoretical orientation

LeMasters, *Battle of the Sexes* (Part One, "Introduction to Social Analysis")

Davis, *Socialization* (Part Two, "Socialization")

Gracey, *Learning the Student Role: Kindergarten as Academic Boot Camp* (Part Two, "Socialization")

McGee, *Deviance as Variance from Norms* (Part Five, "Social Deviance")

Chambliss, *The Saints and the Roughnecks* (Part Five, "Social Deviance")

Silberman, *Poverty and Crime* (Part Five, "Social Deviance")

II. Readings illustrating the use of social research methods

A. Use of questionnaires and interviews

Lever, *Sex Differences in the Complexity of Children's Play and Games* (Part Two, "Socialization")

Kohn, *Social Class and Parental Values* (Part Three, "Social Stratification")

Murray, *The Abolition of* El Cortito, *the Short-Handled Hoe* (Part Three, "Social Stratification")

Marx, *Religion: Opiate or Inspiration of Civil Rights Militancy?* (Part Four, "Institutions and Their Interrelationships")

Dreier, *The Position of the Press in the U.S. Power Structure* (Part Four, "Institutions and Their Interrelationships")

Freeman, *On the Origins of Social Movements* (Part Six, "Social Change")

B. Use of observation

1. Participant observation

    LeMasters, *Battle of the Sexes* (Part One, "Introduction to Social Analysis")

    Roache, *Confessions of a Househusband* (Part Three, "Social Stratification")

    Freeman, *On the Origins of Social Movements* (Part Six, "Social Change")

2. Nonparticipant observation

    Lever, *Sex Differences in the Complexity of Children's Play and Games* (Part Two, "Socialization")

    Gracey, *Learning the Student Role: Kindergarten as Academic Boot Camp* (Part Two, "Socialization")

C. Use of available data

Lever, *Sex Differences in the Complexity of Children's Play and Games* (Part Two, "Socialization")

Murray, *The Abolition of* El Cortito, *the Short-Handled Hoe* (Part Three, "Social Stratification")

Dreier, *The Position of the Press in the U.S. Power Structure* (Part Four, "Institutions and Their Interrelationships")

Bowles and Gintis, *Beyond the Educational Frontier* (Part Four, "Institutions and Their Interrelationships")

Smelser, *Processes of Social Change* (Part Six, "Social Change")

Cottrell, *Death by Dieselization* (Part Six, "Social Change")

Freeman, *On the Origins of Social Movements* (Part Six, "Social Change")

D. Use of field experiment

Pearce, *Gatekeepers and Homeseekers* (Part Three, "Social Stratification")

Cross-Reference Table of Readings and Core Concepts

Readings by Number and Author	Social Analysis	Socialization	Social Stratification	Institutions	Social Deviance	Social Change
PART ONE						
Introduction to Social Analysis						
1. Bates	□					■
2. Eitzen	□		■			
3. Poloma	□					
4. Rose	□					
5. Inkeles	□	■	■	■	■	
6. LeMasters	□	■	■			■
PART TWO						
Socialization						
7. Davis	■	□				
8. Lever	■	□	■	■		
9. Gracey	■	□		■		
PART THREE						
Social Stratification: Class, Race, and Gender						
10. Berger and Berger	■		□			
11. Kohn	■	■	□	■		
12. Murray	■		□	■		■
13. Pearce	■		□			■
14. Roache	■	■	□	■		■
15. Wiley	■		□			

Note: This cross-reference table shows at a glance the core concepts covered in each reading. Open squares (□) identify those readings in the left-hand column whose *main* topic corresponds to the core concept indicated. The solid squares (■) identify those readings from other parts of the book that also touch on the core concepts indicated.

Cross-Reference Table of Readings and Core Concepts

Readings by Number and Author	Social Analysis	Socialization	Social Stratification	Institutions	Social Deviance	Social Change
PART FOUR						
Institutions and Their Interrelationships						
16. Mack and Bradford	■	■		□		
17. Marx	■		■	□	■	■
18. Dreier	■		■	□		
19. Kanter	■	■	■	□		■
20. Bowles and Gintis	■	■	■	□		■
PART FIVE						
Social Deviance						
21. McGee	■		■		□	
22. Chambliss	■		■		□	
23. Silberman	■	■	■	■	□	
PART SIX						
Social Change						
24. Smelser	■		■	■	■	□
25. Cottrell	■			■		□
26. Freeman	■		■		■	□

PART ONE

Introduction to Social Analysis

THE SOCIOLOGICAL
PERSPECTIVE

Throughout your life you will hear and probably use many different explanations for the ways people behave, or how much money they have, or what is happening to the divorce rate, or the ways people respond to a tragedy or a crisis. One of the things all of us as human beings do is try to understand the world around us and our places in that world. As the first reading indicates, we draw on many areas of human understanding (and sometimes misunderstanding) to explain these matters. For instance, the differences we observe in people's behavior may be explained by differences in individual personalities. The hard-working office employee is a "diligent" person while the not so hard-working person is said to be "unmotivated" or "lazy." Sometimes to explain these differences we fall back on old stereotypes: The diligent male worker is diligent because he is a man, while the diligent female worker is just trying to be like a man. Spiritual or moral composition may also be used to account for certain behaviors: The "spiritually strong" can handle tragedy better than the "weak" can. We cite economic conditions to explain rising or falling marriage or divorce rates or crime rates or suicide rates. We use all of these kinds of explanations in an attempt to understand the world we live in.

The first reading, "The Sociological View of Human Behavior," presents one more approach to explaining such issues. The reading does not present specific answers but rather begins to build a perspective, a point of view, that will allow you to view the world through the unique and characteristic lens of sociology. This lens directs your attention to social behavior, social organization, and social change. As you read the article, note the explanations of these three phrases and how they combine to form the basis for the generalizing science of sociology. To reach a fuller understanding of this perspective, note how it deals with the unique or individual characteristics of those engaged in *social* behavior. To understand *patterns* of interdependent behavior, why is it necessary to treat individual characteristics in this way?

After reading the first selection you may be tempted to say, "I already use this perspective to understand the questions raised above." You are probably right. When we say that people behave the way they do because of the environment in which they live, we are practicing an unsophisticated form of sociological analysis. When we attribute juvenile delinquent behavior to a "broken home," we are doing the same. But such amateur sociologizing is quite different from the perspective and techniques that will be laid out in the remainder of this book. The sociology you will learn here is much more systematic and detached than that practiced by most people. For instance, the nonsociologist may arrive at explanations based on inaccurate or selective observations, missing certain things or looking only for certain things. The amateur may overgeneralize or use illogical reasoning. For example, a man may read about two delinquents who did not come from broken homes and conclude that broken homes have nothing to do with becoming a delinquent. Having decided that, the man may fall into yet another trap: He stops looking at the relationship between delinquency and broken homes. Such pitfalls cause errors in explanation—and this is just a partial list of the various problems we may run into. The systematic and objective sociology you will see in the remainder of this book will show how professional sociologists try to avoid these problems.

Look at the title of this book again; it alerts you to the two sides of sociology Bates introduces, *Structure and Process*. Bates states that sociology is concerned with "how human social behavior is organized and how this organization changes over time." "How human social behavior is organized" is a long way of saying "structure." The structure of anything—an automobile, an organization, an English sentence, or a human society—is the regularity or pattern of the various parts. The parts are arranged together in some orderly way. When we talk about the structure of an automobile, we refer to the regularities that appear across many automobiles. The structure of organizations directs our attention to (usually) hierarchical authority, written rules, and job specialization. The structure of an English sentence is usually subject-verb-object, a pattern that is not typical in some other languages. The structure of social behavior refers to regularities that occur across social behavior, as Bates shows in his classroom example. Of course, regularities occur at all levels of social behavior, from two-person interactions to interrelationships among several societies.

But all of this presents a relatively stable picture of social behavior, since the patterns are seen as regular and predictable. The dynamic side of social behavior is found in the other of the pair of words in the title of this book: *process*. When Bates says, "how this organization changes over time," he is referring to the process side of sociology. When he speaks of social change, he is talking about process. However, there is more to the notion of process than what is usually caught up in the concept of social change. Process also includes the dynamic quality of human social behavior, in which people interact together in an ongoing series of mutual activities. You act, I respond, you respond to me, and on it goes—we *inter*act. Although we can observe patterned regularities in social behavior, we can also see that social behavior is in a dynamic state of "becoming." Thus sociology is concerned with *both* structure *and* process.

One word of warning! As Bates points out, the key words *social behavior, social organization,* and *social change* may appear deceptively simple. This reading only begins to build the total sociological perspective. The other sections of Part One—dealing with theoretical orientations, methods of social research, and basic concepts—will furnish more foundation for this perspective. The remaining parts of the book fill out the perspective, allowing you to reexamine some of your explanations for the way people behave, or how much money they have, or what is happening to the divorce rate, or the ways different people respond to a tragedy or a crisis.

1
The Sociological View of Human Behavior

Alan P. Bates

MODELS FOR UNDERSTANDING BEHAVIOR

The term "model" may be applied to fairly inclusive pictures we acquire of what the world is like and what orientations toward it are appropriate. In the normal course of events each of us acquires a number of models of the experi-

Reprinted from *The Sociological Enterprise* by Alan P. Bates. Copyright © 1967 by Houghton Mifflin Company. Used with permission of the publisher.

enced world. For any one of us, society is the main source of these world views. We do not invent them ourselves, although each individual version differs slightly from any other. They come to us little by little, from our parents, the activities of childhood play groups, the adult lives going on around us as we grow up, from books, television, school, and many other places. Our own physical and psychological characteristics interact with the incoming models as the years go by. Slowly the pictures of what the world is (and ought to be) take form in our developing minds.

From the human point of view the world is infinitely various and many models of what it is like are possible. The process of acquiring new points of view about experience need not end at any particular point in an individual's life cycle. It is possible at any age to acquire a new way of looking at familiar things and hence to discover, as it were, a new world. Perhaps part of what we mean by continued growth in adult life is the ability to acquire new perspectives.

The sociological model of human behavior is not inherently more difficult to grasp than are others, yet in practice problems are often encountered. This is so primarily because more familiar perspectives interfere. Everyone has extensive informal and sometimes formal training in several of these more familiar perspectives. For example, nearly everyone has a good deal of general knowledge these days about the structure and functioning of the human body and how physiological factors may influence behavior. Each of us uses a biological model to help us understand some of our experience.

We are equally accustomed to thinking about behavior in psychological terms. Words like "mind," "personality," and "motive" are signposts that direct us toward the individual's psychological organization as a source of conduct. "My friend behaves that way because he has an introverted personality," we say, and curiosity as to what lies back of the friend's actions is satisfied. Psychological models of behavior are exceedingly popular today. Moral perspectives on experience are just as well known. Here, behavior is perceived and related to by comparing it to standards of right and wrong, good and evil. "He is a good man," one says, or "You had no right to do that." When one talks this way he expects to be understood even if not always agreed with.

Sometimes deliberately, sometimes quite unthinkingly, people use one or another of such models to help them come to terms with virtually every experience in life. Through them each person can draw on the accumulated knowledge and wisdom of the human species. In their broadest forms each perspective is available to all, even though each is also the subject of highly specialized study. One need not be a professional psychologist to think about life in essentially psychological terms.

But people do not often think about experience in sociological terms. Sociology came late in the intellectual history of mankind and its specialized approach to understanding behavior has not yet become common knowledge, even among the educated. One does not grow up absorbing its essential point of view as one does with older models. As a consequence, when a person first meets sociology, as in an introductory course, the tendency is to fit the contents of the field into nonsociological perspectives already known. This is not done deliberately, of course, but the result is that sociology's most important contribution to understanding is lost.

To the social aspects of human experience sociology brings a unique and valid perspective unlike any other. It is not a better perspective than those provided by alternative models; it is different. Each of the major models which have evolved over time address themselves to some, but never all of the facets of that complex creature, man. Each is especially appropriate in some situations, but not in all circumstances. Both these statements are true of sociology too. Each perspective looks at the human scene and abstracts from the whole those features to which it is particularly sensitive. No model is sensitive to all the ways in which human behavior may be perceived as significant and orderly. Sociology, in taking its place alongside older perspectives, adds a new dimension to man's understanding of man without supplanting older orientations. . .

SOCIOLOGY'S PERSPECTIVE

Sociology overlaps its sister fields in many ways, but, like each of them, it has a distinctive orientation toward its subject matter. Most broadly and fundamentally, it is concerned with how human social behavior is organized and how this organization changes over time. Just now these words may convey little meaning, or may have a deceptive simplicity, but they state the case for what is unique in the point of view of sociology. The key words in this statement are "social behavior," "organization," and "change."

Social Behavior

As a specialist, the sociologist is not interested in all behavior which affects and is affected by other people, only in that which is interpersonally relevant. Social behavior, a very inclusive notion, refers to all behavior meeting this criterion. Quite a few specialists are interested in social behavior, so we must push further in order to grasp the sociologist's particular concern. We come close to the heart of the matter by stating that the sociologist is chiefly interested in being able to make *general* statements about social behavior—that under such-and-such circumstances a given kind of behavior is likely to occur. Inkeles puts it well in saying that the primary concern of the sociologist is "in the study of those aspects of social life which are present in all social forms."[1]

Such a statement means that the sociologist is interested in such things as the organization of American cities, the way in which power is distributed in groups, the relationship between masculine and feminine roles, the factors which produce conforming and deviating behavior, the ways in which change is induced or resisted (not to mention many other problems, of course). By the same token he is not, as a specialist, concerned with the Boston Tea Party, the Wagner Labor Relations Act, the family life of the American president, a quarrel between two young lovers of his acquaintance, or the personality of his mother-in-law.

We must be as clear as possible about this. In its purest form the sociological frame of reference does not take into account the idiosyncrasies of single persons or of separate historical occurrences. Or, looking at an individual case from this perspective, it will be seen as a single instance of a more general class of similar instances, deviating to a greater or lesser extent from the characteristics of the class. In other words, sociology is or aspires to be a generalizing science. In this it is like many other sciences. Human physiology is not the physiology of a single organism but of a class of organisms, and the characteristics of the class do not precisely describe all the attributes of a single case. As a science psychology is not concerned with the behavior of one particular human, but with that of classes of humans *seen as individuals*. The sociologist also is interested in the behavior of people, but only that behavior which links people together, at a level at which he can generalize about classes of such behavior.

Here is an example of a sociological generalization: "In American cities there is an inverse relation between the incidence of reported crime and distance from the center of the city." Note that there is no reference to any particular city, no mention of which persons actually commit crimes, or what kinds of personalities they have, only a statement of the relation between a condition and a class of social behavior. Here is another. "The higher the rank of a person within a group, the more nearly his activities conform to the norms of the group."[2] Again, no particular group is mentioned, the nature of the norms is not specified, and the many differences among group members are ignored.

When one first encounters the sociological perspective and begins to grasp its nature, an initial reaction may be that it omits one of the most important things about human behavior: that which is unique in each occurrence and in each person. Actually, the sociologist does not mean to belittle in any way such elements in human experience. In his personal life he is as sensitive to them as is anyone else. He does argue that there is a level of human behavioral organization, the social level, which is of enormous importance, and about which it is possible to develop a generalizing science which deliberately ignores the individual case in order to be able to discover how human behavior is socially organized.

Social Organization

The sociologist is interested in organized social behavior. Put very generally, this means that behavior which links together individuals or groups of individuals is not random or haphazard. It has the properties of orderliness, pattern, repetitiveness, hence predictability. Here is a college classroom. During a particular semester at nine o'clock each morning, Monday through Friday, the room is filled with college students. Each goes without hesitation to a certain chair. A minute or two later a professor enters, stands at the front of the classroom, facing the students, and begins to talk. Most of the students write in notebooks. A few whisper covertly to one another. At the end of fifty minutes a bell rings, the professor ends his comments, the students close their notebooks, and all leave the room. We have here an identification and short description of an instance of *social* organization even though it does not use the technical language of sociology. It is clear that the behavior of these persons with respect to each other is patterned. This is true even though there are minor variations in the specific sequence of actions from one class meeting to the next. Our example includes no information about the psychological characteristics of students or teacher; it does not even mention the nature of the course, or whether it is advanced or elementary. We recognize a single specimen of a large class of social situations having a familiar kind of social organization which, by the way, significantly channels a good deal of human activity.

It is the *pattern of interdependent behavior* which interests the sociologist. This is the kind of unit he studies, not the individuals who participate in the pattern. He knows perfectly well that there are important differences between the class members and that from the viewpoint of another model, say, the psychological, these differences would be of first importance. But not for the sociologist. What is crucial for him is that all these persons, *despite their differences*, behave with respect to each other in an orderly, predictable fashion. Furthermore, he is not at all surprised to find that the patterned behavior of the people in this class closely resembles that of innumerable other classes, each with its own set of "unique" personalities and other special characteristics. Without knowing anything of the attributes of individuals in a given class he can know a good deal about how people will behave in this category of situations precisely because such settings are socially organized.

True, he can't say a great deal about the psychological organization of individual students from knowledge of this kind of social organization. But by the same token, we cannot learn much about the social structure of college classrooms from the summated personality characteristics of college students. These are simply different levels of behavioral organization, interdependent to be sure, but not the same.

The order the sociologist sees in the social life of men is not perfect. Evidence of organization is sought in the pattern and predictability of actual behavior, but it is always true that some of the behavior in every situation does not fit the pattern and conform to the prediction. Similarly, if organization is described in cultural terms, it will be found that there is seldom, perhaps never complete agreement among all the actors on what behavior is called for in a particular real-life drama. There may even be radical disagreement on the cultural prescriptions. On the other hand, the fact that a group exists at all testifies that it is to some degree socially organized. Social organization is a "more or less" matter, and the sociologist is interested in differences in the degree of organization and the consequences for understanding behavior.

Social Change

The general statement about the sociological outlook made a few pages back indicated that this orientation is concerned not only with stability in social life but also with change. Consider the college classroom illustration again. It is possible to describe this situation as though there were no time dimension, and the sociologist often does this when he is primarily concerned with revealing the "structural" characteristics of a social situation. So we say that the classroom is organized so that the students sit in orderly rows facing the front of the room, each student occupying a particular spot in the arrangement. The instructor faces them, standing at the front. Interaction flows between the students and the instructor for the most part, with little student–student communication; students show more deference to the teacher than vice versa; and so on.

Such a description has a static quality. The fact is that what we see as social organization only becomes manifest with the passage of time, as was better suggested in our first reference to the classroom. First this event takes place, then that. We say there is organization and structure because the *sequence* of events is repetitive and predictable. The next session of the class will correspond closely to this one. Paradoxically, one form of change is a kind of absence of change. Since the pattern of events repeats itself over and over, we can observe change only as we watch the unfolding of a single manifestation of a pattern which itself does not alter.

A more familiar notion of change as applied to social organization involves some alteration in the patterned character of social behavior. The *pattern* is different, and presumably will not return to its former state. In a strict sense even very stable social organizations always undergo at least minor alterations through time. Our hypothetical college class will not have quite the same social organization ten weeks after its first session even though the main features of the structure appear to be the same. Similarly, on a larger scale, college classes in general are conducted somewhat differently today than their "sociological ancestors" were two or three generations ago.

Sociologists are interested in both cross-sectional, structural approaches to social phenomena and in time-dimensional, change approaches. Neither is inherently more important than the other. Both present fundamental problems to the discipline. The stability of social life and the inevitable accompanying change are taken for granted by laymen, but to sociologists they are a Janus-faced mystery that forever challenges.

Notes

1. A. Inkeles, *What Is Sociology?* Foundations of Modern Sociology Series. Englewood Cliffs, N.J.: Prentice-Hall, 1964, p. 16.

2. G. C. Homans, *The Human Group.* New York: Harcourt, Brace, 1950, p. 141. This is Homans' famous "rank-conformity" hypothesis, which stimulated much research and discussion subsequent to its publication.

MAJOR THEORETICAL ORIENTATIONS

Bates tells us that the term *model* refers to "fairly inclusive pictures we acquire of what the world is like and what orientations toward it are appropriate." He mentions biological and psychological models. Then he goes on to present the sociological model, highlighting patterns of social organization and the sequences of events that produce or change them. The sociological perspective leads us to examine the social world, but that world has many, many features. Which of the many features in the social world should we pay attention to? Which ones can we let fade into the background as relatively unimportant?

Within the sociological perspective are several models of the social world. These models represent general theoretical orientations operating to help us make sense out of the bewildering mass of social organization we see. Each orientation identifies the features of social organization that are crucial from its point of view. In explaining how perspectives work, Bates says, "Each perspective looks at the human scene and abstracts from the whole those features to which it is particularly sensitive." Just as the sociological perspective abstracts social organization from the complete human scene, so the theoretical orientations *within* sociology abstract certain features of social organization as the ones to which they are sensitive. Of the several theoretical orientations in sociology today, we will consider the three major ones: functional theory, conflict theory, and symbolic interactionism. The first two focus on structure, while the third focuses on process.

The functional model highlights the order and stability in society. It sees society as a *system,* a set of interrelated parts in which each part affects and is affected by at least one other part. Functional theorists concentrate on stable patterns of interrelated parts, often examining exactly how the parts are related to each other and what part they play in the whole. In this orientation a *function* is a consequence that one part has for another part or for the entire pattern in which it is embedded. For example, the functions of the family are often identfied as nurturing children and teaching them how to behave as "good members" of the society: keeping family members fed, clothed, and ready to participate in the society; providing emotional satisfaction and support; and so on.

The functions of a part may be *manifest* (intended or recognized and understood) or *latent* (unintended or not recognized and understood). They may be *positive* (leading to the smooth operation of the system) or *negative* (leading to problems in the operation of the system). Note that the second set of distinctions is not that of good or bad, which are moral judgments. It simply refers to how the system is operating—smoothly or roughly—whether you approve of the system or not. In a classic example of functional analysis, Robert Merton shows that old-time political bosses in cities helped illegitimate *and* legitimate business people to get special favors that helped their businesses prosper and provided poor newcomers to the city with jobs and desperately needed help in times of crisis. In identifying the latent positive functions of political bosses, Merton is showing how the system operates, not whether he approves or disapproves of the system. Students understand well the positive and negative manifest functions of grades (rewarding performance, producing anxiety), along with the positive and negative latent functions (providing generalized feelings of self-worth, leading to cheating), no matter how they personally feel about grading. (Notice that latent functions may become manifest. The "latent" functions of grading are fairly well recognized and understood now.)

The conflict model also focuses on the organization of society, but it highlights a quite different feature. To conflict theorists, power relations of dominance and subordination are the crucial features of social organization. They show that some people are able to claim more than "their share" of power and resources and to maintain this favored position. For example, conflict theorists point out that in 1983 the richest 5 percent of the population of the United States held just over one-half of the country's total wealth, while the top 1 percent held about one-third of this wealth. Conflict theorists demonstrate the interconnections between great wealth, control of economic resources, and control of political decision making in favor of the wishes of those who control the wealth. Conflict theorists show that structures of dominance greatly benefit the few at the expense of the many. In this model stability may be precarious, since conflict over scarce resources is the basic fact of life.

In the selection that follows, Eitzen lays out the basic ideas in the functional and conflict models, both of which are concerned with the structure of society. He then compares the assumptions about society on which these models rest. In a note Eitzen says that the order or functional model has dominated American sociology since the 1930s. In the eleven years since the Eitzen piece was published however, the situation has changed dramatically. Among theorists concerned with societal structure, the conflict model has become more and more accepted as an extremely fruitful way in which to conceptualize society. (After the Eitzen article, we will take up the third major theoretical orientation in sociology, shifting to a much different level of analysis.)

2
Social Systems: Order and Conflict

D. Stanley Eitzen

The analyst of society begins with a mental picture of its structure. For the scientist, this image (or model) influences what he looks for, what he sees, and how he explains the phenomena that occur within the society.

Among the characteristics of societies is one—the existence of segmentation—that is the basis for the two prevailing models of society. Every society is composed of parts. This differentiation may result from differences in age, race, sex, physical prowess, wisdom. family background, wealth, organizational membership, economic specialty, or any other characteristic considered to be salient by the members. The fundamental question concerning differentiation is this: what is the basic relationship among the parts of society? The two contradictory answers to this question provide the rationale for the two models of society—order and conflict.

Reprinted from *Social Structure and Social Problems in America* by D. Stanley Eitzen. Copyright 1974 by Allyn and Bacon, Inc. Used with permission of the publisher. Footnotes have been renumbered.

One answer is that the parts of society are in harmony. They cooperate because of similar or complementary interests and because they need each other to accomplish those things beneficial to all (e.g., production and distribution of goods and services, protection). Another answer is that the subunits of society are basically in competition with each other. This view is based on the assumption that the things men desire most (wealth, power, autonomy, resources, high status) are always in short supply; hence competition and conflict are ubiquitous social phenomena.

THE ORDER MODEL

The order model[1] attributes to societies the characteristics of cohesion, consensus, cooperation, reciprocity, stability, and persistence. Societies are viewed as social systems, composed of parts that are linked together into a boundary-maintaining whole. The parts of the system are basically in harmony with each other. The high degree of cooperation (and societal integration) is accomplished because there is a high degree of consensus on societal goals and on cultural values. Moreover, the different parts of the system are assumed to need each other because of complementary interests. Because the primary social process is cooperation and the system is highly integrated, all social change is gradual, adjustive, and reforming. Societies are therefore basically stable units.

For order theorists, the central issue is: What is the nature of the social bond? What holds the group together in a boundary-maintaining whole? This was the focus of one of the most important figures in sociology, Emile Durkheim, the French social theorist of the early 1900s. The various forms of integration were used by Durkheim to explain differences in suicide rates, social change, and the universality of religion.[2]

One way to focus on integration is to determine the manifest and latent consequences of social structures, norms, and social activities. Do these consequences contribute to the integration (cohesion) of the social system? Durkheim, for example, noted that the punishment of crime has the manifest (intended) consequences of punishing and deterring the criminal. The latent consequence of punishment, however, is the societal reaffirmation of what is to be considered moral. The society is thereby integrated through belief in the same rules.[3]

Taking Durkheim's lead, sociologists of the order persuasion have made many penetrating and insightful analyses of various aspects of society. By focusing on *all* the consequences of social structures and activities—intended and unintended, as well as negative (malintegrative)—we can see behind the facades and thereby understand more fully such disparate social arrangements and activities as ceremonials (from rain dances to sporting events), social stratification, fashion, propaganda, and even political machines.[4]

THE CONFLICT MODEL

The assumptions of the conflict model are opposite from those of the order model. The basic form of interaction is not cooperation but rather competition which often leads to conflict. Because the individuals and groups of society compete for advantage, the degree of social integration is minimal and tenuous. Social change results from the conflict among competing groups and therefore tends to be drastic and revolutionary. The ubiquitousness of conflict results from the dissimilar goals and interests of social groups. It is, moreover, a result of social organization itself.

The most famous conflict theorist was Karl Marx, who, after examining history, theorized that there exists in every society (except, Marx believed, in the last historical stage of communism) a dynamic tension between two groups—those who own the means of production and those who work for the owners. The powerful will use and abuse the powerless, thereby "sowing the seeds" of their own destruction. The destruction of the elite is accomplished when the dominated unite and overthrow the dominants.

Ralf Dahrendorf, a contemporary conflict theorist, has also viewed conflict as a ubiquitous phenomenon, not because of economic factors as Marx believed, but because of other aspects of social organization. Organization means, among other things, that power will be distributed unequally. The population will therefore be divided into the "haves" and the "have-nots" with respect to power, Since organization also means constraint, there will be a situation in all societies where the constraints are determined by the powerful, thereby further ensuring that the "have-nots" will be in conflict with the "haves." Thus, the important insight that conflict is endemic to social organization.[5]

One other emphasis of conflict theorists is that the unity present in society is superficial because it results not from consensus but coercion. The powerful, it is asserted, use force and fraud to keep society running smoothly, with benefits mostly accruing to those in power.

The basic duality of social life can be seen by summarizing the opposite ways in which order and conflict theorists view the nature of society. If asked, "What is the fundamental relationship among the parts of society?" the answers of order and conflict theorists would disagree.

Table 1

The Duality of Social Life: The Assumptions of the Order
and Conflict Models of Society

	Order Model	Conflict Model
Question	What is the fundamental relationship among the parts of society?	
Answer	Harmony and cooperation.	Competition and conflict.
Why	The parts have complementary interests. Basic consensus on societal norms and values.	The things people want are always in short supply. Basic dissensus on societal norms and values.
Degree of integration	Highly integrated.	Loosely integrated. Whatever integration is achieved is the result of force and fraud.
Type of social change	Gradual, adjustive, and reforming.	Abrupt and revolutionary.
Degree of stability	Stable.	Unstable.

This disagreement leads to and is based upon a number of related assumptions about society. These are summarized in Table 1.

One interesting but puzzling aspect of Table 1 is that these two models are held by different scientific observers *of the same phenomenon.* How can such different assumptions be derived by experts of society? The answer is that both models are correct. Each focuses on reality—but only part of that reality. Scientists have tended to accept one or the other of these models, thereby focusing on only part of social reality for at least two reasons: (1) one model or the other was in vogue at the time of the scientist's intellectual development;[6] or (2) one model or the other made the most sense for the analysis of the particular problems of interest—e.g., the interest of Emile Durkheim, who devoted his intellectual energies to determining what holds society together, or the fundamental concern of

Karl Marx, who explored the causes of revolutionary social change.

Notes

1. This model is most often referred to in sociology as the functional or structural-functional model. It is the basis for the analysis of American society by Robin M. Williams, Jr. Robin M. Williams, Jr., *American Society: A Sociological Interpretation,* Third Edition (New York: Alfred A. Knopf, 1970).

2. Emile Durkheim, *Suicide,* John A. Spaulding and George Simpson (trans.), (New York: The Free Press, 1951) originally published in 1897; Emile Durkheim, *The Division of Labor in Society,* George Simpson (trans.), (New York: The Free Press, 1933), first published in 1893; and Emile Durkheim, *The Elementary Forms of Religious Life,* Joseph Ward Swain (trans.), (New

York: Collier Books, 1961), first published in 1912.

3. Emile Durkheim, *The Rules of the Sociological Method,* (Eighth Edition), (Glencoe: The Free Press, 1938), pp. 64-75.

4. See Robert K. Merton's *Social Theory and Social Structure* for an excellent discussion of sociological research from the order (functionalist) perspective. Robert K. Merton, *Social Theory and Social Structure,* (Second Edition), (Glencoe: The Free Press, 1957), pp.19-84.

5. This is a very superficial account of a com-plex process that has been fully described by Ralf Dahrendorf. Ralf Dahrendorf, *Class and Class Conflict in Industrial Society* (Stanford, Calif.: Stanford University Press, 1959).

6. Order theorists have dominated American sociology since the 1930s. This has led to the charge by so-called radical sociologists that the contemporary sociology establishment has served as the official legitimator of the system—not the catalyst for changing the system. *Sociological Inquiry* 40 (Winter, 1970).

Another Theoretical Orientation

Although the functional and conflict models of social organization rest on different assumptions about the nature of society, they share a concern with *structure,* the patterned arrangement of parts. In the third major model the structure fades into the background, while the spotlight focuses on people in face-to-face interaction, on *process.* This is the symbolic interactionist model, and its very name includes the elements of social organization to which it is sensitive. Symbolic interactionists study people interacting through symbolic communication (the shared meanings of language), developing these shared meanings and working out joint interpretations of their common activities.

While there are many variants within the interactionist tradition, we will offer the classic version of symbolic interactionism developed by Herbert Blumer. In fact, it was Blumer who (in 1937) came up with the name *symbolic interactionism* for this particular model of society. At that time he was trying to systematize the many ideas of George Herbert Mead, the founding father of this model. You will meet Mead's ideas about interaction in Part Two.

In the selection to follow, Margaret Poloma presents Blumer's three basic premises and illustrates each of them, showing the interactionist vision of the dynamic nature of social life. We see people, acting and reacting together, modifying their actions in light of the actions of others, interpreting their own behavior and the behavior of others, working out shared meanings and joint lines of action. It is this ever-changing configuration of ongoing processes that becomes social structure, the focus of concern in the other two models. When you have finished reading Poloma's discussion of symbolic interactionism, go back and look again at the issues raised by Eitzen in his comparative table on the functional and conflict models. What are the assumptions that symbolic interactionists make about social life?

3
Symbolic Interaction

Margaret M. Poloma

For Blumer (1969:2) symbolic interactionism rests on three premises. These premises are as follows:

1. "That human beings act toward things on the basis of the meanings that things have for them."
2. That these meanings are derived from "the social interaction that one has with one's fellows."
3. That these meanings are modified through an interpretive process.

There is nothing inherent in an object that provides meaning for the person. Take as an example the meaning that may be attached to a snake. For some, a snake is a vile reptile; for naturalists, it is another link in the delicate balance of nature. Whether a person instantly kills a harmless snake in his/her garden or watches it spellbound by nature's beauty depends on the meaning the person ascribes to this object. These meanings are derived from interaction with others. The son whose father was a natu-

ralist and who himself was schooled early in the operation of the animal world may respond quite differently from the lad whose only contact with the snake comes from reading the Genesis account of Adam and Eve's encounter with the serpent. All objects are similarly encountered—not directly, but with meanings attached to them. These meanings are derived from interaction with others, particularly with significant others. As Blumer (1969:4–5) observes, "The meaning of a thing for a person grows out of the ways in which other persons act toward the person with regard to the thing. Their actions operate to define the thing for the person." If a parent responds favorably toward a child who is not afraid of a garden snake, the child will continue such behavior. If, however, parents and playmates both show disapproval of the child, the child may modify not only his/her behavior but the meaning attached to the object.

It is important to remember, however, that our nature lover and snake hater do not automatically internalize two extreme meanings of the object *snake*. Blumer (1969:5) asserts:

The actor selects, checks, suspends, regroups, and transforms the meanings in light of the situation in which he is placed and the direction of his action. Accordingly, interpretation should not be regarded as a mere automatic application of established meanings but as a formative process in which meanings are used and revised as instruments for the guidance and formation of action.

We might use the illustration of a young female's accepting a ride home every evening from a married male co-worker as an example of this interpretive process. She may accept the ride as simply a gesture of friendliness and neighborliness. On the evening that he asks her if she would like to stop at a local lounge for a drink before going home, another stimulus is introduced that she will have to interpret. Let us suppose that our young woman interprets this action simply as a friendly gesture and stops for a drink. He then proceeds to discuss some of his marital difficulties with her and indicates that he wishes his wife were more like her. The young woman interprets this as an invitation to become romantically involved, at least in a casual way, and begins to decline rides from her co-worker. She begins to question his motivation for being so helpful to her and also his willingness to confide in her. It is possible that she has misinterpreted the married man's message; he may have seen her simply as a good friend. What becomes important is the meaning that she attaches to the question, "Do you need a ride home tonight?" rather than the question itself.

Blumer asserts that persons do not act because of some "forces" out there (as structural functionalists seem to imply) nor because of "inner forces" (as psychological reductionists suggest). Blumer (1969:80) argues:

Instead of the individual being surrounded by an environment of preexisting objects which play upon him and call forth his behavior, the proper picture is that he constructs his objects on the basis of his ongoing activity. In any of his countless acts—whether minor, like dressing himself, or major, like organizing himself for a professional career—the individual is designating different objects to himself, giving

them meaning, judging their suitability to his action, and making decisions on the basis of the judgment. This is what is meant by interpretation or acting on the basis of symbols. . . .

The action of human beings is permeated with interpretation and meaning. This action is fitted together and comprises what functionalists have termed *social structure.* Blumer (1969:17) chooses to refer to this social phenomenon as *joint action* or "a social organization of conduct of different acts of diverse participants." Each of these acts flows in processual form, and each interlinks with the processual acts of others. Action for Blumer is far more than the single performance described in Goffman's account of impression management. People engaged in joint action comprise the social structure. An institution such as a church, a business corporation, or a family is simply a "collectivity that engages in joint action." Yet these institutions are not static structures, for the behavior linkages are never identical (although they may be similar) even when patterns are well established. Consider the example of a family comprised of a husband, a wife, and one child. This family is in the continual process of day-to-day living. The marital relationship when the child is two months old may be quite different from when the child is six years old. Similarly the husband's career may assume a greater importance as he climbs the organization ladder, which also affects his family life. There is no simple definition of a husband's role, a wife's role, or parental roles. They develop within the context of the familial structure, which is constantly in a state of flux, responding to the symbolic interactions within the family unit. Blumer (1969:19) asserts the priority of interaction to the structure when he states that it is "the social process in group life that creates and upholds the rules, not the rules that create and uphold group life." In other words, norms, as discussed by structural functionalists, do not determine the behavior of individuals; individuals act in concert to uphold the norms or rules of behavior. A structural functionalist emphasizes that people are products of their respective societies; a symbolic interactionist stresses the other side of the coin, namely, that social structure is the result of persons in interaction. . . .

For Blumer, then, the study of society must be a study of joint action rather than a preoccupation with what he feels to be nebulous systems and elusive functional prerequisites. Society is a result of symbolic interaction among persons, and it is precisely this aspect that should be of concern to sociologists. . . .

Rather than asserting the priority and dominance of the group or the structure, Blumer (1969:84–85) views group action as a collection of individual actions: "Human society is to be seen as consisting of acting people, and the life of the society is to be seen as consisting of their actions." Blumer extends this idea to point out that such group life is a response to situations in which persons find themselves. These situations may be structured, but Blumer cautions against ignoring the importance of interpreta-

tion even in relatively fixed institutions. Blumer (1969:78) observes the following two differences between the structural functionalist and the symbolic interactionist views of society:

First, from the standpoint of symbolic interaction the organization of human society is the framework inside of which social action takes place and is not the determinant of that action.

Second, such organization and changes in it are the product of the activity of acting units and not of "forces" which leave such acting units out of account.

Reference

Blumer, Herbert
    1969   *Symbolic Interactionism: Perspective and Method.* Englewood Cliffs, N.J.: Prentice-Hall, Inc.

Choosing a Theoretical Orientation

You have now met the three major theoretical orientations within the broader sociological perspective. Which of these three models of social organization is correct? Recall what Bates said about the nature of perspectives in general: "Each perspective looks at the human scene and abstracts from the whole those features to which it is particularly sensitive." Thus each of these models is correct—about the presence of those features it considers important. Are there some stable relationships of parts in society? Of course there are. Are there some structures of dominance in society? Of course there are. Are people engaged in ongoing processes of symbolic communication and interaction? Of course they are. Structures of interrelated parts, including dominance structures, and processes of interaction and change are part of social organization.

Then what good are these models of society, if each is only partial and the elements crucial to all three are present in social organization? We cannot take into account all of social organization at one time—there is too much. It is too vast and bewildering to make sense of in one gulp, so to speak. But we can select the *crucial* features and pay attention to them. Such a partial view is exactly what each of these three models of social organization offers. Each model isolates for us what matters—what explains or needs explaining—and lets the other features fade into the background. It serves as a lens, sharpening some features, while other less important features remain hazy.

But on what basis does a researcher select one or another of these models to use in directing his or her attention? The choice may depend on the nature of the problem and the researcher's views as to which of these models is most likely to provide insight into that particular problem. Or it may depend on which model the researcher believes to be most accurate about the crucial realities of social organization, whatever the problem.

In any case, it is clear that each of the three models can be used for any aspect of social organization. It is equally clear that what you see will depend rather heavily on which model you choose to direct your observation.

METHODS OF SOCIAL RESEARCH

Up to this point we have examined the important questions of what the sociological perspective is, why we use it, and what theoretical models lie within it. But how do we use it? The answer: by applying the methods of science to social behavior. In the first section, The Sociological Perspective, we pointed out several differences between amateur sociologizing and systematic social analysis. These included differences in observation, logic, generalization, and suspension of inquiry. Methods of scientific research are important tools sociologists use to guard against such pitfalls of careless social analysis.

In the next reading Jerry Rose points out how doubt and evidence are crucial parts of any scientific inquiry. He then shows how sociologists apply scientific methods, collecting empirical evidence to provide accurate descriptions and explanations of the social world, in order to allay doubt. Be sure you see the importance of evidence in this battle with doubt. Does *all* evidence need to point to the same conclusion in order to allay doubt? Must knowledge be "incapable of being doubted?" (Immediately following the Rose reading you will find a short discussion of the three important techniques sociologists use to gather data or evidence.)

Although the scientific method encompasses many steps, Rose chooses to focus on four points that seem especially troublesome in sociology. Problems of objectivity, measurement, sampling, and causation, although not unique to sociology, are of special concern, primarily because sociologists gather their data from or about human subjects. Is it easier to remain objective when studying reproduction of fruit flies than when studying incidence of child abuse? Although bias may enter into both situations, is it the same kind of bias? Why might the sociologist be more prone to bias than the biologist?

The problem of measurement is the next one raised by Rose. Is it more straightforward to measure increases in size of fruit flies than to measure decreases in prejudice among children bused to another school? In the first case, a scientist can pull out a ruler and measure the fruit flies. It would have to be a very precise (and very small!) ruler, yet we all know the principles involved in measuring size. But do we have a ruler that allows us to measure amount of prejudice? Well, we do not have a standard ruler, but we can make a ruler. How do we know if it is any good? This is exactly the question Rose raises in his discussion of *validity* and *reliability*. Note the importance of these two concepts for any "ruler."

The next problem Rose addresses is sampling. Is it more accurate to assemble a colony of fruit flies and argue that this colony behaves like any other colony than it is to take a city neighborhood and argue it is like any other neighborhood? Rose discusses the problem of representativeness of samples; how does one know that the sample is like all of the other "pieces" in the population? What are the different ways to sample from the population? Note that with all of the different techniques of sampling Rose discusses, there is always a trade-off; there are advantages and disadvantages to each of them.

Finally, Rose takes up the very "sticky" problem of causal inferences. This is an especially important problem in the social sciences since, most of the time, sociologists lack the controlled laboratory environment of the natural and physical sciences. For example, in the natural sciences it is obvious that, when some foreign material is introduced into a colony of fruit flies in a controlled laboratory environment and many of the flies die, the foreign material probably caused the death. But can a researcher be equally sure that the busing of children caused an increase or decrease in prejudice on the part of these children? This section of the reading probably will be tough going. Pay particular attention to the difference between correlation and causation. Mistaking correlation for causation is one of the pits into which the amateur may fall. Slowly work your way through Rose's discussion of contingency analysis and the two statistics, chi-square and the coefficient of correlation. Spend a bit of time on the *logic* of these. Don't be discouraged if the first time through you do not completely understand these concepts. It may take a few passes before you are comfortable with the ideas in this section.

4
Methods in Sociological Study

Jerry D. Rose

SOCIOLOGY AND THE SCIENTIFIC METHOD

As we noted at the start, the sociologist holds no monopoly in his interest in understanding human behavior. Human behavior is grist not only for the social scientist but for the novelist, the essayist, the playwright, the poet. In the mill of his mind the creative writer turns over the behavior of his fellows and, depending upon his motivation, produces a view of humanity— or of a very small piece of it—that will arouse, or placate, educate, or simply entertain and inform his readers. . . .

If the sociologist is not distinguished from the artist by his *aims*, however, he clearly is distinguished from him in his *methods*. Sociology attempts to apply the methods of science to the understanding of human behavior. Men of letters are not scientists; the sociologist is, or he at least aspires to apply scientific methodology to his study of human behavior. The essence of this method is a suspension of judgment about the apparent facts in a given area until any hypothesis that has been formulated is supported overwhelmingly by empirical evidence. Two features of this definition of the scientific method will now be discussed.

Doubt

The scientist is sensitive—some critics would say overly sensitive[1]—to the "error" of accepting as fact some proposition that is in fact false. The

Reprinted from *Introduction to Sociology,* 1st ed., by Jerry D. Rose. Copyright © 1971 Houghton Mifflin Company. Used with permission of the publisher.

prototype of the scientific attitude is Descartes' seventeenth century exercise in "methodological scepticism,"[2] in which he proposes to doubt literally everything until it can be established on the level of absolute certainty, that is, to "make it a rule to trust only what is completely known and incapable of being doubted."[3] This rule can be carried to a ridiculous extreme, of course, as in the story of a scientist riding on a train whose companion points out the window and says, "Look, those sheep have been shorn," to which the scientist replies, "To be sure, they have been shorn on one side."

Contrary to Descartes, the modern scientific attitude takes account of the likelihood that most or all of our knowledge is inferential or probabilistic in nature. If we waited for knowledge which is "incapable of being doubted," we apparently should wait forever to find any propositions that we can "trust." Still, the scientist is likely to be less trusting of his impulses and intuitions than is the artist. Scientific attitudes demand and scientific procedures provide for systematic generation of empirical *evidence* for or against any proposed facts.

Evidence

How does one gather scientific evidence for or against a proposition that will allow him to suspend his suspended judgment and reach a conclusion about some matter of fact? What counts as evidence for or against the proposition?

The basic scientific method for accumulating evidence is the method of empirical *observation*; one uses his sensory faculties—sight, hearing, taste, touch, and smell—to apprehend the facts of the world. The chemist sees the changes of color and texture that accompany the mixing of chemical reagents; the sociologist hears men saying certain things to their fellow men, or to himself. These observations are recorded in painstaking detail, and one's conclusions must be strictly consistent with the facts that one has observed in the empirical world.

This fact-gathering may or may not be preceded by some tentative idea of what the final conclusion might be. One model of scientific operation is the idea of the *inductive* method: the investigator begins with a set of observed facts on which he can base some overall conclusion or some abstract *theory* about the facts in a particular area of study. The frequently cited model of the inductive method is Darwin's description of the laborious biological observations by which he finally arrived at the theory of natural selection.[4] However, much scientific investigation is in the nature of hypothesis-testing. Hypotheses are tentative statements about the facts in a particular area of study. One frequent justification of scientific *theory* (e.g., Darwin's theory of natural selection or Freud's libido theory of human psychology) is that it allows the investigator to hypothesize facts before he has gathered them; he then proceeds *deductively* from an existing theory to a specific hypothesis about some phenomenon.

Whether he proceeds from a basis of induction or deduction, the scientist must devise observational "tests" of the facts that he is investigating. Frequently scientists think in terms of entities that are unobservable by the senses: light waves, for example, or the superego. To make any observations at all about such phenomena, he must develop operations that provide the rules for determining what sensory observations will be treated as evidence for or against a proposition.[5] Much of the uncertainty and controversy in science arises from disagreements about the appropriateness of using a particular operation as a measure of some unobservable phenomenon. (A familiar example: Do intelligence tests *really* measure intelligence?)

Assuming his ability to develop adequate measures of some phenomenon, the scientist is frequently faced with a problem of *interpreting* the data that his observations have generated. What does it all mean? is a question that will arise in any science as the scientist confronts the hard facts of his area of study. Even if all scientific effort were concerned with testing specific hypotheses (it is not), the process of hypothesis-testing would generate many puzzling facts that have yet to be explained scientifically.

Some students have found encouragement in the frequency in scientific research of *serendipity*: the discovery of new facts for which one was not looking at the time of their discovery.[6] An antibiotic drug, penicillin, was supposedly discovered serendipitously, and the story of the apple falling on Newton's head before he "discovered" the law of gravity is a popularized version of the fact that, frequently, the scientist must be "hit on the head" by facts before he recognizes their scientific value. Whatever the degree of importance one assigns to serendipitous findings, it is clear that much scientific thought is post-factum and involves the problem of interpreting the meaning of preexisting facts. This situation leads to one of the persisting criticisms of scientific interpretations; that is, being after the fact, the interpretation represents a plausible explanation of the facts but does not preclude the possibility that someone else may dream up an alternate interpretation that is equally plausible.[7]

In the balance of this [reading] we shall consider some of the problems and proposed solutions to the problems of applying scientific methods to sociological subject matters. In the light of the foregoing discussion, the reader may need to remind himself from time to time that these methodological problems are not unique to sociology. If sociological research is sometimes (or always) characterized by slipshod methodology, we may at least take some comfort in the realization that the development of knowledge which is "completely known and incapable of being doubted" is an extremely difficult feat in *any* line of scientific inquiry.

PROBLEMS IN OBJECTIVITY

The sociologist, like any scientist, is expected to take a quite different stance toward the material of his study than does the artist or literary person. Self-expression is the ideal stance of the artist, as indicated in Cooley's approving characterization of Goethe's writing which allows the reader to "get the feeling of something calm, free, and onward which is Goethe himself, and not to be had elsewhere."[8] The scientist, by contrast, is expected to disengage his own personality from his scientific findings, producing results that can be verified by any other scientist who uses the same methods of study. In the realm of human behavior, that novelist who writes about social life as *he* has experienced it is considered "authentic." The social scientist is discouraged from allowing his own biased sample of social experience to substitute for the whole of human behavior. In every respect, the rule is one of subjectivity for the artist, objectivity for the scientist.

The social scientist does not, however, derogate the importance for scientific discovery of the element of subjectivity, either his own or that of persons in the subjectively oriented professions. The beginning of sociological investigation is frequently the provocative hypothesis or hunch, and literary sources may be rich mines of material for the sociologist's hypotheses.[9] The insights on human behavior of a Dostoevsky, a Goethe, or a Shakespeare may be more illuminating than the most sophisticated sociological theories. But, valuable as these insights may be as starting points for sociological study, they do not enter the body of sociology proper until they have been tested with research instruments that are independent of the brilliant intuitions of individual thinkers.

The positivistic program advocated by Comte aimed at removing sociology from the realm of speculation and establishing it as an objective or research science.[10] Comte's fellow countryman, Emile Durkheim, shared this vision of an objective sociology and, in his *Rules of Sociological Method,* urged that the sociologist must "eradicate all preconceptions" and deal with facts rather than with his ideas about social facts.[11] The eminent German sociologist Max Weber devoted major essays to the problem of objectivity or "value-neutrality" in sociology, arguing that the sociologist may well be involved in partisan political activity to stimulate his intellectual curiosity but that, as a social scientist (e.g., a teacher of sociology), he must leave out his personal biases, remembering always that a "podium is not a pulpit."[12]

Objectivity is easily articulated as an ideal but not so easily practiced, perhaps especially so in the social sciences. It is quite common in treatises on social science to note that the control of personal bias is an especially difficult feat when the subject matter is human behavior.[13] Whether concerned with the study of prejudice, or voting, or lovemaking, the social scientist is trying to understand behavior in which he himself is engaged. This is in contrast with, say, the geologist, who studies phenomena with which he does not personally identify.

This contrast in the ease of maintaining objectivity in the social and physical sciences can easily be overdrawn. The working habits of the professional scientist in any field are such that he tends to develop preferences for finding one set of facts rather than another. Scientists develop hypotheses or theories which they publish, thereby committing themselves professionally. The reluctance with which a geologist gives up his hypothesis about the surface of the moon, despite the introduction of new facts, suggests that, even in the physical sciences, human preference is an ever-present factor.

Most scientific fields recognize individual bias and control it by institutionalizing a system of internal checks by which one scientist's biased thinking is reviewed by other scientists, who presumably operate with other kinds of bias. However, there are many flaws in this system. A scientist may be too specialized for many others to be able to check his work. The weight of an investigator's reputation or mere politeness toward a colleague may produce in the reviewers a reticence to criticize.[14] The training of scientists still involves indoctrination in the necessity of individual intellectual integrity. Exercising this integrity may be more difficult for the social scientist, who is influenced by his identification with his subject matter as well as by his professional commitments.

PROBLEMS IN MEASUREMENT

When the poet writes that "these are the times that try men's souls," he is making a statement about social conditions that no one is inclined to reject because the poet does not specify *how much* men's souls are currently being tried. The scientific interest is quite different. When the physical scientist describes a chemical element, it is not sufficient to call it a light or a heavy element; the chemist, at the least, will be expected to identify the different elements by different degrees (more or less) of weight (a measuring device which will allow such relative measurements is called an *ordinal scale*). Better, the weights of different elements might be described as falling at a point along a continuous scale (e.g., so many pounds and ounces) that will tell one by *how much* the weight of a given element exceeds that of any other element (*interval scales* permit such measurements).

Likewise, the sociologist will seldom be content to assert that "times are trying" or that "there is a lot of unrest on college campuses today." There are any number of sociological questions that assume the capacity to make accurate measures of, say, the amount of unrest now compared with five years ago, or in Europe compared with the United States, or in one situation compared with another.

The two criteria of accurate sociological measures are *reliability* and *validity*.[15] A reliable measure is one which yields the same results upon repetition of the measuring procedure or upon application by other investigators. Reliability is one indication of the objectivity of sociological knowledge: a judgment, for example, about the degree of unrest is not subject to the vagaries of viewpoints of persons making the judgment if this trait is measured by reliable instruments. A valid measure is one which in fact measures whatever it is purported to measure. The validity of a measure of unrest might be challenged by arguing that sociologists are not really measuring unrest but only the degree of willingness or reticence of people to express discontent in interviews.

Of the two kinds of measurement problems—reliability and validity—the degree of reliability of a sociological measure can be much more easily determined. The degree to which measuring scales yield comparable results upon repeated measurement can be stated in precise mathematical terms.[16] Validity, however, can only be inferred, never proven. If we want to know, for example, whether we are really measuring social unrest, we have no perfect device for reassuring ourselves. We might consider whether our measure has "face validity"; that is, whether, in the judgment of ourselves or some panel of experts, it appears obvious that the questions we ask people are well designed to measure their degree of discontent. But what is obviously valid to one investigator may be just as obviously invalid to another investigator with another set of intuitions. Even if all investigators were to agree on the face validity of a measure, they could not be sure of its validity. Sociology itself will teach us that forty million Frenchmen *can* be wrong (at least to the extent that what is judged as right in one place may be judged as wrong elsewhere, or that what seems right today may be proven wrong tomorrow) and that a panel of seven experts can indeed all operate under the same illusions.

We might also infer validity by comparing results yielded by a measure with unknown validity with results yielded by a measure with known validity, much as psychologists validate a new test of intelligence by determining whether people make scores on it comparable to scores they make on some established or standard test. The rub here, of course, is that we have made an inference about the validity of the established measure. All we actually measure by these techniques is the reliability of different measures of the same characteristics. It is still possible that we err (albeit "reliably") in *all* our measures.

Finally, we might resort to some form of *scaling* technique.[17] A *scale* involves a number of measures of the same characteristic and is constructed on the theory that the sum total or pattern of responses on a number of measurement items will be more valid than a single measurement. Any professor who bases exam grades on the total number of correctly answered questions is using a kind of scaling technique. If the students' grades were based on a single question, a student might well claim that his grade was an invalid measure of his overall knowledge of the course materials ("You just happened to hit me with the one thing I didn't know" or "My pencil slipped"). But if the student missed thirty-five out of forty questions, he would appear foolish if he made such arguments. Similarly, in measuring unrest, if a subject answers one question about the degree of his contentment in negative terms, it may be that the investigator accidentally hit upon the one area of dissatisfaction in an otherwise contented existence. However, we are unlikely to attribute to accident those similar events that occur repeatedly. A pattern of discontented responses allows a more valid inference that a subject is, in fact, discontented.

Although scaling is a common and reputable way of dealing with the problem of validity, it is not a panacea. Anyone who has objected to a course examination on the grounds that the professor's questions are too vague or that the expected pattern of responses is too idiosyncratic to the professor's way of thinking will recognize the problem. High and low total scoring on a number of items, instead of measuring the course knowledge as intended, may measure the student's ability to parrot the professor or the text or may reflect the student's familiarity with testing rules-of-thumb such as, on a true-false question, the statement is false if the words *always* or *never* are used or, on a multiple choice question, the alternative with the most words is the correct one. Similarly, a generalization like "men display more social unrest than women" may be challenged (even though research shows this to be the case) if, for any reason, men are simply more willing to admit their discontent when certain kinds of questions are used.

To deepen a bit the perplexity introduced by the problem of validity of sociological measures, consider the problem of what may be called "observer effect." The problem, briefly, is whether or not a person's awareness that his behavior is being observed will alter his behavior. Most of us have experienced the sensation of stage fright or seen the effects of an audience on the behavior of the inveterate ham. With the physical scientist, observer effect is much less a problem. When the physicist measures the temperature of a liquid, he is not likely to be much concerned with the question of whether the insertion of the thermometer into the thermal system being measured will itself change that temperature. The sociologist, in assessing the validity of his measuring techniques, must consider a variety of problems involving the reactions of people to the act of observation: the hostility of subjects to a questionnaire, the constraints imposed by an interviewer taking notes, the fear of self-incrimination, and so forth.

In dealing with observer effect, the investigator can resort to various tricks of the researcher's trade.[18] An assurance of anonymity may neutralize a subject's fear of negative consequences if certain answers are given. Note-taking may be eliminated in favor of an unobtrusive tape recorder. *Projective* techniques—questioning people more indirectly about sensitive matters—may be used. The rapport of the investigator with his subjects is a concern of virtually every sociological study.[19] But even when all the tricks are used by a trained and skillful investigator, he can never be sure that the behavior he observes or is told about corresponds to the behavior that occurs in the absence of his investigations.[20]

There seems to be no ultimate solution to the problem of the validity of sociological measures. Sociologists employ a wide variety of validating techniques, but the usual understanding is that we strive for the most valid possible measure, knowing that we shall never entirely succeed.

PROBLEMS IN SAMPLING

Even assuming that our measures of behavior are valid, the problem remains that, given the limited amount of time, energy, and money that can be devoted to sociological investigations, it is unlikely that we shall be able to apply our valid measuring instruments to all possible instances of the kind of behavior we are studying. A study of unrest on American college campuses, for example, would be able to measure the degree of discontent avowed or displayed by only a limited number of students or faculty. To deal with this situation, the sociologist typically *samples* human behavior and, on the basis of a limited number of observations made on that sample, he hopes to generalize about the behavior of persons in a larger *universe* or *population.* This generalization has to be based on an *inference,* since the sociologist cannot prove that people whose behavior he has not observed are behaving in the same way as those he has observed. A major problem in sociological methodology is the construction of samples for study that will insure that the inference is a valid one.[21]

A *representative* sample is the aim of the sociologist because it is this kind of sample that permits a valid inference about a larger population. A sample is representative when the various elements of a population are represented in the sample in the same proportion that they constitute in the population from which the sample was drawn. A sample of college students is representative with reference to sex if, in a college with 75 percent females, there are 75 percent females in the sample. A *biased* sample is one in which some population elements are underrepresented and others are overrepresented. A class in introductory sociology (a frequent "sample" in sociological studies) would, in most colleges, have an overrepresentation of freshmen and sophomores and an underrepresentation of upperclassmen (as well as, probably, some other kinds of bias in the kinds of people who are found in such a course).

A representative sample, like a valid measure, is easier said than done. Some techniques can be mentioned, along with some of their difficulties and limitations. The most familiar technique is the *random sample.* Contrary to the popular conception that a random sample is an arbitrary selection of cases for study ("I just went around randomly and talked to any student I happened to run across"), a random sam-

ple employs a technique that eliminates entirely the arbitrary or willful element in sample selection. A random sample begins with an enumeration (listing) of all members of a population (a roster of members of a labor union, for example) and selects cases from that list by a mechanical procedure similar to drawing names from a hat, or selecting the cases whose numbers correspond to a group of numbers drawn from a table of random numbers. The investigator thus may exercise *no* discretion in the selection of his sample for study.

The value of random samples can well be emphasized. A random-sampling technique is likely, with a degree of probability that can be stated statistically, to generate a representative sample, since the likelihood of persons from various elements of the population being included in the sample is directly proportional to the numbers of each kind of persons in the population. (Thus, a random sample is sometimes called a *probability sample.*) Obviously, the size of the sample is important in determining this probability. In a population with half females, the probability of randomly selecting an all-male sample of two or three persons is quite high (like the chance of flipping a coin and getting "heads" three times in a row). However, the probability of such a chance selection of a fifty-person all-male sample from such a population is extremely slight.

Random samples, though valuable, have their limitations. In the first place, they assume an enumeration of the population, and for many populations that the sociologist would study there is no such listing. (Where would you find a complete enumeration of unwed mothers or Italian-American residents of a city?) They assume, also, that the investigator will be able to study all the cases selected for his sample. In a random sample of the residents of a city, some of the sample persons may be extremely difficult to locate and many may refuse to cooperate with the study (e.g., refuse to grant an interview or return a questionnaire). This would introduce a possible bias if those who cooperate are different in any way relevant to the research from those who refuse to cooperate. (It is sometimes thought, for example, that only those persons cooperate with researches on sex behavior who have "nothing to hide" or "much to brag about" sexually.)

Some of these problems may be skirted by the adoption of other sampling techniques. Even without a names-and-addresses listing of the persons in a population, we may know enough about the general composition of the population to give us leads in constructing a sample. We may know, for example, that 40 percent of unwed mothers are under seventeen years of age, and that 55 percent of Italian-Americans are men. We may construct a *quota sample* in which we select enough persons of each type to correspond to their proportions in the population. We can thus construct by design a sample that is representative with reference to the criteria of representativeness (e.g., age, sex, marital status, social class) that we may think are relevant to the results of our research.

The limitation of the quota-sampling method should be clear. We have allowed an arbitrary element to remain. Assume that the sample must contain twelve women to be representative with reference to sex, but the question of *which twelve* are to be chosen from the population is left to the investigator's discretion. The bias may come if there is some criterion of representativeness that we have not considered but that affects the outcome of our research. The investigator might use his discretion to select *twelve pretty women;* if physical attractiveness affects the behavior being studied (attitudes toward the opposite sex, for example), we could not infer that the behavior measured in our sample would be found with equal frequency in a population with a different proportion of attractive and unattractive women. Most of the public opinion polls in the United States use a quota-sampling technique, and some of the error in their results comes from the inability of the pollsters to know precisely which population variations (e.g., age, sex, region of country, or religious affiliation) will be relevant to variations in public opinion on a given issue; they are never quite sure, therefore, which criteria to use in constructing a quota sample.

Finally, the least respected but probably most used sampling technique involves the use of what can be called a *convenience sample,* that is, a sample of those persons who happen to be available to be studied. Two familiar recruitment techniques are (1) advertising for volunteers or for paid participants in a study, and (2) the use of a captive audience such as the members of a school classroom or employees of a company that will give them time off to participate in a study. The biasing possibilities in such samples are obvious. College freshmen are not "the world," and what is true of their behavior may not be true of "real-life" people. However, such samples do have the advantage of their label—convenience—and it may be possible to dismiss the significance of a given form of bias by showing that, in relevant respects, the sample of available subjects is reasonably typical of some wider population. For example, introductory sociology students may not be a bad representation of college underclassmen if most or all students at a given college take such a course. If the sample *is* biased in some significant way, it is at least possible to take the bias into account and exercise the proper caution in any suggestion of a generalization of one's findings.

PROBLEMS IN CAUSAL INFERENCE

The measurement and sampling problems we have just discussed refer to the sociologist's problem of providing accurate *descriptions* of some of the facts about human behavior. Another side of sociological interest in human behavior is its concern with the *explanation* of human behavior: *Why* is there more campus unrest today than yesterday? *Why* is there more unrest on the large campuses? etc. Human behavior is a *variable,* and sociology is concerned with explaining this variability. The explantation of a given kind of behavior presupposes the existence of measuring and sampling operations that indicate the frequency of that behavior, but the problems of explanation have only begun when these other problems are solved.

Correlation

Sociological explanation, like scientific explanation in general, begins with the attempt to discover *correlations* in the phenomenal world. Correlation means covariance, the tendency for variation in one variable to accompany variations in other variables. The Boyles Law and Charles Law of physics state the covariance of the variables of temperature, pressure, and volume. A sociological study of, for example, campus unrest would tend to try to discover variations in other social conditions that are correlated with variations in campus unrest. Questions might be raised, for example, about whether unrest varies with (1) the time of the school year (more of it around examination time, for example), (2) the social-class composition of the student body, and (3) the degree of "social distance" between faculty and students. These are all *variables,* and the sociologist may hypothesize a correlation between one or more of such variables and the variable of campus unrest.

The introductory student should acquaint himself with a few of the technicalities involved in the reporting of sociological correlations. Two major devices for the demonstration of correlation will be discussed.

The first device may be called the technique of *contingency analysis,* used especially when one or more of the correlated variables is a discrete (either-or) kind of variable. Suppose a sociologist of campus unrest observed that, during the disturbances on American campuses that occurred in the spring of 1970, some colleges closed early in accommodation to student demands while other colleges remained in operation to the end of the semester. The sociologist might believe that there is a correlation between closing or not closing and, say, the kind of financial support—private or public—on which the school is primarily dependent. Each college in a sample of 100 colleges is classified on these two variables. There are four combinations of closing policy and type of financial support; any correlation would show up in an uneven distribution of closing policies in the schools with the two types of financial support. We might tabulate our 100 cases as follows:

CLOSING POLICY

TYPE OF FINANCIAL SUPPORT		Closed Early	Stayed Open	
	Private	40	10	50
	Public	20	30	50
		60	40	100

According to the table, there *appears* to be a relationship between the two variables, i.e., a private school was more likely than a public one to close early.

If we want a more precise statement of the probability of a relationship between these two variables we may use a *test of statistical significance.* Very frequently, the *chi*-square test is used in such cases.[22] To understand something of the logic of the *chi*-square test, let us construct a table that would show the distribution of measurements on these two variables if there were *no* relationship between the two variables. Such a no-relationship or theoretical frequency table would be as follows:

CLOSING POLICY

TYPE OF FINANCIAL SUPPORT		Closed Early	Stayed Open	
	Private	30	20	50
	Public	30	20	50
		60	40	100

Since half of the sample's schools are private and half are public, half of the schools that closed early should be private and half should be public, etc. The *chi*-square statistic is arrived at by computing the degree of discrepancy between this theoretical frequency of cases in each cell and the actual or measured distribution (the first model); the greater the discrepancy, the greater the *chi*-square value. The statistical significance of this value is determined by consulting a statistical table which indicates the probabilty that any apparent correlation of the variables is actually the result of "chance" factors (such as the kind of sample we happen to have drawn). The *smaller* the size of this number, the greater the investigator's confidence that there is actually a relation between the variables. A limitation of this technique is that it does not indicate the degree of correlaltion or "strength of association" of the variables. A probability of .001 does *not* indicate ten times as much correlation as does a probability of .01; it simply reflects that much greater confidence that there is *some* relationship.

Dissatisfaction with this limitation of contingency analysis has led many sociologists to prefer another technique that does not have this limitation, namely, some form of a *coefficient of correlation*.[23] This technique is useful when variables are measured on a *continuous* scale, i.e., where measurements yield scores on both variables. To consider again our campus unrest example, our interest in the relationship between the type of financial support and the closing policy may have been based on the view that the governing boards of private colleges are composed of wealthier people who are more sympathetic to the aims and tactics of student protest. We might, now, measure our 100-case sample of colleges on two variables: (1) the average income of the members of the governing board of each college and (2) the number of public statements by board members of each college that indicate sympathy for student protest. Each college would receive a numerical "score" for each of these two variables and a coefficient of correlation would show the degree of covariance of these scores.

The mathematics involved in computing a coefficient of correlation need not concern us here; suffice it to understand the meaning of a given correlation. Coefficients of correlation range from a perfectly negative correlation of -1.0 to a perfectly positive correlation of $+1.0$, with *no* correlation at the midpoint of 0. Negative correlations mean that an individual or institution with a high value on one variable is likely to have a low value on another (colleges with wealthy board members have few sympa-

thetic public statements by board members). Positive correlations show similarity of value on the two variables (colleges with wealthy board members have many sympathetic public statements by board members).

The magnitude of a correlation (.40, for example) indicates the degree to which variability in one variable can be accounted for by variation in another variable. The degree of this predictability is not, however, the decimal of the given coefficient, but the mathematical square of this value. A .40 correlation indicates 16 percent variability accounted for, .30 means 9 percent, etc. This information is useful to the student in assessing the scientific value of a given coefficient of correlation. The statistical probability that a correlation of a given magnitude indicates *some* relationship between variables can be computed, as in the case of a *chi*-square of a given value. Correlations on the order of .20 to .30 are often reported as being statistically significant. When the reader is reminded that correlations of this magnitude account for only 4 to 9 percent of variability, he may want to question whether the correlation is very significant in terms of its power to explain the phenomenon in question.

Causality

So far we have, by design, said nothing about any *causal* relation between variables. We have not spoken, for example, of the causes of campus unrest. However, when the sociologist (or the man in the street) asks for explanations of phenomena, he does want to know what forces or factors have produced the phenomenon in question, whether it be a crime wave, an economic depression, or a championship football team. Philosophers like David Hume might argue that we experiece "concomitant variation" (correlation) and imagine cause-and-effect relations only as a matter of "habit"; but it is a strongly ingrained habit in human thought, and the sociologist takes it over.

The terms *independent variable* and *dependent variable* are used to denote cause and effect, respectively. The demonstration of correlation is necessary but not sufficient to support an inference that variation in one variable "causes" variation in another. For one thing, even if the variables are causally connected, it is not always possible to determine which is cause and which is effect. If there is a high correlation between poverty and mental illness, it may be that being poor is a causal factor in becoming mentally ill, but it may also be that the expense incurred by mental illness is a causal factor in precipitating poverty. (There may also, of course, be an interaction or mutual dependence of variables—the proverbial vicious circle.) Our judgments in these matters are likely to be rather intuitive. If there is a correlation between wealth and liberalism in social attitudes, we may doubt that liberalism contributes very much to a person's becoming wealthy, whereas wealth does make it possible for one to indulge in the "luxury" of liberalism in the *noblesse oblige* style. Such judgments, being intuitive, are subject to controversy because of variations in individual intuition.

Another and probably more serious problem in inferring causality from correlation appears when we reflect that two classes of events may be correlated without there being *any* causal connection between them. The blooming of the dogtooth violet and the northward migration of the bobolink coincide closely in time, but no one would seriously suggest that flower-blooming is the cause of bird migration or that bird migration is the cause of flower-blooming. Clearly they are both dependent variables (effects) of a third variable, the change of the seasons.

A closely analogous situation often exists in sociological explanation and creates a major problem in causal inference. Consider again the hypothetical correlation of financial support of colleges and their responses to student demonstrations. The fact that the private colleges are more likely to close early could mean that financial support is a determinant of school policy in such cases, but it is also quite possible that both financial support and school policy are dependent effects of a third variable, say, the social-class composition of the student body. If colleges with "upper-class" student bodies are privately supported colleges and are also col-

leges where the pressure of student demands to close early is greater (as a reflection of upper-class life styles), then the pattern of coincidence of private financial support and early school-closing may have no more causal significance than does the correlation of flower-blooming and bird migration. The influence of third . . . variables is an ever-present problem in the making of causal inferences.

There are, of course, long-established scientific techniques for dealing with the effects of intervening variables. The physical scientist's laboratory experiment is an attempt to study the effects of one variable on another by holding constant all other variables. The typical small-groups experiment uses control and experimental groups in which the situation of each group is identical except for the introduction of one variable (say, the raising or lowering of group morale) whose effects the investigator wants to study.[24]

Many kinds of sociological explanation are not amenable to such treatment, however. Were the sociologist interested in the effects of capital punishment in encouraging or discouraging capital crimes, he might suspect that any correlations are the result of intervening variables; for example, the lower rates of capital crimes in those states that have abolished capital punishment may mean simply that general social enlightenment has produced both a reduction in crime and a reduction in the severity of punishment. He might be tempted to wish himself in a position to impose on one state an elimination of capital punishment (his experimental group) and impose on an otherwise similar state a maintenance of capital punishment (his control group). Any differences in the subsequent capital crime rates of the two states could properly be ascribed to the effects of the treatment. But, of course, the sociologist is restrained from making some of the experiments that could answer difficult questions of explanation either by his lack of political power or by his ethical notions about appropriate ways of treating human subjects.[25]

Fortunately, there are alternatives to experimental manipulation in dealing with the effects of [third] variables. One possibility is that, while sociologists are seldom in power positions that would allow them to make random assignments of subjects for different experimental treatments, other people *do* sometimes make such assignments and, in a sense, set up experiments for us. Students may be assigned to one section or another of a class, to one dormitory roommate or another on an essentially random basis. The alert sociologist can use such situations as "natural experiments" in the factors that influence human behavior.

Another possibility is that one may, by statistical manipulation of data, control for the effects of a third variable. This is done by computing some kind of *partial correlation,* the correlation that remains between two variables when the effects of a third variable have been held constant. The assertion, for example, that the correlation of mode of financial support and college response to student demonstration is accounted for by the higher social-class composition of the private schools would have to be rejected if it could be shown that, *within* a group of colleges with student bodies of equivalent class standing, the private ones are more likely to respond favorably to the student demonstrations. Here we have the statistical equivalent of the "holding constant" of intervening variables by laboratory controls. Although we obviously cannnot *impose* any lack of variation in social-class composition of student bodies at different colleges, we can see whether correlations of our independent and dependent variables hold up within a subgroup of our sample for which there is no variation of class position.[26]

A critic of sociological explanations (and sociologists tend to be their own severest critics) may point out that causal inferences based on such statistical manipulations are always risky because it is always possible that the investigator has overlooked some hidden variable that is influencing his results. If you believe that human behavior is the resultant of a complex of causal factors that are hopelessly intertwined, you may doubt that the human mind will ever be able to apprehend all the obscure interconnections of things. The sociologist is continuously made aware of these problems by the criticism of his research by his colleagues, if not by himself.

For the nth and final times in this [reading] it must be said that there are no ultimate answers to the problem of applying scientific methodology to the study of human behavior. When sociology was characterized, at the outset, as an "intellectual enterprise," it was in the author's mind that sociology is, for those who choose to indulge in it, a tantalizing, often frustrating, sometimes rewarding effort to apply a discipline of method to the recalcitrance of human behavior. When asked why he studied sociology, Max Weber was said to have replied, "To see how much I can stand." In so answering, he may well have had in mind the incredible complexity of human behavior and the necessity for the student of that behavior to exercise continuous and critical self-consciousness about his methods of study.

SUMMARY

A contemporary sociologist, C. Wright Mills, has criticized some of his colleagues for a "methodological inhibition," an overconcern for "how to do it" in research that leads to a poverty of imagination in insightful understanding of human behavior.[27] The reader may suspect by now that this criticism is justified, that with all the things that can go wrong in sociological research, the sociologist must be discouraged from attempting anything really bold or creative.

It has not been the purpose of this [reading] to scare the reader into extreme caution in his own research or extreme skepticism about the validity of the research done by others. Rather, the aim has been to introduce the reader as frankly as possible to the problems faced daily by practicing sociologists. Sociological investigation is carried on in a pervasive atmosphere of criticism that is likely to be painful to the recipient but is a necessary part of the system of checks and balances by which sociological findings are kept honest.

We have discussed three troublesome areas of methodological concern in sociology: (1) the problem of developing reliable and valid measures of human behavior; (2) the problem of constructing representative samples that allow an inference from a limited number of measurements to a wider universe of human behavior; and (3) the problem of apprehending the relationships, especially cause and effect, between different aspects of human behavior. In none of these areas is there any easy solution to the problem; but in none is the sociologist completely bereft of techniques for dealing with the problem. Research *style* is as important a consideration in sociology as it is elsewhere. Just as there may be graceful or clumsy styles of public address or lovemaking, there are sociologists who command the respect of their colleagues for the elegance of their methodological style, and others whose styles are best overlooked in the interest of charity.

Notes

1. William James, "The Will to Believe" in *The Will to Believe, and Other Essays in Popular Philosophy,* new ed. (New York: Longmans, Green, 1937).

2. John H. Randall, Jr., and Justus Buchler, *Philosophy: An Introduction* (New York: Barnes & Noble, 1942), p. 93.

3. Ibid., p. 79.

4. Sir Gavin De Beer, *Charles Darwin* (Garden City, N.Y.: Doubleday, 1965).

5. Carl G. Hempel, "A Logical Appraisal of Operationism," in Philipp Frank (ed.), *The Validation of Scientific Theories* (Boston: Beacon, 1956), pp. 52–58.

6. Robert K, Merton, *Social Theory and Social Structure* (Glencoe, Ill.: Free Press, 1956), pp. 103–108.

7. Ibid., pp. 93–95.

8. Charles H. Cooley, *Human Nature and the Social Order* (New York: Scribner's, 1902), p. 110.

9. Lewis Coser, *Sociology Through Literature* (Englewood Cliffs, N.J.: Prentice-Hall, 1963).

10. *The Positive Philosophy of Auguste Comte,* trans. by Harriet Martineau (London: Bell, 1896).

11. Emile Durkheim, *The Rules of Sociological Method,* trans. by Sarah A. Solovay and John H. Mueller (Chicago: University of Chicago Press, 1938).

12. Max Weber, *The Methodology of the Social Sciences,* trans. by Edward A. Shils and Henry A. Finch (Glencoe, Ill.: Free Press, 1949).

13. One of the earliest examples was Herbert Spencer, *The Study of Sociology* (New York: Appleton, 1902).

14. One of the problems of becoming an expert or a "big name" in a scientific field is that other scholars are often more inclined to cite the expert's work with approval as a way of gaining prestige for themselves than they are to criticize the work of a "great man." See Norman Storer, *The Social System of Science* (New York: Holt, Rinehart & Winston, 1966).

15. Claire Selltiz et al., *Research Methods in Social Relations,* rev. ed. (New York: Holt, Rinehart & Winston, 1961), pp. 154–186.

16. J. P. Guilford, *Psychometric Methods,* 2nd ed. (New York: McGraw-Hill, 1954), pp. 373–398.

17. Selltiz et al., *Research Methods in Social Relations,* Ch. 10.

18. Aaron V. Cicourel, *Method and Measurement in Sociology* (New York: Free Press of Glencoe, 1964), Chs. 2 and 3; Eugene J. Webb et al., *Unobtrusive Measures* (Chicago: Rand McNally, 1966).

19. For discussion of the problem of establishing rapport in participant-observer situations, see William F. Whyte, *Street Corner Society* (Chicago: University of Chicago Press, 1943), Appendix; John Dollard, *Caste and Class in a Southern Town* (Garden City, N.Y.: Doubleday, 1957); Leon Festinger et al., *When Prophecy Fails* (Minneapolis: University of Minnesota Press, 1956), Methodological Appendix.

20. In addition to observer effect, the reverse situation, namely, the effect of his subjects on the observational powers of the observer, has also been discussed. See John F. Glass and Harry H. Frankiel, "The Influence of Subjects on the Researcher: A Problem in Observing Social Interaction," *Pacific Sociological Review,* 11(1968): 75–80.

21. For a general discussion of problems in sampling, in this case revolving around the failure of the public opinion polls to predict the outcome of the 1948 presidential election, see Rensis Likert, "Public Opinion Polls," *Scientific*

American, 179 (Dec., 1948): 7–11. For a more recent discussion, see Gideon Sjoberg and Roger Nett, *A Methodology for Social Research* (New York: Harper & Row, 1968), pp. 144–159.

22. Sidney Siegel, *Nonparametric Statistics for the Behavioral Sciences* (New York: McGraw-Hill, 1956).

23. Bernard S. Phillips, *Social Research Strategy and Tactics* (New York: Macmillan, 1966), pp. 45, 46.

24. See, for one example, Muzafer and Carolyn Sherif, *Reference Groups* (New York: Harper & Row, 1964).

25. For one discussion of the ethical problems involved in social research, see Edward A. Shils, "Social Inquiry and the Autonomy of the Individual," in Daniel Lerner (ed.), *The Human Meaning of the Social Sciences* (Cleveland: World, 1959), pp. 114–157.

26. An example of a study which deals in this way with intervening variables is Samuel A. Stouffer, *Communism, Conformity and Civil Liberties* (Garden City, N.Y.: Doubleday, 1955).

27. C. Wright Mills, *The Sociological Imagination* (New York: Oxford University Press, 1959).

Collecting the Data

Although the Rose reading singles out four very important points in the scientific method for closer examination, one other point deserves extended treatment—data collection or methods of observation. In sociology, researchers gather information using a number of different techniques that can be grouped under three broad headings: questionnaires and interviews, observation, and available data. The first technique, *questionnaires and interviews,* uses questions to gather information directly from the subject. The researcher either presents these questions in the form of a written questionnaire or asks them directly in a person-to-person interview. You are probably quite familiar with the questionnaire format; you have, no doubt, filled out many of them in your life, although not all of them have been made up by sociologists. The questionnaire format is a series of questions about the subject that the subject fills out. The interview technique differs in that the subject is asked the questions by someone else (the researcher or a trained interviewer). The questions may or may not be as structured in the interview. Sometimes an interviewer simply has a list of areas that must be covered during the interview. The areas can be covered in any order and in any way, just so long as they are covered. Job interviews are often conducted in this way. In contrast, in many public opinion polls, interviewers ask very specific questions in a predetermined fashion. Both of these interviewing variations are widely used in sociology.

The second broad category of data collection is *observation.* In this case a researcher does not ask questions directly but rather observes some event or series of events and carefully records the data observed. This technique also comes in two varieties. In the first, the observer becomes directly involved in the event being recorded—a technique called participant observation. In the second, the observer assumes the role of observer only. A researcher interested in observing soccer crowd behavior who chooses to become a member of the crowd in order to collect the information is engaged in participant observation. An adult researcher who observes children playing on a school playground is engaged in the nonparticipant type of observation.

The third general type of data collection is not really "collection" in the usual sense of that word. Instead, the third technique uses *available data*—that is, data that have already been collected, although sociologists usually use these data for some purpose other than originally intended. Examples of available data are the U.S. Census, personal diaries, newspaper and magazine articles, TV shows, court records, minutes of meetings, historical records, and data collected by another researcher. Each year thousands of pieces of data are generated in this country and in all the other countries of the world. These are not always in the form of statistics or numbers, as the previous examples demonstrate. Many of these data can be used in research. For instance, if you were interested in the question of whether or not the portrayal of women in women's magazines has changed in the last thirty years, you could examine the contents of fictional accounts involving women from a sample of women's magazines from the 1950s, 1960s, 1970s, and 1980s. These would give you a good picture of the changing portrayal of women across time. If you were more interested in seeing the difference between the portrayals in men's versus women's magazines today, you could easily compare the contents of two representative sets of magazines. (Incidentally, such analysis of the contents of documents, magazines, newspapers, and so on, is known as content analysis.) Throughout the rest of this book, you will see numerous examples of these three broad categories of data collection techniques.

BASIC CONCEPTS

Social structure, role, class, interaction, norms, and *culture*—these are all parts of the vocabulary of basic concepts sociologists use in analyzing the social world. A concept is a mental image that is formed by looking at many cases of a particular object or event and identifying the characteristics they have in common. The word *chair* is a concept. When we see the word, we form a mental image of this object in our minds. How did we arrive at this particular mental image? By looking at lots of things people sit on and abstracting a set of common characteristics from them: They each had four legs, a seat, and a back. Concepts are tools for making sense out of the world; we categorize and simplify through the use of general concepts. *House* is a concept used to identify a particular type of dwelling. We use it to categorize and simplify the world of physical living facilities. Whenever we use the term *house* we create an image that allows us to distinguish a house from a high-rise apartment, a tent, and an old station wagon. So it is with all concepts. They tell us what to look for and what does not fit.

In the following reading, Alex Inkeles lays out the basic set of important concepts used by sociologists. Sociological concepts tell us what to pay attention to as we sort the social world in new ways. Although the concepts used in this section may look familiar, you will see that they have technical definitions often differing from their more common usages. Sociologists, like any other scientists, have come to depend on these shared technical definitions in order to communicate efficiently and accurately with each other. These same basic concepts are used in all sections of this book. As you read the rest of this book, you will learn other concepts used to understand and portray a social world.

In a very few pages Inkeles takes you through the structure and process of societies by introducing the units of social organization; the nature of social relationships; conformity, variation, and deviance; and stratification and mobility. The concepts discussed in each of these areas furnish you with the basic vocabulary of sociology. It is important to realize that these are not simply words and their definitions that you need to learn. These concepts are analytical tools; they allow you to "see" your world. For instance, look at the concept *role*. Two points need to be made about the use of this concept. First, the word *role* is probably not new to you. You already know about roles in plays—people learn lines and act out certain parts or characters. Although very similar, the sociological definition is much more detailed. Second, knowing the sociological definition allows you to "see" roles as important components of a society. Let's look at Inkeles' definition of *role* and see what these two points mean. Inkeles says that roles are "definite sets or complexes of customary ways of doing things, organized about a particular problem, or designed to attain a given objective." By knowing this definition, your attention is directed to these clusters of customary ways of doing things. Without the definition, you might answer the question What is a student? by saying, "Someone who studies." With the definition of *role* we can direct your attention beyond studying to a cluster of "customary ways of doing things." So we ask, "What is the student role?" The word *role* directs your attention to "definite sets or complexes . . ." and you are able to see that *student* means so much more than studying. It may mean going to class, sitting in certain seats in the classroom (whether assigned or not), accepting directions from professors, dressing like other students, cooperating on assignments, and acting like a student around Mom and Dad. When we ask, "What is the role of daughter?" your attention is drawn to the cluster of customary ways of being a daughter. Each of the concepts and its definition, then, not only teaches a vocabulary necessary for efficient communication but also gives you a set of tools for seeing the world around you.

As you read through Inkeles' dictionary of concepts (notice that he is rather abstract), ask yourself these questions about each one. Where does the concept focus your attention? On individuals as actors? On collections of individuals? Or on the larger society without paying much attention to individuals? We need all of these levels for a complete understanding of the social world. Also notice that even though our basic concepts focus on different levels, they are all interrelated. For instance, while individuals interact in patterned ways through roles, these *sets* of patterns in specific areas are called institutions—the family, the economy, and so on. Note that interaction patterns are ongoing processes; once they crystallize, they become part of the structure of society. You might try to trace some of the other interrelationships among the concepts at the different levels.

Although Inkeles does not mention it, you should tie these basic concepts back to the theoretical orientations discussed in the second section of Part One. Do some of these concepts fit better into one theoretical orientation rather than another? Are some equally at home in any orientation? Although there are no clear-cut answers to these last questions, you may see some regularities. Because functionalists and conflict theorists often think in terms of structure, the basic concepts that relate to the patterning or structuring in societies are more likely to fall under these theoretical orientations. The concepts referring to structure include *norms, primary groups, culture, stratification, institutions,* and *society.* As you have seen before, structure refers to the organization or framework of social behavior—it is how behavior is patterned. All of these concepts define and describe frameworks for behavior. Interactionists, however, tend to concentrate more on interaction processes, paying less attention to the concepts with more structural meaning. But the world is not so neat! Interaction processes in roles are structured or patterned and, thus, are of concern to the people interested in structure. Inkeles uses roles to describe institutions, a basic structural concept. Conversely, interactionists look at norms and groups as fundamental parts of interaction in a society. More important than pigeon-holing the concepts into some single orientation is being aware that the concepts are used for different purposes in the different models. The definitions stay the same, but the focus and relative importance change.

One final word about the reading. Although the use of the word *man* as a general concept to refer to *all* human beings is still a debated issue, we (the editors) do not feel that this usage is appropriate. However, in the interests of preserving Inkeles' article in its original form, we have left the generic *man* in the text.

5
Basic Elements of Social Life

Alex Inkeles

THE UNITS OF SOCIAL ORGANIZATION

Man is endlessly inventive. But his greatest invention is non-invention, the skill of transmitting intact and unchanged from one generation to the next the fundamental ways of doing things which he learned from the generation which preceded him. Children are conceived and reared, houses built, fish caught, and enemies killed in much the same way by most of the members of any society; and these patterns are maintained for relatively long periods of time. From the perspective of those in each new generation, and for the society as an enduring, historical entity, this process of cultural transmission yields enormous economy. Thanks to it, each generation need not rediscover, at great cost in time and subject to great risk of failure, what those coming before have already learned. Not only is knowledge thus conserved, but the basis for communal life, resting on common information and understanding, is thus established. Since all those in each generation receive more or less the same cultural heritage from the preceding generation, they can more easily relate to one another and more effectively coordinate their actions.

The grand total of all the objects, ideas, knowledge, ways of doing things, habits, values, and attitudes which each generation in a society passes on to the next is what the anthropologist often refers to as the *culture* of a group. The transmission of culture is man's substitute for the instincts whereby most other living creatures are equipped with the means for coping with their environment and relating to one another. Yet it is more flexible than instinct, and can grow; that is, it can store new information, infinitely more rapidly than the process of mutation and biological evolution can enrich the instinctual storehouse of any other species.

From Folkways to Institutions

Custom, or alternatively, *folkways,* are the terms most commonly applied to the specialized and standardized ways of doing things common to those sharing a particular culture. The term can be applied to as small a social act[1] as a man's lifting his hat and saying "hello" on passing a woman he knows, or to as large and complex a set of events as the speeches, ceremonies, parades, and fireworks which grace the celebration of the Fourth of July in the United States. Custom, then, is any standardized and more or less specialized set of actions which is routinely carried out according to a generally accepted pattern in a given group. If the custom is not only routinely followed, but is, in addition, surrounded by sentiments or values such that failure to follow the expected pattern would produce strong sanctions from one's group, it is referred to as part of the *mores*. This distinction between folkways and mores lay at the heart of the work of the noted American sociologist William Graham Sumner.[2]

The association among customs is not random. Definite sets or complexes of customary ways of doing things, organized about a particular problem, or designed to attain a given objective, can be readily identified in any human community. Such a cluster of customary ways of doing things we designate a *role*. Roles are generally recognized and defined by the participants in a social system. They are, therefore, intimately tied to a set of expectations about which acts go with which others, in what sequence and under which conditions. Certain roles are open and can be assigned to anyone. A child asked to go out and rake the leaves has been temporarily assigned a role. He will be expected to follow a certain broadly defined sequence of acts, including putting the rake back in the garage when he is through. Any other child in the family might have been asked, and would have been expected to proceed in the same way.

Other roles are more highly specialized and become specific to particular individuals. When this degree of formalization exists, in particular when we use a specific name, title, or similar designation for certain role incumbents, then a social *position* has been created. The term "status" is most commonly applied to such positions, but since this use of the term is easily confused with another, as in Vance Packard's *The Status Seekers*, as meaning prestige or standing in the community, we will speak either of "positions" or "status-positions." Within our family system we obviously do not recognize the status-position of "leaf-raker." In the occupational realm, however, where the degree of specialization is very much greater, we do recognize such rather narrowly defined positions as "stoker" on a coal ship or "fireman" on a train.

A *status-position*, then, is a socially recognized designation, a position in *social* as against geographical space, to which individuals may be assigned and which confers on the incumbent a set of rights and obligations. The rights and obligations constitute the role which the incumbent is expected to play. Positions may vary in the range and specificity of the roles they involve. In my status-position as rider on a public bus, my chief right is to be transported more or less directly to my destination. My obligations are largely limited to paying my fare, and not causing any disturbance to the other passengers. When I step into the position of husband

or father, however, I acquire a large and complex set of roles involving a series of quite diffuse rights and obligations.

The paths of assignment to status-positions are generally distinguished on grounds of whether the position is ascribed or achieved. *Ascribed* status-positions are those to which individuals are more or less automatically assigned on the basis of accidents of birth. Age and sex form the most obvious bases for such ascription, and often color, caste, family line, and religion determine the assignment. *Achieved* status-positions are those in which a person is placed because of some action or attainment on his part. In our society political office and occupation or profession provide the most important examples of achieved positions, but one can treat the status-position of husband and wife in the same way. Certain achieved positions may be open only to those with prior qualifications on the basis of ascription, and many positions once open mainly to achievement are captured by a particular group and converted into ascribed positions.

Just as social acts may be aggregated into customs, and sets of such actions aggregated in roles, so a more complex structure of roles organized around some central activity or social need may be aggregated into an *institution*. . . .

Institutions lie at the center of sociological attention. They constitute the main building blocks of society. The number of institutions and the degree of their specialization vary from society to society. High civilizations and modern large-scale industrial societies are characterized by the intensive specialization of institutions organized around delimited problems of social life, and by the extensive internal elaboration of sub-systems within the larger institutions.

We must, therefore, think in terms of small-scale and large-scale institutions, and of complexes of institutions which form sub-systems within the larger society. At least four major sets or complexes of important institutions are recognized by most sociologists. It will be evident, however, that each group could readily be broken up into several . . . categories.

First, are the *political institutions*, concerned with the exercise of power and which have a monopoly on the legitimate use of force. Institutions involving relations with other societies, including war, are also considered to fall into the political category. Second, there are the *economic institutions,* concerned with the production and distribution of goods and services. *Expressive-integrative* institutions, including those dealing with the arts, drama, and recreation, represent a third set. This group also includes institutions which deal with ideas, and with the transmission of received values. We may, therefore, include scientific, religious, philosophical, and educational organizations within this category. *Kinship institutions,* the fourth main category, are principally focused around the problem of regulating sex and providing a stable and secure framework for the care and rearing of the young.

Although it is helpful and to a degree accurate to think of institutions as organized mainly around *one* central problem of social existence, it is misleading to assume that each institution's contribution to social life is limited to that main concern. Each major institutional complex participates in and contributes in a number of ways to the life of the community. The family, for example, may be, and often is, itself a productive enterprise, and it always engages in the distribution of goods and services. Economic institutions not only produce goods and services but must have an internal order which involves the control of force and the exercise of legitimate authority. These considerations have led sociologists to make a distinction between social structures conceived of in either the analytic or the concrete sense. When speaking of *concrete structures,* they refer to the institutions we are also familiar with—families, courts, factories, and the like. By *analytic structures* they mean the whole set of social ways, spread over many concrete institutions, whereby a society manages to effect the production and distribution of goods, the control of force, and its other basic functional needs. For example, when we speak of "the structure of authority" in the analytic sense, we mean the way in which authority is organized and exercised not only in political affairs but also in the neighborhood, the church, the school, the family, and even in informal groups. Analytic structures are, therefore, constructs, products of the mind, abstracted from the concrete reality of a set of specific institutions.

A set of institutions constitutes a *social system,* of which the institutions may be thought of as sub-systems. The term "social system," like many others in sociology, is used to describe quite different levels of complexity. Thus, it is not uncommon to speak of the social system of a unit as small as a village or even a street-corner gang, and of those as large as a nation. Despite the ambiguity this introduces, it is at the present stage of our development a term without which we seem unable to manage.

Three elements are relevant to a definition of *community.* A community exists (1) when a set of households is relatively concentrated in a delimited geographical area; (2) their residents exhibit a substantial degree of integrated social interaction; and (3) have a sense of common membership, of belonging together, which is not based exclusively on ties of consanguinity. The example most commonly used, most familiar, and most directly accessible, is that of the peasant village. In such a village the peasants and their families usually live in fairly close proximity, and their common residence area is clearly demarcated and known to them. Most of the villagers' interaction is with other residents of the same village. The inhabitants will commonly consider themselves of the village, know its name, acknowledge their membership in the community, and be defined by and treated by those from other communities in accord with the standing of the village from which they come.

The *neighborhood* is simply a more limited form of community, but otherwise, it has the same characteristics. There is a physically distinctive territory, the inhabitants interact with one another relatively often, and they have a sense of belonging together. The neighborhood is usually the smallest residential unit, other than the household, recognized by sociology. The latter is not, customarily, spoken of as a community because it is predominantly organized on the basis of kinship.

As the size of a group inhabiting a given

territory increases, there is an almost inevitable decrease in the probability of interaction between any two individuals chosen at random. When interaction between the average member and any other decreases beyond a certain point, the appropriateness of speaking of a community may be slight. In other words, physical proximity does not in itself make a community. A census tract arbitrarily and mechanically imposed on the map of a city does not bear any important relation to the more natural communities which develop in the different sections of a city. In what sense can the 10 million inhabitants of New York City be considered members of "a" community? In reply we might say that direct face-to-face interaction can be replaced to some degree by symbolic interaction, including that fostered by the media of mass communication. And a *sense* of common membership can be reinforced by external—i.e., legal or political—inducements to think of oneself as part of a specified community. . . .

Society: National and Worldwide

There is a type of social system larger than the institution and different from the community. Yet it is not automatically present whenever there is a set of institutions, nor does it automatically arise from every set of communities. It constitutes the largest unit with which sociology is ordinarily concerned, and is designated a *society.*

In *The Structure of Society* Marion Levy proposed 4 criteria which must be met by a group before it may be considered a society: The group must be capable of existing longer than the life span of the individual; it should recruit its new members at least in part by means of sexual reproduction; it should be united in giving allegiance to a common complex "general system of action"; and that system of action should be "self-sufficient."[3] The last of these criteria merits a few words of further explanation. By "system of action" we mean the total set of customs, values, and standard ways of acting which are commonly manifested by a group having relatively enduring mutual social relations. Systems of action may be relatively

limited and moderately simple. For example, the relations between the teachers and pupils in a school represent the system of action specific to the school. We consider a system of action "self-sufficient" only if the rules, customs, and technology of a given group provide resources, knowledge, and legitimate power which normally arise in the course of social life.

According to this definition, the ordinary township in the United States, despite its high material culture and complex organization, would not be considered a society. It does not have the power to organize its own defense, and as a rule to deal with a murder it is obliged to rely on county or state police, courts, jails, and the like. A monastery would not qualify, even if its rules covered murder, because it makes no provision for sexual recruitment of new members. But these are essentially technical reservations. A simpler, although somewhat macabre, way to think about whether a group qualifies as a society would be to imagine that all other communities in the world except this one were suddenly to disappear. If there were a good chance that the surviving community would go forward in substantially its present form through subsequent generations, then it qualifies as a society. Most primitive tribes, however small, and virtually all nation-states clearly meet this requirement. If a community could not survive under such a severe test, or could do so only by developing or elaborating many new institutional arrangements, such as a system of law and justice for which it formerly depended on a larger social system, then it does not qualify as a true society.

One can argue that the increased speed of travel, and the interlocking nature of world economy and international politics have, in effect, made a single, interacting community of all the people on earth. From this perspective one would maintain that there is a *worldwide social system.* Participation in this system is partly on an individual basis; partly on the basis of informal groups, as in the relations between relatives dispersed in different countries; and partly between more formally organized entities, such as companies doing business internationally, or international welfare organizations such as the Red Cross. The greatest portion of the interaction which characterizes the global social system, however, is accounted for by relations between the nation-states as units, or at least between individuals and groups acting as representatives or agents of such national units. These activities include diplomatic relations, the control of trade and movement, and war.

Whether the system of action in which the nations of the world participate constitutes a true worldwide *society,* in the sense in which we use the term, is certainly open to question. The issue hinges by our definition on the existence of shared, self-sufficient system of action. On this test the world community seems seriously lacking. Very few values are shared by the majority of the world's people and fewer still are shared by their governments. Accepted mechanisms for the peaceful settlement of disputes, an indispensable element in any society, are poorly developed at the international level. The United Nations notwithstanding, there is no organized authority with the power to compel the nation-states' obedience to group decisions. We are today probably further from having a truly global society than the world knew under the hegemony of Rome or at the height of the power of the Church in medieval Europe. Yet there is reason to feel that since World War II we have come closer to developing a world society than was true at any point in the past few centuries.

THE NATURE OF SOCIAL RELATIONSHIPS

In exploring the basic elements of social organization, we identified the institution, the community, and the society, each reflecting a different degree of completeness as a system of social action. But pursuing this line we neglected another set of distinctions which has an equally long and honorable place in sociology. One major mode of sociological analysis focuses mainly on the frequency and the qualities of *social relationships.* This approach can be applied to all the groups we have already discussed. It cuts across institutions, households, neighborhoods, community, and society.

The smallest unit to which sociological analysis is applied is *"the social act."* It has been written about at length by leading sociological thinkers such as Max Weber and George Herbert Mead,[4] but it remains an elusive concept and something difficult to measure. Most theorists apparently have in mind the smallest unit of directly visible action which has a reasonably clear shared meaning for both the actor and others with whom he is in contact. The instantaneous flick of the eyelid may serve as a simple example. If I merely "blink" spontaneously, especially as a reflex, the act is physical, but not social. But if I "wink," meaning to communicate the idea—"I am with you"—to someone I believe able to read the sign, then the movement of my eyelid is "a social act." If the other person responds by nodding or smiling, and he intends thereby to communicate receipt of the signal from me, then his nod is also "a social act." Taken together this sequence represents *a simple social interaction.* Social relationships may be conceived as made up of sets and patterns of such interaction sequences.

These ideas obviously invite numerous complications. We may ask, for example: Is an act social if I alone give it meaning? Is it social if it has no particular meaning for me, but has meaning for others? What about "internal" acts, which no one else can directly observe? Different, but equally difficult, is the task of setting limits to the begining and end of any social act. If I not only wink but also laugh and say, "Very funny," should each of these units be considered a social act, or only the entire sequence? It is obvious that challenging difficulties face those who aspire to classify and measure interaction in empirical research.

One can easily be tempted to see in the sociological concepts of "the act" and "the relationship" an analogy with the atom and the molecule in physics and with the cell and tissue in biology. These are the basic units of which are built all the larger and more complex structures relevant to the respective disciplines. It will be no surprise, therefore, that many leading sociological theorists sought to develop a set of terms to distinguish different types of relationship and to increase our understanding of them. Sociological writing is replete with schemes for classifying social relationships, varying greatly in complexity, sophistication, and thoroughness. Perhaps the most honored is Charles Cooley's distinction between primary and secondary relationships.[5] A primary relationship, according to Cooley, is one in which intimate face-to-face association and cooperation predominate, as a result of which individuals become fused into a common whole epitomized by stress on "we" rather than "I." Similar, and equally well-known distinctions, were elaborated by Tönnies in Germany[6] and by Durkheim in France.[7]

Not only have these distinctions endured, but so have the difficulties of using the concepts with any degree of precision. As Kingsley Davis has pointed out, Cooley's stress on "we" feeling cannot be taken as the distinctive element in a primary group since this same feeling is to some degree necessary for any enduring community. It must exist even in the great nations, in which there clearly can be face-to-face contact between only a small proportion of the members.[8]

The obvious difficulty is that concepts such as Cooley's primary group and Tönnies' gemeinschaft assume the factual coherence of a set of discrete aspects of relationships which may or may not combine in reality as the sociologist thought they would. Such concepts are, in other words, rather global summaries; they refer to the hypothetical rather than to the empirically demonstrated. One of the tasks of those following Cooley and Tönnies, therefore, has been to designate more precisely what are the aspects of any relationship. The underlying justification for these efforts at conceptual clarification is, of course, the hope that more precise conceptual distinctions will encourage more exact observation and measurement. The accumulation of data based on direct observation would enable us more accurately to describe the actual pattern of association between various dimensions of interaction which is assumed to exist when we use concepts such as "the primary group."

One distinction we obviously must make in describing any relationship is that between quantitative and qualitative aspects. The quantitative elements include, first and foremost, the number of people participating in the system of action, their concentration or dispersion in geographical space, the frequency with which they interact with one another, and the relative duration of their association.

The qualitative aspects of the interaction are less easy to agree about. Kingsley Davis distinguishes 5 characteristics which, when combined with certain information concerning the quantitative aspect (which he calls "physical conditions") serve him as a basis for discriminating primary from secondary relationships.[9] He gives examples of these at the level of both the dyad and the larger group. His scheme is given in Table 1.

Professor Davis' scheme is a variant on one more widely known, developed by Talcott Parsons.[10] He uses a set of 5 "pattern variables" to distinguish the aspects of any social relationship. According to Parsons, each time we act, and in each role in which we act, we are, in effect, emphasizing one or another side of the 5 basic divisions. If a role is specific, our relationship is limited to one particular narrowly defined exchange; if it is diffuse, our involvement will extend over a wide variety of problems or relationships. We stress either affectivity (that is, feeling, emotion, and gratification), or affective neutrality, which means we place more emphasis on instrumental or moral considerations. We manifest particularism when we give special consideration to people because of their relationship to us, whereas if we evidence universalism, we treat more or less alike all who come before us in a given status-position. If my treatment of you is mainly on the basis of what you are in yourself, in contrast to what you do or have done, I stress quality over performance. When my concern is mainly to advance the goals of the group, I display a collectivity-orientation, whereas if I am most concerned to advance my own interests through our relationship, I stress self-orientation. Described in these terms, the relations of husband and wife, and indeed all nuclear family relations, tend to be diffuse, affective, and particularistic, and reflect stress on quality and collectivity-orientation. The relationship between a clerk and a customer would be at the opposite pole on each dimension. . . .

Table 1

Primary and Secondary Relationships

Primary			
Physical Conditions	Social Characteristics	Sample Relationships	Sample Groups
Spatial proximity	Identification of ends	Friend-friend	Play group
Small number	Intrinsic valuation of the relation	Husband-wife	Family
Long duration	Intrinsic valuation of other person	Parent-child	Village or neighborhood
	Inclusive knowledge of other person	Teacher-pupil	Work-team
	Feeling of freedom and spontaneity		
	Operation of informal controls		

Secondary			
Physical Conditions	Social Characteristics	Sample Relationships	Sample Groups
Spatial distance	Disparity of ends	Clerk-customer	Nation
Large number	Extrinsic valuation of the relation	Announcer-listener	Clerical
Short duration	Extrinsic valuation of other person	Performer-spectator	Professional association
	Specialized and limited knowledge of other person	Officer-subordinate	Corporation
	Feeling of external constraint	Author-reader	
	Operation of formal controls		

Kingsley Davis, *Human Society* (New York: Macmillan, 1957), p. 306.

The Study of Values

Although the most dramatic advances in the direct observation of interpersonal relations and the measurement of interaction have been made in the laboratory, significant progress is also being made in studying relationships in real life. These studies, however, more often deal with *values* about human relations rather than with behavior directly observed.

The term "values" has almost as much importance in sociology as the terms "institution" and "social system." Individuals, groups, organizations, societies, and cultures are all spoken of as "having," "expressing," and "pursuing" values. Like many another sociological term, "values" carries a heavy load indeed. In the many definitions of values proposed by sociologists and anthropologists, the common element lies in the recognition of values as an expression of the ultimate ends, goals, or purposes of social action. Values deal not so much with what is, but with what ought to be; in other words, they express moral imperatives. Thus, when Weber identified the importance to Benjamin Franklin of sobriety, strict ethics in business relations, and the avoidance of indulgence, he was describing Franklin's values. Almost any conceivable aspect of any relationship can be, and somewhere probably has been, made an object of value. Honesty and duplicity, silence and loquaciousness, stoicism and emotionality, restless activity and passive acceptance, all have been deeply valued in different societies.

Much the same range of human qualities and aspects of relationships are recognized in most societies, the main differences between cultures being in the value they put on these qualities as important or minor, good or bad. One values aggressiveness and deplores passivity, another the reverse. And a third gives little attention to this dimension altogether, emphasizing instead the virtue of sobriety over emotionality, which may be quite unimportant in either of the other cultures.[11]

As was true in the study of interactions, it was only after World War II that social scientists went beyond merely defining and discussing values and began actively to measure their nature and distribution. One of the most complex and interesting of these efforts has been carried out by Florence Kluckhohn. She began by defining certain basic "common human problems for which all peoples, at all times must find some solution."[12] All societies, she maintained, adopt some value position with regard to man's relation to other men, to nature, to time, and to activity. She argued that all cultures had discovered pretty much the same range of positions or alternatives one might take with regard to these life problems, but that different cultures placed different *value* on the various alternatives.

To establish her point Dr. Kluckhohn studied 5 small communities, each with an apparently distinctive way of life but all inhabiting the same area in the American Southwest. The groups included a Mormon settlement, one of ex-Texans, a village of Spanish-Americans, and both Zuñi and Navaho Indian reservations. To samples from each community she presented the same set of basic human situations, and recorded the alternative solutions they preferred. She found that the groups were indeed different, and "no two of the cultures chose exactly the same pattern of preferences on any of the (value) orientations."[13]

The two English-speaking groups were most alike, although differing in important respects. They seemed to represent one pole, the Spanish-Americans the other, with the Indian groups falling somewhere between. For example, the Texans were more individualistic rather than concerned with the extended family group, were oriented to the future rather than to the past, inclined to see man as over nature rather than as subjugated to it, and on the activity dimension were predominantly interested in "doing." By contrast, the Spanish-Americans stressed lineality (the principle which sees the individual mainly in terms of his relation to an ordered succession of social positions enduring through time); they were more oriented to the present than to the future; they viewed man as subjugated to nature; and they strongly preferred "being" over "doing." . . .[14]

CONFORMITY, VARIATION, AND DEVIANCE

The social order depends on the regular and adequate fulfillment of the role obligations incurred by the incumbents of the major status-positions in a social system. It follows that the most important process in society is that which insures that people do indeed meet their role obligations. The processes of conformity, variation, and deviance are, therefore, among the most crucial with which sociology concerns itself.

Most people assume, almost glibly, that they know the meaning of conformity. It means doing what you are supposed to do, as exemplified by the child who puts on his rubbers when his mother tells him to, the pupil who does his homework assignment, the motorist who stops his car at the intersection until the policeman signals that he may proceed, and the citizen who honestly pays his taxes. In all these examples the status-position is clear-cut, the behavior required explicit and limited, the rules unambiguous, and the power to enforce conformity physically embodied and close at hand. Sociology starts here with what we all know and accept; conformity to role obligations rests in good part on *sanctions*: the power of others—individuals, groups, and the community—to enforce their expectations by the use of reward and punishment.

The ultimate negative sanction is, of course, death. Negative sanctions range through all forms of physical force down to mild restraint. They include, as well, psychological punishments from the most degrading public humiliation, through ridicule, to mild forms of censure such as are implicit in many nominally friendly jibes and critical jokes. Negative sanctions may be effected not only in doing, but in not doing. In our psychological-minded era, everyone has become familiar with the idea of the "withholding of love" as a sanction parents apply to control their children.

There is an obvious difficulty in relying on sanctions to insure conformity to crucial role obligations: Someone must always be around to observe what happens and to dispense rewards and punishment. Although we are all to some extent our brothers' keepers, no society could manage even a small part of its diverse tasks if conformity to role obligation rested solely on such ubiquitous supervision. *Motivation*, the readiness and desire of the individual to fulfill his role obligations is, therefore, an indispensable underpinning which supports the network of roles and insures the reasonably smooth flow of social activity without excessive social investment in supervision by others. Finally, neither sanctions nor motivation to perform can be successful where the incumbent of status-position does not understand clearly what is required of him.

When an individual has incorporated within himself knowledge and appropriate skills necessary to the fulfillment of a role, and when he accepts the value or appropriateness of the action, sociologists speak of his having "internalized" the role and its psychological underpinnings. The term *socialization* is used to describe the process whereby individuals learn their culture, both in its most general form and as it applies to particular roles. Although it usually refers to the learning of children, the term "socialization" may be used in exactly the same sense to describe adults learning what is required of them in a new job or some other status-position which they are entering.

A complaint long directed against anthropologists, and sometimes made with equal justice about sociologists, is that they too readily assume that the members of society hold the same values and beliefs and share a common pattern of action. In trying to develop a "model" of any society, the social scientist almost inevitably gives us a simplified picture which gravely understates the variety and diversity of attitude and behavior found in most societies. Cultural norms and ways of doing things seldom involve rigid and uniform requirements. They usually permit a fairly wide range in the way things are done. We are expected to cross streets at the crossing, but people cross them at all places and in all ways without, in most cases, very much being made of the fact. Even with regard to the most fundamental issues of life, most cultures do not hold a single unified set of beliefs. Rather, they harbor both dominant and quite acceptable variant values.[15] Most Americans are either present or future oriented, but it is quite acceptable to look to and value the past. Indeed, some social groups in some sections of the country, notably New England and the South, rest their social distinction in part on their preoccupation with the past.

Deviance, then, is not necessarily inherent in every departure from a commonly accepted standard, nor in holding any minority view. This would be statistical deviance, but not social deviance. *Social deviance* arises when the departure from accepted norms involves action about which the community feels strongly, so strongly as to adopt sanctions to prevent or otherwise control the deviant behavior. In other words, deviant behavior is not merely oblique to dominant or "core" values, but is antithetical to them. The point is clear-cut in the case of major crimes. But the issue can also become clouded, and the designation "deviant" very ambiguous. Exceeding the speed limit on the highway is against the law. Is it still deviance if almost everyone does it? In Mississippi local citizens engaged in armed resistance to United States marshals trying to carry out an order of a Federal Court instructing them to effect the enrollment of a Negro in the University of Mississippi. The local grand jury in Mississippi wished to send the marshals, not the rioters, to jail. Obviously, what is deviant may be different from the perspective of different groups participating in the same larger system of action. Landlords owning property near crowded army camps may, for substandard housing, charge the dependents of mobilized soldiers much higher rents than those commonly collected in their region. Are they merely following the accepted business practice in taking advantage of an opportunity for profit, or is their action a deviation from moral norms? . . .

STRATIFICATION AND MOBILITY

There is no society known which does not make some distinction between individuals by ranking them on some scale of value. The most ubiq-

uitous is that between men and women. But such distinctions may rest on almost any basis, involving either ascribed or achieved status. Even in the societies with the simplest technology, the good hunter is distinguished from the poorer one and is generally accorded prestige or higher standing in the community. The more complex the technology, the greater the specialization, the more extensive the degree of social differentiation, the more bases are established for differential valuation.

Such prestige rankings are often referred to as status rankings. It is [in] that sense of the word that almost everyone has come to know of "The Status Seekers." Many radical religious and political philosophies treat all such distinctions as invidious, and indeed evil. They urge the establishment of a world in which these distinctions no longer exist, and instead all men are *valued* as equal. Most sociologists are dubious of the possibility of creating such a society, and the unhappy fate of most utopian communities makes this skepticism warranted. There is good reason to assume that ranking people is inherent in man, and that no society will ever be without it.

Differential valuation is unfortunately commonly confused with differential possessions, such as skill, power, or economic resources. Sociologists insist on keeping these categories quite distinct. Exploring the actual relation between differential possessions and differential prestige is one of the more important and interesting tasks the sociologist can find. The interrelations are by no means obvious or simple. Prestige may be used to win access to economic advantage, and both power and money may be used to buy standing in the community—or at least the outward evidences of respect and prestige.

The individuals in any society may be placed on a scale or hierarchy of value expressing the prestige or respect in which each person is held. Those sharing more or less comparable standing will then form a *prestige group,* or stratum. In some societies these arrangements are formal and explicit. They may be religiously sanctioned, as in the Indian caste system, and even enforced by law. Similarly, individuals may be placed on a scale of possessions, separately for political power, land, and money. Those having similar shares of power or wealth can be grouped and considered as forming a stratum, or *class,* in the hierarchy of possessions.

When we speak of the stratification system in any society we refer to the nature of its hierarchies of possessions and status, the bases for assignment to positions in their hierarchies, and to the relations between the two hierarchies and among groups within each hierarchy. No problem in sociology has received more attention in the last 3 decades, and probably no other has been the subject of more confusion. This attention stems in good part not only from the basic importance of the issues but also from the special role which the theory of stratification plays in the Marxist scheme.

Notes

1. The term *social act* is defined and discussed . . . in the section on social relationships, p. 42.

2. William Graham Sumner, *Folkways* (Boston: Ginn, 1906), 692 pp.

3. Marion Levy, *The Structure of Society* (Princeton: Princeton University Press, 1952), p. 113.

4. Max Weber (A. Henderson and Talcott Parsons, trans.), *Theory of Economic and Social Organization* (New York: Oxford University Press, 1947), especially pp. 88–122; George Herbert Mead (C. W. Morris, ed.), *Mind, Self and Society* (Chicago: University of Chicago Press, 1934), and (C. W. Morris, ed.), *The Philosophy of the Act* (Chicago: University of Chicago Press, 1950).

5. Charles H. Cooley, *Human Nature and the Social Order* (New York: Scribner, 1902).

6. Ferdinand Tönnies (C. P. Loomis, trans.), *Fundamental Concepts of Sociology* (New York: American Book, 1940).

7. Émile Durkheim (G. Simpson, trans.), *The Division of Labor in Society* (Glencoe, Ill.: The Free Press, 1949). . . .

8. Kingsley Davis, *Human Society* (New York: Macmillan, 1957), p. 303.

9. *Ibid.,* pp. 294–298.

10. Talcott Parsons, *The Social System* (Glencoe, Ill.: The Free Press, 1951).

11. For one general reference see Charles Osgood, *The Measurement of Meaning* (Urbana: University of Illinois Press, 1957).

12. Florence Kluckhohn and Fred L. Strodtbeck, *Variations in Value Orientation* (New York: Harper & Row, 1961), p. 10.

13. *Ibid.,* p. 172.

14. *Ibid.,* p. 170*ff.*

15. Florence Kluckhohn and Fred L. Strodtbeck, *Variations in Value Orientations* (New York: Harper & Row, 1961). The terms of dominant and variant values have been proposed by Florence Kluckhohn. Her comparative study of values in the American Southwest . . . gives ample evidence for the point made here.

SOCIAL ANALYSIS AT WORK: AN EXAMPLE

We have covered a great deal of material up to this point without offering any concrete extended illustrations of what was being said. In a very real way the rest of the book serves as such an extended illustration. *Everything* discussed in this first part—the sociological perspective, theoretical orientations, methods of research, and basic concepts—will appear in the reading selections yet to come in the book. The upcoming readings will also add much to what has already been said, including new concepts, refinements of concepts already introduced, and the application of theoretical orientations and research methods to concrete situations. But to show how all of these work together in a quick example, we are going to take you on a trip to a bar, The Oasis.

The following reading comes from E. E. LeMasters's *Blue-Collar Aristocrats*, an in-depth participant observation study of a family-type blue-collar tavern in a small suburban town in the Midwest. LeMasters called the regular patrons "blue-collar aristocrats" because the men were employed in skilled-craft occupations at the top of the blue-collar world—as carpenters, plumbers, operators of heavy equipment, and so on. LeMasters spent about six years "hanging out" at The Oasis, observing nearly fifty men and women who were "regulars" at the tavern. He was careful to catch the weekly cycle of events so as not to overrepresent some special activity or event. When LeMasters started "hanging around" the tavern, some of the regular patrons pegged him as either an undercover agent for the state liquor commission or an alcoholic. When asked why a college professor was drinking in a blue-collar tavern, LeMasters told the regulars that his time with them helped him to understand American society and relieved the boredom of constant association with white-collar people. After about a year of participant observation, he "leaked" the idea that he might write a book about the tavern life, an idea that eventually became accepted among the tavern regulars. Throughout his study one of his skills served him in good stead with the regulars. He was a skilled pool player.

In this selection LeMasters relates his conversations with the husbands about their wives (and about women in general) and with the wives about their husbands (and about men in general). As you read the selection, ask yourself these questions. How do the men view the women? LeMasters points out that the men want their wives to behave like "traditional women" rather than "modern women" with one striking exception. What is the exception? How did it evolve? What implications does it have for change in the relationship between the men and the women? How do the women view the men? What is differential social change, and how has it influenced interactions at The Oasis?

The sociological perspective is nicely illustrated in this selection. We see social behavior, social organization, and social change, the three components identified earlier by Bates. Thus, both structure and process are included in the events unfolding at The Oasis. This reading demonstrates especially well the interrelationship between structure and process. As you read the exchanges over sex-role definitions, you will see that many references are made to now existing patterns of sex roles while other references (especially those made by the women) are made to the changes in sex roles that are in the process of occurring as these people speak. If you could magically extend these conversations twenty-five years into the future, what would the patterns be? Structure and process seem to reflect each other in a reciprocal relationship.

The symbolic interactionist theoretical orientation shows clearly in this selection, with its concern for meanings (in this case, of sex roles). LeMasters offers quotation after quotation from individuals, exploring the processes of interaction between husbands and wives. He also talks the language of functionalism, saying that the males have evolved a female sex role that is "eufunctional" (has positive consequences) for themselves, if not for their wives. While he gives examples of conflict between husbands and wives, LeMasters shows it as an interaction process in the symbolic interactionist framework rather than as a societal structure of dominance, as would a conflict theorist.

As mentioned, LeMasters used the participant observation form of data collection. What particular problems do you suspect this caused in this setting? How might he have solved the four problems of social research outlined in Rose's article—the problems of objectivity, measurement, sampling, and causation? Given that LeMasters wanted to capture everyday life in a blue-collar tavern, could he have gathered his information in any other way?

Several of the basic concepts introduced in Inkeles' reading can be found here. Of course, the entire reading represents a slice of blue-collar culture with its folkways and mores. Equally important is the concept of role and its partner, status-position. At The Oasis we see both ascribed and achieved status-positions enter into the battle. The real conflict is not just men versus women but men/husbands versus women/wives. All of this reflects two broader concepts, the kinship institution and primary relationships. Finally, LeMasters introduces a small segment of life found in a particular social class, the working class. More specifically, he introduces one prestige group, the blue-collar aristocrats.

As you read the article try to see how the four major tools of analysis—the sociological perspective, theoretical orientations, methods of social research, and basic concepts—are woven together to produce a systematic description of this one small segment of social life. You will see this same interweaving in all of the other readings in this book. It is these four components of sociological thinking that allow us to answer questions about the way people behave, or how much money they have, or why the divorce rate is going up or coming down, or how people respond in a crisis. It is these four components that you will become more familiar with when you see them applied in other areas, as social life unfolds in the remainder of this book.

6
Battle of the Sexes

E. E. LeMasters

"Women are so goddamn sneaky."
—*Statement by a man at The Oasis*

INTRODUCTION

In any society one of the functional imperatives is to evolve some system whereby the two sexes

Reprinted from *Blue Collar Aristocrats* by E. E. LeMasters. Copyright 1975 by the Regents of the University of Wisconsin System. Used with permission of the publisher. Footnotes have been renumbered.

can work together effectively. It is my belief that this has not been accomplished in the blue-collar group covered in this study.[1]

In an earlier examination of blue-collar marriages, Lee Rainwater came to this conclusion: "Working class men, even more than men in general, tend to think of women as temperamental, emotional, demanding, and irrational; they are sometimes in deadly earnest when they, with the hero of *My Fair Lady*, ask with exasperation, 'Why can't a woman be more like a man?' They think that women do silly things:

51

They cry for no reason, they argue in petty ways about the things a man wants to do, and they are always acting hurt for no apparent reason."[2] Some of these attitudes were found in this study and will be examined in this [reading]—as will the ideas the women at The Oasis have concerning men.

This discussion is limited to generic items—males and females looking at each other as two different species. How for example, does women's liberation look at the level of the blue-collar aristocrat? Are blue-collar men and women suffering from differential social change—that is, are the women more contemporary than the men? . . .

THE MEN VIEW THE WOMEN
Suspicion, Distrust, and Fear of Women

It is difficult, if not impossible, to talk with the men at The Oasis about the opposite sex without feeling that they view women with suspicion and distrust. In many ways these blue-collar men feel the same way about women as they do about Negroes.

One man said: "The trouble with American women is they don't know their place. I was in Japan after World War II and by God those women know who is boss. You tell one of them babes to jump and all they ask is, 'how high?' But an American woman will say, 'why?'"

Another man said: "You take that woman who wants to run the school board.[3] Hell, when I moved to this town twenty years ago there weren't any women on the school board—it was all men. Now you go up there and the whole damn room is full of women.[4] No wonder the taxes are going up."

"Women are so damn sneaky," another man said. "You never know what they're up to."

I asked him to give an example.

"Well, you take my wife—if she wants a new sweeper or stove or something like that for the house she won't come right out and say so. Instead, she starts to drag me around the stores until I finally figure out what she's up to—then we either buy the damn thing or we don't.

Sometimes it's weeks before I even know what she's looking for."

I asked him if he thought his wife was extravagant in what she bought.

"No, she's a damn good manager, but she's so sneaky. I never know what's coming next."

I asked one of the wives at The Oasis to comment on the above statement. She was caustic: "That woman's husband is so damn tight with a dollar that she'd never get anything for the house if she let him know what she was up to. Fortunately, he is dumber than an ox and she can usually outsmart him."

You get the feeling that the women, having less power, feel that they have to outmaneuver the men to get what they want.

Some of the men at the tavern seem to resent the position women have won for themselves in American society in recent decades. One man, a plumber, put it this way: "I don't mind their being equal," he said, "but some of them want to run the whole damn show. They're just like the niggers—give them an inch and they'll take a mile."

The men complain that the women are unpredictable and moody.

"I came home the other night and the wife was crying. I figured I must have done something wrong but I couldn't think what it was.

"Anyhow, she was crying so I asked her what the trouble was."

"'Nothing,' she said.

"'Then what in the hell are you crying for?,' I asked.

"It took me ten minutes to find out she was crying because she got a letter that her favorite uncle died—Uncle Joe.

"You know how old that old bastard was? Ninety-four! And she's crying because he finally kicked the bucket!"

One man laughed and said: "I'll bet you were scared before you found out what she was crying about."

"Hell, yes, I thought maybe she found out I had ordered that new deer rifle she doesn't think we can afford."

Another man said: "Isn't it funny how women cry over the damndest things?"

Then he added: "The last time I cried was

when the Packers lost the championship." The men laughed.

I asked one of the women at The Oasis about this complaint from the men that their wives cry too much.

"Sure, they cry," she said. "If you were married to some of these dumb bastards you would cry too."

She was warming up to the subject.

"These guys don't cry—they get drunk, or chase women, or go shoot a deer or something. But women cry. It's good for them—a hell of a lot better than getting drunk or leaping into bed with somebody."

The men seldom complain that their wives are "dumb": it tends to be the opposite, that the women are crafty, sly, devious, or scheming.

"I never can figure out what in the hell she is up to," one man observed about his wife.

"The other night, for example, I was watching a baseball game on television and I noticed her sitting there in her nightgown brushing her hair—usually she just goes to bed when a game is on but this night she didn't.

"Finally, about the eighth inning, I realized what was up—she was in the mood for some loving.

"I shut that goddam set off in one second flat and in two minutes we were in the sack.

"Now why in the hell didn't she come right out and tell me what she wanted?"

I asked a wife at the tavern to comment on the above incident.

"Well," she said, "women have learned that men like to think of themselves as great seducers. They don't want their wife to chase them all over the house when she wants to go to bed with them, so the women play it coy. They undress in front of their husband, or sit around in their nightgown, as this wife did, and pretty soon the husband gets the message and makes a pass and the wife responds. This makes the guy feel that he is irresistible—which is what they like."

On the positive side the men have certain expressions for a woman they like: she is a "good sport," or a "good mother," or a "good manager," or a "helluva good woman."

One never hears a man at The Oasis make a negative reference to his own mother. He might refer to his father as a "no good sonofabitch" but never his mother. Sisters are usually referred to in a positive tone also. Any hostility the men express toward women is focused either on their wife (or former wife) or on some woman activist in the community.

The Ideal Woman

What sort of woman do these men really want? What kind can they live with happily? Our material would suggest the following ideal:

1. A woman who is content to live along the lines of what some social scientists have called "segregated sex roles"; in other words, in a female world that is largely isolated or blocked off from the world of men.

   One man put this point into these words: "I hate a goddamn woman messing in my affairs—always asking 'Where are you going?' 'What time you gonna be back?' I always answer: 'Going where I have to and back soon as I can.'"

2. A woman who is willing to spend time and effort on her home and children. "If there's anything I can't stand," a carpenter said, "it's a woman who keeps a dirty house or lets her kids run loose all day. I figure if a woman can't take care of the house and the kids she shouldn't get married."

3. A woman who keeps herself neat and clean. A wife doesn't have to be beautiful, but she must take some pride in her appearance.

4. A woman who is sexually responsive. Her willingness to have sexual relations when the man feels like it is more important than her appearance or her body. In other words, it is absolute guarantee against sexual frustration that these men are looking for, not beauty or some vague sexual ecstasy.

5. A woman who is reliable and faithful. When a blue-collar aristocrat spends a lot of time with his male buddies he likes to be sure that his children are being cared for properly and that his wife is home minding her business. Above all she must not be "running around" with some other man. This would expose the

husband to ridicule and lower his status in the male peer group.

In general, it would seem that these men like traditional rather than modern women. There is one striking exception, however: almost all (over 90 percent) of these men are willing to have their wives work outside of the home. This represents a modification of the traditional wife model that these men have learned to live with. For some of the older men this change dates back to the economic crisis of the 1930s when they were unable to support their families and their wives had to find some sort of work. For some of the younger or middle-aged men the acceptance of outside employment by wives and mothers dates back to World War II, when labor shortages and a national crisis made it imperative that wives and mothers hold outside jobs if at all possible.

It could be said that these men have evolved a female model that is extremely functional for them: it allows them great freedom; guarantees them good care of their homes and their children; assures them of sexual satisfaction; protects them against ridicule and gossip; and at the same time gives them economic aid when they need it.

When the writer discussed this wife model with one of the women at The Oasis, her comment was: "Why in the hell wouldn't they like a wife like that? It's a damn good deal for them."

One has the feeling that traditional women of the above type are becoming increasingly scarce in American society and that sooner or later the blue-collar aristocrats will have to face the fact that the slaves are in revolt.

Women's Liberation

To say that the drive to liberate women frightens the men in this study is an understatement. As one man said: "It scares the hell out of me." For centuries men have dominated Western society[5] and now they face the prospect that their world, and their power, may have to be shared with women. This prospect leaves them feeling gloomy—or angry.

"What in the hell are they complaining about?" one man asked. "My wife has an automatic washer in the kitchen, a dryer, a dishwasher, a garbage disposal, a car of her own—hell, I even bought her a portable TV so she can watch the goddamn soap operas right in the kitchen. What more can she want?"

Most of the wives at The Oasis are willing to settle for the "good life" described above. They know they have it better than their mothers had it, and the male-female arrangement gives them enough room to maneuver so that they do not feel "hemmed in" or stifled. As one woman said: "If my husband says 'no' to something I can always take him to bed and get a new vote."

One has the impression, however, that the younger women at the tavern are less philosophical about these issues and are more determined to have sexual equality. One of them told me that she claims the same right to "run around" that the men have; she also says that her husband has as much responsibility for their children as she has. This woman is considered a deviant at the tavern now, but sometimes deviants represent the wave of the future.

The older women—those over forty—have very little, if any, tolerance for the militant women's liberationists. This is because the women at the tavern are "gradualists"; they (and their husbands) do not favor social revolution in any form.

One wonders to what extent the attitudes of the men toward women in this study have been formed by the nature of their work: they spend all day, five days a week, in an exclusively male world. I, in contrast, have worked with women (and even under their supervision) for thirty-five years. It could be argued, of course, that being deprived of the company of women all day would make these men anxious to associate with women after work—but this does not seem to be true of the men at The Oasis. These men seem to prefer the company of men.

THE WOMEN VIEW THE MEN

The most common negative reference to the men is that they are "dumb." I once asked one of the women what she meant by this.

"Well, for one thing, they do everything in the book a woman doesn't like and then they can't understand why she loses her enthusiasm for them."

I asked her to be more specific.

"Well, they drink too much; they spend too much time away from home; they often run around with other women; they spend too much money—is that enough or do you want more?"

"Why do you think women marry these men?"

"Because they don't have any choice—the other men aren't any better."

A frequent complaint by the women is that the men drink "too much."

"How often have you seen a woman drunk in here?" one of the wives asked me.

"Four or five times."

"OK. How often have you seen a man drunk in here?"

"Fifty to seventy-five times."

"OK. How would you like to be the little woman at home when daddy comes in with a snootful?"

"Not much."

"OK. That's what women have to put up with."

"And another thing," she added, "if a woman gets too much in here the men think she's *disgusting*—if a man gets too much he's *funny!* I don't get it." She ordered another beer and stared into her glass, contemplating the sad state of the male-female world.

The women complain that the men are "selfish." One woman put it this way: "These guys would go deer hunting if their mother was on her death bed. They think first of themselves. When our kids were small we could never have a birthday party on the right day for one of them because it was the week that the pheasant season opened. Wouldn't you think that kids are more important than pheasants?"

The women also object to what they consider to be sexual promiscuity in the men. This came out when I took a graduate seminar group to the tavern one evening. In the group was a rather vivacious girl in her twenties who made quite a hit with the men. Several of them, mar-

ried as well as single, danced with the girl, bought her drinks, and plied her with quarters for the juke box.

A few evenings later one of the wives who had witnessed the above incident made a few comments. "That was quite a student you brought over the other night. I thought some of the older men would have a stroke dancing with her. I think Herman[6] was the only guy that didn't make a play for her."

It is literally true that an attractive woman can excite most of the men at the tavern just by walking in the door. If she is unattached (not married to a regular patron of The Oasis) the atmosphere will be charged with expectation: who will make the approach first? And how?

It may be that attractive men have a similar impact on women at the tavern but if so the women conceal their reaction—at least most of them do.

During the years of this study two or three women did appear at the tavern with an obvious sexual interest in the male customers. These women did not conceal their sexual interest, nor attempt to be coy. They were like the men in that their attraction to certain men was highly visible.

The reaction of both sexes to these women was interesting: the men regarded them as "whores" or "sluts," while the wives considered them "sick." Nobody could view them the way similar men are viewed at The Oasis: as people with an insistent sexual need that has not been satisfied.

The basic attitude of men and women at The Oasis toward each other seems to be that of wary distrust. They know they need each other, but at the same time they are never sure how an alliance or truce will work out.

DIFFERENTIAL SOCIAL CHANGE AND THE TWO SEXES

To what extent are the two sexes truly compatible or incompatible? Man's ancestors were mammals and primates, neither of which are noted for close and continuous male-female association. Of course, man's great plasticity makes it possible for him to adapt to almost any cultural system if he has been properly socialized. But at the same time there must be some behavior systems which are more congenial than others to males. As Orville G. Brim, Jr., says, it is easier to make a boy out of a boy than it is to make a boy out of a girl.[7]

Is male-female "togetherness" what men really want or is it something they will have to accept because modern society cannot function under any other arrangement?

It is not being suggested here that males are superior to females, or that sexual equality is not a desirable goal. The question is whether men like to spend their free hours with their own sex or the opposite sex.

It is difficult to talk with the men and women who frequent The Oasis without feeling that somehow these two groups of people are not very compatible. The men in this study prefer the company of other men.[8] They are fiercely independent, determined not to be domesticated or henpecked by a "damn woman," and the women are equally determined not to be relegated to some nineteenth-century Victorian family style that their feminine ancestors struggled to overthrow.

To phrase this in sociological language one might say that these two sexes, at the blue-collar level, have experienced differential social change during the last few decades: the women have had a glimpse of equalitarian marriage as portrayed in the soap operas and in women's magazines and have liked what they have seen, whereas the men have been horrified (or frightened) by the same glimpse.

And so the battle lines are drawn, with each couple carrying on the struggle in their own way. One wife said that she first began to feel like a *person* after her marriage when she took a job and established her own checking account. "I was damn sick and tired of being dependent on my husband for every dime I needed," she said. "When I first got my own checking account, opened with my own money, I used to go around town buying little things for the kids and myself and writing a check for every little purchase—I was like a child with its first allowance. It felt wonderful."

With some couples the struggle for equality leads to bitterness, and the marriage may be terminated. In other cases the wife concedes defeat and retires to her home and her children. And in a few, the man surrenders, knuckles under, and is seen at The Oasis no more.

This struggle, or conflict, can best be seen among the young couples who have begun rearing their families. If the man continues to spend a lot of time at the tavern when his wife is busy with preschool children, it is apparent that he has won the struggle and has emerged victorious, his freedom and independence intact. But if the man seldom appears at the tavern after his first or second child has arrived, then it seems likely that his wife has prevailed. If the young father reduces the amount of time he spends at the tavern, then the chances are that some sort of compromise has been reached.

This battle or struggle is often not apparent in young married couples who have not had their first child; at that point the wife is still employed outside of the home, has her own income, and retains much of the freedom and independence she had while single. The big test for these couples comes when they begin to have children—and one has the impression that some of the marriages begin to slide downhill at this point.

Margaret Mead has argued that no human society has ever really achieved sexual equality.[9] Efforts toward this end have characterized American society since at least the latter part of the nineteenth century, reaching a climax at the end of World War I when women won the right to vote.[10]

In subsequent decades they also won the right to smoke, drink liquor, enjoy sex, go to college, work outside of the home, and divorce their husbands for a variety of reasons. Out of this social revolution has emerged the so-called "modern American woman."

In the past this struggle for emancipation on the part of women has been experienced largely at the middle and upper-class levels in American society, but now it is also being fought out at the blue-collar level. Thus many of the skilled workers at The Oasis are only now facing demands from their wives that white-collar men had to face decades earlier.

It has been stated many times in this [reading] that these blue-collar aristocrats are extremely independent persons—in the mass society they refuse to be homogenized. Maybe it is because they know, or sense, that the computer will never replace a good bricklayer; that toilets will always have to be installed by a plumber; or that only a skilled carpenter can make your house look the way you want it to.

And yet one has the feeling that eventually these men are going to lose their fight against social change (out of deference to them we will not call it progress). They are opposed to sexual equality, racial equality, mass production of houses, and many other features of modern society. In a very real (or literal) sense these men are *reactionary*—that is, they yearn for the America that began to disappear yesterday or the day before. One can see this in their attitude toward women, in their gloomy view of the welfare state, and in their hostility toward blacks demanding equality. Perhaps this generation of blue-collar aristocrats can survive free and undomesticated in their marriages, but their sons may be in for a rude awakening a few years hence.

One thing seems clear: the parents of these men did not prepare them to live happily with modern women, to enjoy them as companions (except in bed), while the women were not properly socialized to be good companions for men (even in bed). One is reminded of a point made by David Riesman and his associates in *The Lonely Crowd:*[11] namely, that some parents socialize their children for a world that no longer exists. This would seem to be what happened to some of these men. It may turn out, as our society changes, that the two sexes will become completely compatible, even at the blue-collar level. But this does not appear to be the case today.

Notes

1. For a general analysis of the male-female relationship in human society, see Margaret Mead, *Male and Female* (New York: William Morrow & Co., 1949).

2. Lee Rainwater, *And the Poor Get Children* (Chicago: Quadrangle Books, 1960), p. 77.

3. He was referring to a local woman who was a candidate for the school board.

4. Actually, as of the 1960s, men still made up a substantial majority of the local school board.

5. For a scholarly analysis of how men have dominated Western society, see Charles W. Ferguson, *The Male Attitude* (Boston: Little, Brown & Co., 1966). For the feminine version, see Elaine Kendall, *The Upper Hand* (Boston: Little, Brown & Co., 1965).

6. Herman is about seventy years old.

7. See Orville G. Brim, Jr., *Education for Child Rearing* (New York: Russell Sage Foundation, 1959).

8. In a very controversial book, Lionel Tiger has argued that men tend to seek male companionship because male bonding was crucial for human survival in man's early history. See his analysis, *Men in Groups* (New York: Random House, 1969). For some interesting and provocative replies to Tiger and the men who agree with him, see Michele Hoffnung Garskof, ed., *Roles Women Play: Readings toward Women's Liberation* (Belmont, Calif.: Brooks/Cole Publishing Company, 1971).

9. Mead, *Male and Female.*

10. For an excellent historical analysis of the feminist movement in the United States, see William L. O'Neill, *Everyone Was Brave: The Rise and Fall of Feminism in America* (Chicago: Quadrangle Books, 1969).

11. David Riesman et al., *The Lonely Crowd,* rev. ed. (New Haven: Yale University Press, 1961).

PART TWO

Socialization

READINGS 7–9

In Part One of this book we laid out a basic framework for understanding social behavior. We turn now to a number of specific components of social behavior and the unique way that sociologists view these different components. This section of the book and all the sections that follow have a format that should lead you to a better understanding of the important components of social behavior. Each part begins with a keynote article that presents a comprehensive overview of a particular area of sociological concern. This keynote reading defines fundamental concepts and shows how these concepts direct attention to particular aspects of the social world. The keynote selection is followed by several illustrative readings that examine topics raised in the keynote reading. These more specific readings illustrate and amplify important points and also extend the concepts from the keynote reading into new areas. The first component of social behavior to be considered is socialization.

What makes us human? Although you may give many answers to this question, depending on which perspective you choose to take, sociologists would answer it by saying that to be human is to be a *social* being. To be human is to take part in the structure and process of social behavior. But this is not as easy as it may appear. To be a social being requires constant learning and practice. To a sociologist, we learn to be what we are. We are taught every day through direct and indirect interaction with other social beings (also known as people). This teaching-learning process is called *socialization*. You are going through some of it at the very moment you read these words. You are indirectly interacting with the social being who wrote these particular words. You do not know that person's sex, age, race, or anything else about that person, with the possible exception that she or he can write a comprehensible English sentence. Yet the person who wrote these very words is teaching you some of what it means to be a social being.

But socialization does more than mold individual personalities. It is the process we use to pass on what we know about our world, what we believe in, and how we act. We become what we are through interacting with others, but what we are is very much a reflection of the ongoing social organization we are "trained" for. The most immediate example of this is the educational process you are now involved in. The educational institution, remember, is one of the major elements of a social system. One of its important functions is to socialize the members of a society. But look at what this socialization involves. You are taught reading, writing, and arithmetic so that you can operate effectively in this society. But you are also taught to show up on time, do work that is assigned to you, operate under formal hierarchical authority, work in groups, obey the rules, and so on. Now, ask yourself, "Why must I learn these things?" The answer is obvious. If you did not learn these things, society as we know it would not exist. In the same way, when we learn to become conventionally defined boys and girls, and eventually men and women, we are developing our individual personalities, but we are also internalizing or learning what the larger society expects boys and girls and men and women to be. At The Oasis bar, the fights really centered on the perpetuation of conventional sex roles. The men wanted to maintain the culture they had been trained for. The women were caught by their own socialization— they knew what was expected by the men and they also knew that they could be something else. The media and their experience in white-collar jobs had taught the women what it meant to be more "liberated" women. Socialization, then, is twofold. It molds individuals into social beings and, in so doing, serves to keep the social world going with a degree of predictability.

The keynote reading for this part is taken from the classic *Human Society* by Kingsley Davis. First published in 1948, this statement on socialization contains the basic sociological argument on the development of human personality and the passing on of human society. Davis begins his statement by examining the still turbulent heredity-environment argument. What are the basic ideas presented by the two sides? Does Davis argue that these two models are mutually exclusive? Can you think of current issues on which representatives of these two schools of thought have engaged in public debate? Recognizing the nondeterministic nature of both sides, Davis next presents the characteristics of the unsocialized organism, the raw material of the socialization process. What is the significance of reflexes, instincts, urges, and capacities in the formation of individual personality, according to Davis? Why is his discussion of Anna and Isabelle, the isolated children, crucial to his discussion of the raw material?

A very important section of the Davis reading is the discussion of
George Herbert Mead's stages of development of the self and the
components of the self. Mead's ideas form a central core in the
sociological approach to socialization. You will see these ideas reflected in the illustrative readings in this part and throughout the
book. Mead discusses the development of self in two stages, the
play stage and the game stage. Although Davis does not name these
stages as is conventionally done today, he does give detailed accounts of what happens in each of them. When Davis is describing
the process of taking the role of a single other, he is describing
what is usually called the play stage. When Davis introduces the
game of baseball into the discussion of Mead's ideas, he has
switched the focus to the game stage. Be sure to note what happens
to the self in each of these stages, and the differences between the
two stages. Look at how the "other" changes in the two stages.
Once the self is fully developed, what are its components?

Observe the very important role of other people (both concrete
and abstract) in Mead's theory. When people use Mead's theory
they often speak of the "significant (or particular) other" and the
"generalized other." A significant other for you is some specific person who occupies a particularly important position for you at this
point in your life. A parent and a boyfriend or girlfriend are examples of significant others. In the formation of self, interaction with
these people is especially important. Davis only makes passing reference to the phrase, "significant other," but his discussion describes the all-important function of these persons in the molding
of a self. The generalized other is identified and discussed by
Davis. As you read the last section of the article, take special note
of the generalized other. What is it? What function does it have in
socialization? These points will show you why Mead sees the self as
reflexive.

One of the three major theoretical orientations, symbolic interactionism, evolved from the approach to socialization developed by
Mead. Recall that Mead is considered to be the founder or intellectual parent of the symbolic interactionist school. Note the role
played by symbols and symbolic communication in the development
of self. You may want to review Margaret Poloma's reading on symbolic interactionism (and its introduction) in Part One of this book.

Following the keynote selection are two readings that extend the
discussion of socialization beyond Davis's rather abstract reading. In
the first, "Sex Differences in the Complexity of Children's Play and
Games," Janet Lever examines the important stages of development
identified by Mead. She arrives at some rather revealing conclusions about the role of play and games in the socialization of boys

and girls. In the second reading, "Learning the Student Role: Kindergarten as Academic Boot Camp," Harry L. Gracey amplifies the keynote selection by taking readers back to kindergarten to find out what is *really* learned in that setting. You probably never thought of all the fun and games as "basic training." Although we have not included a reading on adult socialization in this part, you will find some excellent examples in other parts of the book. The first can be found in Part One in "Battle of the Sexes." The women at The Oasis had been socialized as adults into what they saw as a new role for women. The second example is in Part Three of this book. In Joel Roache's "Confessions of a Househusband" you will see a husband and wife each "resocialized" into portions of the other's role. Although Roache writes in a slightly humorous vein (on the surface), he provides a graphic example of the power of adult socialization. Once you grasp the general principles and specific procedures set forth in this section, you should have no trouble seeing how these apply from birth right up to the moment of death in old age.

7
Socialization

Kingsley Davis

The paradox of human society—that it has a unity and continuity of its own and yet exists solely in the minds and actions of its members—can be resolved only by understanding how the newborn individual is molded into a social being. Without this process of molding, which

Reprinted with minor deletions from *Human Society* by Kingsley Davis. Copyright 1948 and 1949 by Macmillan Publishing Company, Inc. Used with permission of the author.

we call "socialization," the society could not perpetuate itself beyond a single generation and culture could not exist. Nor could the individual become a person; for without the ever-repeated renewal of culture within him there could be no human mentality, no human personality. Both the person and the society are alike dependent on this unique process of psychic amalgamation whereby the sentiments and ideas of the culture are somehow joined to the capacities and needs of the organism.

No one understands the process thoroughly. It is still as mysterious as photosynthesis or organic aging. Yet it is a common meeting ground of all the sciences dealing with man; for here in the problem of socialization, biology and sociology, psychiatry and anthropology come together. Each of the human sciences has something it wants to learn about the process, and each has something it can contribute. If a science is interested in man at all it is interested in the subtle alchemy by which the human animal is transmuted into the human being. If the essential mystery has not yet been solved, this does not mean that nothing is known about the process; much is known, and only a fraction can be suggested here.

THE ROOTS OF PERSONALITY

In addition to socialization there are other factors affecting the individual, and the relation of these to our topic must be considered. In this matter, however, there is much confusion because of the perennial failure to distinguish between an abstraction and a concrete entity. Out of this confusion grow such loose phrases as "the individual and his environment" and such fruitless questions as "Which is more important, heredity or environment?" One might as well discuss a book in terms of ideas versus ink, or plot versus format. . . .

Terms such as "heredity" or "environment" do not refer to anything tangible but to an abstraction. To treat them as if they were on the same level as the concrete individual, as in phrases like "the individual and his environment," is to invite complete muddlement. Of course "the individual" may be viewed as an abstraction, but in this case it is necessary to be clear as to what level of abstraction and system of discourse one is employing.

Any given individual is, in part, a product of two distinct modes of transmission, one hereditary and the other social. The first operates through the mechanism of genes, chromosomes, and human reproduction; it relates to the general level of reality designated as biological and is studied by a special branch of biological science called "genetics." The second op-

erates through the mechanism of habituation, learning, and symbolic communication; it relates to the general level of reality designated as socio-cultural, and is dealt with by a branch of social science which may be called "the study of socialization" or sometimes "social psychology" or "psycho-sociology." The accompanying diagram [Figure 1] attempts to give a simplified picture of the situation. Obviously no concrete individual is the product of either of these modes of transmission alone. He is always a product of both, and this means that both modes of transmission are mutually interdependent, each being a necessary condition of the other.

The complexity extends further than this, however. Not only is the individual a product of these two dynamic processes of transmission, but he is also a product of several different kinds of environment. Neither genetic nor communicative transmission can occur in man without a geographic, a biological, a cultural, and an interpersonal environment. For this reason the individual is just as much an outgrowth of the environments as he is a result of the two kinds of dynamic transmission.

Obviously if a complete explanation of the concrete individual is to be given, all the elements in the environments and all the mechanisms in the two kinds of transmission must be taken into account. Such, however, would be a Herculean task and a useless one. Science is not so much interested in a complete explanation of the concrete entity as it is in an analysis of the kinds of factors that are involved. It divides the labor; it elaborates conceptual systems capable of handling different types or levels of causation; it singles out only certain aspects of concrete entities for explanation. Only by such methods of logico-empirical abstraction can the task of scientific understanding be accomplished. Only in this way can the behavior of individuals be statistically predicted.

The danger of abstractions lies not in the abstractions themselves but in the failure to recognize them as such. They simply represent aspects of reality; on the concrete level they stand in a relation of mutual interdependence, being independent only as abstractions. Each

Figure 1

Diagram of Factors Affecting the Concrete Individual

Bio-physical Environment   Socio-cultural Environment

Genetic Transmission	Social Transmission
Transmitting mechanism: *Organic Reproduction*	Transmitting mechanism: *Symbolic Communication*
Emergent level: *Biological*	Emergent level: *Socio-cultural*
Science involved: *Genetics*	Science involved: *Study of Socialization*

Concrete Individual

science elaborates its scheme of explanation by assuming the other aspects and concentrating on the one in which it is interested. Thus only by assuming the influence of the genetic and geographical factors to be constant can the sociologist deduce consequences from variations in the socio-cultural factors. And vice versa, only by assuming the influence of the socio-cultural factors to be constant can the biologist deduce consequences from variations in the genetic factors. In other words each science of man, like any other science, approaches its task with an "as if" attitude. It reasons as if a certain type of factor were alone operative. In reality this is never the case, but it enormously speeds up scientific progress to make the hypothetical assumption. The main hazard is that the layman often forgets, as does the scientist occasionally, that the reasoning is hypothetical. He tends to assume that a given conceptual system describes concrete reality *in toto* and thus he lands in a kind of determinism, oversimplified and untrue. He then engages in futile battles with people who expound the determinism of other fac-

tors. Thus arises the war of the determinisms, a war of vague words and bad logic.

The Heredity-Environment Controversy

The question, "Which is more important, heredity or environment?" illustrates the pitfalls. In the first place there is no such thing as "the" environment. There are many different environments, and what is environmental in one sense may be not so in another. Thus from the point of view of genetics the body is an environment in which the reproductive cells multiply and receive nourishment; whereas from the point of view of ecology the body is what the environment surrounds. In the second place the question wrongly assumes that environment and transmission are somehow opposed, so that if the one is important the other cannot be. Since, however, organisms are perpetuated through germ cells and nourished in an environment they obviously depend on both of these factors. In the third place the question makes a comparison without stating the terms of reference. It uses the term "important" but does not say for what. Finally, the question confuses necessary with sufficient conditions. A necessary condition is one that must be present if another factor is to operate. From the standpoint of a biologist a woman speaks because she has the organic capacity (it is assumed that somebody teaches her to speak). If, however, the question is why she speaks Chinese rather than some other language, this is not a sufficient explanation. Speaking Chinese is a cultural datum; and only a cultural explanation—in this case, the fact that she was reared in a Chinese society—can give a sufficient answer.

In trying to explain particular traits observers frequently commit what may be called "the family history fallacy." If the forebears exhibit the same trait as the descendant, one says that it "runs in the family." Traits, however, are transmitted from parent to child in two different ways—one by genetic transmission, the other by communicative transmission. If a child has an unusually flat head and his ancestors before him had the same sort of flat head, the likely conclusion is that this is a genetic trait, "in the blood." If it were an English child the conclusion would probably be correct. But if it were a Hopi child it would not be correct, because the Hopi Indians flattened the heads of their babies by tight lashing to the cradles. The Samoans, in turn, deliberately flattened the skull by the application of stones.

If the women in several generations of the same family have been prostitutes, the fact is likely to be ascribed to a "hereditary taint," though it would seem much easier and less mystical to recall that mothers can teach their daughters to be prostitutes. In fact, occupations are frequently transmitted from parent to child, but never through the genes.

The family history fallacy arises from the fact that genetic transmission occurs only through the parent-child channel and that communicative transmission occurs very largely through this channel. For this reason one must always ask if the trait in question is the sort which *could* be physically inherited. If it is primarily symbolic, like language, one may infer that the sufficient cause lies in the social sphere. The fact that successive generations of a given family all speak English need not lead one to infer that this a biological trait. If the trait is primarily physical, like the shape of the head, one may form the hypothesis that it is genetically caused (provided this does not blind one to the possibility of social causation). More crucial, however, is the necessity of asking whether or not the trait conforms to the known rules of genetic or cultural transmission. Does it appear for example in successive generations in such a manner as to conform to Mendelian principles? Or does it appear in such a manner as to indicate social transmission (e.g., in connection with social position and social norms)?

From a research point of view a great aid in overcoming the family history fallacy is the fact that social transmission is not limited to the parent-child relation. This makes it possible to separate the two kinds of transmission. Adopted children can be investigated to see in what ways they resemble their foster parents more than their biological parents; and identical twins can be studied to see in what ways they resemble

each other more when reared together than when reared apart. Another great aid lies in cultural relativity. Since human beings are all of one species, any trait which varies from one culture to another is not likely to be adequately explained in biological terms.[1] The basic principle underlying all these methods is to hold one kind of factor constant while allowing the other kind to vary. This simply amounts to applying experimentally or statistically the abstraction practiced in theory.

THE UNSOCIALIZED ORGANISM

A human being's dependence on the social environment begins long before he is born—with the folkways and mores governing his parents' courtship and marital selection, with the customs concerning pregnancy, with the whole system of cultural practices surrounding the family. His parents, socialized creatures when they conceived him, previously had to learn the sexual act. Conception took place in a socially defined situation important for the child's subsequent status. Techniques of prenatal care current in the community affected his chances of being born and of being healthy. In sum, the social circumstances preceding his birth not only made his life possible but also laid down to a great extent the kind of life he was to lead.

But it is not until birth that direct socialization begins. Hence it is worthwhile to inquire what the individual, as an organism, has at birth that is relevant to the process of socialization. The things he has may be divided into four admittedly overlapping categories: capacities, reflexes, "instincts," and urges.

1. Reflexes. Plainly, the severest limitation upon socialization is supplied by the automatic and rigid responses of the organism. Such responses, or reflexes, are attached to a given stimulus and, if learned at all, are acquired by a minimum of organic experience in relation to the physical environment. The pupil of the eye automatically contracts in strong light, the glands of the mouth salivate at the taste of sugar, the muscles of the arm contract at the prick of a pin, urination occurs with fullness of the bladder, etc. A catalogue of all the reflexes is impossible to make. The whole autonomic nervous system is reflex in character, including breathing, heartbeat, peristalsis, and digestion. Without its reflexes the organism could not live. Yet since the reflexes are automatic and rigid, they are unlearned and in many cases unmodifiable. They set limits on what the organism can and will do, but they are hardly the bases out of which socialization arises.

2. Instincts. Much debate has always attended the use of the term "instinct," especially as applied to human behavior. Biologists define as instinctive any behavior that originates in an urge or appetite, involves some sort of perception of the external world, is peculiarly fixed and mechanical, is dependent on inherited structure and therefore characteristic of the species, and, though compulsory or necessary, is at the same time highly adaptive or functional (without the organism being aware of its ultimate significance).[2] It is plain why so much debate has surrounded the concept, for it is practically synonymous with the life process itself. Broad and complex, it embraces elements which need not occur together or which seem incompatible.

The human being at birth probably has no complete instinct but only certain elements of them, such as reflexes and urges. Given these plus his capacities, all of his subsequent behavior is partly learned and is hence not instinctive. Consequently the explanation of human behavior in terms of instincts is fallacious.

At one time almost any form of behavior was ascribed to some instinct. If a boy and girl fell in love it was due to the "instinct to reproduce the race." If they quarreled it was due to the instinct of pugnacity. If the quarrel resulted in a reconciliation it was due to the gregarious instinct; or if the boy fled, it was due to the self-preservation instinct. It was, in short, a type of explanation that explained everything (too much too easily). It was purely *post hoc*; it could seemingly "explain" why a thing had happened but could give no basis for predicting what had not yet happened. At its worst it was a redundant explanation, similar to the brilliant conclusion that opium causes sleep because of its dormitive powers or that sap goes up in trees because that is the nature of sap. At its best it was an explanation *obscurum per obscurius* (explaining an unknown by something still more unknown). To explain war, for example, as being the result of the "combative instinct" merely makes the problem harder. We know little enough about all the forms that human warfare has taken, but we know still less about this mysterious instinct. We have a rough idea in social and historical terms why war came to the United States in 1917 and 1941 rather than other years, but we have no idea why an instinct should suddenly have erupted at those times. Such an explanation, therefore, may be emotionally satisfying because the unknown is mysterious and hence magically superior, but it is not scientifically acceptable.

3. Urges. What is variously referred to as impulse, drive, tension, urge, or appetite provides firmer ground for analysis of human behavior. As previously noted, the organism has certain needs that must be met. Unless they are met it develops increasing tension and restlessness until it encounters a stimulus capable of relieving the tension. Thus the urges represent a dynamic force behind behavior. Whereas in the instinctive behavior of animals the satisfaction of the appetite is tied to only one or a few stimuli, in man it tends to be (except on the reflexive level) rigidly tied to none. A very wide range of stimuli can satisfy the various urges. Which stimuli do satisfy them becomes a matter of learning. The urges, not the reflexes, provide an organic bridgehead, a starting point, for the process of socialization.

4. Capacities. Intelligence is regarded as man's important attribute because it enables him to compensate for the limitations of his body. He can run only so fast, lift only so much, fight only so well. He must therefore rely upon techniques that enlarge or extend what capacities he has. Though his learning capacity exceeds that of any other animal, it is nevertheless limited. Curiously enough, however, even this limitation can be overcome by the development of culture.

Presumably his innate intellectual capacity could be increased by a eugenic program (itself a cultural phenomenon), but barring this the use of his capacity, in the sense of learning more and more, could still be increased by the development of new instructional and incentive techniques. Human mentality is like a box—the way to get more into it is to pack things systematically. No limit can be foreseen to the possible increase of man's intellectual efficiency through new techniques of socialization.

At present no human being learns as much as he could under more favorable circumstances, for his learning ability is never used to maximum capacity. Every society uses defective instructional techniques, appeals occasionally to wrong motives, taboos certain kinds of knowledge, and has a limited culture. The last factor—limited culture—may seem the most important cause for the failure to teach individuals all they can absorb, until it is recalled that no society ever transmits its whole culture to any one person. The amount that given individuals absorb is more a function of the techniques and incentives utilized than of the size of the culture. Actually the main societal consideration is not the maximum use of the individual's capacity in the sense of mere learning but the maximum incorporation of his productive effort with that of others. If the collective activities are well organized, a small but specialized contribution from each person will have more effect than a much greater individual contribution in a poorly integrated system. For this reason a lot depends on how much use is made of individual differences in amount and kind of capacity. All told, societies vary enormously in their waste of human learning ability, but they all waste it. Since modern scientists have such difficulty in perfecting teaching techniques, in measuring capacities and talents, and in motivating people to learn, there is little wonder that societies have also bungled the job.

ISOLATED CHILDREN: WHAT THEY SHOW

One line of evidence showing the role of socialization in human mentality and human be-
havior and demonstrating how utterly limited are the resources of the organism alone, is afforded by extremely isolated children. Since with these individuals physical development has proceeded to an advanced point with practically no concomitant social influence, they reveal to what degree the stages of socialization are necessarily correlated with the stages of organic growth. They enable us to see what an unsocialized mind (and body) is like after developing beyond the point at which normal minds have been socially molded.

Two such cases have been seen by the writer.[3] The first was the case of an illegitimate child called Anna, whose grandfather strongly disapproved of the mother's indiscretion and who therefore caused the child to be kept in an upstairs room. As a result the infant received only enough care to keep her barely alive. She was seldom moved from one position to another. Her clothing and bedding were filthy. She apparently had no instruction, no friendly attention.

When finally found and removed from the room at the age of nearly six years, Anna could not talk, walk, or do anything that showed intelligence. She was in an extremely emaciated and undernourished condition, with skeleton-like legs and a bloated abdomen. She was completely apathetic, lying in a limp, supine position and remaining immobile, expressionless, and indifferent to everything. She was believed to be deaf and possibly blind. She of course could not feed herself or make any move in her own behalf. Here, then, was a human organism which had missed nearly six years of socialization. Her condition shows how little her purely biological resources, when acting alone, could contribute to making her a complete person.

By the time Anna died of hemorrhagic jaundice approximately four and a half years later, she had made considerable progress as compared with her condition when found. She could follow directions, string beads, identify a few colors, build with blocks, and differentiate between attractive and unattractive pictures. She had a good sense of rhythm and loved a doll. She talked mainly in phrases but would repeat words and try to carry on a conversation.

She was clean about clothing. She habitually washed her hands and brushed her teeth. She would try to help other children. She walked well and could run fairly well, though clumsily. Although easily excited, she had a pleasant disposition. Her improvement showed that socialization, even when started at the late age of six, could still do a great deal toward making her a person. Even though her development was no more than that of a normal child of two to three years, she had made noteworthy progress.

A correct interpretation of this case is handicapped by Anna's early death. We do not know how far the belated process of socialization might ultimately have carried her. Inevitably the hypothesis arises that she was feebleminded from the start. But whatever one thinks in this regard, the truth is that she did make considerable progress and that she would never have made this progress if she had remained isolated. Of course, she was not completely isolated. Had she been, she would have died in infancy. But her contact with others was almost purely of a physical type which did not allow of communicative interaction. The case illustrates that communicative contact is the core of socialization. It is worth noting that the girl never had, even after her discovery, the best of skilled attention. It took her a long time to learn to talk, and it is possible that once she had learned to talk well the process of socialization would have been speeded up. With normal children it is known that the mastery of speech is the key to learning.

The other case of extreme isolation, that of Isabelle, helps in the interpretation of Anna. This girl was found at about the same time as Anna under strikingly similar circumstances when approximately six and a half years old. Like Anna, she was an illegitimate child and had been kept in seclusion for that reason. Her mother was a deaf-mute and it appears that she and Isabelle spent most of their time together in a dark room. As a result Isabelle had no chance to develop speech; when she communicated with her mother it was by means of gestures. Lack of sunshine and inadequacy of diet had caused her to become rachitic. Her legs in particular were affected; they "were so bowed that as she stood erect the soles of her shoes came nearly flat together, and she got about with a skittering gait."[4] Her behavior toward strangers, especially men, was almost that of a wild animal, manifesting much fear and hostility. In lieu of speech she made only a strange croaking sound. In many ways she acted like an infant. "She was apparently utterly unaware of relationships of any kind. When presented with a ball for the first time, she held it in the palm of her hand, then reached out and stroked my face with it. Such behavior is comparable to that of a child of six months."[5] At first it was even hard to tell whether or not she could hear, so unused were her senses. Many of her actions resembled those of deaf children.

Once it was established that she could hear, specialists who worked with her pronounced her feebleminded. Even on nonverbal tests her performance was so low as to promise little for the future. "The general impression was that she was wholly uneducable and that any attempt to teach her to speak, after so long a period of silence, would meet with failure."[6] Yet the individuals in charge of her launched a systematic and skillful program of training. The task seemed hopeless at first but gradually she began to respond. After the first few hurdles had at last been overcome, a curious thing happened. She went through the usual stages of learning characteristic of the years from one to six not only in proper succession but far more rapidly than normal. In a little over two months after her first vocalization she was putting sentences together. Nine months after that she could identify words and sentences on the printed page, could write well, could add to ten, and could retell a story after hearing it. Seven months beyond this point she had a vocabulary of 1,500–2,000 words and was asking complicated questions. Starting from an educational level of between one and three years (depending on what aspect one considers), she had reached a normal level by the time she was eight and a half years old. In short, she covered in two years the stages of learning that ordinarily require six.[7] Or, to put it another way, her I.Q. trebled in a year and a half.[8] The speed with which she reached the normal level of mental development seems analogous to the recovery of body weight in a growing child after an illness, the recovery being achieved by extra fast growth until restoration of normal weight for the given age. She eventually entered school where she participated in all school activities as normally as other children.

Clearly the history of Isabelle's development is different from that of Anna's. In both cases there was an exceedingly low, or rather blank, intellectual level to begin with. In both cases it seemed that the girl might be congenitally feebleminded. In both a considerably higher level was reached later. But Isabelle achieved a normal mentality within two years, whereas Anna was still markedly inadequate at the end of four and a half years. What accounts for the difference?

Perhaps Anna had less innate capacity. But Isabelle probably had more friendly contact with her mother early in life, and also she had more skillful and persistent training after she was found. The result of such attention was to give Isabelle speech at an early stage, and her subsequent rapid development seems to have been a consequence of that. Had Anna, who closely resembled this girl at the start, been given intensive training and hence mastery of speech at an earlier point, her subsequent development might have been much more rapid.

Isabelle's case serves to show, as Anna's does not clearly show, that isolation up to the age of six, with failure to acquire any form of speech and hence missing the whole world of cultural meaning, does not preclude the subsequent acquisition of these. Indeed, there seems to be a process of accelerated recovery. Just what would be the maximum age at which a person could remain isolated and still retain the capacity for full cultural acquisition is hard to say. Almost certainly it would not be as high as age fifteen; it might possibly be as low as age ten. Undoubtedly various individuals would differ considerably as to the exact age.

Both cases, and others like them, reveal in a unique way the role of socialization in personality development. Most of the human behavior we regard as somehow given in the species does not occur apart from training and example by others. Most of the mental traits we think of as constituting the human mind are not present unless put there by communicative contact with others. No other type of evidence brings out this fact quite so clearly as do these rare cases of extreme isolation. Through them it is possible "to observe *concretely separated* two factors in the development of human personality which are always otherwise only analytically separated, the biogenic and the sociogenic factors."[9]

THE DEVELOPMENT OF THE SELF

The heart of socialization is the emergence and gradual development of the self or ego. It is in terms of the self that personality takes shape and the mind comes to function.

The self develops out of the child's communicative contact with others. Contact is at first on a physical level, and in this phase the infant's stability and continuity seemingly come from several sources: his body, which furnishes a constant flow of internal stimuli and has regularly recurring needs; his external surroundings, which constantly bombard his awakening senses and have a certain stability; his attendants, who observe a certain regularity in ministering to him. Consequently the possibility for forming habits is there from the beginning. Such activities as sucking the thumb and swinging suspended toys tend to be done repeatedly in the same way, and later the child shows a strong tendency toward "ritualistic" conformity to behavior patterns already established, as every parent knows. Thus the element of persistence, of conservation, so essential for the notion of the self, is present from the start.[10]

The self, however, has a character different and apart from that of the physiological organism proper, a development and a structure of its own. It is not there at birth but arises in the interplay of social experience. Parts of the body—toes, teeth, tonsils—can be lost without any corresponding loss to the self. Only when the loss has a real social meaning (as when a young girl loses a leg or becomes facially disfigured, or when it involves the organism's capacity for thought and feeling— as when the brain is injured or a gland has a tumor) does the change make a difference for the self. In these cases the effect of the bodily change clearly illustrates the separate character of the self. The latter is a psychic, not a physical entity.

George H. Mead has pointed out that an essential characteristic of the self is its reflexive character.[11] By this he means that the self can be both subject and object to itself; it can reflect upon itself or, as we often put it, can be self-conscious. Mead then says that the essential problem of selfhood or self-consciousness is "How can an individual get outside himself in such a way as to become an object to himself?" He can do it only through others, by temporarily assuming the role of other persons and looking at himself, so to speak, through their eyes. He learns to imagine how he appears to others, to imagine how others judge this appearance and then to react himself to this judgment as he imagines it. Unless the attitudes are in his mind they cannot affect the self; and unless they are attributable to others, they cannot be acquired. Thus by adopting toward himself the attitudes that others take toward him, he comes to treat himself as an object as well as a subject.

In acquiring the attitudes of others toward himself, the individual is not merely passive. He explores and finds out because the satisfaction of his wants greatly depends on others' attitudes toward him. In fact, the expression of attitudes by his fellows soon becomes so important to him that he wants and demands attention. He has a powerful incentive to understand their attitudes, because otherwise he could not predict or control what happens to him. The child early learns that one of the most important ways of controlling his destiny is by influencing the feelings of others toward himself. Since attitudes are matters of meaning, they can be known only through the mechanism of symbolic communication. Hence the child must learn to utilize the symbols by which attitudes are communicated, so that he can conjure up the attitudes of others in his own imagination and in turn communicate his own reactions to others in the light of what he imagines their judgments to be. In order to communicate with others he must himself be able to respond to what he communicates, else he would have no notion of the meaning of what he says and does. Once he has acquired the attitudes of others as part of himself, he can judge how another person will respond by how he himself responds to the words he utters. He not only hears himself but responds to himself; he talks and replies to himself as truly as the other person talks and replies to him.

"The self, as that which can be object to itself, is essentially a social structure, and it arises in social experience." It could not conceivably arise outside of social experience. After it has arisen it contains the social system actively within itself, and so in a way can provide its own social interaction. The person can carry on a conversation with himself. What he says, or thinks he might say, calls out a certain reply in himself (as he takes the role of the other). This reply leads him to say something else, and so on. Thus a person, once he is socialized, can remain solitary for a long time without ceasing to enjoy a certain kind of social interaction. Eventually, however, he must have an audience. Otherwise he cannot check the accuracy of his own responses; his imaginings become barren, repetitive, and divorced from reality.[12] But the very process of thinking is simply an inner conversation in which the individual responds to what he himself says and in turn replies himself to his own response.

It is astonishing how early in life the infant learns to take the role of the other. By the age of two it plays at being mother, baby, or sister. In doing so it views the situation from the standpoint of the person in question, and acts accordingly. The attitudes thus imitated are often those taken toward the infant itself. Thus a child of two may examine a doll's dress, pretend to find it wet, reprimand it, and take it to the bathroom. Such a child has already internalized the attitudes of others. By putting itself in the role of the other it can then respond to its own words and acts in terms of the meaning they would convey to the other person. In this way the self develops and grows.

In an organized game, such as baseball, the child must be ready to take the role of everyone else in the game. "He must have the responses of each position involved in his own position.

He must know what everyone else is going to do in order to carry out his own play."[13] The organization of reciprocal responses is contained in the rules of the game. In so far as the child has grasped the rules of the game and thus can participate in the mutual responses that constitute the actual play, he has acquired within himself an organized system of roles. His specific response is controlled by his sense of the whole system of responses. These are not so much the responses of particular persons as of positions.

The community or social group, like baseball, has an organized character. And as it takes shape in the organization of the self, a process of generalization occurs. What were earlier for the child the attitudes of particular other persons, now become the attitudes of everybody in the given situations. This justifies Mead's term, "the generalized other." As the individual incorporates into himself the system of mutually related attitudes in the community with reference to the common activites and goals of the group as a whole, he becomes a complete self, a social product in the fullest sense.

Of course, not all of the attitudes acquired by the individual are equally general. Many of them apply to particular classes and groups, but even these are integrally related to the most general attitudes of the entire community. When a person puts himself in the place of the generalized other and thus judges his own conduct, he is reflecting in himself the organization of the community at large. The self, then, is a structure of attitudes, not a group of habits. There are some habits that have nothing to do with the systems of attitudes, and the attitudes, while they may be habitual, are distinguished by the fact that they are acquired through communicative interaction with others. No sharp line can be drawn between our own selves and the selves of others, since our own selves function in our experience only in so far as the selves of others function in our experience also.

The reflexive character of the self can be phrased in terms of the "I" and the "me." "The 'I' is the response of the individual to the attitudes of the others; the 'me' is the organized set of attitudes of others which one himself assumes," and to which the "I" responds. The "me" is what is remembered and reflected upon; the "I" is what remembers and does the reflecting.[14] The "me" is the self that one is aware of, the "I" is the unpredictable response. A player can throw the ball to another player because he knows what the rest expect of him. Their expectations are his "me." But exactly how he will respond—whether he will make a brilliant play or an error—neither he nor anybody else knows. The response at the moment of action is the "I"; it is the dynamic unpredictable aspect of the self. As soon, however, as the "I" has acted, it can be remembered and reflected upon; it then becomes a part of the "me." The player has in him all the attitudes of others calling for a certain response, and this is the "me" of the situation; his response at the moment when made is the "I." The "I," then, is always acting in that infinitely small moment when the future becomes the present. It always contains an element of novelty. It resolves in a partially unexpected fashion the conflicting elements of the situation. It is what gives the person a sense of freedom and initiative. The "me" calls for a response in a given situation but the exact character of the response is not completely determined, being morally, not mechanically, necessary. Plainly the "I" and the "me" are separate aspects of the same thing. Taken together they constitute the personality as it appears in social experience. If the self did not have these two aspects there could be no conscious responsibility, and there could be no novelty.

"The self is not something that exists first and then enters into relationship with others." It is something that develops out of social interaction and is constantly changing, constantly adjusting, as new situations and conflicts arise. It assumes the prior existence of a social order and yet is the vessel in which and through which the order continues.

Notes

1. The converse, that any trait appearing in all cultures can be explained in biological terms, is not necessarily true because there may be purely cultural traits, transmitted by socialization, which are essential for human and societal survival and are therefore found in all cultures.

2. Wm. Morton Wheeler, *Essays in Human Biology* (Cambridge: Harvard University Press, 1939), pp. 38–39.

3. The material that follows is condensed, with permission of the publisher, from two papers by the writer: "Extreme Social Isolation of a Child," *American Journal of Sociology,* Vol. 45 (January 1940), pp. 554–564; and "Final Note on a Case of Extreme Isolation," *ibid.,* Vol. 50 (March 1947), pp. 432–437. The literature on feral and extremely neglected children has been summarized by J. A. L. Singh and Robert M. Zingg, *Wolf-Children and Feral Man* (New York: Harper, 1942). This source contains a full bibliography up to the date of publication. Since that time several articles have appeared, mostly devoted to the question of whether or not so-called "wolf-children" have actually existed. This aspect of the subject has been, in the writer's opinion, magnified beyond its importance.

4. Francis N. Maxfield, "What Happens When the Social Environment of a Child Approaches Zero," unpublished manuscript.

5. Marie K. Mason, "Learning to Speak after Six and One-Half Years of Silence," *Journal of Speech Disorders,* Vol. 7 (1942), p. 299.

6. *Ibid.*

7. *Ibid.,* pp. 300–304.

8. Maxfield, *op. cit.*

9. Kingsley Davis, in a foreword in Singh and Zingg, *op. cit.,* pp. xxi–xxii.

10. Cf. Jean Piaget, "Principal Factors Determining Intellectual Evolution from Childhood to Adult Life" in *Factors Determining Human Behavior* (Cambridge: Harvard University Press, 1937), pp. 35–36.

11. *Mind, Self, and Society* (Chicago: University of Chicago Press, 1934), Part III. Much of the present section is paraphrased from Mead's brilliant discussion.

12. Mead, *op. cit.,* pp. 140–141.

13. *Ibid.*

14. Mead, *op. cit.,* p. 175.

8
Sex Differences in the Complexity
of Children's Play and Games

Janet Lever

Editors' Introduction

In the keynote reading for this part Davis described the play and game stages of Mead's theory of the development of the self. In reference to Mead's game stage Davis said, "In an organized game, such as baseball, the child must be ready to take the role of everyone else in the game. 'He must have the responses of each position involved in his own position. He must know what everyone else is going to do in order to carry out his own play.'" This statement suggests that important social learning occurs in a complex game such as baseball. In fact, the game of baseball serves very well to point out the importance of games and the generalized other in the development of the self. Mead used it to make a general point that he assumed described and explained the development of *all* people. Since Mead's time our society has become increasingly aware that the socialization of some people is sometimes dramatically different from that of others. One of the major differences in socialization that has received much attention in the past several years is that between the sexes. It is not that sociologists have just discovered that little boys are raised differently from little girls (that has been known for several hundred years), but rather, sociologists are beginning to sort out the subtle ways in which this difference occurs and to understand the ramifications of this differential socialization for both males and females. In this vein Janet Lever returns to the basic ideas presented by Mead and raises the questions: If important social skills are learned while playing complex games, is there evidence that suggests boys and girls engage in games of equal complexity? If not, what are the consequences?

Lever is doing something quite common in sociology—she is taking a theory and expanding or elaborating on it. She is not arguing that Mead is wrong; she is saying he did not go far enough in his analysis of the development of the self. Look for the ways Lever's work goes beyond that of Mead, as she takes the theory in new directions.

Symbolic interactionism is the obvious guiding theoretical orientation in this reading. You should tie Lever's use of this orientation back to the discussion of the symbolic interaction orientation in Part One of this book, which pointed out that symbolic interaction is concerned with *process*. As you saw in the keynote reading in this part, this orientation forms the basic structure for understanding the socialization process. We develop selves through symbolic interaction with others. Be sure to refer back to Davis for the stages of self that Mead describes. How do these stages enter into Lever's analysis? Why does Lever say that ". . . boys develop the ability to take the role of the *generalized other* while girls develop empathy skills to take the role of the *particular other*?" (Lever's "particular other" is the same as the "significant other" identified in the introduction to the Davis reading.) To answer this, ask yourself, What happens to *other* as games become more complex? Finally, what are the consequences that might result from the differences Lever finds in children's play and games?

In recalling the earlier discussion of the sociological perspective, you should remember that both structure and process are included within it. Although the theoretical orientation of this reading focuses on process, Lever is showing once again the interrelationship between process and structure. Games have rules; they are almost always played in the same way. In other words, games have patterns or regularities—they have structure. But interaction within these structured games is what contributes to the development of the self. So, there are interaction processes within structures, producing differential socialization of boys and girls.

This study of play and games is a methodological gold mine. Lever uses four different data collection techniques: nonparticipant observation of children in school yards, semistructured interviews, written questionnaires, and content analysis of diaries kept by children in her study. Half of her fifth-grade sample was selected from a suburban school; the other half from two urban schools. Lever chose predominantly white middle-class schools for her study. Also, notice that she uses a series of "dimensions" or aspects of complexity for categorizing the games children play.

So far we have just listed the many facets of the methodology of this reading. The real question is, How do these facets combine to make this a very good methodological study? Look at the six dimensions of complexity first. When you get to this point in the reading, stop for a moment and think about games you play or used to play. Without using Lever's complexity dimensions, decide if a certain game is complex. Then analyze the same game, using the six dimensions. You will see why this multidimensional approach is so good—it is more accurate and relatively easy to use.

With the complexity issue still in mind, you can also look at the four data collection techniques. After you have read the selection, go back and single out one of the dimensions of complexity. What do the different data collection techniques tell you about this dimension? You will notice that they are complementary; that is, observation of children gives information that cannot be gotten through the analysis of diaries and vice versa. If you want further verification of the worth of this approach, stop and ask yourself, What would have happened if she had just observed playgrounds?

Look at Lever's sample. She selected certain schools to ensure that differences in social classes or races would not account for differences in socialization (perhaps lower-class males engage in different types of games or black females are more likely to play team sports). By selecting predominantly white middle-class schools, Lever avoided this problem. Since only whites were included in her sample, race could not be the cause of any difference. Likewise, since only middle-class children were included, social class was removed as a cause of the differences. (This should give you an idea for expanding Mead's theory even further: Look at the complexity of games across different social classes and races as well as sexes.) Watch how Lever's methodological choices, especially the use of four different data collection techniques, solve problems of validity (are we really seeing what we think we are seeing?) in this study.

The cognitive development theorists in psychology, most notably Jean Piaget, have traced the growth in knowledge and perceptions through the various stages of childhood. To date, little has been done to chart the parallel development of interpersonal skills needed as the child moves from the egocentric orientation of the family to the community of children found in the school. George Herbert Mead

Reprinted from *American Sociological Review* 1978, Vol. 43 (August): 471–483, by permission of the American Sociological Association and the author.

This research was supported by an N.I.M.H. dissertation fellowship. I would like to thank Stanton Wheeler, Louis W. Goodman, and R. Stephen Warner for their guidance and criticism, and the Yale Child Study Center for its help in securing access to the public schools. I also thank John Meyer, Allan Schnaiberg, Marshall Shumsky, and the anonymous reviewers for their careful reading and discussion of an early draft of this paper.

(1934) initiated this line of thought with his classic essay on the child's learning to regard the "self as object" and "take the role of the other." Unfortunately, few have followed Mead's example.

Significantly, both Mead and Piaget recognized the rich learning environment provided in play. Mead credits the child's shift from aimless play to the realm of structured games as a crucial step in the development of role taking. Piaget (1965), through a close study of the game of marbles, meticulously explains how children develop moral values while they play rule-bounded games. Aside from Mead and Piaget, little attention has been paid to the world of play and games in the study of childhood socialization.[1]

This study follows in the Mead and Piaget tradition by focusing on play and games as situations in which crucial learning takes place, but it goes beyond Mead's and Piaget's work in three important ways. First, Mead and Piaget each rests his analysis on a single game, whereas this study is based on a wide range of play and game activities. Second, both Mead and Piaget ignore sex differences in play. Mead's solitary example is the boys' game of baseball, but he does not tell us how girls, who are less familiar with team play, learn the same role-taking lessons. Piaget mentions, almost as an afterthought, that he did not find a single girls' game that has as elaborate an organization of rules as the boys' game of marbles, but he too fails to draw out the implications of his observation. A central concern of this study is to explore sex differences in the organization of children's play and to speculate on the sources as well as the potential effects of those differences.

Third, the paper highlights a specific dimension of play hitherto disregarded, namely, the *complexity* of the learning experience. I shall define complexity in more detail below, but it includes many of those attributes associated with the emergence of modern industrial society, such as division of labor, differentiation, heterogeneity, and rationalization (Simmel, 1955; Tonnies, 1955; Durkheim, 1893; Weber, 1967; Parsons and Smelser, 1956). My basic thesis is that the play activities of boys are more complex than those of girls, resulting in sex differences in the development of social skills potentially useful in childhood and later life.

METHODOLOGY

A variety of methods was used to gather as much data as possible in one year, 1972. In total, 181 fifth-grade children, aged 10 and 11, were studied. Half were from a suburban school and the other half from two city schools in Connecticut. The entire fifth grade of each school was included in the study. Three schools were selected whose student populations were predominantly white and middle-class—a choice made deliberately because of the possibility that race and class distinctions would confound the picture at this stage of exploratory research.

Four techniques of data collection were employed: observation of schoolyards, semistructured interviews, written questionnaires, and a diary record of leisure activities. The diary was a simple instrument used to document where the children had actually spent their time for the period of one week. Each morning, under the direction of the researcher, the children filled out a short form on which they described (1) what they had done the previous day after school, (2) who they did it with, (3) where the activity took place, and (4) how long it had lasted. Half the diaries were collected in the winter and half in the spring. The questionnaire, designed to elicit how children spend their time away from school, also was administered by me inside the classroom. I conducted semistructured interviews with one-third of the sample. Some were done in order to help design the questionnaire and diary; others were done later to help interpret the results. I gathered observational data while watching children's play activity during recess, physical education classes, and after school.[2]

MEASURING COMPLEXITY

In common usage, the word "complex" means something that is made up of a combination of elements. Sociologists similarly have applied the term to describe the amount of functional differentiation in any social unit, from a small group or a large organization, to society as a whole. Based on the ideal type of complex organization, regardless of the scale of the collectivity, there is general agreement that increases in any of the following six attributes constitute greater complexity (Etzioni, 1969; Blau and Schoenherr, 1971):

1. division of labor based on specialization of roles
2. interdependence between individual members
3. size of the membership
4. explicitness of the group goals
5. number and specificity of impersonal rules and
6. action of members as a unified collective

Borrowing from the work of some contemporary students of games (Roberts et al., 1959;

Redl et al., 1971; Avedon, 1971; Eifermann, 1972), I developed operational definitions for these six dimensions of complexity as they apply to the structure of play and games:

1. Role Differentiation. For the purposes of this study, activities are to be considered low in role differentiation if the same behavior is required or expected from all players. For example, in the game of checkers, each player is equipped with the same number of pieces and is expected to move them in accordance with the same rules. Role differentiation is to be scored medium if one player has more power and acts differently from the undifferentiated group of other players. This describes all central-person games such as tag and hide-and-seek. An activity is to be scored high on role differentiation if three or more distinct game roles are present. For example, in the game of baseball, the pitcher has a different task to perform than the shortstop whose task is different from the center fielder and so on.

2. Player Interdependence. An activity is to be judged low on the dimension of interdependence of players when the performance of one player does not immediately and significantly affect the performance of other players. For example, in the game of darts, one person's score does not interfere with the next player's score for the round. On the other hand, in the game of tennis, each player's move greatly affects the other's so that game has high interdependence of players.

3. Size of Play Group. This is a simple count of the number of players engaged in an activity. In this analysis, a group of three or fewer children is considered low on this dimension of complexity.

4. Explicitness of Goals. The explicitness of goals is found in the distinction between play and games. *Play* is defined as a cooperative interaction that has no stated goal, no end point, and no winners; formal *games*, in contrast, are competitive interactions, aimed at achieving a recognized goal (e.g., touchdown; checkmate).

Goals may involve tests of physical or mental skills, or both. Formal games have a predetermined end point (e.g., when one opponent reaches a specified number of points; end of ninth inning) that is simultaneous with the declaration of a winner or winners. The same basic activity may be either play or games. For example, riding bikes is play; racing bikes is a game.

5. Number and Specificity of Rules. Sometimes the word "rule" is broadly used to refer to norms or customs. Here the term is used in a narrower sense and refers to explicit rules which (a) are known to all players before the game begins, (b) are constant from one game situation to the next, and (c) carry sanctions for their violation. Play as defined above never has rules, whereas games always are governed by them. But games do vary by the number and specificity of their rules. Some games, like tag and hide-and-seek, have only a few rules; other games, like baseball and monopoly, have numerous well-established rules.

6. Team Formation. A team is a group of players working collectively toward a common goal. Play, as defined above, is never structured by teams. Games, on the other hand, are to be divided into those requiring team formation when played with three or more persons and those prohibiting or excluding team formation. Within the category of games with team formation are included both those games where teammates play relatively undifferentiated roles, as in tug-of-war or relay races, and those that require coordination between teammates playing differentiated positions, as in baseball.

In order to test the hypothesis that boys' play and games are more complex in structure, I examine closely the type and frequency of the play activities of both sexes as they occur in public and private places. The evidence for private play is in the diary data, reporting after school and weekend play. Diary data are important because they reflect a large number of incidents, a wide range of activities, and a free choice of both games and playmates. The evidence for public play, based on observational data collected mostly during recess and gym periods, reveals the rich texture of the play world, replete with dialogue that helps the researcher understand the meanings children attribute to different play forms.

Diary Data

The diary responses reflect activities played inside or around the home in the hours after school. From over 2,000 diary entries, 895 cases of social play were isolated for this analysis.[3]

They represented 136 distinct play activities which were then scored by the author and three independent coders.[4] The operational definitions of the six dimensions of complexity were presented to the coders, along with descriptions of play activities derived from the children's interviews. The activities were then rated along each of the six dimensions. All games were given ratings based on the children's own reports of how a game is played most typically at the fifth grade level.[5]

Table 1 presents the basic data. To develop

Table 1

Coding and Complexity Scores of the Most Frequently Listed Diary Activities

	Girls	Boys	Total
Type I. Complexity Score=0			
one role (0); low interdepedence (0); play (0) no rules (0); no teams (0).			
1. listen to records (g) 11. exploring woods (b)			
2. listen to radio (g) 12. hiking (g)			
3. drawing (g) 13. horseback riding (g)			
4. painting (g) 14. grooming horses (g)			
5. work with clay (g) 15. take a walk (g)			
6. build things (b) 16. jump roofs (b)			
7. ice skating (g) 17. climb trees (b)			
8. roller skating (g) 18. sled ride (b)			
9. bike riding 19. launch rockets (b)			
10. mini-biking (b) 20. fly kites (b)			
Type I:	42% (179)	27% (126)	34% (305)
Type II. Complexity Score=1			
A. one role (0); high interdependence (1); play (0); no rules (0); no teams (0).			
21. cheerlead practice (g) 23. dancing (g)			
22. singing (g) 24. catch (b)	(13)	(14)	(27)
B. one role (0); low interdependence (0); game (1); few rules (0); no teams (0).			
25. bowling (g) 28. paddle pool (b)			
26. skittle bowl (b) 29. race electric			
27. pool (b) cars (b)	(17)	(42)	(59)
Type II:	7% (30)	12% (56)	10% (86)

(continued)

Table 1

continued

	Girls	Boys	Total
Type III. Complexity Score=2			
A. two or more roles (1); high interdependence (1); play (0); no rules (0); no teams (0).			
30. dolls (g) 32. jumprope (g)			
31. indoor fantasy (g) 33. outdoor fantasy (b)			
(e.g., school, house) (e.g., Army, FBI, Batman)	(72)	(19)	(91)
B. two roles (1); low interdependence (0); game (1); few rules (0); no teams (0).			
34. tag, chase (g) 36. kick the can (b)			
35. hide-and-seek (g)	(38)	(23)	(61)
C. One role (0); high interdependence (1); game (1); few rules (0); no teams (0).			
37. simple card games (g) 38. 2-square; 4-square	(21)	(29)	(50)
Type III:	31% (131)	15% (71)	22.5% (202)
Type IV: Complexity Score=3			
one role (0); high interdependence (1); game (1); many rules (1); no teams (0).			
39. chess (b) 41. board games (g)			
40. checkers (b) (e.g., Monopoly, Parcheesi)			
Type IV:	8% (35)	15% (70)	12% (105)
*Type V: Complexity Score=4			
one role (0); high interdependence (1); game (1); many rules (1); team formation (1).			
Type V:	2% (9)	1% (5)	1.5% (14)
Type VI: Complexity Score=5			
two or more roles (1); high interdependence (1); game (1); many rules (1); team formation (1).			
42. football (b) 46. soccer (b)			
43. ice hockey (b) 47. kickball (g)			
44. baseball (b) 48. punch ball (b)			
45. basketball (b) Type VI:	10% (43)	30% (140)	20% (183)
Total Social Play:	100% (427)	100% (468)	100% (895)

*Infrequently played activities, exemplified by Newcombe (g) and Capture the Flag (b).

an overall complexity score, five of the dimensions were dichotomized and assigned either a low or high value (0,1).[6] (The sixth dimension, size of group, varied from one play situation to the next and was tabulated independently.) The five dichotomous attributes yield thirty-two possible combinations; however, only nine occurred empirically. In Table 1 they are organized from lowest to highest complexity (scores from 0 to 5). Only the forty-eight activities that appeared in the diaries ten or more times are used to exemplify this scoring procedure, but all social play activities, even those less frequently mentioned, are included in the tabulations.[7] By age ten, play activities are generally known to be sex segregated. The "g" or "b" after each activity in Table 1 indicates whether it is played predominantly by girls or boys; the absence of a letter implies that the sexes engage in the activity with roughly equal frequency.

Table 1 yields two important findings. First, it shows the great variety regarding levels of complexity in the games played by children of similar age. Mead and Piaget, by focusing on only a single game, could not show the range of experiences available within the play world. Fully a third of the activities were low on all the measured dimensions of complexity. Another fifth were high on all. Children exposed to one or the other of these types of play are likely to be learning very different skills. Second, if we can agree that games provide differential learning environments, then we must assume differential effects for boys and girls. Boys experience three times as many games at the highest level of complexity and over twice as many boys' activities are located in the top half of the complexity scale.[8]

Table 2 views the data from a different perspective by showing the sex distribution separately for each of the six dimensions. Although greater complexity in boys' activities is demonstrated for all six, the major finding of Table 2 is seen on the fourth dimension, explicitness of goals. Sixty-five percent of boys' activities were competitive games compared to only 37% of girls' activities. In other words, *girls played more* while *boys gamed more*. This difference is not merely a function of boys' playing more team

Table 2

Sex Differences on the Six Dimensions of Complexity in Play and Games

Dimensions of Complexity	Girls	Boys
1. Number of roles (3 or more roles)	18% (427)	32% (468)
2. Interdependence of players (high interdependence)	46% (427)	57% (468)
3. Size of play group (4 or more persons)	35% (427)	45% (468)
4. Explicitness of goals (game structure)	37% (427)	65% (468)
5. Number of rules (many rules)	19% (427)	45% (468)
6. Team formation (teams required)	12% (427)	31% (468)

sports. Only 140 of the 305 games played by boys were team sports. Eliminating team sports for both sexes, we would still find 54% of the boys' activities and 30% of the girls' activities competitively structured. Sedentary games, like chess and electric race cars, are as important as sport in reflecting boys' greater competitiveness.

Nor is it the case when girls do participate in competitive games that they experience the same level of complexity as their male peers. The games girls play have fewer rules, and less often require the formation of teams.[9] In summary, the data from children's diaries show strongly that boys, far more often than girls, experience high levels of complexity in their play and games.

Observational Data

Observations of children at play during recess, gym classes, and after school also indicate very distinct play patterns for boys and girls. As in the diary data, boys' activities were found to be more complex. The following descriptions of a few selected play activities illustrate the way in which each of the dimensions of complexity is expressed. Greater attention is given to girls' games as they are less familiar to adults. Some implications of differential organization of play are suggested, but their elaboration awaits the discussion section.

1. Role Differentiation. The largest category of girls' public activity was the same as their private activity, namely, single-role play. These were cooperative activities with both or all parties doing basically the same thing such as riding bikes, roller skating, or ice skating. A minority of girls' activities were competitive games. Observing recess periods for a year, I saw only one instance of a spontaneously organized team sport, namely, kickball. The activities that appeared most regularly during recess were the traditional girls' games, like hopscotch, which are turn-taking games with only one game role present at a given time. Each player, in specified sequential order, attempts to accomplish the same task as all other players. A few turn-taking games have two distinct roles: for example, in jumprope there is the role of rope turner and that of rope jumper. The other girls' games I observed frequently at recess were central-person games, the most popular being tag, spud, and Mother May I. These games also have only two roles—the "it" and the "others." Power is usually ascribed in these games through "dipping rules" like "odd-man-out."

Boys at this age have largely stopped playing central-person games except as fillers; for example, they might play tag while waiting for a bus or after so many team members have been called home to dinner that their previous game has disintegrated. The great majority of observed games were team sports with their multiple roles. Besides distinctions based on positions and assigned tasks, there were also distinctions in power between team captains and their subordinates. Sometimes the leaders were appointed by teachers, but more often the children elected their captains according to achievement criteria.[10] After school especially, I observed boys in single role activities, some noncompetitive, like flying kites and climbing trees, but most competitive like tennis, foot races, or one-on-one basketball.

2. Player Interdependence. There are many types of player interdependence: (1) interdependence of action between members of a single group; (2) interdependent decision making between single opponents; (3) simultaneous interdependence of action with one's own teammates and an opposing group of teammates.

Very little interdependence was required of those girls engaged in single role play; coaction rather than interaction is required of the participants. Also, little interdependence was required of those playing turn-taking games. Even though the latter activity is competitive, the style of competition is indirect, with each player acting independently of the others. That is, one competes against a figurative "scoreboard" (Player A → norm ← Player B). Participation in such games is routinized and occurs successively or after the previous player's failure; that is, opponents do not compete simultaneously. Interdependent decision making is not necessary in turn-taking games of physical skill as it may be in some of the popular board games.

When girls do play interdependently, they tend to do so in a cooperative context where there is interdependence of action between members of a single group. This type of interaction is best exemplified (but rarely observed) in the creation of private fantasy scenarios. One public example occurred when seven girls from one school took the initiative to write, produce, and act out a play they called "Hippie Cinderella." They stayed indoors at recess and rehearsed almost daily for three weeks in preparation for presentation to the entire fifth-grade class.

When boys compete as individuals, they are more likely to be engaged in direct, face-to-face confrontations (Player A ⇆ Player B). Interdependent decision making between single opponents is necessary in games like tennis or one-on-one basketball that combine strategy with physical skill. More often, boys compete as members of teams and must simultaneously coordinate their actions with those of their teammates while taking into account the action and strategies of their opponents. Boys interviewed expressed finding gratification in acting as representatives of a collectivity; the approval or disapproval of one's teammates accentuates the importance of contributing to a group victory.

3. Size of Play Group. Observations made during recess periods showed boys playing in much larger groups than girls to a far greater extent than appeared in the diary data. Boys typically were involved in team sports which require a large number of participants for proper play. Boys in all three schools could play daily, depending on the season, in ongoing basketball, football, or baseball games involving ten to twenty-five or more persons. Girls were rarely observed playing in groups as large as ten persons; on those occasions, they were engaged in cooperative circle songs that seemed to emerge spontaneously, grow, and almost as quickly disintegrate. More often, girls participated in activities like tag, hopscotch, or jumprope, which can be played properly with as few as two or three participants and seldom involve more than five or six. In fact, too many players are considered to detract rather than enhance the fun because it means fewer turns, with longer waits between turns. Indeed, Eifermann (1968), after cataloging over 2,000 children's games, observed that most girls' games, like hopscotch and jacks, can be played alone, whereas the great majority of boys' games need two or more players.

4. Explicitness of Goals. In the recess yards, I more often saw girls playing cooperatively and boys playing competitively. Some girls engaged in conversation more than they did in play (see Lever, 1976:481). Others, like those who initiated the circle songs and dances, preferred action governed by ritual rather than rules. For example, the largest and most enthusiastic group of girls witnessed during the year of research was involved in a circle chant called "Dr. Knickerbocker Number Nine." Twenty-four girls repeated the chant and body motions in an outer circle, while one girl in the center spun around with eyes closed. She then stopped, with

arm extended, pointing out someone from the outer circle to join her. The ritual chant began again while the new arrival spun around; this procedure continued until nine persons had been chosen in similar random fashion to form the inner circle. Then the ninth person remained in the circle's center while the others resumed their original positions and the cycle would begin anew.

Although this activity appeared monotonous to the observer because it allowed the participants little chance to exercise physical or mental skills, these ten-year-olds were clearly enjoying themselves. Shouts of glee were heard from the circle's center when a friend had been chosen to join them. Indeed, a girl could gauge her popularity by the loudness of these shouts. For some the activity may provide an opportunity to reaffirm self-esteem without suffering any of the achievement pressures of team sports.

Even when girls engaged in presumably competitive games, they typically avoided setting precise goals. In two schools, I observed girls playing "Under the Moon," a popular form of jumprope. The first person hops in and jumps once, in any fashion of her choosing, and then hops out. She then enters again and does two jumps, usually though not necessarily, different from the first. She increases her jumps by an increment of one until she has jumped ten times. Her turn over, she then becomes a rope turner. There was no competition exhibited between players. They participated for the fun of the turn, not to win. Even if the jumper trips the rope, she is allowed to complete her turn. If the jumper competes, it is with herself, as she alone determines whether to attempt an easy jump or a more difficult one.

The point is that girls sometimes take activities in which a comparison of relative achievement is structurally possible (and sometimes normatively expected) and transform them into noncompetitive play. Girls are satisfied to keep their play loosely structured. For example, in the game of jacks, girls can say before beginning, "The first to finish 'double bounces' is the winner." More often, however, they just play until they are bored with the game. Players may or may not verbalize "you won," and recognize who has advanced the most number of steps. Boys grant much more importance to being proclaimed the winner; they virtually always structure their games, be it one-on-one or full team basketball, so that the outcomes will be clear and definite.

5. Number and Specificity of Rules. This investigator also observed, reminiscent of Piaget, that boys' games more often have an elaborate organization of rules. Girls' turn-taking games progress in identical order from one situation to the next; prescriptions are minimal, dictating what must be done in order to advance. Given the structure of these games, disputes are not likely to occur. "Hogging" is impossible when participation is determined by turn-taking; nor can fouls occur when competition is indirect. Sports games, on the other hand, are governed by a broad set of rules covering a wide variety of situations, some common and others rare. Areas of ambiguity which demand rule elaboration and adjudication are built into these games. Kohlberg (1964) refines Piaget's thesis by arguing that children learn the greatest respect for rules when they can be used to reduce dissonance in ambiguous situations.[11]

Because girls play cooperatively more than competitively, they have less experience with rules per se, so we should expect them to have a lesser consciousness of rules than boys. On one of those rare occasions when boys and girls could be watched playing the same games, there was striking evidence for a sex difference in rule sensitivity. A gym teacher introduced a game called "newcombe," a simplified variation of volleyball, in which the principal rule is that the ball must be passed three times before being returned to the other side of the net. Although the game was new to all, the boys did not once forget the "3-pass" rule; the girls forgot it on over half the volleys.

6. Team Formation. Team formation can be seen as a dimension of complexity because it indicates simultaneously structured relationships of cooperation and conflict. In turn-taking games, girls compete within a single group as independent players, each one against all others. Boys compete between groups, acting interdependently as members of a team. Team formation is required in all of their favorite sports: baseball, football, basketball, hockey, and soccer. Only a few girls in each school regularly joined the boys in their team sports; conversely, only a few boys in each school avoided the sports games. Questionnaire data support these observations. Most boys reported regular participation in neighborhood sports games. In addition, at the time of the study 68% said they belonged to some adult-supervised teams, with a full schedule of practice and league games. In fact, some of these fifth graders were already involved in interstate competitions.

The after-school sports program illustrates boys' greater commitment to team competition. Twenty girls from the third, fourth, and fifth grades elected captains who chose teams for newcombe games. Only seven of those girls returned the following week. In contrast, after-school basketball attracted so many boys that the fifth graders were given their own day. The teacher called roll for the next two weeks and noted that every boy had returned to play again.

Thus observational data, like the diary data, support the basic hypothesis that boys' play activities are more complex in structure than those of girls. Boys' play more frequently involves specialization of roles, interdependence of players, explicit group goals, and larger group membership, numerous rules, and team divisions. This conclusion holds for activities in public as well as in private. It suggests a markedly different set of socialization experiences for members of each sex.

DISCUSSION

Sources of the Sex Difference

What is it that produces these distinct play patterns for boys and girls? The answer is mostly historical and cultural and holds true for much of Europe as well as the United States. While the rise of recreational physical activities in the late nineteenth century was enjoyed by women and men alike, the organized team sports which flourished at the same time were limited to participation by males (Paxson, 1917). The combined beliefs in the masculine nature of sport and the physiological inferiority of females led early twentieth century educators to lobby for competitive athletics for boys while restricting the physical education of girls to gymnastic exercises and dance. The emphasis on competitive athletics for males was reinforced by the view that sport served as a training ground for future soldiers ("the battle of Waterloo was won on the playing fields of Eton") and by the growing interest in spectator sports in which the dominant performers were young men (Cozens and Stumpf, 1953). Despite some outstanding individual female athletes in golf, tennis, and track and field, there was no development of interest in women's team sports. This situation is only now beginning to change.

Evidence generated in connection with Title IX of the Education Amendments Acts shows the extraordinary sex difference with respect to the allocation of funds for athletic programs from the primary grades through college. In 1969 the Syracuse New York School board allocated $90,000 for boys' extracurricular sports compared to $200 for girls' sports. In rural Pennsylvania, the Fairfield area school district set its 1972–73 budget at a ratio of 40:1 in favor of male athletes whose interscholastic competition begins in earnest by fifth grade. Even at Vassar, where sports for women are given great attention, the boys' athletic budget was double that of girls, although they comprised only one-third of the student body (Gilbert and Williamson, 1973).

Of course, it is not only the schools that encourage boys' and restrict girls' athletic participation. Parents act as the conveyor belts for cultural norms, and it is no less the case for norms pertaining to sport. Male children are quick to learn that their demonstrations of athletic skill earn the attention and praise of adults. Many fathers show more emotion and enthusiasm for professional sports than anything else. Girls at young ages may not be actively discouraged from sports participation, but they are told

that they are "tomboys," which is understood to be a deviant label. In the recent Little League debate, psychologists, parents, and coaches voiced their concern for the masculinization of female athletes, and the possible damage to young male egos when girls defeat boys in public (Michener, 1976). This cultural legacy is still with us, even though we now appear to be on the verge of radical change.

Historical analysis of children's games confirms that boys are playing more team sports now than ever before. Equally important, boys have drifted away from loosely structured play towards more formally organized competitive games (Sutton-Smith and Rosenberg, 1971). Evidence presented here supports this picture. It appears that the growing cultural emphasis on sports and winning has carried over to nonphysical activities and made them more competitive, and that, to date, it has had this effect to a far greater extent for boys than for girls.

Consequences of the Sex Differences

Boys' games provide a valuable learning environment. It is reasonable to expect that the following social skills will be cultivated on the playground: the ability to deal with diversity in memberships where each person is performing a special task; the ability to coordinate actions and maintain cohesiveness among group members; the ability to cope with a set of impersonal rules; and the ability to work for collective as well as personal goals.

Team sports furnish the most frequent opportunity to sharpen these social skills. One could elaborate on the lessons learned. The rule structure encourages strategic thinking. Team sports also imply experience with clear-cut leadership positions, usually based on universalistic criteria. The group rewards the individual who has improved valued skills, a practice which further enhances a sense of confidence based on achievement. Furthermore, through team sports as well as individual matches, boys learn to deal with interpersonal competition in a forthright manner. Boys experience face-to-face confrontations—often opposing a close friend—and must learn to depersonalize the attack. They must practice self-control and sportsmanship; in fact, some of the boys in this study described the greatest lesson in team sports as learning to "keep your cool."

Girls' play and games are very different. They are mostly spontaneous, imaginative, and free of structure or rules. Turn-taking activities like jumprope may be played without setting explicit goals. Girls have far less experience with interpersonal competition. The style of their competition is indirect, rather than face to face, individual rather than team affiliated. Leadership roles are either missing or randomly filled.

Perhaps more important, girls' play occurs in small groups. These girls report preferring the company of a single best friend to a group of four or more.[12] Often girls mimic primary human relationships instead of playing formal games, or they engage in conversation rather than play anything at all. In either case, there are probable benefits for their affective and verbal development. In Meadian terms, it may be that boys develop the ability to take the role of the *generalized other* while girls develop empathy skills to take the role of the *particular other.*

That the sexes develop different social skills in childhood due to their play patterns is logical conjecture; that those social skills might carry over and influence their adult behavior is pure speculation. Indeed, the weight of evidence indicates that life experiences are vast and varied; much can happen to intervene and change the patterns set during childhood. Still, there is so much continuity between boys' play patterns and adult male roles that we must consider whether games serve a particular socializing function.

This idea is now popular. In a recent best seller on managerial leaders, Maccoby (1976) describes the 250 executives he studied as gamesmen who organize teams, look for a challenge, and play to win. The same social skills may be equally helpful in lower level bureaucratic jobs or other settings, like trade unions and work crews, where complexity of organization is also found. One need not endorse the world of organizations, bureaucracy, sharp competition, and hierarchy to recognize it as an integral part of modern industrial society.

The unfortunate fact is that we do not know what effect playing games might have on later life. We do not know, for example, whether the minority of women who have succeeded in bureaucratic settings are more likely to have played complex games. A recent study offers a modicum of supporting data. Hennig and Jardim (1977) portray their small sample of twenty-five women in top management positions as former tomboys. It is also the case that elite boarding schools and women's colleges, many of which stress team sports, have been credited with producing a large portion of this nation's female leaders. I would not want to argue that competitive team sports are the only place to learn useful organizational skills. Surely, the skills in question can be learned in nonplay settings in both childhood and adulthood. Nevertheless, it can be argued that complex games are an early and effective training ground from which girls traditionally have been excluded.

CONCLUSION

Children's socialization is assumed to have consequences for their later lives. Sociologists have looked to the family and the school as the primary socializing agents. In contrast, this analysis focused on the peer group as the agent of socialization, children's play as the activity of socialization, and social skills as the product of socialization. The data presented here reaffirm Mead's and Piaget's message that during play children develop numerous social skills that enable them to enjoy group membership in a community of peers.

The data also demonstrate that some games, when analyzed structurally, provide a highly complex experience for their young players while others do not. By itself, the notion of complexity adds to our appreciation of games as important early training grounds. However, the evidence of differential exposure to complex games leads to the conclusion that not all children will learn the same lessons. Here the approach to play and games differs dramatically from that of Mead and Piaget who presumed social and moral development as a normal part of the growth process and, therefore, did not make problematic the different experience of boys and girls. One implication of this research is that boys' greater exposure to complex games may give them an advantage in occupational milieus that share structural features with those games. At the very least, the striking similarity between the formula for success in team sports and in modern organizations should encourage researchers to give serious attention to play patterns and their consequences.

Notes

1. Among others who have recognized the importance of play in childhood socialization are Roberts and Sutton-Smith, 1962; Stone, 1971; Bruner et al., 1976.

2. See Lever (1974:65–108) for a detailed description of the methodology.

3. There were 2,141 activities recorded in the children's diaries. Five hundred eight entries were eliminated from this analysis because they were descriptions of nonplay activities like attending church services, doing homework or household chores, or going to the doctor. Another 527 items were eliminated because they reflected pastimes rather than actual play. This category included: watching television; reading books, comics or newspapers; going to the movies; going for an auto ride; and talking on the telephone. Television viewing, by far, accounts for most of the entries in this category. Of the remaining 1,106 play activities, 211 were not included because they were instances of the child's playing alone rather than in the company of others. Because the complexity dimensions reflect interpersonal skills, pastimes and solitary play are not relevant. However, it should be noted that there was no sex difference in the number of leisure hours spent with the television (15 to 20 hours/week) or playing alone (about 20% of all play).

4. The coders included the headmistress of a private elementary school who previously had taught fifth-graders for over a decade, a graduate student who had been a camp counselor for ten-year-olds for several years, and an assistant professor of sociology. Overall, the judges agreed on over 90% of the items coded.

5. Such reports were especially needed because separate groups of children may play the same game somewhat differently, while even the same children do not necessarily play a game in identical fashion from one occasion to the next. It is also important to note that children modify adult games, so that a game like pool, which has complicated rules for adults, usually is played according to simple rules by children.

6. To justify linking the six dimensions, a factor analysis was run on the 136 activities. There was only one factor present, and all six dimensions were a part of it (the lowest degree of communality was .60); I have referred to this single factor as "complexity." While it may be argued that some dimensions add more complexity than others, the absence of guidelines encourages equal weighting at this time.

7. See Lever (1974:394–7) for a complete list of games recorded in the children's diaries.

8. Because some children reported more activities than others, there is the possibility that these results, based on activities as the units of analysis, reflect the extreme scores of a few individuals and are not representative of the sample as a whole. To guard against such misinterpretation, I made the individuals the units of analysis. To do so, I used the same dichotomization and point system displayed in Table 1 and added the sixth dimension, size of play group, as it appeared in each of the 895 entries. Once each activity could be given a complexity score (now zero to six), an average complexity score could be ascertained for each child based on the entire week's social play report. Seventy percent of the boys, compared with 36% of the girls, had average complexity scores of 3.0 or higher—a fact which further sustains the hypothesis.

9. Fifty-one percent of the games girls play (n = 158) contain many rules, compared with 69% of the boys' games (n = 305). Looking only at games with three or more participants, we note that boys played 26% more games which called for team formation.

10. In response to the interview question "Who are the fifth-grade leaders?" the boys in all three schools answered that the best athletes/team organizers rightly held that position. In contrast, most girls hesitated with the question, then named persons who had power, but credited their aggression rather than particular valued skills. They equated giving directives with assertiveness and gave that behavior negative labels like "bossy" or "big mouth." Some openly stated that leaders acted less than ladylike and were not envied for their power. Attitudes that underlie Kanter's (1977:201) "mean and bossy woman boss" stereotype obviously are set at a very young age.

11. See Lever (1976:482–3) for a description of sex differences in the handling of quarrelling in games.

12. It is important to note that, according to their questionnaire responses, the minority of thirty girls who reported playing complex games during the diary week also indicated a preference for larger friendship groups. The fact that the sex difference in size of friendship cliques disappears when controlling for complexity of game experience is one indication of the importance of this classification scheme.

References

Avedon, Elliott M.
  1971   "The structure elements of games." Pp. 419–26 in Elliott M. Avedon and Brian Sutton-Smith (eds.), The Study of Games. New York: Wiley.

Blau, Peter and R. A. Schoenherr
  1971   The Structure of Organizations. New York: Basic Books.

Bruner, J. S., A. Jolly, and K. Sylva
  1976   Play: Its Role in Development and Evolution. New York: Penguin.

Cozens, Frederick and Florence Stumpf
  1953   Sports in American Life. Chicago: University of Chicago Press.

Durkheim, Emile
  [1893] The Division of Labor in Society.
  1964   New York: Free Press.

Eifermann, Rivka
  1968   "School children's games." Final Report, Contract No. OE-6-21-010. Department of Health, Education and Welfare; Office of Education, Bureau of Research. Unpublished paper.
  1972   "Free social play: a guide to directed playing." Unpublished paper.

Etzioni, Amitai
  1969   A Sociological Reader on Complex Organization. New York: Holt.

Gilbert, Bil and Nancy Williamson
  1973   "Sport is unfair to women." Sports Illustrated 38 (May 28):88–98.

Hennig, Margaret and Ann Jardim
  1977   The Managerial Woman. New York: Doubleday.

Kanter, Rosabeth Moss
  1977   Men and Women of the Corporation. New York: Basic Books.

Kohlberg, Lawrence
  1964   "Development of moral character and moral ideology." Pp. 383–431 in M. L. Hoffman and L. W. Hoffman (eds.), Review of Child Development Research, Vol. 1. New York: Russell Sage.

Lever, Janet
  1974   Games Children Play: Sex Differences and the Development of Role Skills. Ph.D. dissertation, Department of Sociology, Yale University.
  1976   "Sex differences in the games children play." Social Problems 23:478–87.

Maccoby, Michael
  1976   The Gamesman. New York: Simon and Schuster.

Mead, George Herbert
  1934   Mind, Self, and Society. Chicago: University of Chicago Press.

Michener, James A.
  1976   Sports in America. New York: Random House.

Parsons, Talcott and Neil J. Smelser
  1956   Economy and Society: A Study in the Integration of Economic and Social Theory. London: Routledge.
Paxson, Frederic L.
  1917   "The rise of sport." Mississippi Valley Historical Review 4:144–68.
Piaget, Jean
  1965   The Moral Judgment of the Child. New York: Free Press.
Redl, F., P. Gump, and B. Sutton-Smith
  1971   "The dimensions of games." Pp. 408–18 in Elliott M. Avedon and Brian Sutton-Smith (eds.), The Study of Games. New York: Wiley.
Roberts, John M., M. J. Arth, and R. R. Bush
  1959   "Games in culture." American Anthropologist 61:597–605.
Roberts, John M. and Brian Sutton-Smith
  1962   "Child training and game involvement." Ethnology 1:166–85.
Simmel, Georg
  1955   The Web of Group Affiliations. Trans. by Reinhard Bendix. New York: Free Press.
Stone, Gregory P.
  1971   "The play of little children." Pp. 4–17 in R. E. Herron and Brian Sutton-Smith (eds.), Child's Play. New York: Wiley.
Sutton-Smith, B. and B. Rosenberg
  1971   "Sixty years of historical change in the game preference of American children." Pp. 18–50 in R. E. Herron and B. Sutton-Smith (eds.), Child's Play. New York: Wiley.
Tonnies, Ferdinand
  1955   Community and Association. Trans. by Charles P. Loomis. London: Routledge.
Weber, Max
  1967   From Max Weber: Essays in Sociology. Trans. and ed. by H. H. Gerth and C. Wright Mills. New York: Oxford University Press.

9
Learning the Student Role: Kindergarten as Academic Boot Camp

Harry L. Gracey

Editors' Introduction

So far in this part we have set forth the basic sociological approach to the important socialization process, with special attention paid to George Herbert Mead's theory of the development of self. We have seen how Mead's theory can be expanded to cover important differences in the socialization of boys and girls. We now turn to a more formal setting for socialization, the school classroom.

When sociologists study what it is that children learn in school classrooms, their interests go well beyond the usual "reading, 'riting, and 'rithmetic." They are concerned with what children learn from the structure of the school and classroom and the interaction patterns within them. Harry Gracey brings these interests to the kindergarten classroom and finds that the important thing children learn there is how to be a student. According to Gracey, what is this student role and how is it being taught?

Gracey begins by saying that education *serves* the society created by the economic, political, and military institutions. In Part One of this book, Alex Inkeles identified institutions as the "main building blocks of society" (p. 39). He characterized them as "a more complex structure of roles organized around some central activity or social need" (p. 39). He then went on to classify institutions into several broad types. Notice what Gracey adds to the classification of institutions—they no longer all exist on the same level. Education seems to be the institution in which people are trained or socialized to operate within a given set of political, economic, and military institutions. Education, then, plays a secondary role in society. But notice how important this secondary role is. Gracey wants to show that learning the student role prepares these children for roles in society beyond that of student. How does he go about doing this? Does he make a convincing case? Is his case overdrawn in any way?

Gracey's article illustrates two of the three major theoretical orientations. In the symbolic interactionist orientation, he focuses on everyday life in the kindergarten and provides detailed descriptions of interaction patterns between teacher and pupils and among the children themselves. He shows the teacher's efforts to construct meanings, while the children share their own meanings in the "holes" in the official structure. Meanings, you will recall from Part One, are crucial to the premises of symbolic interactionism; we act toward objects on the basis of socially defined and learned meanings. However, while Gracey focuses on the small-scale interaction processes in the kindergarten, he also shows how they relate to the larger societal structure. In the conflict orientation, Gracey shows children learning to take their place in a hierarchy of constraint and authority without raising any persistent questions about it. So the teacher is molding these children by furnishing meanings that are compatible with the major institutions in the society. The children, although usually compliant, do not cooperate fully in accepting these meanings—yet. Once again, you can see the interplay of structure and process.

Gracey used nonparticipant observation, sitting in kindergarten classrooms and watching what happened. You have now seen observation used in three settings: The Oasis tavern, school playgrounds, and now classrooms. Although this is an obviously useful technique for data collection, it does have a problem that should be pointed out. Whenever observation is used, the possibility exists that the presence of the observer may alter the behavior of the subjects. This is especially a problem when the observer is different from those being observed, such as an adult observing children or a woman observing men. At The Oasis tavern this did not seem to be a problem after a short while, since LeMasters was accepted as a regular. In her study of children's games, Lever does not say whether or not this was a problem, but it is safe to assume that it was not. Why? If you recall, all of her techniques of data collection accumulated compatible information—they corroborated each other. If the observational data had been altered because of the presence of the observer, the data would probably not have fit so well with those data collected in other ways. But what about adding an adult observer to a kindergarten classroom? Would this create a problem? What information does Gracey give about this problem? Do you think Gracey could have gathered better data by using some other method of data collection? Gracey also interviewed kindergarten teachers. Why did he do this? Did he gain anything by using both observation and interviews with teachers?

INTRODUCTION

Education must be considered one of the major institutions of social life today. Along with the family and organized religion, however, it is a "secondary institution," one in which people are prepared for life in society as it is presently organized. The main dimensions of modern life, that is, the nature of society as a whole, is determined principally by the "primary institutions," which today are the economy, the political system, and the military establishment. Education has been defined by sociologists, classical and contemporary, as an institution which serves society by socializing people into it through a formalized, standardized procedure. At the beginning of this century Emile Durkheim told student teachers at the University of Paris that education "consists of a methodical socialization of the younger generation." He went on to add:

It is the influence exercised by adult generations on those that are not ready for social life. Its object is to arouse and to develop in the child a certain number of physical, intellectual, and moral states that are demanded of him by the political society as a whole and by the special milieu for which he is specifically destined. . . . To the egotistic and asocial being that has just been born, (society) must, as rapidly as possible, add another, capable of leading a moral and social life. Such is the work of education.[1]

The educational process, Durkheim said, "is above all the means by which society perpetually

Reprinted with permission of Macmillan Publishing Co., Inc. from *Readings in Introductory Sociology*, 3d ed., by Dennis H. Wrong and Harry L. Gracey, eds. Copyright © 1977 by Macmillan Publishing Co., Inc.

This article is based on research conducted with the Bank Street College of Education under NIMH Grant No. 9135. The study is more fully reported in Harry L. Gracey, *Curriculum or Craftsmanship: Elementary School Teacher in a Bureaucratic System*. Chicago, University of Chicago Press, 1972.

recreates the conditions of its very existence."[2] The contemporary educational sociologist, Wilbur Brookover, offers a similar formulation in his recent textbook definition of education:

Actually, therefore, in the broadest sense education is synonymous with socialization. It includes any social behavior that assists in the induction of the child into membership in the society or any behavior by which the society perpetuates itself through the next generation.[3]

The educational institution is, then, one of the ways in which society is perpetuated through the systematic socialization of the young, while the nature of the society which is being perpetuated—its organization and operation, its values, beliefs and ways of living—are determined by the primary institutions. The educational system, like other secondary institutions, *serves* the society which is *created* by the operation of the economy, the political system, and the military establishment.

Schools, the social organizations of the educational institution, are today for the most part large bureaucracies run by specially trained and certified people. There are few places left in modern societies where formal teaching and learning is carried on in small, isolated groups, like the rural, one-room schoolhouses of the last century. Schools are large, formal organizations which tend to be parts of larger organizations, local community School Districts. These School Districts are bureaucratically organized and their operations are supervised by state and local governments. In this context, as Brookover says:

The term education is used . . . to refer to a system of schools, in which specifically designated persons are expected to teach children and youth certain types of acceptable behavior. The school system becomes a . . . unit in the total social structure and is recognized by the members of the society as a separate social institution. Within this structure a portion of the total socialization process occurs.[4]

Education is the part of the socialization process which takes place in the schools; and these are, more and more today, bureaucracies within bureaucracies.

Kindergarten is generally conceived by educators as a year of preparation for school. It is thought of as a year in which small children, five or six years old, are prepared socially and emotionally for the academic learning which will take place over the next twelve years. It is expected that a foundation of behavior and attitudes will be laid in kindergarten on which the children can acquire the skills and knowledge they will be taught in the grades. A booklet prepared for parents by the staff of a suburban New York school system says that the kindergarten experience will stimulate the child's desire to learn and cultivate the skills he will need for learning in the rest of his school career. It claims that the child will find opportunities for physical growth, for satisfying his "need for self-expression," acquire some knowledge, and provide opportunities for creative activity. It concludes, "The most important benefit that your five-year-old will receive from kindergarten is the opportunity to live and grow happily and purposefully with others in a small society." The kindergarten teachers in one of the elementary schools in this community, one we shall call the Wilbur Wright School, said their goals were to see that the children "grew" in all ways: physically, of course, emotionally, socially, and academically. They said they wanted children to like school as a result of their kindergarten experiences and that they wanted them to learn to get along with others.

None of these goals, however, is unique to kindergarten; each of them is held to some extent by teachers in the other six grades at Wright School. And growth would occur, but differently, even if the child did not attend school. The children already know how to get along with others, in their families and their play groups. The unique job of the kindergarten in the educational division of labor seems rather to be teaching children the student role. The student role is the repertoire of behavior and attitudes regarded by educators as appropriate to children in school. Observation in the kindergartens of the Wilbur Wright School revealed a great variety of activities through which children are shown and then drilled in the behavior and attitudes defined as appropriate for school and thereby induced to learn the role of student. Observations of the kindergartens and interviews with the teachers both pointed to the teaching and learning of classroom routines as the main element of the student role. The teachers expended most of their efforts, for the first half of the year at least, in training the children to follow the routines which teachers created. The children were, in a very real sense, *drilled* in tasks and activities created by the teachers for their own purposes and beginning and ending quite arbitrarily (from the child's point of view) at the command of the teacher. One teacher remarked that she hated September, because during the first month "everything has to be done rigidly, and repeatedly, until they know exactly what they're supposed to do." However, "by January," she said, "they know exactly what to do [during the day] and I don't have to be after them all the time." Classroom routines were introduced gradually from the beginning of the year in all the kindergartens, and the children were drilled in them as long as was necessary to achieve regular compliance. By the end of the school year, the successful kindergarten teacher has a well-organized group of children. They follow classroom routines automatically, having learned all the command signals and the expected responses to them. They have, in our terms, learned the student role. The following observation shows one such classroom operating at optimum organization on an afternoon late in May. It is the class of an experienced and respected kindergarten teacher.

AN AFTERNOON IN KINDERGARTEN

At about 12:20 in the afternoon on a day in the last week of May, Edith Kerr leaves the teachers' room where she has been having lunch and walks to her classroom at the far end of the primary wing of Wright School. A group of five and six-year-olds peers at her through the glass doors leading from the hall cloakroom to the play area outside. Entering her room, she straightens some material in the "book corner" of the room, arranges music on the piano, takes colored paper from her closet and places it on one of the shelves under the window. Her room is divided into a number of activity areas through the arrangement of furniture and play equipment. Two easels and a paint table near the door create a kind of passageway inside the room. A wedge-shaped area just inside the front door is made into a teacher's area by the placing of "her" things there: her desk, file, and piano. To the left is the book corner, marked off from the rest of the room by a puppet stage and a movable chalkboard. In it are a display rack of picture books, a record player, and a stack of children's records. To the right of the entrance are the sink and clean-up area. Four large round tables with six chairs at each for the children are placed near the walls about halfway down the length of the room, two on each side, leaving a large open area in the center for group games, block building, and toy truck driving. Windows stretch down the length of both walls, starting about three feet from the floor and extending almost to the high ceilings. Under the windows are long shelves on which are kept all the toys, games, blocks, paper, paints and other equipment of the kndergarten. The left rear corner of the room is a play store with shelves, merchandise, and cash register; the right rear corner is a play kitchen with stove, sink, ironing board, and bassinette with baby dolls in it. This area is partly shielded from the rest of the room by a large standing display rack for posters and children's art work. A sandbox is found against the back wall between these two areas. The room is light, brightly colored and filled with things adults feel five- and six-year-olds will find interesting and pleasing.

At 12:25 Edith opens the outside door and admits the waiting children. They hang their sweaters on hooks outside the door and then go to the center of the room and arrange themselves in a semi-circle on the floor, facing the teacher's chair, which she has placed in the cen-

ter of the floor. Edith follows them in and sits in her chair checking attendance while waiting for the bell to ring. When she has finished attendance, which she takes by sight, she asks the children what the date is, what day and month it is, how many children are enrolled in the class, how many are present, and how many are absent.

The bell rings at 12:30 and the teacher puts away her attendance book. She introduces a visitor, who is sitting against the wall taking notes, as someone who wants to learn about schools and children. She then goes to the back of the room and takes down a large chart labeled "Helping Hands." Bringing it to the center of the room, she tells the children it is time to change jobs. Each child is assigned some task on the chart by placing his name, lettered on a paper "hand," next to a picture signifying the task—e.g., a broom, a blackboard, a milk bottle, a flag, and a Bible. She asks the children who wants each of the jobs and rearranges their "hands" accordingly. Returning to her chair, Edith announces, "One person should tell us what happened to Mark." A girl raises her hand, and when called on says, "Mark fell and hit his head and had to go to the hospital." The teacher adds that Mark's mother had written saying he was in the hospital.

During this time the children have been interacting among themselves, in their semi-circle. Children have whispered to their neighbors, poked one another, made general comments to the group, waved to friends on the other side of the circle. None of this has been disruptive, and the teacher has ignored it for the most part. The children seem to know just how much of each kind of interaction is permitted—they may greet in a soft voice someone who sits next to them, for example, but may not shout greetings to a friend who sits across the circle, so they confine themselves to waving and remain well within understood limits.

At 12:35 two children arrive. Edith asks them why they are late and then sends them to join the circle on the floor. The other children vie with each other to tell the newcomers what happened to Mark. When this leads to a general disorder Edith asks, "Who has serious time?"

The children become quiet and a girl raises her hand. Edith nods and the child gets a Bible and hands it to Edith. She reads the Twenty-third Psalm while the children sit quietly. Edith helps the child in charge begin reciting the Lord's Prayer; the other children follow along for the first unit of sounds, and then trail off as Edith finishes for them. Everyone stands and faces the American flag hung to the right of the door. Edith leads the pledge to the flag, with the children again following the familiar sounds as far as they remember them. Edith then asks the girl in charge what song she wants and the child replies, "My Country." Edith goes to the piano and plays "America," singing as the children follow her words.

Edith returns to her chair in the center of the room and the children sit again in the semi-circle on the floor. It is 12:40 when she tells the children, "Let's have boys' sharing time first." She calls the name of the first boy sitting on the end of the circle, and he comes up to her with a toy helicopter. He turns and holds it up for the other children to see. He says, "It's a helicopter." Edith asks, "What is it used for?" and he replies, "For the army. Carry men. For the war." Other children join in, "For shooting submarines." "To bring back men from space when they are in the ocean." Edith sends the boy back to the circle and asks the next boy if he has something. He replies "No" and she passes on to the next. He says "Yes" and brings a bird's nest to her. He holds it for the class to see, and the teacher asks, "What kind of bird made the nest?" The boy replies, "My friend says a rain bird made it." Edith asks what the nest is made of and different children reply, "mud," "leaves" and "sticks." There is also a bit of moss woven into the nest and Edith tries to describe it to the children. They, however, are more interested in seeing if anything is inside it, and Edith lets the boy carry it around the semi-circle showing the children its insides. Edith tells the children of some baby robins in a nest in her yard, and some of the children tell about baby birds they have seen. Some children are asking about a small object in the nest which they say looks like an egg, but all have seen the nest now and Edith calls on the next boy. A number of children say,

"I know what Michael has, but I'm not telling." Michael brings a book to the teacher and then goes back to his place in the circle of children. Edith reads the last page of the book to the class. Some children tell of books which they have at home. Edith calls the next boy, and three children call out, "I know what David has." "He always has the same thing." "It's a bang-bang." David goes to his table and gets a box which he brings to Edith. He opens it and shows the teacher a scale-model of an old-fashioned dueling pistol. When David does not turn around to the class, Edith tells him, "Show it to the children," and he does. One child says, "Mr. Johnson [the principal] said no guns." Edith replies, "Yes, how many of you know that?" Most of the children in the circle raise their hands. She continues, "That you aren't supposed to bring guns to school?" She calls the next boy on the circle and he brings two large toy soldiers to her which the children enthusiastically identify as being from "Babes in Toyland." The next boy brings an American flag to Edith and shows it to the class. She asks him what the stars and stripes stand for and admonishes him to treat it carefully. "Why should you treat it carefully?" she asks the boy. "Because it's our flag," he replies. She congratulates him, saying, "That's right."

"Show and Tell" lasted twenty minutes and during the last ten one girl in particular announced that she knew what each child called upon had to show. Edith asked her to be quiet each time she spoke out, but she was not content, continuing to offer her comment at each "show." Four children from other classes had come into the room to bring something from another teacher or to ask for something from Edith. Those with requests were asked to return later if the item wasn't readily available.

Edith now asks if any of the children told their mothers about their trip to the local zoo the previous day. Many children raise their hands. As Edith calls on them, they tell what they liked in the zoo. Some children cannot wait to be called on, and they call out things to the teacher, who asks them to be quiet. After a few of the animals are mentioned, one child says, "I liked the spooky house," and the others chime in to agree with him, some pantomiming fear and horror. Edith is puzzled, and asks what this was. When half the children try to tell her at once, she raises her hand for quiet, then calls on individual children. One says, "The house with nobody in it"; another, "The dark little house." Edith asks where it was in the zoo, but the children cannot describe its location in any way which she can understand. Edith makes some jokes but they involve adult abstractions which the children cannot grasp. The children have become quite noisy now, speaking out to make both relevant and irrelevant comments, and three little girls have become particularly assertive.

Edith gets up from her seat at 1:10 and goes to the book corner, where she puts a record on the player. As it begins a story about the trip to the zoo, she returns to the circle and asks the children to go sit at the tables. She divides them among the tables in such a way as to indicate that they don't have regular seats. When the children are all seated at the four tables, five or six to a table, the teacher asks, "Who wants to be the first one?" One of the noisy girls comes to the center of the room. The voice on the record is giving directions for imitating an ostrich and the girl follows them, walking around the center of the room holding her ankles with her hands. Edith replays the record, and all the children, table by table, imitate ostriches down the center of the room and back. Edith removes her shoes and shows that she can be an ostrich too. This is apparently a familiar game, for a number of children are calling out, "Can we have the crab?" Edith asks one of the children to do a crab "so we can all remember how," and then plays the part of the record with music for imitating crabs by. The children from the first table line up across the room, hands and feet on the floor and faces pointing toward the ceiling. After they have "walked" down the room and back in this posture they sit at their table and the children of the next table play "crab." The children love this; they run from their tables, dance about on the floor waiting for their turns and are generally exuberant. Children ask for the "inch worm" and the game is played again with the children squirming down the

floor. As a conclusion Edith shows them a new animal imitation, the "lame dog." The children all hobble down the floor on three "legs," table by table, to the accompaniment of the record.

At 1:30 Edith has the children line up in the center of the room; she says, "Table one, line up in front of me," and children ask, "What are we going to do?" Then she moves a few steps to the side and says, "Table two over here, line up next to table one," and more children ask, "What for?" She does this for table three and table four and each time the children ask, "Why, what are we going to do?" When the children are lined up in four lines of five each, spaced so that they are not touching one another, Edith puts on a new record and leads the class in calisthenics, to the accompaniment of the record. The children just jump around every which way in their places instead of doing the exercises, and by the time the record is finished, Edith, the only one following it, seems exhausted. She is apparently adopting the President's new "Physical Fitness" program in her classroom.

At 1:35 Edith pulls her chair to the easels and calls the children to sit on the floor in front of her, table by table. When they are all seated she asks, "What are you going to do for work-time today?" Different children raise their hands and tell Edith what they are going to draw. Most are going to make pictures of animals they saw in the zoo. Edith asks if they want to make pictures to send to Mark in the hospital, and the children agree to this. Edith gives drawing paper to the children, calling them to her one by one. After getting a piece of paper, the children go to the crayon box on the righthand shelves, select a number of colors, and go to the tables, where they begin drawing. Edith is again trying to quiet the perpetually talking girls. She keeps two of them standing by her so they won't disrupt the others. She asks them, "Why do you feel you have to talk all the time," and then scolds them for not listening to her. Then she sends them to their tables to draw.

Most of the children are drawing at their tables, sitting or kneeling in their chairs. They are all working very industriously and, engrossed in their work, very quietly. Three girls have chosen to paint at the easels, and having donned their smocks, they are busily mixing colors and intently applying them to their pictures. If the children at the tables are primitives and neo-realists in their animal depictions, these girls at the easels are the class abstract-expressionists, with their broad-stroked, colorful paintings.

Edith asks of the children generally, "What color should I make the cover of Mark's book?" Brown and green are suggested by some children "because Mark likes them." The other children are puzzled as to just what is going on and ask, "What book?" or "What does she mean?" Edith explains what she thought was clear to them already, that they are all going to put their pictures together in a "book" to be sent to Mark. She goes to a small table in the play-kitchen corner and tells the children to bring her their pictures when they are finished and she will write their message for Mark on them.

By 1:50 most children have finished their pictures and given them to Edith. She talks with some of them as she ties the bundle of pictures together—answering questions, listening, carrying on conversations. The children are playing in various parts of the room with toys, games and blocks which they have taken off the shelves. They also move from table to table examining each other's pictures, offering compliments and suggestions. Three girls at a table are cutting up colored paper for a collage. Another girl is walking about the room in a pair of high heels with a woman's purse over her arm. Three boys are playing in the center of the room with the large block set, with which they are building walk-ways and walking on them. Edith is very much concerned about their safety and comes over a number of times to fuss over them. Two or three other boys are pushing trucks around the center of the room, and mild altercations occur when they drive through the block constructions. Some boys and girls are playing at the toy store, two girls are serving "tea" in the play kitchen and one is washing a doll baby. Two boys have elected to clean the room, and with large sponges they wash the movable blackboard, the puppet stage, and then begin on the tables. They run into resistance from the children who are working with construction toys on the tables and do not want to dismantle their structures. The class is like a room full of bees, each intent on pursuing some activity, occasionally bumping into one another, but just veering off in another direction without serious altercation. At 2:05 the custodian arrives pushing a cart loaded with half-pint milk containers. He places a tray of cartons on the counter next to the sink, then leaves. His coming and going is unnoticed in the room (as, incidentally, is the presence of the observer, who is completely ignored by the children for the entire afternoon).

At 2:15 Edith walks to the entrance of the room, switches off the lights, and sits at the piano and plays. The children begin spontaneously singing the song, which is "Clean up, clean up. Everybody clean up." Edith walks around the room supervising the clean-up. Some children put their toys, the blocks, puzzles, games, and so on back on their shelves under the windows. The children making a collage keep right on working. A child from another class comes in to borrow the 45-rpm adaptor for the record player. At more urging from Edith the rest of the children shelve their toys and work. The children are sitting around their tables now and Edith asks, "What record would you like to hear while you have your milk?" There is some confusion and no general consensus, so Edith drops the subject and begins to call the children, table by table, to come get their milk. "Table one," she says, and the five children come to the sink, wash their hands and dry them, pick up a carton of milk and a straw, and take it back to their table. Two talking girls wander about the room interfering with the children getting their milk and Edith calls out to them to "settle down." As the children sit many of them call out to Edith the name of the record they want to hear. When all the children are seated at tables with milk, Edith plays one of these records called "Bozo and the Birds" and shows the children pictures in a book which go with the record. The record recites, and the book shows the adventures of a clown, Bozo, as he walks through a woods meeting many different kinds of birds who, of course, display the characteristics of many kinds of people or, more accurately, different stereotypes. As children finish their milk they take blankets or pads from the shelves under the windows and lie on them in the center of the room, where Edith sits on her chair showing the pictures. By 2:30 half the class is lying on the floor on their blankets, the record is still playing and the teacher is turning the pages of the book. The child who came in previously returns the 45-rpm adaptor, and one of the kindergarteners tells Edith what the boy's name is and where he lives.

The record ends at 2:40. Edith says, "Children, down on your blankets." All the class is lying on blankets now, Edith refuses to answer the various questions individual children put to her because, she tells them, "it's rest time now." Instead she talks very softly about what they will do tomorrow. They are going to work with clay, she says. The children lie quietly and listen. One of the boys raises his hand and when called on tells Edith, "The animals in the zoo looked so hungry yesterday." Edith asks the children what they think about this and a number try to volunteer opinions, but Edith accepts only those offered in a "rest-time tone," that is, softly and quietly. After a brief discussion of animal feeding, Edith calls the names of the two children on milk detail and has them collect empty milk cartons from the tables and return them to the tray. She asks the two children on clean-up detail to clean up the room. Then she gets up from her chair and goes to the door to turn on the lights. At this signal the children all get up from the floor and return their blankets and pads to the shelf. It is raining (the reason for no outside play this afternoon) and cars driven by mothers clog the school drive and line up along the street. One of the talkative little girls comes over to Edith and pointing out the window says, "Mrs. Kerr, see my mother in the new Cadillac?"

At 2:50 Edith sits at the piano and plays. The children sit on the floor in the center of the room and sing. They have a repertoire of songs about animals, including one in which each child sings a refrain alone. They know these by heart and sing along through the ringing of the 2:55 bell. When the song is finished, Edith gets up and coming to the group says, "Okay, rhyming words to get your coats today." The children raise their hands and as Edith calls on them, they tell her two rhyming words, after which they are allowed to go into the hall to get their coats and sweaters. They return to the room with these and sit at their tables. At 2:59 Edith says, "When you have your coats on, you may line up at the door." Half of the children go to the door and stand in a long line. When the three o'clock bell rings, Edith returns to the piano and plays. The children sing a song called "Goodbye," after which Edith sends them out.

TRAINING FOR LEARNING AND FOR LIFE

The day in kindergarten at Wright School illustrates both the content of the student role as it has been learned by these children and the processes by which the teacher has brought about this learning, or, "taught" them the student role. The children have learned to go through routines and to follow orders with unquestioning obedience, even when these make no sense to them. They have been disciplined to do as they are told by an authoritative person without significant protest. Edith has developed this discipline in the children by creating and enforcing a rigid social structure in the classroom through which she effectively controls the behavior of most of the children for most of the school day. The "living with others in a small society" which the school pamphlet tells parents is the most important thing the children will learn in kindergarten can be seen now in its operational meaning, which is learning to live by the routines imposed by the school. This learning appears to be the principal content of the student role.

Children who submit to school-imposed discipline and come to identify with it, so that being a "good student" comes to be an important part of their developing identities, *become* the good students by the school's definitions. Those who submit to the routines of the school but do not come to identify with them will be adequate students who find the more important part of their identities elsewhere, such as in the play group outside school. Children who refuse to submit to the school routines are rebels, who become known as "bad students" and often "problem children" in the school, for they do not learn the academic curriculum and their behavior is often disruptive in the classroom. Today schools engage clinical psychologists in part to help teachers deal with such children.

In looking at Edith's kindergarten at Wright School, it is interesting to ask how the children learn this role of student—come to accept school-imposed routines—and what, exactly, it involves in terms of behavior and attitudes. The most prominent features of the classroom are its physical and social structures. The room is carefully furnished and arranged in ways adults feel will interest children. The play store and play kitchen in the back of the room, for example, imply that children are interested in mimicking these activities of the adult world. The only space left for the children to create something of their own is the empty center of the room, and the materials at their disposal are the blocks, whose use causes anxiety on the part of the teacher. The room, being carefully organized physically by the adults, leaves little room for the creation of physical organization on the part of the children.

The social structure created by Edith is a far more powerful and subtle force for fitting the children to the student role. This structure is established by the very rigid and tightly controlled set of rituals and routines through which the children are put during the day. There is first the rigid "locating procedure" in which the children are asked to find themselves in terms of the month, date, day of the week, and the number of the class who are present and absent. This puts them solidly in the real world as defined by adults. The day is then divided into six periods whose activities are for the most part determined by the teacher. In Edith's kindergarten the children went through Serious Time, which opens the school day, Sharing Time, Play Time (which in clear weather would be spent outside), Work Time, Clean-up Time, after

which they have their milk, and Rest Time, after which they go home. The teacher has programmed activities for each of these Times.

Occasionally the class is allowed limited discretion to choose between proffered activities, such as stories or records, but original ideas for activities are never solicited from them. Opportunity for free individual action is open only once in the day, during the part of Work Time left after the general class assignment has been completed (on the day reported the class assignment was drawing animal pictures for the absent Mark). Spontaneous interests or observations from the children are never developed by the teacher. It seems that her schedule just does not allow room for developing such unplanned events. During Sharing Time, for example, the child who brought a bird's nest told Edith, in reply to her question of what kind of bird made it, "My friend says it's a rain bird." Edith does not think to ask about this bird, probably because the answer is "childish," that is, not given in accepted adult categories of birds. The children then express great interest in an object in the nest, but the teacher ignores this interest, probably because the object is uninteresting to her. The soldiers from "Babes in Toyland" strike a responsive note in the children, but this is not used for a discussion of any kind. The soldiers are treated in the same way as objects which bring little interest from the children. Finally, at the end of Sharing Time the child-world of perception literally erupts in the class with the recollection of "the spooky house" at the zoo. Apparently this made more of an impression on the children than did any of the animals, but Edith is unable to make any sense of it for herself. The tightly imposed order of the class begins to break down as the children discover a universe of discourse of their own and begin talking excitedly with one another. The teacher is effectively excluded from this child's world of perception and for a moment she fails to dominate the classroom situation. She reasserts control, however, by taking the children to the next activity she has planned for the day. It seems never to have occurred to Edith that there might be a meaningful learning experience for the children in re-creating the "spooky house" in the classroom. It seems fair to say that this would have offered an exercise in spontaneous self-expression and an opportunity for real creativity on the part of the children. Instead, they are taken through a canned animal imitation procedure, an activity which they apparently enjoy, but which is also imposed upon them rather than created by them.

While children's perceptions of the world and opportunities for genuine spontaneity and creativity are being systematically eliminated from the kindergarten, unquestioned obedience to authority and rote learning of meaningless material are being encouraged. When the children are called to line up in the center of the room they ask "Why?" and "What for?" as they are in the very process of complying. They have learned to go smoothly through a programmed day, regardless of whether parts of the program make any sense to them or not. Here the student role involves what might be called "doing what you're told and never mind why." Activities which might "make sense" to the children are effectively ruled out and they are forced or induced to participate in activities which may be "senseless," such as the calisthenics.

At the same time the children are being taught by rote meaningless sounds in the ritual oaths and songs, such as the Lord's Prayer, the Pledge to the Flag, and "America." As they go through the grades children learn more and more of the sounds of these ritual oaths, but the fact that they have often learned meaningless sounds rather than meaningful statements is shown when they are asked to write these out in the sixth grade; they write them as groups of sounds rather than as a series of words, according to the sixth grade teachers at Wright School. Probably much learning in the elementary grades is of this character, that is, having no intrinsic meaning to the children, but rather being tasks inexplicably required of them by authoritative adults. Listening to sixth grade children read social studies reports, for example, in which they have copied material from

encyclopedias about a particular country, an observer often gets the feeling that he is watching an activity which has no intrinsic meaning for the child. The child who reads, "Switzerland grows wheat and cows and grass and makes a lot of cheese" knows the dictionary meaning of each of these words but may very well have no conception at all of this "thing" called Switzerland. He is simply carrying out a task assigned by the teacher *because* it is assigned, and this may be its only "meaning" for him.

Another type of learning which takes place in kindergarten is seen in children who take advantage of the "holes" in the adult social structure to create activities of their own, during Work Time or out-of-doors during Play Time. Here the children are learning to carve out a small world of their own within the world created by adults. They very quickly learn that if they keep within permissible limits of noise and action they can play much as they please. Small groups of children formed during the year in Edith's kindergarten who played together at these times, developing semi-independent little groups in which they created their own worlds in the interstices of the adult-imposed physical and social world. These groups remind the sociological observer very much of the so-called "informal groups" which adults develop in factories and offices of large bureaucracies.[5] Here too, within authoritatively imposed social organizations people find "holes" to create little subworlds which support informal, friendly, unofficial behavior. Forming and participating in such groups seems to be as much part of the student role as it is of the role of bureaucrat.

The kindergarten has been conceived of here as the year in which children are prepared for their schooling by learning the role of student. In the classrooms of the rest of the school grades, the children will be asked to submit to systems and routines imposed by the teachers and the curriculum. The days will be much like those of kindergarten, except that academic subjects will be substituted for the activities of the kindergarten. Once out of the school system, young adults will more than likely find themselves working in large-scale bureaucratic organizations, perhaps on the assembly line in the factory, perhaps in the paper routines of the white collar occupations, where they will be required to submit to rigid routines imposed by "the company" which may make little sense to them. Those who can operate well in this situation will be successful bureaucratic functionaries. Kindergarten, therefore, can be seen as preparing children not only for participation in the bureaucratic organization of large modern school systems, but also for the large-scale occupational bureaucracies of modern society.

Notes

1. Emile Durkheim, *Sociology and Education* (New York: The Free Press, 1956), pp. 71–72.

2. *Ibid.*, p. 123.

3. Wilbur Brookover, *The Sociology of Education* (New York: American Book Company, 1957), p. 4.

4. *Ibid.*, p. 6.

5. See, for example, Peter M. Blau, *Bureaucracy in Modern Society* (New York: Random House, 1956), Chapter 3.

PART THREE

Social Stratification: Class, Race, and Gender

READINGS 10–15

In his reading in Part One Alex Inkeles says, "There is no society known which does not make some distinction between individuals by ranking them on some scale of values. The most ubiquitous is that between men and women. But such distinctions may rest on almost any basis, involving either ascribed or achieved status" (p. 47). Sociologists use the term *social stratification* to refer to this pattern of ranking, which often rests on such bases as power, prestige, and material resources.

The term *stratification* comes from geology, in which it refers to layers of different kinds of rock. Sociologists use it to refer to the societal pattern that is composed of "layers" of people, each layer including those people of roughly similar rank. These layers are often referred to as social classes. The pattern of ranking in a society is an important form of social organization, with pervasive effects on daily life. However, just as the fish are the last to notice the water, people may find these effects so "natural" that the source goes unexamined. Sociologists have been very interested in examining the stratification structure, since it has such broad influences. In fact, every part in this book contains at least one selection in which social stratification plays a major part.

In our society each person starts with a social class position that is ascribed—by the position of the family in which he or she is reared. Later the person may or may not change that position, since adult class position is achieved—by the amount of the valued resources of wealth, income, education, and occupational prestige that the individual or the adult family has been able to garner. This, of course, is related to where the person starts—reared in a particular family, with its particular set of opportunities or lack of opportunities. Some complicating factors crosscut the stratification structure of social classes. These are the ascribed factors of race and gender. They also must be taken into account for a full under-standing of the kind of social organization called social stratifica-tion.

The keynote reading in Part Three comes from two chapters, "The Stratified Community" and "The Stratified Society," in Peter Berger and Brigitte Berger's *Sociology: A Biographical Approach*. The authors lay out the basic concepts of *class, race, life-styles,* and *mobility*. (Since the authors do not deal with gender, that important topic will be introduced later, along with an illustrative reading.) Notice the three different ways of studying stratification that result from using different criteria for ranking. As you read *any* study of strati-fication, be sure to notice which type of criterion the author is us-ing. Does using one criterion rather than another make any differ-ence? Notice how Berger and Berger use the term *life-style*. How do life-styles vary across the stratification structure? Note the complex interrelationships among life-styles, class, and race.

Berger and Berger include considerable discussion of theories of stratification—explanations as to why stratification is found in every known society (or abstract descriptions of its crucial dimensions). Some of these theories are directly related to two of the three ma-jor theoretical orientations in sociology. Karl Marx's theory of strat-ification rests on ideas of domination and coercion by those who control production. As you have already discovered, Marx is the founder of the conflict theoretical orientation. The functional theo-retical orientation is represented by Kingsley Davis and Wilbert Moore's theory. (Be sure to examine the critiques of the Davis-Moore theory by Melvin Tumin and conflict theorists.) The sym-bolic interactionist model of social organization offers no theory of stratification. Why do you think this is so?

In the material on social mobility be sure to look for these three strands: (1) the changing shape of the occupational structure and its consequences for stratification; (2) any shifts in income distribu-tion across time; and (3) comparisons of the American stratification structure with the stratification structures of other Western indus-trialized societies.

The keynote selection is followed by five illustrative readings that consider various aspects of class, race, gender, and social mobility. Melvin Kohn's "Social Class and Parental Values" was the first in a long series of studies showing how social class (with its characteristic occupational conditions) affects what parents want their children to be like. He shows how class-related values and life-styles are unwittingly maintained in the socialization process.

In his reading titled "The Abolition of *El Cortito*, the Short-Handled Hoe," Douglas Murray discusses the efforts of farm workers engaged in intensive agriculture to improve their unhealthy working conditions. In the conflict tradition, he shows how these efforts raise larger issues about the control of agricultural production and production in general.

The next two selections explore some of the dimensions of race and gender, those factors cutting across the class structure. Diana Pearce explores the meaning of the term *institutional racism* in her "Gatekeepers and Homeseekers: Institutional Patterns in Racial Steering." She shows how institutional racism operates in the housing market, as real estate agents deal with clients who differ by race. Joel Roache describes his experiences in "Confessions of a Househusband," raising some very important issues about sex roles and the way they affect our lives. He concludes with some insights about power relationships in the family, in the work place, and in any hierarchical structure (which includes the entire stratification structure).

The introductions to Pearce's and Roache's readings on race and gender are somewhat different from other introductions. Since the keynote selection is quite old, we provide in those introductions some new data on the situations in these areas. The person on the street may have little specific information and think that there are no longer any problems in the areas of race and gender—that everything has changed and former problems have been solved. Since that is *far* from the case, we want to set the record straight with some basic information about race and gender in the current scene.

This part of the book closes with Norbert Wiley's "The Ethnic Mobility Trap and Stratification Theory." In spite of the title, the selection is primarily about social mobility and only tangentially about ethnicity. The usual metaphor of the mobility structure in societies such as ours is a ladder on which people climb, step by step. But Wiley develops a different picture that provides some interesting insights as to how mobility actually works.

The stratification structure is an extremely important kind of social organization. As we've said before, while there is a collection of readings on stratification in this part of the book, there is at least one selection relevant to the stratification structure in every other part as well.

10
The Stratified Community and Society

Peter L. Berger
Brigitte Berger

MEETING DIFFERENT TYPES OF PEOPLE: SOCIAL DIFFERENTIATION

To grow up in society is to learn more and more about how very different people are from each other. Little boys are different from little girls; all children have something in common against adults; there are old people and young people; there are Protestants and Catholics; there are people who speak with an accent; there are doctors, teachers, babysitters, mailmen, policemen and handymen. All these people are not just different as individuals, but they are different as social types. That is exactly the point: differences are made in society between people not only because of their individual characteristics but because of the larger groups to which they belong.

Broadly speaking, it is this experience which underlies what sociologists commonly call *social*

Reprinted from *Sociology: A Biographical Approach, Second, Expanded Edition,* by Peter L. Berger and Brigitte Berger. © 1972, 1975 by Peter and Brigitte Berger. Used with permission of Basic Books, Inc., Publishers, New York. Footnotes have been renumbered.

differentiation. A very basic question for the sociological analysis of any society is the manner in which it is differentiated, that is, the social typology which is operative in that society for the classification of its members. Learning this typology is one of the basic tasks of socialization. However, hand in hand with the experience of social differentiation goes another experience. People are not only different from each other in terms of their assignment to a certain typology but they are *ranked* differently in accordance with these assignments. The doctor is not only different from the handyman but he is deemed to occupy a higher position in society. This, of course, is not so with all cases of social differentiation. The doctor is generally deemed to be on the same level as the lawyer. *Some* differences, then, have a kind of altimeter attached to them—as soon as we know which social type an individual belongs to, we are in a position to say how high up he is in the ranking scale of society. This phenomenon of ranking is what sociologists call *social stratification*, and the various ranks are called *strata.*

Little Johnny is the son of a doctor. Little Jimmy is the son of a handyman. Their meetings (say, in a public school or public playground) are occasions of mutual wonder and, quite possibly, terror. Not only is it very clear that little Johnny has more money invested in him than little Jimmy, and not only does this particular difference have all sorts of obvious consequences—from the size of the family residence to the quality of Johnny's dental care—but there are many other differences not so readily translated into money terms. Johnny has been taught a whole set of "good manners" which, to Jimmy, just look plain sissy. Jimmy, on the other hand, appears to Johnny as frighteningly prone to violence. In situations of conflict in which Johnny has recourse to verbal argument, Jimmy is ready to fight with his fists. But if Johnny is frightened by Jimmy's physical aggressiveness, he is also fascinated by Jimmy's independence. At an age when Jimmy is free to roam not only the playground but the whole neighborhood, Johnny is still accompanied everywhere he goes by mother, mother's helper, babysitter or other irritating adults. The language of the two boys differs, too. Jimmy probably has a more colorful repertoire of obscenities, but Johnny is much more free to use whatever obscenities he knows, even at home. Music that Johnny has learned to appreciate as beautiful is just dull noise to Jimmy—and quite possibly, vice versa. Moral judgments differ as well. Thus little Jimmy may find it perfectly natural for a black child to be chased from the playground, while Johnny may develop acute guilt feelings about this act of persecution.

In all of this, for both boys there takes place a process by which the essentials of stratification are learned. Needless to say, the full implications of what is learned become clear only much later. This learning process not only conveys information about the world but provides measurements to place others on a ranking scale. Much more basically, because of the fundamental dynamics of socialization that we have discussed earlier, the same learning process leads to a definition of self. The child learns to identify *himself* within a ranking scale. And normally, the social patterns, manners, tastes and values that go with his particular rank become important ingredients of his identity. To be sure, he

may later rebel against these, but they will nevertheless have played a very important part in the shaping of his biography in society. . . .

CLASS, RACE AND ETHNICITY

The phenomena of stratification that we have just alluded to are those which are commonly called (not only by sociologists but in ordinary usage) phenomena of *class*. Just what this term may mean we will discuss presently; for the moment, suffice it to say that all the differences between Johnny and Jimmy that we have just talked about are those deriving from the different class positions of their respective families. In American society, however, the experience of stratification is further complicated by two other factors, namely, those of *race* and *ethnicity*. The latter is a term coined by American sociologists and peculiarly applicable to American society only. It refers to those cultural traits retained by immigrant groups to this country from their original home culture. If, for example, Johnny's parents are the grandchildren of Yiddish-speaking Jewish immigrants from Eastern Europe, while Jimmy's father was born in Greece, there is likely to be a strong ethnic component to their mutual bewilderment that will be added to the experience of class differences. It is quite clear that if Jimmy's father should be black rather than of Greek origin, the sharpness of the experience of difference will be very much increased. Both race and ethnicity are intertwined with class in America, making for an extremely complex and often hard-to-analyze stratification system. . . .

CRITERIA FOR RANKING: OBJECTIVE, SUBJECTIVE OR MAJORITY VOTE

A conceptual problem suggests itself as soon as we talk about ranking. It can be expressed in the form of a one-word question—*whose?* Are we talking about the ranking being undertaken by an outside observer such as the sociologist? Are we talking about the rank that the individual being ranked gives to himself? Or are we talking about the ranking engaged in by others in the individual's situation? These three possibilities already suggest three quite distinct approaches to the study of stratification. First, stratification can be analyzed in terms of objective criteria set by the sociologist. Take the matter of possessions and learning. Even a cursory study of stratification in American society will reveal that both income and education are important factors by which people's rank is determined. Thus middle-class individuals have more income and more education than working-class individuals. The sociologist, based on whatever reasoning of his own, might now draw dividing lines between the middle class and the working class on the basis of these two factors. Thus anyone having more than x amount of income would be defined as middle class, while anyone having less than y amount of education would be assigned to the working class; more precisely, a scale would be worked out in which the factors of income and education taken together would decide where an individual is placed in terms of the class system. Needless to say, other criteria could be used in the construction of such a scale.

Second, stratification could be analyzed in terms of the subjective consciousness of the people in question. Most simply, individuals can be asked how they view themselves in terms of class. In America, incidentally, it has been found that when asked this question the great majority of people reply that they consider themselves to be middle class (which, taken at face value, would create utter havoc with the neat differentiating scheme concocted by our first sociologist above). And third, stratification can be studied in terms of the way in which people see each other. Thus, if one wants to locate a particular individual in terms of stratification, one can ask a variety of people where *they* would locate him, and then make his assignment on the basis of some kind of majority vote. The same method, obviously in a more complicated way, can be used to stratify an entire community.

Now, quite clearly there can, and will be,

considerable discrepancies between the results achieved by these three methods. The sociologist using objective criteria may place individual A in the working class. Individual A, informed of this assignment through some mismanagement of research, will fly into a rage and denounce the research project as a Communist plot. A, of course, has always thought of himself as middle class. But there may be equal disagreement between his self-ranking and the way in which others (not counting the sociologist) rank him. Nor is there any assurance that a careful matching of all the others' rankings will, in the end, have much relationship to objective criteria worked out by the sociologist. One should not draw hasty conclusions from these discrepancies. It is, of course, possible that the sociologist is an armchair philosopher who thinks up criteria that have nothing to do with the social reality he is investigating. It is also quite possible, however, that people living in a particular situation are quite ignorant of the real forces that determine their lives. Indeed, it is quite possible that the very rage with which our individual A responds to his classification by the sociologist derives from his own lingering suspicion that he may be living in a great illusion as to his own position in the world. Put simply: sociologists can be very wrong about the reality of other people's lives, but people can also be quite wrong about the reality of their own lives. Being in a situation is no guarantee whatever that one understands it. (If this were not so, sociology would be a waste of time.) . . .

KARL MARX: THE CONCEPT OF CLASS

The most influential approach to the study of stratification has been that of Marxism.[1] This is so not only in terms of direct influence but also in terms of having been the provocation for alternative approaches to the phenomenon. . . . It was Marx who made the concept of class a central one for the sciences of man. Everyone who followed him (be it historian, economist or social scientist) had to confront Marx's ideas about class. Indeed, the greater part of studies

on stratification taking place within the sociological tradition proper has been a result of this
confrontation with the Marxist approach.

THE KEEPERS AND THE TAKERS: THE STRUGGLE OVER SCARCE RESOURCES

For Marx, class is determined by the relationship of a group to the means of production. He
understood this relationship rather narrowly in
terms of the ownership of the means of production. Thus classes are defined by how much
or how little their members own not only of the
wealth of a society but of the means by which
this wealth is produced. Some later Marxist
scholars have modified this definition by placing
less emphasis on the legal matter of ownership,
instead stressing the element of control over the
means of production. They have insisted that
the really important determinant of class position is not so much what an individual can legally call his own but over what resources he
has effective command. Be this as it may, the
Marxist approach to stratification, and its concept of class itself, is basically an *economic* one.
This is very much related to the basic Marxist
conception of society as such. What society is
essentially all about is a struggle over the scarce
resources that human beings want or need. Different groups of people, for various historical
reasons, have differential access to these resources. History is the story of the struggle between groups over this control. In other words,
history is the story of the struggle between
classes. In the Marxist approach, therefore,
class is not only an important but the central
category for any analysis of society.

In different historical situations, the class
struggle can be quite complex and involve a
number of groups with different characteristics.
Fundamentally, however, the Marxist approach
sees the struggle as between two fairly clearly
defined groups, the haves and the have-nots. In
terms of the society of his day (that is, early
nineteenth-century capitalist society in Europe),
Marx saw the fundamental struggle as taking
place between the bourgeoisie and the proletar-

iat. By Marx's time, the old upper class—the
aristocracy—had pretty much been eliminated
as an important social group in most European
societies. It was the old middle class—the bourgeoisie—which had taken effective control, at
least since the French Revolution. This bourgeoisie was the capitalist class which both owned
and controlled the economic machinery of these
societies. The proletariat, on the other hand, is
defined in terms of its lack of ownership and
control. The relationship between bourgeoisie
and proletariat is seen as a relationship of exploitation and oppression. Political disputes
(such as the revolutionary turmoils of nineteenth-century France and Germany that Marx
wrote about) are only the surface manifestations
of the underlying conflict between classes. For
reasons that we cannot go into here, Marx
thought that the inevitable outcome of this
struggle would be a victorious proletarian revolution. While Marx's economic approach
stresses the objective factors that determine
stratification, he was also very much aware of
the subjective dimension, which he called that
of *class consciousness*. Very often, he insisted,
there is a discrepancy between the objective circumstances of class and the subjective awareness
that people have of their position in the class
system. Quite often, people may delude themselves about their real position in society, in
which case Marx speaks of *false consciousness*.
One of the important preconditions of successful revolution by an exploited class is precisely
the growth of class consciousness, that is, of the
awareness of people that they are indeed an
oppressed group that has a common destiny.

A Marxist approach to stratification has
been, and still is today, of obvious attractiveness
to those who would like to radically transform
society. Marx himself, of course, deliberately
constructed his theory with that purpose in
mind. There is also, however, an intellectual
attraction to the Marxist approach that is quite
independent of its political uses. However complex the Marxist analysis of a particular situation might become, its fundamental intellectual
thrust is toward simplification. When all is said
and done, every social situation resolves itself
into a struggle between those who want to hold

onto their prerogatives and those who want to take these away. This approach thus has a way of seeming to cut through irrelevant details to the essentials of any situation.

CLASS, STATUS, POWER: WEBER'S THREE-FOLD APPROACH

Next to the Marxist approach, the most influential approach to the topic of stratification has been that initiated by Max Weber.[2] As we have previously pointed out, Weber's entire approach to sociology was, in many ways, a long-lasting confrontation with Marx. This was very much the case with his approach to stratification. Weber felt that Marx's approach to these matters was far too simple and was, for this reason, likely to lead to a distorted view of stratification phenomena. To counteract this alleged simplicity of Marxism, Weber proposed a three-fold conceptual scheme. More precisely, he suggested that there were three quite different types of stratification.

First, there were the phenomena which, like Marx, he called *class*. Although Weber placed less emphasis on ownership of property than Marx did, he agreed with Marx that in this type of stratification the fundamental dynamic was economic. A class is understood by Weber as a group of people with similar *life chances*. This means that, because of a certain commonality of access to scarce resources, there exists the strong probability that people within one class will have similar biographies in terms of what they will actually achieve in this particular society.

Second, there is a quite different type of stratification based on *status*. Status simply refers to the degree of social esteem that is bestowed on an individual or a group. Needless to say, there is very frequently a close relationship between class and status. But this is not a necessary or universal relationship. Thus there are cases in which people occupy a high position in the class system but do not attain comparable status. A simple example of this would be a wealthy parvenu trying to crash an aristocratic society. Conversely, there may be people, or

groups, with high status that occupy relatively low positions in the class system. An example of this is the military in many societies. Closely related to the concept of status is Weber's concept of the *estate* as a stratum. An estate (the word here is, of course, used not in the sense of real estate but as, for example, when people spoke of the bourgeoisie as the third estate at the time of the French Revolution) is understood by Weber as a social group into which an individual is born and in which he remains by virtue of adherence to what Weber calls a code of honor. It follows that moving up in an estate system is considerably more difficult than moving upward in a class system. In the latter, the main mechanism of mobility is the acquisition of economic means. That, of course, is not enough in an estate system; one can buy any number of things, but one cannot buy the accident of one's birth—no matter how much money one has, one remains stuck with that. Actually, in a perfect estate system, it would not be possible for anyone to move up, although, because of breaches of the code of honor, it might be possible for some people to move down. In actual fact, there are possibilities of movement in an estate system, one of the most important ones being marriage. By marrying the right person, one can, as it were, correct the accident of birth.

And third, according to Weber, there is stratification based on *power*. Again, this may or may not be related to either class or status. Power is defined by Weber, rather simply, as the capacity to carry through one's intentions in society even against resistance. In discussing stratification based on power, Weber also uses such terms as political class or party. Other sociologists have preferred to use the term elite. Whatever term is used, it is quite clear that societies are stratified not only in terms of people's access to scarce resources, and to status, but also to power. Some groups are more powerful than others. The third type of stratification, then, is political.

The Weberian approach to stratification has been very influential in non-Marxist sociology, both in Europe and in this country. Its attraction lies in the fact that it provides a much more complex and calibrated conceptual scheme than the Marxist one. No attempt is made here to reduce the varieties of stratification phenomena to some one underlying force (though Weber would agree with Marx to the extent that he also regards modern society as primarily a class society and thus as primarily determined by economic forces). Weber, like Marx, was very much aware of the possible discrepancies between objective and subjective location in the stratification order. However, unlike Marx, Weber did not reduce this dimension to the question of class consciousness. Class, status and power here serve as a system of coordinates within which just about any question of stratification can be investigated.

THE STRUCTURAL-FUNCTIONALISTS: MOTIVATING INDIVIDUALS TO KEEP THE SYSTEM FUNCTIONING

The structural-functionalist school in American sociology has produced its own approach to stratification.[3] This was very influential for a while, though it is probably fair to say that it has been in decline in recent years. Whatever criteria may be used to determine location in the stratification system (and some sociologists of this school have been influenced more by Weber), the emphasis here is on stratification as maintaining the functioning of society by providing motivation and rewards for the members of society. It is necessary that certain tasks in society be carried on, and it is further necessary that people expend effort in performing these tasks. In order for people to do this, they must be motivated, and the best motivation comes from rewards being attached to successful performance of these tasks. In other words, stratification functions as a carrot-and-stick system. It is as if society were saying to people: "Do what you are expected to do and you will attain or maintain a rank that has certain privileges. Refuse to do what you are expected to do and you will either never get such rank or, if you now hold it, you will be thrown out of it." Unlike the Marxist emphasis on struggle, the emphasis

here is on the integration and stability of society. In terms of Weber's trilogy, status is emphasized much more strongly than either class or power.

CRITIQUES OF THE DAVIS-MOORE HYPOTHESIS

In its sharpest way, as formulated above, the structural-functionalist approach to stratification has been associated with two American sociologists, Kingsley Davis and Wilbert Moore, and has consequently come to be known as the "Davis-Moore Hypothesis." This has not only been criticized by sociologists of different orientations but within the camp of structural-functionalists themselves. Melvin Tumin has pointed out that attainment of the "rewards" of the stratification system is dependent on the previous development of the attitudes and habits conducive to such attainment, and that these are available only to a limited number of people. In other words, Tumin has tried to show that the Davis-Moore view exaggerates the "openness" of the class system (presumably following general American ideology in this respect). Talcott Parsons has also modified the structural-functionalist approach to stratification, having started out with a position very close to the Davis-Moore Hypothesis and subsequently moving further away from it. Parsons particularly emphasized the necessity of understanding values and norms as they operate in stratification. It is not enough to understand the concrete, material "rewards" of the system, but the subtle network of normative judgments that people make both about the "rewards" and the means to attain them. What all structural-functionalist positions have in common is their perspective on stratification as part of a functioning social system, though they differ in how they look upon the complexity and the specific character of these functions. Indeed, values and norms (such as those motivating people to achieve) can themselves be viewed as "functional" for the maintenance of the social system.

The structural-functionalist approach has been attractive to many American sociologists because, in accordance with widely held American values, it emphasizes achievement and its rewards as against the much nastier imagery that both the Marxist and the Weberian approaches suggest. The major assumption of this approach is that the de facto system of stratification actually does function so as to maintain the integration and stability of society as a whole. This, many critics have argued, is quite an assumption and one that has very little support from the empirical evidence. Marxist critics, indeed, would maintain that the structural-functionalist approach to stratification is nothing but the theoretical elaboration of a widely prevalent form of false consciousness in American society. The major ingredient of this false consciousness is the illusion that people can make it to the top if only they will do what is expected of them. Structural-functionalists might reply to such critics that even illusion may be functional in maintaining the integration and the stability of a society. To say that a society is functioning is not necessarily to say that its order is an expression of either truth or justice.

THE CASTE SYSTEM AND AMERICAN RACIAL STRATA

Despite these overall differences in approach, there is general concurrence in American sociology on the usage of the two terms, class and status. Whatever the differences in general approach, almost everyone agrees that the former term refers to economically based and the latter to non-economically based forms of ranking. Because of the peculiar racial situation in America, the additional concept of caste has been added to the general terminology regarding stratification.[4] The term originally derives from India, but it has been given a much more general significance by American sociologists. By caste is meant a stratum into which one is born, within which one must marry and out of which (at least theoretically) there is no exit. In a continuum of rigidity, one might thus place the concept of class at one end, this concept of caste at the other, and Weber's concept of estate in the middle.

The concept can, of course, be applied quite successfully to racial stratification in America, and, indeed, it was specifically coined for such

application. Needless to say, the addition of this concept makes the analysis of stratification even more complex. This is especially so because everyone familiar with the situation realizes that caste and class are very much related in the American situation. Thus, while it is true that, generally speaking, it is impossible for a black person to move into the white stratum (except by "passing," that is, by pretending not to be black), there are very wide class differences within the black group and these class differences have a lot to do with the way in which the racial situation is experienced. What is more, if one applies objective class criteria, a great part of the black group would fall below the middle class in American society. Some Marxist analysts of the American situation have used this latter fact to arrive at the conclusion that the conflict between the races in America is simply another manifestation of class struggle. Rather few non-Marxist sociologists would go along with this position, but it is quite clear that the American stratification system cannot be understood unless both caste and class are taken into consideration.

LIFE-STYLE: DIFFERENCES BETWEEN CLASSES

Another key concept in American studies of stratification is that of life-style. This concept, originally coined by Weber, refers to the overall culture or way of life of different groups in the society. The differences we have pointed out at the beginning of this [reading] between the worlds of little Johnny and little Jimmy are expressions of different classes' life-style. Some American sociologists have emphasized life-style in lieu of economic factors, and have thought thereby to provide an unambiguously non-Marxist way of studying stratification. This has been particularly true of the studies of stratification in America stimulated by the work of Lloyd Warner.[5] This approach began with an intensive study of the community of Newburyport, Massachusetts, by Warner and his associates (following the usual convention of anonymity in the field, Warner called the community "Yankee City"). Warner's work has stimulated many further investigations into the phenomena of class in America, especially in terms of the differential life-styles of different classes. Critics of this approach, however, have maintained that life-style is a *result* of class position and not, in itself, a determining factor of the latter. Everyone, though, will agree on the reality of the phenomenon of life-style and the fact that there are, indeed, significant differences between the life-styles of different classes. In other words, different strata live in different worlds.

ELMTOWN'S YOUTH, "THE ELITE," "THE GOOD KIDS" AND "THE GRUBBY GANG"

Some of the foregoing considerations might have struck some readers as excessively abstract, as theories having nothing to do with the real lives of people outside of whatever sanctuaries sociologists sit in. Such an impression would be quite erroneous. Ordinary people living in ordinary American communities experience the reality of stratification every day of their lives. What is more, this experience begins very early. A very influential study of the impact of class on adolescents in a Midwestern town was August Hollingshead's *Elmtown's Youth*, published in 1949. Hollingshead's book had a considerable impact beyond sociology proper because it so radically challenged what many Americans then (and some still today) like to believe so strongly, namely, that in some fashion American society is classless, is a society in which no fundamental differences are made between people, and also that the primary locale for training individuals in this kind of democracy is the public school. All these assumptions were blown sky high by Hollingshead's data.[6]

Hollingshead divided the population of Elmtown into five classes (the details of his criteria need not concern us here), ranging from an upper class 1 to a quite depressed lower class 5. He then was able to show in great detail how class position determined just about every aspect of the adolescent's life in this community. Success or failure in school was directly related to class level. For example, in the Elmtown high school, 2.9 percent of children from class 1 failed to pass from one grade to another; the corresponding figure for class 5 was 23.1 percent. To some extent, no doubt, these differences are to be explained in terms of teachers' prejudices. But much more important, the underlying factor is a difference in life-style between classes and the simple fact that the school itself is geared to the life-style of the higher classes and not to that of the lower ones. The private lives of the adolescents, however, are equally dominated by class. For example, Hollingshead found that 61 percent of dates in the Elmtown high school take place between people of the same class, 35 percent between people in adjacent classes and only 4 percent between people whose class position is farther apart than that. One hundred percent of the adolescents in classes 1 and 2 participated in some extracurricular activity of the school; 73 percent of those in class 5 did not participate in anything. The facts of class, while of course not expressed in sociological jargon, were well known to the children and expressed by them in their own terms. Thus Hollingshead found that the adolescents in this high school stratified themselves in three overall categories: "the elite," "the good kids" and "the grubby gang." To a large extent these, as it were, inner stratification categories were related to the class system in the larger community.

THE QUIET LIFE, TRYING HARD AND IMMEDIATE ENJOYMENT: CLASSES IN NEW ENGLAND

We have already mentioned the work of Lloyd Warner and his collaborators which was published at about the same time as Hollingshead's book. Warner divided the community he was studying into six classes, ranging from an upper-upper class (descended from old New England families) to a lower-lower class (a kind of sub-proletariat). He tried to show how each one of these classes had a distinctive life-style that went far beyond the obvious differences in economic resources available. For example, he distinguished between the aforementioned upper-upper class and the lower-upper class, which consisted of much more recent arrivals on that social level. In some instances, lower-upper-class individuals had far more money than upper-upper-class people, yet they tried to emulate as far as they could the life-style of the latter. The best adjective with which to describe that life-style would be "quiet." This is quite different from the life-style of the upper-middle class from which most of the lower-upper individuals had recently come. In the upper-middle class, with whatever measure of taste, the fruits of one's economic endeavor are displayed openly and sometimes with a measure of aggressiveness. By contrast, the upper-class style dictates that wealth be hidden as much as possible. Corresponding to this, there is also a difference in ethos. Put very simply: the overall middle-class ethos is a pushing one. The same values which, in the middle class, are looked upon as showing healthy ambition are regarded as pushiness and vulgarity in the upper class.

Similar differences in ethos exist further down in the social scale. Thus Warner showed that the dividing line between what he called the upper-lower and the lower-lower classes is primarily one of morality. The upper-lower class (what most other sociologists would now call the working class) is poor, in some instances perhaps as poor as members of the stratum below it, but it is animated by an ethos of hard work, discipline and ambition. By contrast, the lower-lower class has no such virtues at all. The prevailing ethos there is one of immediate enjoyment, and there is mainly disdain for the rewards which people in the other strata strive for. In one respect there is actually a curious similarity between the uppermost and the lowest strata in Warner's scheme, and that is in the contempt for the middle-class ethos of driving ambition. That ethos dominates the greatest part of the class system as analyzed by Warner (thus, in a very real way, verifying at least the symbolic significance of the American belief that this is a middle-class society). Going from top to bottom, the middle-class ethos extends from the lower-upper class through the upper-lower. In these strata, everyone is trying hard. All this frenetic activity is viewed with sardonic detachment by people on the two extreme poles

of the system, from the very top and from the very bottom. . . .

CASTE AND CLASS: STATUS COMPENSATION

As we move from stratification by class to stratification by caste (that is, in American terms, as we cross the race line between white and black), we shall continue to encounter this basic phenomenon of differentiated life-styles. However, the phenomenon becomes more complex. The black community itself is divided along class lines. Here too we find distinctive class-bound life-styles, some of which are quite similar to the differences existing between classes in the white community, while others are distinctive to the culture of the black community as such. We also find, however, sharp dividing lines between the two racial communities as a whole—as a result of which there are overall life-styles that are distinctively black, irrespective of class divisions.

An early and very influential study of the relationship of class and caste in an American community was John Dollard's *Caste and Class in a Southern Town*, originally published in 1937.[7] Dollard showed very clearly how the dynamics of caste and class are combined in the everyday life of people in this Southern community. For example, he was particularly interested in the oft-noted fact that lower-class whites show much more intense hostility toward blacks than upper-class whites. One element in this is undoubtedly that there is sharper economic competition at those levels of the social system. There is, however, another very important dimension, which has to do with status as distinct from economic level. In the traditional Southern stratification system, the black community as a whole was ranked below the white community as a whole. Within the white community, however, there were quite sharp class antagonisms and resentments. Caste served as a status compensation mechanism for the lower-class white. Put quite simply: whatever the lowliness of his class position, the lower-class white is irrevocably ranked above the black within the caste system. What is more, the etiquette of relations between the races in the traditional

South makes this fact unambiguously clear every time a white and a black meet. . . .

GETTING AHEAD MEANS BECOMING WHITE?

More recent studies of black communities in America, whatever other changes have taken place, show that one fundamental aspect of the situation has remained very similar, namely, that the higher up a black individual is located on the class scale, the closer he is to the white community in terms of his life-style.[8] Again, of course, there is an economic aspect to this. Middle-class blacks quite simply have the economic resources to participate in a much wider range of activities in the overall white-dominated community than is the case with lower-class blacks. Beyond this obvious fact, however, there are much subtler dynamics of opinion, values, tastes and manners. A middle-class white will much more readily feel at ease with a middle-class black than either he or a working-class white would feel in encountering blacks of lower levels in terms of class. Putting the same observation in terms of the black community itself, it can be said that it has been the lower-class black who has retained a much more distinctively black life-style as against the middle-class black. It is quite possible that the recent upsurge of black nationalism, in its various manifestations, will change this in the direction of producing a much more distinctive black culture that will embrace all classes within the black community. At this time it would be hazardous to make sociological predictions about this. . . .

STATUS ASCRIPTION AND ACHIEVEMENT

Sociologists make the distinction between *ascribed and achieved status*.[9] Ascribed status belongs to the individual by virtue of his birth or some other biographical fact that is not due to his own efforts. For example, both a prince and a leper have a specific status ascribed to them, and there is nothing which the former did to attain it or that the latter can do to get rid of

it. Achieved status, on the other hand, is attained by the individual as a result of his deliberate efforts. Thus a person rising from office boy to office manager (assuming that he is not a relative of the boss) occupies the latter status on the basis of his own achievement. Again, for reasons that have a long history, contemporary society—and especially American society—is permeated with an achievement ethos. The individual is expected to want to achieve better things in life and the society is expected to provide him with the opportunity to do so. Indeed, some psychologists have maintained that socialization in our society instills a strong need for achievement. Most games played by American children are competitive. From early childhood, acts of achievement are applauded and rewarded, and the failure to achieve is presented to the child as a very serious thing indeed.

In terms of the stratification system, this achievement ethos is translated into a mobility ethos, that is, into an ambition by the individual to improve his position in the stratification system, to move upward. In America, this mobility ethos has been, just about from the beginning of American history, an intrinsic element of the national ideology. America is supposed to be the land of opportunity. Ideally, it is supposed to be a society in which *all* status is achieved, a society which discards all distinctions between men that are produced by ascription. This, indeed, was to be the major difference between the new world and the old. The same national ideology proposes that the major institutions of American society should be so arranged as to facilitate such movement by individuals. American free enterprise, American government and (very importantly) the American public school system are permeated with the notion of equality of opportunity—or, if such was deemed to be lacking, with the ideal of equalization of opportunity. . . .

WHERE AM I HEADED? TYPES OF SOCIAL MOBILITY

It is clear . . . that the life chances of an individual are decisively affected by his starting position in terms of the stratification system. One should be very careful how one chooses one's parents. Again, an obvious question follows: To what extent can fortune be corrected? If one has been careless in the choice of parents, what are one's chances of making good this mistake? In sociological terms, this question concerns one's chances of *social mobility*.

Social mobility is defined as any movement within a stratification system. Very often in sociological literature, the term "mobility" is used by itself to designate the same phenomenon. A number of further conceptual clarifications are necessary, though. The distinction is made between *social and geographical mobility*. The latter simply refers to movements of people in physical space and in itself need have no particular relationship to social mobility. For example, nomadic Arabs are constantly moving about in space, but these movements do not normally entail any changes in position on a stratification scale. In our society, however, there is a relationship between these two kinds of mobility. Very often, social mobility requires a geographical movement as well. To take another example: opportunities for social mobility are typically smaller in rural than in urban communities. Consequently, migration of rural people into cities is commonly associated with social mobility, or at least with aspirations to such mobility. A further distinction is made between *upward and downward mobility*. Both concepts refer to social mobility. In terms of American values, it is only upward mobility that is in most people's minds when they speak about the subject. Individuals not only move up, however, but they do move down in the stratification scheme, and it is important to keep this in mind.

There is also *vertical and horizontal mobility*. Only the former refers to social mobility properly speaking, that is, to upward or downward movement within a stratification system. Horizontal mobility refers to changes in social position that remain within the same strata. For example, a schoolteacher who becomes a principal undergoes vertical mobility. But a teacher who changes his subject from mathematics to geography undergoes horizontal mobility that does not, in all probability, affect his rank in the stratification scheme of his profession. A fur-

ther distinction is made between *career and generational mobility* (sometimes also referred to as *intra-generational and inter-generational mobility*). By career mobility (or intra-generational mobility) is meant such movement as occurs within the adult life of one individual—as, for instance, in the movement from teacher to principal. Generational (or inter-generational) mobility, on the other hand, refers to the respective ranks of two successive generations. For example, if the teacher's father was the school janitor, the son has undergone generational mobility, even if, having once become a teacher, he never moves beyond this position.

Finally, the difference is made between *individual and group mobility*. The aforementioned examples, of course, all refer to individual mobility, but it is also possible for entire groups within the stratification system to move. Thus it could happen—perhaps as a result of labor-union activity—that school janitors as a group triple their income, change their designation (say, to "building engineers") and require a college degree for admission to their ranks. In such cases, which are far from rare in our society, all individuals in the group undergo considerable social mobility by whatever criteria one might wish to measure it, despite the fact that then, as now, they are janitors.

MONEY, MARRIAGE, EDUCATION, POLITICS AND "IMPRESSION": FIVE MEANS TO MOBILITY

Within a stratification system such as ours, there are five major mechanisms of upward social mobility for individuals. These are related to each other, of course, but can nevertheless be seen as distinct for purposes of sociological analysis. The first, and probably the most obvious mechanism of mobility, is through economic activity. By hard work, by luck, by connections or by fraud the individual operates within the economic system to improve his position. In most cases this simply means that he increases his income and thus his purchasing capacity—not only for the material but also the non-material benefits of status.

The second mechanism, still much more important than many people would readily recognize, is marriage. That is, a person improves his or her position by "marrying up." Clearly, this mechanism is more readily available for women than for men in our society, but it is by no means limited exclusively to women. The third mechanism of mobility is education. As we have already pointed out, this is very much related to the first mechanism of economic activity and position, but it is nevertheless distinct from it. The efforts of the individual here are primarily exerted not at his place of work or business but in movement through an educational process.

A fourth mechanism of mobility is political. This takes place when improvements in the position of individuals or entire groups are achieved through political pressures, negotiations or guarantees. It is a particularly important mechanism in terms of group mobility. Thus American blacks and other non-white minorities are today using political means to pressure society to grant and guarantee a collective improvement in the position of their members in the stratification system.

Finally, there is a mechanism which is perhaps best described by the term coined for different purposes by the contemporary sociologist Erving Goffman—"impression management." This is mobility achieved through the manipulation of status symbols and personal attraction. It is most readily evident in such social contexts as that of "café society," in which all kinds of hangers-on, confidence men and alleged inside dopesters try to advance themselves by making an impression on those who have already made it in that particular sector of the stratification system. While in terms of the society as a whole this mechanism is probably of minor importance, it is almost certainly one element in the use made by many individuals of the first four mechanisms.

AREAS OF AGREEMENT: THE *SHAPE* OF SOCIAL MOBILITY

How much upward mobility is there in American society? It is very difficult to answer this

question in a direct way. Data about social mobility are surprisingly scarce, and most of them are ambiguous in their implications. There are differences in interpretation caused not only by the ambiguity of the data but by differing theoretical presuppositions of the interpreters. The most accessible data are those concerning occupation and income (the basic data for this, of course, are provided by the United States census). As we have seen, however, class and stratification generally are much subtler phenomena than simply raw expressions of occupational and income standing. There is therefore a problem of relating data on occupation and income to the subtler phenomena of class-related life-style and class consciousness. A full discussion of this topic would completely break the framework of [a reading] such as this, requiring very extensive and at times very complicated treatment. The best we can do here is to summarize a number of trends in social mobility about which there is fairly general agreement among sociologists, and to point out a number of important areas in which there is disagreement.[10]

1. As measured by occuptional mobility between generations (that is, between fathers and sons), there is considerable upward movement, though there are sharp differences in this between different occupational categories. Figures for 1950 indicate that 77 percent of professionals have moved upward to their present position from the position held by their fathers, but only 56 percent of skilled workers and foremen have gone through a similar movement.[11] In other words, a considerable number of individuals manage to improve their position vis-à-vis that of their fathers in terms of occupation, but middle-class individuals are in a more favored position to do this.

2. As measured by occupation, most mobility is between occupational categories that are adjacent or close in status (to which should be added that the relative status of different occupations has remained remarkably the same in recent decades). For example, it is much more likely that the son of an un-

skilled worker will become a garage mechanic than that he will become a lawyer. Similarly, it is more likely that a lawyer's son will become a law professor than the director of a large corporation. The most difficult line to cross remains that between manual and non-manual work. Individuals whose occupation is farming are least mobile.

3. As measured by occupation, mobility rates in America have remained very similar during the last half century. That is, roughly similar proportions of people have moved upward in the occupational structure. Moreover, these mobility rates are quite similar to those prevailing in other Western industrial societies. There is disagreement as to whether mobility into the highest strata of the system has become harder or easier or has remained the same. However, most sociologists who have looked into this aspect of the matter are of the opinion that the highest strata in America have become more closed to newcomers from below.

4. It is likely that most mobility has been the result of changes in the overall occupational structure. An important factor in this has been the increase in demand for clerical, technical and other skilled labor, and a concomitant decrease in the demand for unskilled labor. The same relationship between changes in the occupational structure and mobility seems to prevail in other industrial societies (including the Soviet Union).

5. Education has become the most important mechanism for mobility. This makes particularly serious the vicious-cycle relation between class and education that we have referred to above. This also makes it easy to understand why the educational system has become the main target for political pressure on the part of blacks trying to improve their chances in the society.

6. For the foregoing reasons, mobility has become more difficult, and may actually have decreased, for the lowest strata. This trend has been particularly severe for blacks and other racial minorities. If one combines this fact with the aforementioned opinion of some sociologists that the highest stratum has become relatively closed, an interesting picture emerges with regard to mobility; namely, most mobility takes place in the broad sector *between* the highest and the lowest strata of society; both the top and the bottom of the system participate least in this mobility. Individuals in these two strata are most likely to remain where they are—though this, very obviously, has different connotations at the bottom than at the top. As measured by occupation, it is the middle sectors of the stratification system that have expanded the most. In other words, it is, broadly speaking, the middle class that has grown the most. To some sociologists, this has suggested the image of a diamond to represent the stratification system—as against the pyramid, which has been the apt image for stratification in most older societies.

7. There has been a steady decrease in self-employed individuals. Even professionals are increasingly on payrolls rather than in independent business for themselves.

8. There has been a steady increase in income of almost all strata over the last half century, so that, in absolute terms, almost all strata have experienced upward group mobility. To measure differences in income, economists have coined the term "real income," by which they mean that income figures for different periods are translated into standardized dollars to take cognizance of differences in purchasing power between these periods. Thus, between 1939 and 1950, real income, so defined, increased 176 percent among unskilled workers, 172 percent among skilled workers, 111 percent among clerical workers and 95 percent among proprietors and managers.[12] In terms of income, the entire national pudding has grown very much, and everyone has experienced a slice of this growth. Indeed, for the lower strata this growth in income has been relatively greater.

9. Nevertheless, the income differential between different strata has remained fairly similar over the same period. That is, there

have been no dramatic shifts in the proportions of total national income accruing to different strata, though it is claimed by some that the gaps between the different strata have steadily diminished. It should be noted that although the census provides very reliable data on these matters, it is sometimes difficult to know just how to use them. For example, there are people with very small running incomes who, nevertheless, own their own homes. There are various sources of hidden income in all strata of the population—most spectacularly so in the higher strata. Thus there is also disagreement as to whether the share in the total national income of the highest strata has changed or not.

10. Again, the relations between income and mobility appear to be similar in Western industrial societies, though the increase in total national income has been highest in America. There is disagreement as to whether income differentials are higher or lower in the Soviet Union. There is general agreement that these differentials are everywhere higher in the less-developed societies than in the industrial ones.

Notes

1. References to class are scattered throughout Marx's work. For the beginnings and the basic conceptions of the Marxian theory of class, see Karl Marx, *Early Writings* (New York, McGraw-Hill, 1964).

2. Max Weber, *The Theory of Social and Economic Organization* (New York, Free Press, 1957); Hans Gerth and C. Wright Mills (eds.), *From Max Weber* (New York, Oxford University Press, 1946).

3. The debate was initiated among structural-functionalists by Kingsley Davis and Wilbert Moore, "Some Principles of Stratification," *American Sociological Review,* 10 (1945): 242ff. For modifications of the structural-functionalist approach to stratification, see Melvin Tumin, *Social Stratification* (Englewood Cliffs, N.J., Prentice-Hall, 1967), especially pp. 106ff., and Talcott Parsons, "A Revised Analytical Approach to the Theory of Social Stratification," in Reinhard Bendix and Seymour Lipset (eds.), *Class, Status and Power* (New York, Free Press, 1953), pp. 92ff. For a criticism of the entire approach, see Dennis Wrong, "The Functional Theory of Stratification," *American Sociological Review,* 24 (1959): 772ff.

4. On the general concept of caste, see the article by Gerald Berreman under "Caste" in the *International Encyclopedia of the Social Sciences,* Vol. 2 (New York, Macmillan, 1968), pp. 333ff.

5. Lloyd Warner and Paul Lunt, *The Social Life of a Modern Community* (New Haven, Conn., Yale University Press, 1941).

6. August Hollingshead, *Elmtown's Youth* (New York, Wiley, 1949).

7. John Dollard, *Caste and Class in a Southern Town* (New York, Harper, 1937).

8. See, for example, Andrew Billingsley, *Black Families in White America* (Englewood Cliffs, N.J., Prentice-Hall, 1968).

9. The terms were originally coined by Ralph Linton, a cultural anthropologist, but they have now become common sociological usage.

10. Bendix and Lipset, *op. cit.;* Harold Hodges, *Social Stratification* (Cambridge, Mass., Schenkman, 1964); Joseph Kahl, *The American Class Structure* (New York, Holt, Rinehart & Winston); Gerhard Lenski, *Power and Privilege* (New York, McGraw-Hill, 1966); Seymour Lipset and Reinhard Bendix, *Social Mobility in Industrial Society* (Berkeley, Calif., University of California Press, 1959).

11. Kahl, *op. cit.* These data are derived from a study by the National Opinion Research Center.

12. Hodges, *op. cit.*

11
Social Class and Parental Values

Melvin L. Kohn

Editors' Introduction

In the keynote selection Berger and Berger say that ". . . differences are made in society between people not only because of their individual characteristics but because of the larger groups to which they belong." The following illustrative reading shows how some of these differences are made and how they are passed on from parents to children in the socialization process.

When you notice that this reading was published in 1959, you may well wonder why we have included such an old reading in this book—surely, it is out-of-date by now. In fact, the findings of this study started a research series by Kohn and others that has continued into the mid 1980s and shows no sign of stopping. The basic findings of this study—done in Washington, D.C., in the late 1950s—have been confirmed in both local and nationwide studies in the United States and in studies done in several other countries. We have chosen to include this early version of Kohn's work (rather than a later version) for four reasons. First, it raises a manageable number of issues. Second, although in professional journal format, it is readable, without an excessive number of methodological and conceptual complications. Third, it provides a clear-cut example of the research process, with enough detail to flesh it out. Fourth, its findings are "up-to-date" in light of repeated confirmations here and elsewhere. The replication process (in which a study is repeated) is important in that it provides confidence in research findings.

Originally appearing in *The American Journal of Sociology*, this reading presents the results of survey research on what characteristics parents of the working and middle classes value in their children and why these particular characteristics are valued. As you examine Kohn's findings, note which values for children are *shared* by parents in both classes and which values *differ* by social class of parent. The crucial values in this study are self-direction (acting on the basis of internal standards of conduct) and obedience (following orders given by those in positions of authority). Note how these values are related to working-class and middle-class positions and to the finer gradations in the five levels of social class that Kohn considers. He goes on to include some other factors: mother's occupation and education, religious background, and rural or urban background. Notice how the relationship between social class and parental values is spelled out and made more precise by including these other factors.

In the last section Kohn presents his conclusions, but he does not stop there. In a very important part of the reading, he *interprets* his findings, trying to explain *why* parents on these two different class levels stress self-direction or obedience as valued characteristics for their children. It is this interpretation, in which he takes into account the different occupational worlds known by working-class and middle-class parents, that has led to the continuing interest in this research problem.

The current research explores the characteristics of these different occupational worlds and ties them directly to the differing values that parents hold, showing that parents prepare their children as best they can for the occupational world *as they know it*. What implications does this have for the later class positions of their children?

Think back to the issues Jerry Rose raises (in Part One) about survey research—problems of objectivity, measurement, sampling, and causation—and note how Kohn takes them into account. Kohn begins by proposing his research question. Then he provides full information about his sampling procedures and methods of data collection. Why did he choose to sample in this way? Exactly how did he go about collecting his data? Why did he decide to do it this way? What criteria of social class did he use in placing people on one or another of the class levels included in this study? Note how the question of validity is raised—is the researcher really measuring what he thinks he is measuring? Is Kohn really measuring *values*? What steps does he take to make sure that he is measuring values rather than something else? (What might that something else be?)

This reading shows how the stratification structure of society affects the process of socialization. That process, in turn, has consequences for the maintenance of the structure. As we have said before, structure and process are reciprocal.

We undertake this inquiry into the relationship between social class and parental values in the hope that a fuller understanding of the ways in which parents of different social classes differ in their values may help us to understand why they differ in their practices.[1] This hope, of course, rests on two assumptions: that it is reasonable to conceive of social classes as subcultures of the larger society, each with a relatively distinct value-orientation, and that values really affect behavior.

SAMPLE AND METHOD OF DATA COLLECTION

Washington, D.C.—the locus of this study—has a large proportion of people employed by government, relatively little heavy industry, few recent immigrants, a white working class drawn heavily from rural areas, and a large proportion of Negroes, particularly at lower economic levels. Generalizations based on this or any other sample of one city during one limited period of time are, of course, tentative.

Our intent in selecting the families to be studied was to secure approximately two hundred representative white working-class families and another two hundred representative white middle-class families, each family having a child within a narrowly delimited age range. We decided on fifth-grade children because we wanted to direct the interviews to relationships involving a child old enough to have a developed capacity for verbal communication.

The sampling procedure[2] involved two steps: the first, selection of census tracts. Tracts with

Reprinted from *The American Journal of Sociology*, 64, 4 (January, 1959), 337–351. Used with permission of the publisher, the University of Chicago. Footnotes have been renumbered.

Revision of paper presented at the annual meeting of the American Sociological Society, August, 1957. This is the first portion of a more general inquiry into the relationship of class and family directed by the author and John A. Clausen, with the collaboration and aid of Eleanor Carroll, Mary Freeman, Paul Hanlon, Alexander Shakow, and Eleanor Wolff.

20 per cent or more Negro population were excluded, as were those in the highest quartile with respect to median income. From among the remaining tracts we then selected a small number representative of each of the three distinct types of residential area in which the population to be studied live: four tracts with a predominantly working-class population, four predominantly middle-class, and three having large proportions of each. The final selection of tracts was based on their occupational distribution and their median income, education, rent (of rented homes), and value (of owner-occupied homes). The second step in the sampling procedure involved selection of families. From records made available by the public and parochial school systems we compiled lists of all families with fifth-grade children who lived in the selected tracts. Two hundred families were then randomly selected from among those in which the father had a "white-collar" occupation and another two hundred from among those in which the father had a manual occupation.

In all four hundred families the mothers were to be interviewed. In every fourth family we scheduled interviews with the father and the fifth-grade child as well.[3] (When a broken family fell into this subsample, a substitute was chosen from our over-all sample, and the broken family was retained in the over-all sample of four hundred families.)

When interviews with both parents were scheduled, two members of the staff visited the home together—a male to interview the father, a female to interview the mother. The interviews were conducted independently, in separate rooms, but with essentially identical schedules. The first person to complete his interview with the parent interviewed the child.

INDEXES OF SOCIAL CLASS AND VALUES

Social Class

Each family's social-class position has been determined by the Hollingshead Index of Social

Position, assigning the father's occupational status a relative weight of 7 and his educational status a weight of 4. We are considering Hollingshead's Classes I, II, and III to be "middle class," and Classes IV and V to be "working class." The middle-class sample is composed of two relatively distinct groups: Classes I and II are almost entirely professionals, proprietors, and managers with at least some college training. Class III is made up of small shopkeepers, clerks, and salespersons but includes a small number of foremen and skilled workers of unusually high educational status. The working-class sample is composed entirely of manual workers but preponderantly those of higher skill levels. These families are of the "stable working class" rather than "lower class" in the sense that the men have steady jobs, and their education, income, and skill levels are above those of the lowest socioeconomic strata.

Values

We shall use Kluckhohn's definition: "A value is a conception, explicit or implicit, distinctive of an individual or characteristic of a group, of the desirable which influences the selection from available modes, means, and ends of action."[4]

Our inquiry was limited to the values that parents would most like to see embodied in their children's behavior. We asked the parents to choose, from among several alternative characteristics that might be seen as desirable, those few which they considered *most* important for a child of the appropriate age. Specifically, we offered each parent a card listing 17 characteristics that had been suggested by other parents, in the pretest interviews, as being highly desirable. (These appear down the left margin of Table 1. The order in which they were listed was varied from interview to interview.) Then we asked: "Which three of the things listed on this card would you say are the *most* important in a boy (or girl) of (fifth-grade child's) age?" The selection of a particular characteristic was taken as our index of value.

Later in this report we shall subject this index to intensive scrutiny.

CLASS AND VALUES

Middle- and working-class mothers share a broadly common set of values—but not an identical set of values by any means (see Table 1). There is considerable agreement among mothers of both social classes that happiness and such standards of conduct as honesty, consideration, obedience, dependability, manners, and self-control are highly desirable for both boys and girls of this age.

Popularity, being a good student (especially for boys), neatness and cleanliness (especially for girls), and curiosity are next most likely to be regarded as desirable. Relatively few mothers choose ambition, ability to defend one's self, affectionate responsiveness, being liked by adults, ability to play by one's self, or seriousness as highly desirable for either boys or girls of this age. All of these, of course, might be more highly valued for children of other ages.

Although agreement obtains on this broad level, working-class mothers differ significantly[5] from middle-class mothers in the relative emphasis they place on particular characteristics. Significantly fewer working-class mothers regard happiness as highly desirable for *boys*. Although characteristics that define standards of conduct are valued by many mothers of both social classes, there are revealing differences of emphasis here too. Working-class mothers are more likely to value obedience; they would have their children be responsive to parental authority. Middle-class mothers are more likely to value both consideration and self-control; they would have their children develop inner control and sympathetic concern for other people. Furthermore, middle-class mothers are more likely to regard curiosity as a prime virtue. By contrast, working-class mothers put the emphasis on neatness and cleanliness, valuing the imaginative and exploring child relatively less than the presentable child.[6]

Middle-class mothers' conceptions of what is desirable for boys are much the same as their conceptions of what is desirable for girls. But working-class mothers make a clear distinction between the sexes: they are more likely to regard dependability, being a good student, and

Table 1

Proportion of Mothers Who Select Each Characteristic as One of Three "Most Desirable" in a Ten- or Eleven-Year-Old Child

Characteristics	For Boys		For Girls		Combined	
	Middle Class	Working Class	Middle Class	Working Class	Middle Class	Working Class
1. That he is honest	0.44	0.57	0.44	0.48	0.44	0.53
2. That he is happy	.44*	.27	.48	.45	.46*	.36
3. That he is considerate of others	.40	.30	.38*	.24	.39*	.27
4. That he obeys his parents well	.18*	.37	.23	.30	.20*	.33
5. That he is dependable	.27	.27	.20	.14	.24	.21
6. That he has good manners	.16	.17	.23	.32	.19	.24
7. That he has self-control	.24	.14	.20	.13	.22*	.13
8. That he is popular with other children	.13	.15	.17	.20	.15	.18
9. That he is a good student	.17	.23	.13	.11	.15	.17
10. That he is neat and clean	.07	.13	.15*	.28	.11*	.20
11. That he is curious about things	.20*	.06	.15	.07	.18*	.06
12. That he is ambitious	.09	.18	.06	.08	.07	.13
13. That he is able to defend himself	.13	.05	.06	.08	.10	.06
14. That he is affectionate	.03	.05	.07	.04	.05	.04
15. That he is liked by adults	.03	.05	.07	.04	.05	.04
16. That he is able to play by himself	.01	.02	.00	.03	.01	.02
17. That he acts in a serious way	0.00	0.01	0.00	0.00	0.00	0.01
N	90	85	84	80	174	165

*Social-class differences statistically significant, 0.05 level or better, using chi-squared test.

ambition as desirable for boys and to regard happiness, good manners, neatness, and cleanliness as desirable for girls.

What of the *fathers'* values? Judging from our subsample of 82 fathers, their values are similar to those of the mothers (see Table 2). Essentially the same rank order of choices holds for fathers as for mothers, with one major exception: fathers are not so likely to value happiness for their daughters. Among fathers as well as mothers, consideration and self-control are more likely to be regarded as desirable by the middle class; middle-class fathers are also more likely to value another standard of conduct—dependability. Working-class fathers, like their wives, are more likely to value obedience; they are also more likely to regard it as desirable that their children be able to defend themselves.[7]

We take this to indicate that middle-class parents (fathers as well as mothers) are more likely to ascribe predominant importance to the child's acting on the basis of internal standards of conduct, working-class parents to the child's compliance with parental authority. . . .

CLASS, SUBCULTURE, AND VALUES

In discussing the relationship of social class to values we have talked as if American society

Table 2

Proportion of Fathers Who Select Each Characteristic as One of Three "Most Desirable" in a Ten- or Eleven-Year-Old Child

Characteristics	For Boys		For Girls		Combined	
	Middle Class	Working Class	Middle Class	Working Class	Middle Class	Working Class
1. That he is honest	0.60	0.60	0.43	0.55	0.52	0.58
2. That he is happy	.48	.24	.24	.18	.37	.22
3. That he is considerate of others	.32	.16	.38	.09	.35*	.14
4. That he obeys his parents well	.12*	.40	.14	.36	.13*	.39
5. That he is dependable	.36*	.12	.29*	.00	.33*	.08
6. That he has good manners	.24	.28	.24	.18	.24	.25
7. That he has self-control	.20	.08	.19	.00	.20*	.06
8. That he is popular with other children	.08	.16	.24	.45	.15	.25
9. That he is a good student	.04	.12	.10	.36	.07	.19
10. That he is neat and clean	.16	.20	.14	.09	.15	.17
11. That he is curious about things	.16	.12	.10	.00	.13	.08
12. That he is ambitious	.20	.12	.14	.00	.17	.08
13. That he is able to defend himself	.04	.16	.00*	.18	.02*	.17
14. That he is affectionate	.00	.04	.05	.18	.02	.08
15. That he is liked by adults	.00	.08	.00	.09	.00	.08
16. That he is able to play by himself	.00	.08	.05	.00	.02	.06
17. That he acts in a serious way	0.00	0.04	0.00	0.00	0.00	0.03
N	25	25	21	11	46	36

*Social-class differences statistically significant, 0.05 level or better, using chi-squared test.

were composed of two relatively homogeneous groups, manual and white-collar workers, together with their families. Yet it is likely that there is considerable variation in values, associated with other bases of social differentiation, *within* each class. If so, it should be possible to divide the classes into subgroups in such a way as to specify more precisely the relationship of social class to values.

Consider, first, the use we have made of the concept "social class." Are the differences we have found between the values of middle- and working-class mothers a product of this dichotomy alone, or do values parallel status gradations more generally? It is possible to arrive at

an approximate answer by dividing the mothers into the five socioeconomic strata delineated by the Hollingshead Index (see Table 3). An examination of the choices made by mothers in each stratum indicates that variation in values parallels socioeconomic status rather closely:

1. The higher a mother's status, the higher the probability that she will choose consideration, curiosity, self-control, and (for boys)[8] happiness as highly desirable; curiosity is particularly likely to be chosen by mothers in the highest stratum.
2. The lower her status, the higher the probability that she will select obedience, neatness,

Table 3

Mothers' Socioeconomic Status and Their Choice of Characteristics as "Most Desirable" in a Ten- or Eleven-Year-Old Child

	Proportion Who Select Each Characteristic Socioeconomic Stratum (on Hollingshead Index)				
Characteristic	I	II	III	IV	V
Obedience	0.14	0.19	0.25	0.35	0.27
Neatness, cleanliness	.06	.07	.16	.18	.27
Consideration	.41	.37	.39	.25	.32
Curiosity	.37	.12	.09	.07	.03
Self-control	.24	.30	.18	.13	.14
Happiness	.61	.40	.40	.38	.30
Boys		.48		.40	.27
Girls		.54		.40	.45
Honesty	0.37	0.49	0.46	0.50	0.65
N	51	43	80	128	37

and cleanliness; it appears, too, that mothers in the lowest stratum are more likely than are those in the highest to value *honesty*.

Mothers' values also are directly related to their own occupational positions and educational attainments, independently of their families' class status. (The family's class status has been indexed on the basis of the husband's occupation and education.) It happens that a considerable proportion of the mothers we have classified as working class hold white-collar jobs.[9] Those who do are, by and large, closer to middle-class mothers in their values than are other working-class mothers (see Table 4). But those who hold manual jobs are even further from middle-class mothers in their values than are working-class mothers who do not have jobs outside the home.

So, too, for mothers' educational attainments: a middle-class mother of *relatively* low educational attainment (one who has gone no further than graduation from high school) is less likely to value curiosity and more likely to

Table 4

Working-Class Mothers' Own Occupations and Their Choice of Characteristics as "Most Desirable" in a Ten- or Eleven-Year-Old Child

	Proportion Who Select Each Characteristic		
Characteristic	White-Collar Job	No Job	Manual Job
Obedience	.26	.35	.53
Neatness, cleanliness	.16	.18	.42
Consideration	.39	.21	.05
Curiosity	.10	.04	.00
Self-control	.13	.14	.11
Happiness	.33	.40	.26
Boys	.32	.21	—
Girls	.36	.59	—
N	69	77	19

Table 5

Mothers' Education and Their Choice of Characteristics as "Most Desirable" in a Ten- or Eleven-Year-Old Child

	Middle-Class Mothers Proportion Who Select Each Characteristic			
	Male Child		Female Child	
Characteristic	At Least Some College	High-School Graduate or Less	At Least Some College	High-School Graduate or Less
Obedience	0.11	0.22	0.13	0.29
Neatness-cleanliness	.03	.09	.03*	.23
Consideration	.47	.35	.41	.37
Curiosity	.31*	.13	.31*	.06
Self-control	.33	.19	.19	.21
Happiness	0.50	0.41	0.59	0.40
N	36	54	32	52

	Working-Class Mothers Proportion Who Select Each Characteristic			
	Male Child		Female Child	
Characteristic	At Least High-School Graduate	Less than High-School Graduate	At Least High-School Graduate	Less than High-School Graduate
Obedience	0.29	0.43	0.28	0.32
Neatness-cleanliness	.12	.14	.21	.35
Consideration	.32	.27	.33*	.14
Curiosity	.07	.05	.12	.00
Self-control	.22*	.07	.16*	.08
Happiness	0.27	0.27	0.47	0.43
N	41	44	43	37

*Difference between mothers of differing educational status statistically significant, 0.05 level or better, using chi-squared test.

value (for girls) neatness and cleanliness (see Table 5). A working-class mother of *relatively* high educational attainment (one who has at least graduated from high school) is more likely to value self-control for boys and both consideration and curiosity for girls. The largest differences obtain between those middle-class mothers of highest educational attainments and

those working-class mothers of lowest educational attainments.

Even when we restrict ourselves to considerations of social status and its various ramifications, we find that values vary appreciably within each of the two broad classes. And, as sociologists would expect, variation in values proceeds along other major lines of social demarcation as well. Religious background is particularly useful as a criterion for distinguishing subcultures within the social classes. It does *not* exert so powerful an effect that Protestant mothers differ significantly from Catholic mothers of the same social class in their values.[10] But the combination of class and religious background does enable us to isolate groups that are more homogeneous in their values than are the social classes *in toto*. We find that there is an ordering, consistent for all class-related values, proceeding from middle-class Protestant mothers, to middle-class Catholic, to working-class Protestant, to working-class Catholic (see Table 6). Middle-class Protestants and working-class Catholics constitute the two extremes whose values are most dissimilar.

Another relevant line of social demarcation is the distinction between urban and rural background.[11] As we did for religious background, we can arrange the mothers into four groups delineated on the basis of class and rural-urban background in an order that is reasonably consistent for all class-related values. The order is: middle-class urban, middle-class rural, working-class urban, working-class rural (see Table 7). The extremes are middle-class mothers raised in the city and working-class mothers raised on farms.

Several other variables fail to differentiate mothers of the same social class into groups having appreciably different values. These include the mother's age, the size of the family, the ordinal position of the child in the family, the length of time the family has lived in the neighborhood, whether or not the mother has been socially mobile (from the status of her childhood family), and her class identification. Nor are these results a function of the large proportion of families of government workers included in the sample: wives of government employees do not differ from other mothers of the same social class in their values.

In sum, we find that it is possible to specify the relationship between social class and values more precisely by dividing the social classes into subgroups on the basis of other lines of social demarcation—but that social class seems to provide the single most relevant line of demarcation.

Table 6

Mothers' Religious Background and Their Choice of Characteristics as "Most Desirable" in a Ten- or Eleven-Year-Old Child

	Proportion Who Select Each Characteristic			
Characteristic	Middle-Class Protestant	Middle-Class Catholic	Working-Class Protestant	Working-Class Catholic
Obedience	0.17	0.25	0.33	0.36
Neatness, cleanliness	.08	.15	17	.27
Consideration	.36	.38	.26	.29
Curiosity	.24	.12	.07	.05
Self-control	.28	.15	.15	.09
Happiness	.47	.42	.38	.30
Boys	.48	.32	.35	.13
Girls	0.45	0.52	0.42	0.54
N	88	52	107	56

Table 7

Rural versus Urban Background of Mothers and Their Choice of Characteristics as "Most Desirable" in a Ten- or Eleven-Year-Old Child

	Proportion Who Select Each Characteristic			
Characteristic	Middle-Class Urban	Middle-Class Rural	Working-Class Urban	Working-Class Rural
Obedience	0.19	0.24	0.29	0.42
Neatness, cleanliness	.11	.12	.17	.25
Consideration	.42	.27	.31	.18
Curiosity	.19	.12	.07	.04
Self-control	.20	.33	.15	.11
Happiness	.47	.42	.41	.25
Boys	.44	.47	.28	.25
Girls	0.50	0.37	0.57	0.26
N	141	33	110	55

ADEQUACY OF INDEX OF VALUES

The form in which our major question was asked enabled us to set the same ground rules for all parents. No premium was put on imaginativeness or articulateness. But the fact that we limited their choice to these particular characteristics means that we denied them the opportunity to select others that they might have regarded as even more desirable. However, we had *previously* asked each parent: "When you think of a boy (or girl) of (child's) age, are there *any* things you look for as most important or most desirable?" Only three additional characteristics were suggested by any appreciable number of parents. The first, suggested by a significantly larger proportion of middle- than of working-class parents, was "self-reliance" or "independence"—a result entirely consistent with the rest of this study. The second, variously labeled "friendliness," "co-operativeness," or "ability to get along well with others" was also predominantly a middle-class concern. It indicates that we may have underrepresented the proportion of middle-class parents who value

their children's ability to relate to others. Finally, several parents (of both social classes) said that they considered it desirable that the child not "act too old," "too young," or be effeminate (in a boy) or masculine (in a girl). There seems to be a certain concern, not adequately indexed by our major question, that the child conform to his parent's conception of what constitutes the proper age and sex role.

Of course, parents might have selected other characteristics as well, had we suggested them. These possible limitations notwithstanding, it appears that the index is reasonably comprehensive.

More important than the question of comprehensiveness is whether or not it is really possible for parents to select characteristics as desirable independently of the way that they rate their own children's behavior. Since each parent was later asked to rate his child's performance with respect to each characteristic, we can compare the ratings given by parents who chose a characteristic with those given by parents of the same social class who did not. Parents who chose each characteristic were no more and no less likely to describe their children as excelling in that characteristic; nor were they any more or less likely than other parents to feel that their children were deficient. The parents have not imputed desirability to the characteristics that they feel represent their children's virtues or their children's deficiencies.

The final and most important question: Is it wise to accept someone's assertion that something is a value to him? After all, assertions are subject to distortion.[12] To the degree that we can ascertain that parents act in reasonable conformity to the values they assert, however, we gain confidence in an index based on assertions.

This study does not provide disinterested observations of the parents' behavior. Our closest approximation derives from interviews with the parents themselves—interviews in which we questioned them in considerable detail about their relevant actions. Perhaps the most crucial of these data are those bearing on their actions in situations where their children behave in *disvalued* ways. We have, for example, questioned parents in some detail about what they do when

their children lose their tempers. We began by asking whether or not the child in question "ever really loses his temper." From those parents who said that the child does lose his temper, we then proceeded to find out precisely what behavior they consider to be "loss of temper"; what they "generally do when he acts this way"; whether they "ever find it necessary to do anything else"; if so, what else they do, and "under what circumstances." Our concern here is with what the parent reports he does as a matter of last resort.[13]

Mothers who regard *self-control* as an important value are more likely to report that they punish the child—be it physically, by isolation, or by restriction of activities; they are unlikely merely to scold or to ignore his loss of temper altogether (see Table 8).

To punish a child who has lost his temper may not be a particularly effective way of inducing self-control. One might even have predicted that mothers who value self-control would be less likely to punish breaches of control, more likely to explain, even ignore. They

Table 8

Choice of "Self-control" as "Most Desirable" Characteristic and Most Extreme Actions That Mothers Report They Take When Their Children Lose Their Tempers

	Proportion					
	Middle Class		Working Class		Both	
	Choose Self-control	Don't Choose Self-control	Choose Self-control	Don't Choose Self-control	Choose Self-control	Don't Choose Self-control
Punish physically	0.26	0.20	0.44	0.26	0.32	0.23
Isolate	.20	.11	.11	.12	.17	.11
Restrict activities, other punishments	.06	.05	.17	.14	.10	.10
Threaten punishment	.06	.03	.00	.02	.04	.02
Scold, admonish, etc.	.31	.40	.17	.31	.26	.36
Ignore	0.11	0.21	0.11	0.15	0.11	0.18
	1.00	1.00	1.00	1.00	1.00	1.00
N	35	113	18	113	53	226

do not, however, and we must put the issue more simply: mothers who assert the value are more likely to report that they apply negative sanctions in situations where the child violates that value. This response would certainly seem to conform to their value-assertion.

A parallel series of questions deals with the mother's reactions when her child "refuses to do what she tells him to do." Mothers who assert that they regard *obedience* as important are more likely to report that they punish in one way or another when their children refuse.[14] There is also evidence that mothers who value *consideration* are more likely to respond to their children's "fighting with other children," an action that need not necessarily be seen as inconsistent with consideration, by punishing them, or at least by separating them from the others.[15]

In all three instances, then, the reports on parental reactions to behavior that seem to violate the value in question indicate that mothers who profess high regard for the value are more likely to apply negative sanctions.

INTERPRETATION

Our first conclusion is that parents, whatever their social class, deem it very important indeed that their children be honest, happy, considerate, obedient, and dependable.

The second conclusion is that, whatever the reasons may be, parents' values are related to their social position, particularly their class position.

There still remains, however, the task of interpreting the relationship between parents' social position and their values. In particular: What underlies the differences between the values of middle- and of working-class parents?

One relevant consideration is that some parents may "take for granted" values that others hold dear. For example, middle-class parents may take "neatness and cleanliness" for granted, while working-class parents regard it as highly desirable. But what does it mean to say that middle-class parents take neatness and cleanliness for granted? In essence, the argument is that middle-class parents value neatness and cleanliness as greatly as do working-class

parents but not so greatly as they value such things as happiness and self-control. If this be the case, it can only mean that in the circumstances of middle-class life neatness and cleanliness are easily enough attained to be of less immediate concern than are these other values.

A second consideration lies in the probability that these value-concepts have differing meanings for parents of different cultural backgrounds. For example, one might argue that honesty is a central standard of conduct for middle-class parents because they see honesty as meaning truthfulness; and that it is more a quality of the person for working-class parents because they see it as meaning trustworthiness. Perhaps so; but to suggest that a difference in meaning underlies a difference in values raises the further problem of explaining this difference in meaning.

It would be reasonable for working-class parents to be more likely to see honesty as trustworthiness. The working-class situation is one of less material security and less assured protection from the dishonesty of others. For these reasons, trustworthiness is more at issue for working-class than for middle-class parents.

Both considerations lead us to view differences in the values of middle- and working-class parents in terms of their differing circumstances of life and, by implication, their conceptions of the effects that these circumstances may have on their children's future lives. We believe that parents are most likely to accord high priority to those values that seem both *problematic*, in the sense that they are difficult of achievement, and *important*, in the sense that failure to achieve them would affect the child's future adversely. From this perspective it is reasonable that working-class parents cannot afford to take neatness and cleanliness as much for granted as can middle-class parents. It is reasonable, too, that working-class parents are more likely to see honesty as implying trustworthiness and that this connotation of honesty is seen as problematic.

These characteristics—honesty and neatness—are important to the child's future precisely because they assure him a respectable social position. Just as "poor but honest" has traditionally been an important line of social demarcation, their high valuation of these qualities may express working-class parents' concern that their children occupy a position unequivocally above that of persons who are not neat or who are not scrupulously honest. These are the qualities of respectable, worthwhile people.

So, too, is obedience. The obedient child follows his parents' dictates rather than his own standards. He acts, in his subordinate role as a child, in conformity with the prescriptions of established authority.

Even in the way they differentiate what is desirable for boys from what is desirable for girls, working-class mothers show a keen appreciation of the qualities making for respectable social position.

The characteristics that middle-class parents are more likely to value for their children are internal standards for governing one's relationships with other people and, in the final analysis, with one's self. It is not that middle-class parents are less concerned than are working-class parents about social position. The qualities of person that assure respectability may be taken for granted, but in a world where social relationships are determinative of position, these standards of conduct are both more problematic and more important.

The middle-class emphasis on internal standards is evident in their choice of the cluster of characteristics centering around honesty; in their being less likely than are working-class parents to value obedience and more likely to value self-control and consideration; and in their seeing obedience as inconsistent with both consideration and curiosity. The child is to act appropriately, not because his parents tell him to, but because he wants to. Not conformity to authority, but inner control; not because you're told to but because you take the other person into consideration—these are the middle-class ideals.

These values place responsibility directly upon the individual. He cannot rely upon authority, nor can he simply conform to what is presented to him as proper. He should be impelled to come to his own understanding of the situation.[16] He is to govern himself in such a way as to be able to act consistently with his principles. The basic importance of relationship to self is explicit in the concept of self-control. It is implicit, too, in consideration—a standard that demands of the individual that he respond sympathetically to others' needs even if they be in conflict with his own; and in the high valuation of honesty as central to other standards of conduct: "to thine own self be true."

Perhaps, considering this, it should not be surprising that so many middle-class mothers attribute first-rank importance to happiness, even for boys. We cannot assume that their children's happiness is any less important to working-class mothers than it is to middle-class mothers; in fact, working-class mothers are equally likely to value happiness for *girls*. For their sons, however, happiness is second choice to honesty and obedience. Apparently, middle-class mothers can afford instead to be concerned about their son's happiness. And perhaps they are right in being concerned. We have noted that those middle-class mothers who deem it most important that their sons outdistance others are especially likely to be concerned about their sons' happiness; and even those mothers who do not are asking their children to accept considerable responsibility.

Notes

1. There now exists a rather substantial, if somewhat inconsistent, body of literature on the relationship of social class to the ways that parents raise their children. For a fine analytic summary see Urie Bronfenbrenner, "Socialization and Social Class through Time and Space," in Eleanor E. Maccoby *et al., Readings in Social Psychology*, 3d ed., (New York: Henry Holt & Co., 1958). Bronfenbrenner gives references to the major studies of class and child-rearing practices that have been done.

For the most relevant studies on class and *values* see Evelyn M. Duvall, "Conceptions of Parenthood," *American Journal of Sociology*, LII (November, 1946), 193–203; David F. Aberle and Kaspar D. Naegele, "Middle Class Fathers' Occupational Role and Attitudes toward Children," *American Journal of Orthopsychiatry*, XXII

(April, 1952), 366–78; Herbert H. Hyman, "The Value Systems of Different Classes," in Reinhard Bendix and Seymour M. Lipset (eds.), *Class, Status, and Power* (Glencoe, Ill.: Free Press, 1953), pp. 426–42.

2. I owe a considerable debt of gratitude to Samuel W. Greenhouse, chief of the Section on Statistics and Mathematics, Biometrics Branch, NIMH, for his expert help in sample design, as well as for his advice on general statistical problems of the research.

3. The interviewing staff was composed of Eleanor Carroll, Mary Freeman, Paul Hanlon, and Melvin Kohn. We were aided from time to time by three volunteers from the NIMH staff: Leila Deasy, Erwin Linn, and Harriet Murphy. Field work was conducted between March, 1956, and March, 1957.

We secured the co-operation of 86 per cent of the families where the mother alone was to be interviewed and 82 per cent of the families where mother, father, and child were to be interviewed. Rates of non-response do not vary by social class, type of neighborhood, or type of school. This, of course, does not rule out other possible selective biases introduced by the non-respondents.

4. Clyde Kluckhohn, "Values and Value Orientations," in Talcott Parsons and Edward A. Shils (eds.), *Toward a General Theory of Action* (Cambridge, Mass.: Harvard University Press, 1951), p. 395.

5. The criterion of statistical significance used throughout this paper is the 5 per cent level of probability, based, except where noted, on the chi-squared test.

6. Compare these results with Bronfenbrenner's conclusion, based on an analysis of reports of studies of social class and child-rearing methods over the last twenty-five years: "In this modern working class world there may be greater freedom of emotional expression, but there is no laxity or vagueness with respect to goals of child training. Consistently over the past twenty-five years, the parent in this group has emphasized what are usually regarded as the traditional middle class virtues of cleanliness, conformity, and (parental) control, and although his methods are not so effective as those

of his middle class neighbors, they are perhaps more desperate" (*op. cit.*).

7. A comparison of the values of the fathers in this subsample with those of the mothers in this same subsample yields essentially the same conclusions.

We do not find that fathers of either social class are significantly more likely to choose any characteristic for boys than they are to choose it for girls, or the reverse. But this may well be an artifact of the small number of fathers in our sample; Aberle and Naegele (*op. cit.*) have found that middle-class fathers are more likely to value such characteristics as responsibility, initiative, good school performance, ability to stand up for one's self, and athletic ability for boys and being "nice," "sweet," pretty, affectionate, and well-liked for girls.

8. The choice of happiness is, as we have seen, related to social class for boys only. Consequently, in each comparison we shall make in this section the choice of happiness for *girls* will prove to be an exception to the general order.

9. No middle-class mothers have manual jobs, so the comparable situation does not exist. Those middle-class women who do work (at white-collar jobs) are less likely to value neatness and cleanliness and more likely to value obedience and curiosity.

10. The index here is based on the question "May I ask what is your religious background?"

Even when the comparison is restricted to Catholic mothers who send their children to Catholic school versus Protestant mothers of the same social class, there are no significant differences in values.

Jewish mothers (almost all of them in this sample are middle class) are very similar to middle-class Protestant mothers in their values, with two notable exceptions. More Jewish than Protestant mothers select popularity and ability to defend one's self—two values that are not related to social class.

11. We asked: "Have you ever lived on a farm?" and then classified all mothers who had lived on a farm for some time other than simply summer vacations, prior to age fifteen, as having had a rural background.

Ordinarily, one further line of cultural demarcation would be considered at this point—nationality background. The present sample, however, is composed predominantly of parents who are at least second-generation, United States–born, so this is not possible.

12. But inferring values from observed behavior may not be satisfactory either, for we cannot be certain that we are correctly distinguishing the normative from other components of action. As Robin Williams states: "No student of human conduct can accept uncritically, as final evidence, people's testimony as to their own values. Yet actions may deceive as well as words, and there seems no reason for always giving one precedence over the other" (*American Society: A Sociological Interpretation* [New York: Alfred A. Knopf, 1951], p. 378).

13. This comparison and those to follow are limited to parents who say that the child does in fact behave in the disvalued way, at least on occasion. (Approximately equal proportions of middle- and working-class mothers report that their children do behave in each of these ways.)

14. The figures are 47 versus 29 per cent for middle-class mothers; 36 versus 18 per cent for working-class mothers.

15. The figures are 42 versus 29 per cent for middle-class mothers; 61 versus 37 per cent for working-class mothers.

There is also some indication that *working-class* mothers who value *honesty* have been more prone to insist that their children make restitution when they have "swiped" something, but the number of mothers who say that their children have ever swiped something is too small for this evidence to be conclusive. (The figures for working-class mothers are 63 versus 35 per cent; for middle-class mothers, 38 versus 33 per cent.)

The interviews with the children provide further evidence that parents have acted consistently with their values—for example, children whose mothers assert high valuation of dependability are more likely to tell us that the reason their parents want them to do their chores is to train them in responsibility (not to relieve the parents of work).

16. Curiosity provides a particularly interesting example of how closely parents' values are related to their circumstances of life and expectations: the proportion of mothers who value curiosity rises very slowly from status level to status level until we reach the wives of professionals and the more highly educated businessmen; then it jumps suddenly (see Table 3). The value is given priority in precisely that portion of the middle class where it is most appropriate and where its importance for the child's future is most apparent.

12

The Abolition of *El Cortito*, the Short-Handled Hoe: A Case Study in Social Conflict and State Policy in California Agriculture

Douglas Murray

Editors' Introduction

In the keynote reading Berger and Berger provide considerable discussion of theories of stratification—attempts to make sense of the nature and sources of the class structure. The authors point out Karl Marx's interest in "the relationship of a group to the means of production" (p. 110). They also say that, while ownership of means of production lay at the heart of Marx's theory, later Marxian theorists have been more concerned with *control* of production. The following illustrative reading shows how a simple agricultural tool became a tool of oppressive control as well as a tool of agricultural production. Douglas Murray goes on to show how efforts on behalf of the field workers oppressed by this tool resulted in a major change in the process of production, raising issues beyond this simple agricultural instrument. Although this is the history of one specific case, the implications for the control of workers through the labor process are far-reaching.

    In this reading Murray shows how *el cortito*, a short-handled cultivating hoe, became a source of serious health hazards, oppression of workers, and the focal point of major controversy. This straightforward article traces the emergence and solution of a social problem in several steps. Who were the people who first introduced this type of hoe to California agriculture? In what ways were these people different from the Mexicans who inherited "the short one"? Why were the Mexicans brought into California agriculture in the first place? Why were they forced to use the short-handled hoe? The disastrous physical effects from using the hoe on a continuous basis led to stepped-up union organizing and strike activity. How did the *braceros* program affect these efforts to organize?

In the struggle to counter this new symbol of oppression, what steps were involved? These steps are most significant because they demonstrate the role of government in the process. Notice the original decision of the Industrial Safety Board. Also notice the content of the appeal made to the California Supreme Court, along with the ultimate decision made in the changing political climate in California. According to Murray, what boundaries exist, setting limits to state involvement in the labor process? What questions cannot be answered? What are the larger implications for other work settings and hazardous practices?

As we indicated before, the theoretical orientation that Murray uses is the conflict orientation. In fact, his article comes very close to a Marxist approach in considering the owners and nonowners of means of production. One of Marx's fundamental ideas was that workers would have control of the labor process taken away from them by the owners in an effort to further the exploitation and oppression of those workers. In this case, the introduction of Mexican workers and the imposition of exclusive use of *el cortito* furthered such exploitation and oppression. But later events veered sharply from a Marxian scenario when agencies of the state stepped in and the court decided in favor of the workers. According to Marxian analysis, this would not have happened, since the state is considered to be at the beck and call of the bourgeoisie or owners. But, of course, neither the California Supreme Court nor the governor addressed the larger questions of ownership and ultimate control—just as a Marxist would predict.

Although Murray does not tell us how he did this study, several footnotes and the flow of analysis imply quite a bit about his research methods. First, he used numerous historical documents to reassemble the series of events from a legal and historical standpoint. Second, during the latter part of 1978 and early 1979 he augmented these documents with personal interviews with some of the principal players in these events. A weakness in this reading is the author's failure to discuss his research methods. Were his personal interviews representative of all sides in the dispute?

Think a bit about how this selection fits into the sociological perspective. As Bates points out in his introduction to the perspective in Part One, sociologists are interested in social behavior, social organization, and social change. All three are illustrated in this reading. The workers band together to protest their agonizing tool, while the owners band together to protect their own interests. While these groups and the interactions within and between them represent social organization, the whole process is taking place within the larger realm of social organization known as the societal stratification structure. You can also trace in the reading the processes of social change, as each side responds to the other. Finally, the major social change comes about through the intervention of the legal institution. This is another example of structure and process—and the interrelationship between the two.

Late one afternoon in the spring of 1973, farm workers leaving the fields of the fertile Salinas Valley in central California gathered beside the buses which would take them to the nearby labor camps for the night. They moved nervously about a large pile of short-handled hoes which they had been using that day to thin and weed long rows of lettuce. One farm worker quickly doused the hoes with gasoline; another tossed a match, setting them ablaze. Cries of protest swept through the crowd as the farm workers served their bosses with a defiant notice: no longer would they work with *el cortito*, the short-handled hoe.

Farm workers have protested in the California fields throughout the 20th century, yet most of their attempts to improve agricultural working conditions have met with little success. Often their protests have unleashed repressive measures from growers or local governments. But the struggle over the short-handled hoe was an unusual event in farm worker history. *El cortito* became the focus of California government hearings, a California Supreme Court ruling (*Sebastian Carmona et al. v. Division of Industrial Safety*, January 13, 1975), and ultimately a California administrative edict (Administrative Interpretation No. 62, Division of Industrial Safety, April 7, 1975) banning the tool from further use in the California fields.

The abolition of *el cortito* is an example of the reliance upon administrative and legal institutions by groups challenging specific social conditions, a political phenomenon that has in-

Reprinted from *Social Problems*, 30, 1 (October 1982). Used with permission of The Society for the Study of Social Problems and the author.

Note updates in note 5 (p. 150) concerning current legislation have been furnished by Douglas Murray.

creased significantly in the United States since the 1950s. The civil rights, anti-Vietnam war, and environmental movements have all relied heavily on legal action to force social change or generate popular support for legislative reform. Recent studies of these movements have focused on the resources used to achieve specific goals (McCarthy and Zald, 1977; Oberschall, 1973). Whereas movements in the 19th and early 20th centuries mainly used cultural, community, occupational and other traditional resources (Tilly, 1978), contemporary social movements have relied increasingly upon access to, and mobilization of, state institutions to bring about social change. Legal institutions have played a particularly important role (Black, 1973; Lipsky, 1968). Litigation has attacked social issues ranging from school desegregation (Greenberg, 1959) to environmental degradation (Dunlap, 1981). Studies of litigation generated by social movements have concentrated on the conditions under which legal institutions have become a resource for realizing social movement goals.

This emphasis in contemporary research on the role resources play in bringing about social change neglects the important role these resources play in structuring and redefining the very issues involved. The way a social problem is defined by the government institutions and legal statutes used to resolve it, and the relationship between the original problem and its resolution through state policy, remain relatively unexplored questions.

The abolition of *el cortito* is an example of how social problems are solved within the state arena and how state policy affects the sources of social conflict. This paper explores the origins of the short-handled hoe as a social problem and its subsequent resolution. I examine the process of litigation and state policy formation within the context of the converging social and political forces of the late 1960s and early 1970s. Finally, I look at the relationship between social problems, state policy, and future strategies of the farm-worker movement.

THE ORIGIN OF *EL CORTITO*

The short-handled hoe has not always been an integral part of agricultural production in California. Its introduction and the subsequent conflict it generated are rooted in the early organization of corporate farming. The combination of large land holdings inherited from the Mexican colonial period and the shift to labor-intensive farming transformed California agriculture in the late 19th century. The resulting agribusiness which emerged from this era was characterized by the cultivation of single crops on large tracts of land and the dependence upon a large supply of cheap labor.

The emphasis on labor-intensive farming was accompanied by a need to maintain control over the workers in an effort to assure a profitable return. Direct involvement in the work process to achieve this end was largely unnecessary, however, since most immigrant workers used on the California farms were fleeing extreme economic or political hardships and had no option but to work under whatever terms of employment they were offered.

With such externally imposed discipline, more direct control of the farm workers was unnecessary, and the workers retained a degree of autonomy. Growers[1] relied heavily upon the self-organization of these immigrant workers and the skills they provided. A similar relationship between immigrant workers and employers was also prevalent in the industrial sector in the United States at the same time (Gutman, 1966; Stone, 1974).

It was from this self-organized labor process that the short-handled hoe first emerged. California growers began cultivating sugar beets intensively near the end of the 19th century. Most farm workers on the west coast at this time came from Japan. Like the Chinese farm workers before them (Saxton, 1971), the Japanese were valued for their skills in the intensive cultivation of row crops. Among the techniques the Japanese relied upon was a traditional tool used in Japanese gardening, the short-handled hoe.

Japanese farm workers used the short-handled hoe in conjunction with a variety of tools and techniques over which they had a significant degree of control. They worked in closely knit units called clubs or associations, selecting a secretary from among the group to contract and direct the work (McWilliams, 1971). These farm workers used both short- and long-handled hoes, rotating tasks among themselves to alleviate the strain of using the short-handled hoe.

At first, the Japanese farm workers' knowledge of intensive cultivation and their ability to organize and supervise themselves were prized by growers. But once established as an integral part of production, the farm workers began to demand better wages. Their wages rose 50 percent over a 15-year period and by 1907 they were the highest-paid group of workers in California agriculture (McWilliams, 1971:111). Growers faced the same dilemma as employers in other industries at this time. The degree of autonomy maintained by skilled immigrant workers became the source of leverage in labor's confrontation with capital.

The Japanese farm workers posed a serious threat to California agriculture: they could stop production, often during the crucial harvest period, and drive up the cost of labor. The solution adopted by the growers over the second decade of the 20th century was similar to that used by industrialists in the eastern United States; they recruited a new labor force, one which did not have a history of organization and conflict in California agriculture. To ensure that no such organization developed, the growers increased their control over the labor process.

The new labor force to which the growers turned had been arriving from Mexico as early as the Japanese. They came at first to work on the railroads, and subsequently moved into agriculture as the demand for labor grew. By the end of the 19th century, with the railroads connecting much of Mexico and the United States, the northward migration of workers was increasing (Galarza, 1964). The strategy of economic development pursued in Mexico under the regime of president Porfirio Diaz (1876–1911), of which the railroads were a major part, created not only the vehicle for the northward migration, but the motivation as well. The economic stagnation that grew from this period and the subsequent turmoil of the Mexican Revolution (Goldfrank, 1975) led large numbers of *campesinos* to come north in search of work or to escape political persecution (Hoffman, 1974). The Mexican farm workers, unlike their predecessors, came mainly from regions in Mexico that did not farm intensively. The skills and knowledge of intensive farming, including the use of the short-handled hoe, were not a part of their culture. But the California growers had a greater need for a controllable labor supply than for skilled laborers, and to achieve this control they reorganized the agricultural labor process.

Transformation of the Labor Process

The shift in control of the labor process took subtle forms, often with unseen effects. But the seemingly incremental changes in the first decades of the 20th century had a profound effect on the lives of the farm workers. During this period of transformation, the use of the short-handled hoe emerged as one of the most difficult and oppressive conditions of California farm labor.

Growing resistance and organization by farm workers prompted the growers to form organizations such as the California Farm Bureau Federation to foster "the rational recruitment of seasonal labor" (Chambers, 1952:23). Where Japanese farm workers had selected a secretary from their own ranks to contract work for their crew, the growers began to rely on their own contractors to find workers. The Spanish-speaking farm workers referred to the contractors as *el coyote*. The contractor and his "crew pushers" were responsible for getting maximum productivity out of the labor force; herein lies the beginning of the health hazard posed by the short-

handled hoe. Thinning and weeding became specialized tasks done by gangs of farm workers over larger and larger plots of land. The short-handled hoe began to be used exclusively for thinning and weeding, as the long-handled hoe gradually disappeared from the fields. Growers claimed they preferred the short-handled hoe for its greater accuracy and efficiency, but farm workers and contractors saw a more sinister motive behind the choice of the short-handled hoe. Farm worker Sebastian Carmona recalled a supervisor's response to his objection to the short-handled hoe:

With the long-handled hoe I can't tell whether they are working or just leaning on their hoes. With the short-handled hoe I know when they are not working by how often they stand up (Personal interview, March 1, 1979).

The short-handled hoe was no longer an implement in the repertoire of farm worker tools and techniques for cultivation of row crops. It had become part of the growers' and contractors' repertoire of techniques for the supervision and control of the workers. Hector de la Rosa, another farm worker, described the effects of using this tool:

When I used the short-handled hoe my head would ache and my eyes hurt because of the pressure of bending down so long. My back would hurt whenever I stood up or bent over. I moved down the rows as fast as I could so I could get to the end and rest my back for a moment (Personal interview, March 1, 1979).

Thus, the short-handled hoe also became a means of increasing productivity. Workers moved faster down the rows, in the knowledge that only at the end could they stand up momentarily to rest their backs.

During the 1920s and the Depression years that followed, growers tried to increase productivity and cut costs to maintain a viable profit margin. With the high level of fixed capital and subsequent financing costs, labor became the main target for cost-cutting schemes. The short-handled hoe was seized upon by growers and contractors throughout the region. Its usefulness to growers, and hardship to farm workers, spread as competition standardized agricultural practices in California.

Vivid evidence of changes in the use of the short-handled hoe in California can be found in various written and photographic accounts. References to hoeing activities at the beginning of the 20th century describe it as "squat labor" (Chambers, 1952). Photographs of the pre-1920s period show workers with their head up and hips to the ground.[2] Accounts of later periods describe such work as "stoop labor" (McWilliams, 1971). Photographs show workers with legs nearly straight, head lowered and upper torso parallel to the ground. This position allowed for a faster pace of work, but placed much greater stress on the back.

Use of the short-handled hoe in the stoop position over prolonged periods of time results in a degeneration of the spine, leading to permanent disabilities. This condition was attested to by numerous physicians and medical specialists in hearings on the short-handled hoe held by California's Industrial Safety Board (ISB). The testimony of one physician is indicative of the conclusions reached by the medical experts:

Anybody that's been using the [short-handled hoe] extensively in the field over a ten-year period has got back trouble. Whether or not you're seeing him for tonsilitis or something like that, he still has back problems. He may not be absolutely symptomatic, but that spine is wearing out. He's not going to make it to any retirement age of sixty-five (ISB hearing, May 3, 1973).

The use of the short-handled hoe to increase productivity, and to control labor generally, depends upon an abundance of available workers to replace those who could not keep up the pace. Growers not only expected a high turnover in this work, they actually preferred it. One grower testified during an Industrial Safety Board hearing that the daily turnover in short-handled hoe gangs was "hopefully" 75 to 80 percent (ISB hearing, May 3, 1973). With a steady supply of cheap labor from Mexico, sup-

plemented by a growing population of Mexican-Americans in California, the growers could disregard the destructiveness of the short-handled hoe by relying upon the steady turnover of a transient labor force.

Resistance to *El Cortito*

The farm workers were quick to recognize work with the short-handled hoe as the most difficult and least desirable task. The tool came to be known as *el cortito*, "the short one," a symbol of the oppressive nature of stoop labor. One farm worker, reflecting on the conditions during the 1920s and 1930s, attributed the failing health and premature death of many farm workers indirectly to the short-handled hoe:

In the Sacramento Valley, many of the farm workers would drink wine before going to work to kill the pain in their backs. They would grow old fast, or become sick. When they died people would say it was because they drank. But we knew it was from *el cortito* (Personal interview: Salvatore Gutierrez, March 1, 1979).

Growers and politicians who defended use of the short-handled hoe often argued that farm workers were better equipped physically and culturally to do this kind of work. The testimony of Mervyn Bailey is indicative:

My father ran a crew of Hindus in 1911 in the Salinas Valley in thinning and hoeing beets. Then Japanese. Then we followed with Filipinos. And then the Mexicans. The stoop [laborers], most of them are small or more agile than the ordinary anglo due to their build and the fact that they seem to have a stronger body for the job (*Sebastian Carmona et al. v. Division of Industrial Safety*: Reply to Amicus Brief of Bud Antle, Inc., July 29, 1974:12).

Others argued that the farm workers themselves hadn't objected to the short-handled hoe until social reformers and labor agitators created an issue of it. A recent example of this view was expressed by former U.S. secretary of agriculture Earl Butz:

In California, Mexican farm workers are no longer allowed to use the short-handled hoe they have used for generations; now they are required to use long-handled American type hoes. . . . This is not because the workers or the farmers want to change: but apparently because the city people, driving by, feel more comfortable watching the workers use the kind of hoes that look good through car windows (Perelman, 1977:5).

In fact, use of the short-handled hoe and other working conditions were the focus of many spontaneous and organized protests and strikes by farm workers, particularly in the late 1920s (Galarza, 1970; Hoffman, 1974). Growers and labor contractors reported instances when temporary labor shortages were followed by protests and work stoppages by farm workers over the use of the short-handled hoe (ISB hearing, May 3, 1973:16). That these protests did not spread was more the result of the repressive and often violent response of growers, supported by the police and government agencies, than the result of any cultural heritage or proclivity for stoop labor among the farm workers.[3] Under these conditions, the efforts of farm workers to challenge the use of the short-handled hoe were futile. With the subsequent migration to California of several hundred thousand Dustbowl refugees during the Depression came further exploitation of the farm workers. The "Okies" and "Arkies" became the major source of farm labor during the Depression until the Second World War drew many of them into military service or war-industry jobs. These newly arrived migrants were willing to do any work, including using the short-handled hoe—and for lower wages. Their arrival doomed early union organizing efforts which were developing during the late 1920s among the Mexican farm workers. The Dustbowl migrants refused to cooperate with non-white organizers and workers, and remained unorganizable themselves (Stein, 1973).
    Attempts by farm workers to organize dur-

ing and after the Second World War were continually undermined by state and federal labor and immigration policies. At the urging of powerful agricultural interests the Roosevelt administration initiated a Temporary Worker Program in 1942. This program was to provide Mexican farm workers, under an agreement with the Mexican government, during harvest periods while wartime labor shortages persisted. After the war, Congress passed Public Law 78, known as the Bracero Program, to provide access to temporary workers from Mexico whenever labor shortages occurred. These *braceros* became an important resource for growers in combatting efforts to unionize farm labor. *Braceros* were relied upon heavily until the program was ended in 1964, particularly when strikes or effective union organizing was developing.

The Rise of Farm Worker Power in the 1960s

The recognition of unions following the end of the Second World War helped stabilize working conditions and the labor supply in the industrial sector across the United States, but California agriculture remained unchanged. With government policies such as the Bracero Program assuring an abundant immigrant labor force, the growers saw little need to negotiate with farm workers (Majka, 1978). Without a union, the farm workers saw little improvement in their working conditions, and their protests against the short-handled hoe fell on deaf ears.

The message was clear. If I didn't like working with the short-handled hoe I could quit; there were others to do the work. The contractor didn't have to deal with what the farm workers wanted, so we continued to use *el cortito* (Personal interview: Hector de la Rosa, March 1, 1979).

    Yet, in spite of grower resistance and the barrier posed by the *braceros*, a farm worker union movement was developing. An unsuccessful strike against DiGiorgio vineyards in California's Central Valley in 1947 broke the

AFL-affiliated National Farm Laborers' Union, in large part due to the availability of *bracero* labor. As organizers from this strike scattered throughout the state, they began to organize again (Galarza, 1970). During the 1950s these organizers began to build a base for a successful union throughout California. But the DiGiorgio lesson was clear: the *braceros* had to be overcome if a successful organizing drive was to be sustained.

In the early 1960s the challenge to the Bracero Program was gaining momentum. Congressman Adam Clayton Powell led a campaign on Capitol Hill to end Public Law 78 with the backing of some of the major unions. The use of *braceros* to break strikes and undermine organizing had become well known among organized labor, fueling the opposition to the Bracero Program and support for farm worker organizing. The AFL-CIO and the United Auto Workers provided funds for the union organizing drive. The campaign finally succeeded in November, 1964, when Congress ended the Bracero Program. This set the stage for the changes in California farm labor which would occur over the ensuing decade.

The changing political climate in the fields was not only the result of continuing struggles by farm workers and organized labor. The civil rights movement was changing political institutions and popular consciousness throughout the United States. The middle class was awakened from its post-war somnambulism by the sight of blacks and whites staging sit-ins, demonstrations for equal education and employment, snarling police dogs and the violent reactions of southern bigots. Inner city riots and the rise of the black power movement provided further testimony that a spirit had gripped the oppressed. Students and the clergy became active supporters of movements for social change. The farm workers in California found support coming not only from trade unions, but from urban liberals and students as well. Civil rights activists from the Student Non-Violent Coordinating Committee (SNCC) and the Congress of Racial Equality (CORE) came to the aid of the farm worker union movement.

Less than six months after the end of the Bracero Program, the Coachella Valley in southern California was hit by farm worker strikes. In 1965, cries of *viva la huelga* ("long live the strike") drew national attention to the strike against grape growers in Delano, California. In 1966, two farm worker groups merged into the United Farm Workers (UFW) union, led by Cesar Chavez. The Delano strike gained momentum as a nation-wide boycott of table grapes, which by 1970 "had seriously eroded regular market outlets and substantially reduced grape sales" (Majka, 1978:150), demonstrated that the UFW and California farm workers had gained widespread support across the nation, signaling a significant shift in the historical confrontation between agribusiness and farm laborers.

It was against this background that the short-handled hoe became a focus of farm worker protest. A key factor in the eventual abolition of *el cortito* was the emergence of government institutions as advocates of the farm worker cause, and the state as an arena for the resolution of farm worker demands.

President Lyndon Johnson, in his State of the Union address of January 8, 1964, declared "unconditional war on poverty in America" as part of his campaign to build the "Great Society." Congress quickly passed Johnson's Economic Opportunities Bill of 1964, which he signed in August of that year and which led to creation of the Office of Economic Opportunity (OEO). This agency became a significant component of federal government efforts to both meet and channel the demands of social unrest. The legislation setting up the OEO contained a provision for legal service agencies for the disadvantaged. California Rural Legal Assistance (CRLA) was one of these agencies. The program was created and staffed primarily by young activist attorneys with close links to the civil rights and farm worker union movements. They believed legal action could significantly change the conditions of the oppressed. One CRLA attorney said:

For legal service attorneys, law reform means using the law, either through litigation, legislative or administrative rule-making, to attack the root causes of poverty to enhance the power of the poor (Heistand, 1970:178).

With the belief that a legal solution could reach the "root causes of poverty," together with the CRLA links to the farm workers and a social and political climate receptive to farm worker demands, the conditions were right for the short-handled hoe to become a public issue within the state arena.

EL CORTITO AND THE STATE

In 1969, CRLA attorney Maurice Jourdane and community worker Henry Cantú visited a labor camp for farm workers near Salinas. While taking testimony on housing complaints within the camp, they were challenged by a group of farm workers. As Jourdane recalled:

They had become frustrated over the lengthy process of questioning and checking details. One of them finally said: "This is bullshit! There are real problems for you to deal with, like *el cortito*." The entire group supported his demand. When we left the camp that night we talked and even joked about it some. But several more visits to the camp convinced us that the farm workers were serious, the short-handled hoe was the issue that concerned them (Personal interview, November 28, 1978).

Jourdane and Martin Glick, director of the Salinas CRLA, developed a strategy to transform the farm workers' challenge to the short-handled hoe into a viable issue of legal reform. Jourdane took charge of the campaign from 1969 until its successful conclusion in 1975. He first initiated an extensive research project, then lengthy hearings, litigation and lobbying. The CRLA strategy acknowledged the power and influence of agribusiness and sought to bring the issue into the arena most familiar and potentially most accessible to the attorneys. Agribusiness had traditionally exercised great power within the California state government; its interests were particularly well represented within the administration of Ronald Reagan, governor of California from [1967] to 1974. The CRLA

tried to avoid agencies such as the Department of Food and Agriculture, where the growers' influence was greatest. The attorneys further recognized that most administrative channels were dominated by people who shared Reagan's conservative, antilabor orientation. An avenue was sought which would allow the case to be made quickly and provide a legal appeal should the administrative action fail.

The Administrative Arena

Jourdane chose as his vehicle for change a health and safety standard within Title 8 of the California Administrative Code (Section 3316) which prohibited the use of unsafe hand tools. Jourdane knew this section had traditionally applied to the use of faulty or broken tools, but felt an effort to push for an expanded interpretation was promising since an adverse ruling by the administrative agency could immediately be appealed in the state courts. Seeking a new standard could linger for years in the administrative and legal review process. The choice of strategy reflected not only Jourdane's assessment of the political terrain, but also the principal function and assumption of the OEO mandate—to improve conditions for the oppressed through the courts. Wrote CRLA attorney Fred Heistand:

CRLA . . . has merely tried to implement what the judiciary, at least the Supreme Court, has been saying since the late 1930s: that the courts, not the legislatures, are the branch of government least responsive to immediate pressures, the branch with the greatest flexibility and opportunity, and thereby the greatest responsibility to safeguard and vindicate the rights of the poor (1970:179).

While the judiciary may be the most insulated branch of government, it is also the most selective. Interpretative action is premised upon a historically evolved structure of law and judicial precedence which selects from the array of possible issues, explanations and resolutions, those conditions and interpretations which most nearly approximate the existing legal and social relations (Offe, 1975). The courts can be flexible in their interpretations, and thereby responsive to social problems. But the task remained for the CRLA to develop the issue of *el cortito* in a manner that made the case viable within the established legal parameters. In so doing, the CRLA was redefining the farm workers' issue within the constraints of state policy.

Jourdane petitioned the Industrial Safety Board (ISB) of California's Division of Industrial Safety (DIS) on September 20, 1972, seeking prohibition of the use of *el cortito*.[4] This board held public hearings on complaints of occupational hazards and decided whether existing health and safety standards were applicable. By law, the ISB was composed of representatives of labor, management and the general public, all appointed by the governor. The ISB assembled under the Reagan administration virtually sealed the fate of the farm workers' case. The lone labor representative was the vice-president of Operating Engineers Local 3, San Francisco. The representatives of the public and management sectors included a former FBI agent and corporate director of an oil field equipment manufacturing firm, the supervisor of employee relations for a major gas company, and the owner of a construction company.

The CRLA attorneys were counting on the board's inexperience with both agricultural problems and legal challenges. The DIS had traditionally relied upon the California Attorney General's office for legal counsel and, consequently, the ISB lacked both the legal experience and supporting staff to cope with the intricacies of legal interpretations. The CRLA had set the stage to exploit its own strength and the board's weakness.

The ISB held public hearings on the CRLA petition in El Centro, California, on May 1, 1973, and in Salinas, California, on May 3, 1973. The CRLA came to the hearings with a strong case, built on four years of research and the efforts of a national network of legal aid attorneys, civil rights and farm worker activists, doctors, and the UFW. The attorneys argued that *el cortito* was a health hazard to farm workers. They presented the testimony of 11 doctors familiar with farm worker health problems to

support this claim. The declaration of Dr. David Brooks demonstrates the position held by all the doctors:

I can unequivocally say that the use of this hoe will often cause tissue injury and severe back pain, and later may result in degeneration of the intervertebral discs and other supporting elements of the spine, thereby causing pain, limitation of motion, increased vulnerability to severe injury, and in many cases, complete physical disability (Petition for hearing before the ISB, September 20, 1972: Exhibit M).

The demonstration of an occupational hazard is only part of the process by which a complainant can successfully eliminate a tool or practice under the occupational health and safety codes. A complainant must also meet the requirements of Section 6306 (a) of the California Labor Code, which provides that workers have a right to "such freedom from danger to the life, safety, or health of employees as the nature of the employment reasonably permits." The traditional interpretation of this section has required that not only must a hazard be demonstrated, but it must be shown that a viable alternative also exists, to meet the criteria of "reasonably permits."

The CRLA argued that long-handled hoes were as efficient as short-handled hoes. They presented as evidence the results of a national survey conducted by legal aid agencies in 1971 and 1972 (Petition for hearing before ISB, September 20, 1972:6–10); it showed that the long-handled hoe was used to cultivate the same crops in all other regions of the United States.[5] A representative from a California farm workers' cooperative testified that they had found that workers using long-handled hoes could sustain a productive pace over an entire day and work each day at this pace, while workers using short-handled hoes had fewer productive hours on subsequent days.

It became clear from the CRLA case against *el cortito* that the tool was a symbol to farm workers of the oppressive nature of farm labor. Repeated reference to contractors' and growers' preference for the short-handled hoe as a means of control served to heighten the image of brutality and oppression. Farm workers saw this case as a statement of changing power relations in agriculture.

They felt threatened when the people at the bottom said, "Heh, we're not going to be on our knees no more, we're gonna stand up." They didn't want the farm worker to stand up. Psychologically, that gives them some dignity. . . . When you are kneeling, it's showing humility. The majority of us are Catholics. We've been kneeling for years. It was time for us to overcome these things. We weren't going to be on our knees anymore (Personal interview: Hector de la Rosa, March 1, 1979).

The conflict over the short-handled hoe was symbolic to the growers as well. They saw the CRLA case as part of a growing threat to their power over the workers and the labor process. A spokesman for one of the largest agribusiness firms in the United States repeatedly referred to the case as "the UFW case," although the union played a minor role. The case challenged the grower's prerogatives over labor, as did the union movement, and the two were often indistinguishable to the growers in the overall conflict with farm workers.

The growers were no match for the CRLA. They had traditionally relied upon a government responsive to their interests and pursued questions of agricultural policy in agencies clearly linked to agricultural concerns. They came into this arena with the arguments that had traditionally sustained their demands. Medical evidence of the health hazard of the short-handled hoe was countered with disbelief or claims that sore and tired backs are part of hard work. The testimony of Robert Grainger, a grower in the Salinas Valley, is indicative:

People always complain about back problems. I've thinned and hoed and I'm a great big man. I've thinned lettuce along with workers when I was a younger fellow and I was starting out in the farming business, and it hurts and it hurts badly for about three or four days. Then after that you're in shape (ISB hearing, May 3, 1973:16).

The growers claimed that the short-handled hoe was the traditional tool for thinning and weeding and had not been the subject of complaint prior to the CRLA's intervention. Grainger's testimony again indicates the growers's line of argument:

The people that work for me, and have worked for me, take a great deal of pride in their work that they do, and they want to do it with the short-handled hoe, and we have a wonderful relationship. I have a crew right now. These people are all happy to be there. They're happy to do their work. They want the work done correctly and they do it with the short-handled hoe (ISB hearing, May 3, 1973:15).

Growers made further arguments that the farm workers must stoop to avoid damaging the plants while thinning and weeding, but were unable to provide evidence to support these claims.

Throughout the hearings the growers generally did not try to disprove the CRLA claims. Instead of countering CRLA evidence with their own, the growers seemed satisfied to provide their own opinions and denials as an adequate defense of *el cortito*. In a legal setting such opinions, without the kind of substantiating evidence that the CRLA submitted, would be inadequate in the face of the CRLA case. But the ISB was an administrative board, not a court of law. It was a board composed of appointees of governor Ronald Reagan and reflected the pro-business attitude of the Reagan administration. Consequently the power of the CRLA case was not as persuasive to the ISB as the views of the growers.

After deliberating for two months, the ISB denied the CRLA petition to ban the short-handled hoe on July 13, 1973, claiming the tool had not been demonstrated to be a hazard under Section 3316 of the California Administrative Code, Title 8. The board said a hazardous tool was one that was damaged or improperly maintained, not a tool that was a hazard due to its normal use. The ISB avoided the issues raised by the CRLA case and retreated into the traditionally narrow interpretation of the legal statute applying to unsafe hand tools (Section 3316). The board reiterated the traditional view of worker health and safety in a letter conveying its decision to the CRLA:

There are, in fact, many work operations that hasten aging of various body parts at varying rates according to individual resistance. . . . Very few of these conditions are logically controllable by safety orders, because such orders have few ways of adjusting to the fact that some people are quite resistant to the related aging process (*Sebastian Carmona et al. v. Division of Industrial Safety:* Petition for Writ of Review, October 11, 1973: Exhibit B).

In effect, the ISB placed the blame for injuries resulting from use of the hoe upon the farm workers. In so doing it located the source of the problem in the weakness of the individual worker, the traditional interpretation of occupational hazards (Berman, 1978; Cobb and Sennett, 1973).

The relationship between agricultural interests and the board was further demonstrated by an in-house memorandum, written by board member H. Howard White, which was brought to light by CRLA attorney Maurice Jourdane:

On May 3, 1973, three members of the Board visited a field owned by the largest lettuce grower in the Salinas Valley, wherein workers were using the short hoe. They visited the field with representatives of Interharvest. Mr. White noted in a memo that "We were all watching carefully for any evidence of discomfiture or even low morale, such as expressions or actions, or whatever. I observed literally none. Note that I visited two fields and the same situation existed in both."

Jourdane observed:

It is incredible that board members would go to a field with grower representatives and ex-

pect to see any complaint or indication of low morale by a worker. Obviously, the board has failed to consider how long a worker could expect to retain his job should he indicate dissatisfaction with his work in the presence of grower representatives (Petition for Rehearing, August 3, 1973:17).

On October 11, 1973, the CRLA filed a Petition for Writ of Review with the California Supreme Court. The petition maintained that the ISB had erred in its application of state occupational health and safety standards to the case of the short-handled hoe. The evidence from the original petition to the ISB, along with evidence from the public hearings, was submitted to the court for consideration. But Jourdane introduced one additional argument to the evidence. He stressed the burden to the taxpayer of unemployed farm workers injured by the short-handled hoe. While such an argument had little relevance to the legal code in question, it had a great deal to do with the agenda prepared by CRLA. In anticipating an appeal to the legislative arena and a public which had elected a conservative governor committed to cutting the cost of welfare, this argument successfully linked the case with a broader constituency by appealing not only to their moral sensibilities but their economic interests.

Agribusiness interests filed a brief in support of the ISB ruling. Attorneys for the Bud Antle Corporation, the largest lettuce grower in the world, argued in the brief that banning the short-handled hoe would be disastrous for the industry and consequently the consumer. But the productivity argument had not fared well in the hearings and did not convince the Supreme Court Justices either. On January 13, 1975, the California Supreme Court ruled that the ISB had interpreted its mandate too narrowly. While not ruling directly on the continued use of the short-handled hoe, the ruling did conclude that "the division has given the regulation an unduly narrow interpretation supported neither by the language of the regulation nor by the authorizing statutory provisions" (*Sebastian Carmona et al. v Division of Industrial Safety,* January 13, 1975).

The case came before the California Supreme Court during Jerry Brown's successful campaign for the governorship, based in large part upon a coalition sympathetic to the plight of the farm workers. As Asher Rubin, Deputy Attorney General, State of California, observed at the time of the ruling:

I cannot escape the feeling that the very fact farm workers were the plaintiffs here injected an emotional element into this case which distorted the court's perspective. But *post mortems* are counter productive. The Board and the Division must live with this decision and must conform their approach to the views expressed therein (Memorandum, Asher Rubin to Richard Wilkins, Chief, Division of Industrial Safety, January 15, 1975).

Following the California Supreme Court ruling the farm worker demand that the short-handled hoe be abolished received swift attention. Soon after Brown took office in January, 1975, he met with Cesar Chavez and Rose Bird, the director of the Agricultural and Human Services Agency of which the Division of Industrial Safety was a part, after CRLA complained about possible further delays in a final resolution of the case (Personal interview: Maurice Jourdane, November 28, 1978). Following this meeting Richard Wilkins, the Reagan-appointed Chief of the Division of Industrial Safety, took swift action. On April 7, 1975, he issued Administrative Interpretation Number 62, which stated: "the use of the short-handled hoe shall be deemed a violation of safety order Section 8 CAC 3316."

As DIS personnel later observed:

Wilkins could recognize, like everyone else, the political climate had changed. Jerry Brown was coming in, and the UFW had become an important influence in the new administration (Personal interview: William Becker and Michael Schneider, March 15, 1979).

The traditional strength of agribusiness in California politics had become a factor in undermining Republican political strength by rallying previously inactive sectors of the electorate. The farm worker movement and the liberal coalition within the Democratic party developed an interdependent relationship in opposition to agribusiness and the Republican political establishment during the early 1970s. The issue of *el cortito* became one of many links which cemented these political ties and brought Brown into office. Likewise, Brown's victory became the final step to implementing the California Supreme Court mandate and the farm worker victory.

The administrative interpretation effectively marked the end of the short-handled hoe. Grower efforts to retain its use soon subsided. Bob Antle, head of Bud Antle Inc. and a leader in the fight against the ban of *el cortito*, admitted he was wrong in his opposition to the abolition of the short-handled hoe. Antle compared the use of the short-handled hoe with the long-handled hoe and found the long-handled hoe could be substituted without loss of productivity (*San Francisco Chronicle*, 1975). A few growers have been cited for violation of Section 3316 and have received fines ranging from $100 for first offenses to $500 for second violations. No grower has yet been cited for a third violation, which would receive a fine of thousands of dollars.

The abolition of *el cortito* was heralded as a significant improvement in the conditions of farm labor, and an important victory for the CRLA and attorney Maurice Jourdane.[6] Jerry Brown and the UFW have both repeatedly claimed the banning of the short-handled hoe as one of their contributions to the farm worker cause (Personal interview: Maurice Jourdane, November 28, 1978).

EL CORTITO: THE PROBLEM AND THE SOLUTION

What have the farm workers gained by state intervention into the agricultural labor process? The CRLA case must be evaluated for what it did not accomplish as well as its success. The development of the case in relation to particular government codes, the identification of the problem as a hazardous tool as defined by Title 8, California Administrative Code, Section 3316, and the demonstration of a viable alternative consistent with the requirements of California Labor Code Section 6306 (a) were all part of a process of selective development within the legal arena (Offe, 1975). This arena limits the kind of problems and solutions it will examine. The precondition to protecting the health of the farm worker was the protection of the grower, through the requirement of an alternative means to maintain the existing productive activities and the labor/management relations they sustain. By identifying the problem as the hazardous use of a tool, the statutes deflected the attention away from the hazardous nature of production organized, directed and controlled by a corporation. Lawyers must present their cases with the selective criteria of this legal system in mind. While a changing political environment lends itself to new and more flexible interpretations, as this case demonstrates, there are nevertheless definite limits. The CRLA case did not, and could not, confront the questions of autonomy and control inherent in existing worker/management relations. Nor could the case challenge the organization of corporate agriculture, even though the hazards of *el cortito* are rooted in these conditions.

Clearly, the switch to the long-handled hoe has been an improvement in the conditions of the farm workers. Some growers have reported a significant decrease in Workers Compensation claims for farm worker back injuries since the ban (Personal interview: Maurice Jourdane, November 28, 1978). Conditions for farm worker organizing have also been affected by the ban of *el cortito*. With healthier workers and less turnover, union organizers can work with the same farm workers over entire seasons to build a base for union elections. The political fortunes of Jerry Brown and the UFW continue to be linked through their mutual reliance on state resources to solve problems, as exemplified by the ban on *el cortito*. Current cutbacks in state programs and spending may seriously alter future opportunities for this kind of mobilization around social change in the state arena.

The success of this case has also encouraged worker resistance to other conditions in the agricultural labor process. One farm worker indicated that lessons from the short-handled hoe case are being applied to challenging the hazards of farm worker pesticide exposure (Personal interview: Hector de la Rosa, March 1, 1979). This challenge involves a much more powerful array of interests and political institutions. Thus the case of *el cortito* has not only raised farm worker awareness of worker health issues, but has opened up questions of technology which implicitly question control of the labor process as well. A challenge to pesticide technology could reach much deeper into the organization of agricultural production than the case of *el cortito*.

The example of the CRLA attorneys and the farm workers who campaigned against the short-handled hoe is evidence of the on-going contribution people are making toward improving the conditions under which farm workers and many others must live and work. But the task remains to develop effective strategies and institutions which place more fundamental questions of control and autonomy at the center of these struggles for social change.

Notes

1. The term "grower" applies to those individuals who manage or control the daily decisions of agricultural production. They may be a farmer on a 100-acre farm, or a corporate executive in charge of thousands of acres. The organization of California agriculture is a model of corporate farming. Dominated by large production units, the smaller growers are integrated into the corporate structure through various marketing, labor contracting, financing, and university research institutions. Thus the notion of an independent small farmer has little relevance to the organization of California agriculture. Farms of all sizes are part of an integrated agribusiness structure.

2. See the photographs in the Ira B. Cross Collection, Bancroft Library, University of California, Berkeley.

3. Repression and violence toward farm workers has been a constant theme throughout California history. McWilliams (1971) remains one of the best overall sources for the pre-Second World War era. For an example of the Chinese farm worker experience, see Saxton (1971). Hoffman (1974) and Stein (1973) provide excellent accounts of the farm worker experience during the Depression. Galarza (1964; 1970) and Kushner (1975) are sources for the post-Second World War period.

4. The ISB was a board within the DIS. This division administered the health and safety codes relating to employment. The DIS was part of the Department of Industrial Relations (DIR), which in turn was part of the Agriculture and Human Services Agency, the highest level administrative body in the administration of governor Ronald Reagan [1966]–1974). Under the administration of Jerry Brown (1975 to [1983]), the Agriculture and Human Services Agency has been disbanded and the DIR has become the highest administrative body. The DIS and ISB have been replaced by the Division of Occupational Safety and Health (DOSH), and the California program of the federal Occupational Safety and Health Act of 1970 (Cal/OSHA). Cal/OSHA now enforces the ban on *el cortito*.

5. The accuracy of this survey is questionable. HB 487, a bill to ban the short-handled hoe, was adopted by the Texas Legislature in 1981, accompanied by evidence of its continued use in the state. On June 1, 1983, the Arizona legislature also adopted a ban of the short-handled hoe following a campaign by the UFW. Farm worker opposition to the tool has also been reported in New Jersey, where it is known as *el brazo del diablo*, "the devil's arm."

6. Jourdane later became a legal counsel on the staff of Governor Brown, and was appointed to a judgeship in Superior Court, Salinas, California, on February 26, 1982. He was sworn in by Cruz Reynoso, the first Hispanic on the California Supreme Court, appointed within weeks of Jourdane's appointment. Reynoso, like Jourdane, was an attorney known to have farm worker sympathies.

References

Berman, Daniel
1978   Death on the Job: Occupational Health and Safety Struggles in the United States. New York: Monthly Review.

Black, Donald
1973   "The mobilization of law." Journal of Legal Studies 2:125–149.

Chambers, Clarke
1952   California Farm Organizations. Berkeley: Univesity of California Press.

Cobb, Jonathan, and Richard Sennett
1973   Hidden Injuries of Class. New York: Random House.

Dunlap, Thomas R.
1981   DDT: Scientists, Citizens, and Public Policy. Princeton: Princeton University Press.

Galarza, Ernesto
1964   Merchants of Labor: A Study of the Managed Migration of Farm Workers in California, 1942–1960. Santa Barbara: McNally and Loftin.

1970   Spiders in the House and Workers in the Fields. Notre Dame: University of Notre Dame Press.

Goldfrank, Walter J.
1975   "World system, state structure, and the onset of the Mexican revolution." Politics and Society 5 (4):417–439.

Greenberg, Jack
1959   Race Relations and American Law. New York: Columbia University Press.

Gutman, Herbert G.
1966   Work, Culture and Society in Industrializing America. New York: Random House.

Heistand, Fred J.
1970   "The politics of poverty law." Pp. 160–189 in Bruce Wasserstein and Mark J. Green (eds.), With Justice for Some: An Indictment of the Law by Young Advocates. Boston: Beacon Press.

Hoffman, Abraham
   1974   Unwanted Mexicans in the Great Depression. Tucson: University of Arizona Press.
Kushner, Sam
   1975   Long Road to Delano. New York: International Publishers.
Lipsky, Michael
   1968   "Protest as a political resource." American Political Science Review 62:1144–1158.
McCarthy, John D., and Mayer Zald
   1977   "Resource mobilization and social movements: A partial theory." American Journal of Sociology 82:1212–1241.
McWilliams, Carey
   1971   Factories in the Fields: The Story of Migratory Farm Labor in California. Santa Barbara: Peregrine.
Majka, Theo
   1978   "Regulating farmworkers: The state and the agricultural labor supply in California." Contemporary Crises 2:141–155.
Oberschall, Anthony
   1973   Social Conflict and Social Movements. Englewood Cliffs, N.J.: Prentice-Hall.
Offe, Claus
   1975   "The theory of the capitalist state and the problem of policy formation." Pp. 168–185 in Leon Lindberg, Robert Alford, Colin Crouch, and Claus Offe (eds.), Stress and Contradiction in Modern Capitalism. Lexington, Mass.: D.C. Heath.
Perelman, Michael
   1977   Farming for Profit in a Hungry World. Montclair, N.J.: Allendale, Osman.
San Francisco Chronicle
   1975   "Praise for long hoes." April 15:20.
Saxton, Alexander
   1971   The Indispensable Enemy; Labor and the Anti-Chinese Movement in California. Berkeley: University of California Press.
Stein, Walter J.
   1973   California and the Dustbowl Migration. Westport, Conn.: Greenwood.
Stone, Katherine
   1974   "The origins of job structures in the steel industry." Review of Radical Political Economy (Summer):61–79.
Tilly, Charles
   1978   From Mobilization to Revolution. Reading, Mass.: Addison Wesley.

Case Cited

Sebastian Carmona et al. v. Division of Industrial Safety. 13 C. 3d 313, January 13, 1975. California Supreme Court Number: S.F. 23053.

Codes Cited

Title 8 California Administrative Code, Section 3556 (b). Register 75, No. 13:March 29, 1975. Formerly 8 CAC 3316 (a).
California Labor Code, Section 6306 (a). (West, 1981:343).

Appendix

The following unpublished documents are filed in the Department of Industrial Relations, State of California, 525 Golden Gate Avenue, San Francisco, California. See file titled "The Short-Handled Hoe Matter":

Petition that the Division of Industrial Safety Prohibit the Use of the Short Handle Hoe. September 20, 1972.

Hearing before the Industrial Safety Board, May 1, 1973. El Centro, California (Transcript).

Hearing before the Industrial Safety Board, May 3, 1973. Salinas, California (Transcript).

Petition for Rehearing before the Industrial Safety Board. August 3, 1973.

Memorandum from Asher Rubin, Deputy Attorney General, to Richard Wilkins, Chief, Division of Industrial Safety. January 15, 1975.

Administrative Interpretation Number 62, Division of Industrial Safety. April 7, 1975.

13
Gatekeepers and Homeseekers: Institutional Patterns in Racial Steering

Diana M. Pearce

Editors' Introduction

Our social stratification system sorts people not only on the basis of social class distinctions but also on the basis of such distinctions as race and gender. The latter two are often referred to as distinctions of caste, implying that they are elements of a rigid system of social distinctions that people cannot readily overcome. (While the strict meaning of the term *caste* refers to a hereditary social group in which everyone has the same economic and social position, it is often broadened to refer to the castelike dimensions of race and gender in what is supposed to be an open class system.)

Diana Pearce's illustrative reading deals with the dimension of race. Race clearly is still a very important factor in the life experiences of people in our society. According to the U.S. Census, in 1980 there were 26,488,218 blacks living in the United States, comprising about 12 percent of the population.[1] There is some reason to believe that blacks represent a slightly higher proportion of the population than this. While the census misses a number of people, it appears to miss more urban lower-class people than people in other categories. Since blacks are overrepresented among the urban poor, they are probably systematically undercounted in the census.

The situation of blacks has improved somewhat in recent years. For example, in 1980 black students comprised about 10 percent of all college enrollments, up from 5 percent in 1965. Between 1965 and 1980 white college enrollments increased by about two-thirds, while black enrollments almost tripled.[2] However, although people often think that the economic status of blacks relative to whites also has steadily improved, this is not the case. According to the census (which probably misses some poor blacks), in 1970 black median family income was about 61 percent of that of white families. In 1980 it fell to about 57 percent of median white family income.[3] (The median is the midpoint when all the cases are lined up in order of size. Therefore, median family income is the income at the middle, when all family incomes are ranked from lowest to highest.)

Although blacks represented about 11 percent of all employed persons in 1980, they were heavily overrepresented in some occupations and underrepresented in others. For example, blacks comprised about one-fourth of file clerks, textile operators, and taxi drivers, and just over half of household servants. They comprised about 8 percent of police officers and detectives, 8 percent of accountants, 4.5 percent of sales managers, and 2.1 percent of real estate agents.[4]

It is with this last occupational group that Diana Pearce is concerned. In this reading she examines equality of housing opportunities for blacks and whites, studying the practices of real estate agents in Detroit, Michigan, as they are approached by black couples and by white couples seeking to buy homes. Pearce does not say, but presumably most or all of these real estate agents were white. The home-seeking "couples" were actually research investigators, keeping careful track of their experiences with the agents, the number of houses shown to them, and the quality, price, and location of each house they saw.

In attempting to explain continued residential segregation in an open social and legal context, Pearce begins by focusing on institutional racism. What does she mean by this? How is it usually practiced? Why is it *institutional* racism? Next, ask yourself *how* Pearce collected her data. How did she find out if blacks were being discriminated against by the real estate agents? Look at the evidence on discrimination. Was the discrimination subtle or blatant? What was Pearce's evidence? (You will have to take some time with the section on evidence. However, if you follow Pearce's argument carefully, you will see a nicely constructed test of a theory.) Finally, look at Pearce's conclusions. What modification does she make in the concept of *institutional racism*? Is this modification warranted on the basis of her findings? What policy implications does she discuss? Are only the real estate agents to blame for these practices?

Pearce treats the subjects of discrimination and inequality of opportunity with a conflict orientation. The mere existence of a caste dimension suggests that some group in society is maintaining its advantage at the expense of another group. The practices of institutional racism, as demonstrated in this selection, are subtle ways for whites to maintain their relatively advantaged position over blacks. Go back to the Eitzen reading in Part One and review the assumptions of the conflict and order models of society. It will help you understand the role of institutional racism. Incidentally, you might try to explain the practices outlined by Pearce from the order orientation to see how the arguments differ.

The section of this reading on "Design of the Study" is especially important. This is the only study in this book that illustrates an experiment (in this case, a field experiment). In an experiment the researcher alters the independent variable (in this case, the race of the homeseekers) and examines the results of this alteration, under carefully controlled conditions. Watch how Pearce attempted to "equalize" variables other than the race of these house-seeking couples (age, number of children, amount of education, and so on). Why did she do this? Also, notice how the real estate agents were selected and "tested." Remember that the real estate agents are the real subjects in this experiment. Pearce is changing the race of the homeseekers in order to see the effect this has on the actions of the agents.

This selection clearly demonstrates the practical uses of sociology. Pay special attention to the policy implications of the study, as presented in Pearce's conclusions. Guiding social policy is one of the many practical (and too often ignored) uses of the sociological perspective and of specific research findings.

For additional readings dealing with race, see Gary Marx's study titled "Religion: Opiate or Inspiration of Civil Rights Militancy?" in Part Four and the material on the civil rights movement in Jo Freeman's "On the Origins of Social Movements" in Part Six.

Notes

1. Andrew Hacker, ed., *U/S: A Statistical Portrait of the American People* (New York: Viking Press and Penguin Books, 1983), p. 34.
2. Hacker, p. 247.
3. Hacker, p. 145.
4. Hacker, p. 129.

The segregated housing patterns documented by the Taeubers (1965) from 1940 to 1960 have remained basically unchanged, and seem to show no signs of substantial alteration towards desegregation in the seventies (Hermalin and

Reprinted from *Social Problems*, 26, 3 (February 1979), 325–342, with selected omissions. Used with permission of the Society for the Study of Social Problems and the author.

The author would like to thank the following people whose comments and criticisms of this paper were most helpful: John Tropman, John Johnstone, Diane Colasanto, Dennis Roncek, James Norr, and the anonymous reviewers.

Farley, 1973; Van Valey *et al.*, 1977; Sorenson *et al.*, 1975; deLeeuw *et al.*, 1976). Although more whites may be exposed to token integration (as maintained by Bradburn *et al.*, 1971), the predominant residential experience of Americans today remains that of the monoracial neighborhood. During this same time period, however, the legal supports for discrimination in housing have been largely destroyed. The Supreme Court outlawed racially restrictive covenants in 1948, and twenty years later it declared that all aspects of property transactions must be colorblind (*Jones versus Mayer*), thus broadening the already comprehensive

Fair Housing Act of 1968 just passed by Congress.

White attitudes towards racial integration in housing have also become more positive (Greeley and Sheatsley, 1971; Pettigrew, 1973; Campbell, 1971).[1] The steadily increasing acceptance of equal opportunity in housing over the past several decades has been matched by a decline in the number of whites who believe that they have the right to keep blacks out of their neighborhoods (the percentage decreased from 53 percent in 1963 to 46 percent in 1976 [Taylor et al., 1978]). Although the support for integration of residential neighborhoods fades rapidly above token levels (Farley et al., 1977), white dislike of residential integration is more often expressed by flight than by a fight. On balance, it seems clear that blacks today are not being prevented from moving into all-white neighborhoods by strong and violent resistance of prejudiced white homeowners and landlords to prospective black neighbors.

Three theoretical approaches have been used to explain the paradox of continued segregation and housing inequality within an "open" social and legal context. The first set of theories asserts that the phenomenon is really self-segregation, the result of preferences of blacks, as with other ethnics, to live in segregated neighborhoods. The second suggests that poverty, aided by the inertia of history, has perpetuated segregation. The third suggests that the decline of blatant discrimination of the past has revealed pervasive institutional racism.

Although in this paper we will present data in which we control experimentally for black housing preferences and economic circumstances, it is worth noting some of the previous work that sheds light on the viability of the other hypotheses. First, although black income continues to lag behind white, and the evidence is not at all clear that the gap is closing (Levitan et al., 1975; Farley, 1977), it is also true that black homeownership is considerably less than "expected" on the basis of income. That is, taking white homeownership patterns at various income levels as the expected, blacks do not approach the homeowning percentage of whites (von Furstenberg et al., 1976), nor are

they represented in suburban areas in the proportion expected on the basis of their income or housing expenditures (Hermalin and Farley, 1973). Second, depending in part on how the question is worded, a minority of from 13 percent to one-third of blacks prefer all black neighborhoods (Brink and Harris, 1967; Campbell and Schuman, 1968). As the Taeubers have pointed out, however:

In a society where white prejudice and discrimination against Negroes account for much of the attraction of living within an all-Negro community, and at the same time help account for the exclusion of Negroes from other neighborhoods, it seems impossible to separate coercive and voluntary components of segregation (1965:23).

In contrast to the above interest in the "voluntary" sources of segregation, there is the theory of institutional racism. In this theory racial inequality is seen as the result of the operation of normal rules and procedures that are equally (and often blindly) applied but are unequal in effect. Height requirements or aptitude tests systematically excluding minority applicants are common examples of institutional racism. It is often emphasized that such practices have the effect but not the intent of limiting or excluding minorities from full participation in the life of that institution (see Blauner, 1972). The original formulation of the idea, however, by Carmichael and Hamilton, conceived of the institution as acting *in lieu of* individual action, in ways that were perhaps more subtle but not necessarily less intentional or effective than individual action would have been:

[Institutional racism is] . . . acts by the total white community against the black community. . . . [It is] . . . less overt, far more subtle, less identifiable in terms of *specific* individuals committing the acts. But it is no less destructive of human life (Carmichael and Hamilton, 1967:4; italics in original).

Here, we wish to use institutional racism to describe actions, taken in an institutional context, that produce or continue differential and unequal treatment by race. We do not imply that such actions are unintentional or automatic, only that discriminatory acts are an integral part of the normal/normative *modus operandi* of that institution.

If neither the preferences nor the limited finances of black homeseekers explain housing segregation, does the model of institutional racism describe the operation of the housing market, and thus suggest at least one reason for the persistence of such segregation? In other words, does the housing market, in the course of its normal sequence of operations systematically limit or exclude financially equal blacks from full and equal access to housing?

In order to answer that question, we have chosen to concentrate on one aspect of the housing market. Many individuals and organizations make up the housing market and play a part in any one housing transaction—from the newspaper editor who first runs the ad for the house to the banker who signs the closing papers. But it is the professional real estate agent[2] who plays the key role, for both the market and individual homebuyers (Hempel, 1969). In consumers' eyes, real estate agents (compared to bankers or builders, for example) are frequently seen as the most expert in nearly every aspect of decision making involved in buying a house (Hempel, 1969). As a group they are not only experts, they also control access to housing areas. They are, or can be, community gatekeepers, and often may see their own role as architects of the social structure of the community, and a crucial aspect of the gatekeeper role is the screening of potential residents (Helper, 1969; Palmer, 1955). The advantages to the homebuying public of the real estate agents' professional expertise may come at the price of having the agents exercising their own discretion, for example, about whether to withhold information or exclude some people from certain geographic areas, or both.

We shall approach the problem of whether a model of institutional racism helps explain the paradox of continued housing segregation by focusing on the actual behavior of these key actors in the housing market, real estate agents.

In particular, we will address two questions. First, do real estate agents exercise their discretion and use their expertise in ways that result in treatment that is racially unequal? Second, can the racial practices described here be characterized as institutional racism?

DESIGN OF THE STUDY

The research reported here was part of an experimental field study of real estate agents' practices. In order to answer the first question posed above—whether agent discretion is used to provide racially unequal services—the study was designed to "sample," in as unobtrusive a manner as possible (Webb, 1972), each agent's behavior towards two homeseeker couples who were basically alike except for race. The couples were all in their late twenties, had two children, and needed a house with at least three bedrooms. The woman was not working. The man had a job that required a college education, such as engineer, teacher or office manager, and had a steady work history. Each couple indicated that they were new to homebuying, as well as to the area or community. Each pair of couples visiting a particular agent had roughly the same stated income and savings. (The black couple's income was slightly higher to avoid suspicion.) The incomes were set at approximately 10 percent above the 1970 median income (as reported in the census) of the community in which the particular agent was located. Basically, then, each agent was faced with two homeseeker couples, one white couple and one black couple, who presented the same housing needs and preferences, the same financial abilities, and the same geographic preferences.

The "couples" were actually trained and paid interviewer/participant observers.[3] They did not take notes, except to make "back of the envelope" calculations or jot down addresses, as would be natural for real homeseekers. They quickly acquired good memories, however, and the accuracy of recall was enhanced by the use of an exhaustive Recording Form. Immediately after the visit to the broker, they completed the form, which can be described as a self-administered interview schedule that "debriefed"

Table 1

The Showing of Homes by Real Estate Salespersons

Number of Salespersons Who Showed Homes:	
To the black couple only	2
To both the black and white couples	23
To the white couple only	46
To neither couple	30
Total	97

Note: There were eight additional black couples to whom the salesperson did not offer to show homes, but agreed with the couples' requests to "see homes," only to drive them around and "show" homes as they drove by. Homes were counted as shown only if the couple were taken inside the home by the salesperson.

them on their experience. The form was seven pages long, with an added page for each house seen, and took twenty to thirty minutes to complete. It covered numerous details of the interview and its setting, as well as the agent's words and actions—from their entrance to their exit from the office.[4] Use of this form resulted in finely graded measures of discriminatory behavior by the agents in several areas without creating an artificial and rigid set of stimuli. While the lack of "controls" on the process of the interview resulted in some unique and noncomparable data, it also resulted in a degree of naturalness frequently missing in field experiments. To the extent that we have been successful in creating genuine-appearing homeseekers, the experiences reported here *directly,* not by analogy or extrapolation or reinterpretation, reflect the real-life differences in treatment of black and white couples who seek to buy homes through a real estate agent.

Ninety-seven real estate agents, from the approximately ten thousand in the Detroit metropolitan area (Detroit and its suburbs), were randomly chosen.[5] The interviews were conducted between May, 1974 and March, 1975. Each agent was visited first by a black couple,

and then several weeks later by a white couple. In order to obtain the same agent, the white couple asked by name for the agent seen by the black couple, but used a vague referral rather than the black couple's name such as, "Somebody at the office got your name from a neighbor who just moved from _____ City."[6]

The interviews, which lasted from one to two hours on the average, could be broken into two major parts. (There were no follow-up visits.) First, the agent discussed with the couple their finances, the ins and outs of financing a mortgage, how to select a house that fit their budget and their preferences, advice on FHA and MGIC, and so forth. Second, the agent discussed neighborhoods and/or showed homes to the couple. It is the second part of the interview that is reported and discussed here.

FINDINGS

Frequently the first part of the interview ended with a look at the listings book, which lists all houses currently for sale, arranged by price and geographical area, and including for each house a brief description and a picture. At this point, if the agent did not offer to show homes, the couple requested to see some homes with the salesperson; such requests resulted in ten more *white* couples seeing homes than would have otherwise, while it did not change the number of black couples who were actually shown homes. Overall, the chances of seeing a house on the first visit to a real estate agent are 1 out of 4 if you are black, but almost 3 out of 4 if you are white, other things being equal. Even when homes were shown to blacks, fewer were shown per couple, so that overall only one-fifth of the homes shown were seen by the black couples [Table 1].[7]

Note that there is no mention of the homeowner. In fact few of the couples met homeowners, and if they did, the contact was minimal. This was not accidental, for real estate agents consider themselves to be skilled professional salespeople, and do not wish to have the amateur homeowner sabotage the sale through a well-meaning but disastrous confession about the house's history or faults, or through personally offending the potential buyer. The same was true of the negotiations over purchase price, for again both the buyer's and the seller's agent will emphasize that they are more adequately prepared to bargain effectively than are their inexperienced clients. The end result is that homeseekers may see the homeowner when they are shown the house, but they are unlikely to meet the owner(s) until the closing of the sale. It is not surprising, then, that there were no slammed doors or hurled epithets by homeowners.[8] While the real estate agents may claim that they are acting on behalf of the homeowner, it is rare that anyone but the agent has the opportunity to refuse to show a home or homes to black homeseekers.

The efforts of black homeseekers to be shown homes by the agents were not met with strong or dramatic refusals. Instead, their requests were frequently met with reasonable sounding excuses, such as "no key," "need to make an appointment ahead of time," or with offers to show homes at some later date. In contrast, the same request to see homes, when it came from white homeseekers, was more often honored. Thus, the racially differentiated treatment of homeseekers in the showing of homes by real estate agents is gross in magnitude, but benign in execution. The lack of insult or apparent mistreatment of black couples becomes, upon comparison with the white couples' treatment, a cover that masks unequal treatment.

Comparisons of Homes Shown

We defined discrimination as actions that "limit or exclude financially equal blacks from full and equal access to housing." Many blacks are clearly excluded; but were those who were shown homes also discriminated against? In the latter cases, our real test of discrimination is whether blacks are shown homes that are in the same condition, and in the same areas, as those shown whites. On the assumption that a major cause of residential segregation is black exclusion from white areas, and not the reverse, our primary empirical question is whether blacks have access to predominantly white areas. Not

only have very few whites expressed preferences for moving into all-black neighborhoods, but in the recent instances where whites have attempted to move into central city black neighborhoods, a process sometimes called "gentrification," they have met with little effective black resistance.

Given that being shown homes at all is problematic for the black couple, when they *are* shown homes, how do these homes compare with those shown white couples? Specifically, are the homes shown to blacks and the homes shown to whites characterized by (a) the same prices, (b) the same quality and (c) the same locations? While clearly different, these three characteristics are not independent, for house price is usually seen as the dependent characteristic. That is:

House Price = F(House Location, House Quality).

Thus, the first question is whether there is any variation, by race, in the average house price. As can be seen in Table 2, the homes shown the blacks are systematically less expensive, averaging $3300 less than the homes shown whites (t = 2.69, p < .01).[9] Using the house price equation, there are a number of logical explanations of this difference in prices of homes shown:

1. The *same houses* were shown, but the blacks were quoted lower prices.
2. Houses in the *same location* or neighborhood were shown, but blacks were shown houses of lesser quality (i.e., smaller size, older or poorer condition).
3. Houses of the *same quality* were shown, but in different locations such that the houses shown to blacks were in neighborhoods with generally less expensive homes.

Since the homeseekers did not request to see a specific home, the first explanation seems implausible: in fact only three homes were seen by both black and white couples. Let us examine first the possibility of house quality as the reason for lower house prices of houses shown blacks; note that by quality we are referring to strictly

Table 2

Stated Prices of Homes Shown to Homeseekers, by Their Race

Price Group	Percent of Houses Shown Blacks That Are in Price Group (N = 34)	Percent of Houses Shown Whites That Are in Price Group (N = 123)
$15–19,900	12	2
20–24,900	35	20
25–29,900	24	36
30–34,900	18	24
35–39,900	9	11
40–44,900		6
45–49,900	3	2
Total	100	100
Mean House Price	$26,900	$30,200
Mean Difference = $3300, t = 2.69, p < .01		
Percent told stated price was negotiable	48	38

physical characteristics, such as size and condition of the home. Thus we will use location to refer to all other aspects of a house, such as the neighborhood, quality of schools, crime rate, pollution, and level of amenities and services that might contribute to the selling price of that house.

The homeseekers were asked to record basic descriptive characteristics of each house shown (e.g., number of bedrooms) and then compare the house with others in the neighborhood. As can be seen in Table 3, both in terms of characteristics and in relative comparison to the neighborhood there was no significant difference in the average quality of homes shown blacks and whites. It seems, then, that almost none of the difference in the average price of homes shown is attributable to the poorer quality of houses shown black homeseekers.

In order to determine the importance of location as a determinant of house price differences, the average housing value of the city or suburb where the house was located, the average housing value of the community where the real estate firm was located, and the distance from black population areas were compared by race. First, the cities and suburbs where the real estate firms were located were rank-ordered by mean value of owner-occupied housing units using the 1970 census figures, and the sample was divided into thirds. That is, a third of the salespersons visited were in offices located in higher-priced housing communities, a third were in medium-priced communities, and a third were in lower-priced communities. The expected distribution of houses shown, then, would be that roughly a third of the houses shown would fall in each housing value group. Although *all* the homeseekers were shown housing lower in value than would be expected from the communities' housing values, compared to whites, blacks were shown disproportionately more houses in lower-priced communities [Table 4].

It is apparent then, that some of the difference in the prices of houses shown stems from the location of the houses, for the mean housing value in the communities where blacks were

Table 3

Characteristics of Neighborhoods and Houses Shown by Race of Homeseekers

Characteristics of Houses Shown	Percent of Houses Shown to Blacks (N = 34)	Percent of Houses Shown to Whites (N = 124)	Chi-Square	Significance Level
Quality				
Three or more bedrooms	99	100	.53	n.s.
Basement	97	85	3.12	n.s.
Garage	93	80	.70	n.s.
Single Family	100	100	—	—
Isolated from other houses	6	1	.65	n.s.
Comparison to Other Houses in Neighborhood:				
Size				
Same as other houses in neighborhood	74	80		
Neighborhood houses varied in size	13	4		
Other	13	16		
	100	100	3.49	n.s.
Style				
Similar in style to other houses	59	72		
Neighborhood houses varied in style	26	13		
Other	3	15		
	100	100	3.48	n.s.
Age				
Similar in age to other houses	90	83		
Neighborhood houses varied in age	10	7		
Other	0	10		
	100	100	3.52	n.s.

shown housing is about $700 lower for blacks than the mean housing value of the communities where whites were shown homes. Nevertheless, much of the house price differences of $3300 remains unexplained. An anomalous finding that also remains unexplained is the high percentage of homes shown to blacks in *higher* priced areas; we will return to this later.

Some of the effect of house location may be due to racial composition, both of the immediate neighborhood and of those nearby. To examine this possibility, each of the homes shown was located on a census map and the 1970 racial composition of the tract and the block was recorded. Panels A and B of Table 5 quite clearly portray that the likelihood of a white couple seeing a home in a block or tract with black families was quite low (less than 10 percent for either block or tract). Similarly, two out of three of the black couples were also shown homes in all-white census tracts, and almost all of the remaining one-third were shown homes in areas with quite small percentages of blacks (1 to 15%). A similar pattern for the block data may be discerned. Clearly, most of the homes shown to both blacks and whites were in areas that were all-white in 1970.

It is not unlikely that some of these areas that were all white in 1970 became racially mixed between 1970 and 1975, or were likely to become so in the near future. To assess this possibility, three measurements were made from each house to the nearest black population area.[10] These were: distance from the house to the nearest census tract that was 5 to 49 percent black; distance to the nearest tract that was 50 to 89 percent black; and distance to the nearest tract that was 90 to 100 percent black. Clearly there was not a random distribution of the homes shown to blacks and whites (Table 6). Well over half the homes shown to blacks were within one mile of areas with 5 to 49 percent black population, and only a quarter of the homes shown whites were within a mile of such areas. The same difference in patterns is apparent for each measure—with striking regularity. Almost half the black couples' houses were within two miles of ghetto areas (90 to 100% black tracts). In sum, houses shown to blacks were nearly a mile closer to black areas, on the average, than the houses shown to whites.[11]

To assess the importance of distance from black population areas on the difference in prices of houses shown, distance from black areas[12] was correlated with house price for both races. For both blacks and whites, the correlation between house price and distance from ghetto areas is less than might be expected, but it is much greater for blacks than whites (.39 and .16 respectively). This suggests that distance from black population areas is only important relatively close to those areas. Because the houses shown to whites average over a mile

Table 4

Firms Visited and Location of Houses Shown, by Housing Value Group and by Race of Homeseekers

Housing Value Group[a]		Percent of Couples of Each Race Sent to Firms in Group	Percent of Homes Shown in Cities and Suburbs in Group to:	
			Blacks	Whites
Lower-Priced Communities		34	61	51
Medium-Priced Communities		32	5	32
Higher-Priced Communities		34	35	16
		100	100	100
	(N)	(97)	(31)[b]	(109)[b]
Mean Housing Value of Communities Where Houses Shown		$25,442	21,481	22,185

[a]Mean housing values for cities and suburbs as reported in the 1970 census; communities with mean housing values of $22,800 or less were in the lower-priced group; those with housing values between $22,900 and $25,700 were in the medium-priced group; and those with housing values over $25,700 were in the higher-priced group.
[b]The total N's in this table are somewhat reduced from previous tables because some houses could not be located, and some were unincorporated areas and/or outside the Detroit SMSA.

Table 5

Racial Composition of Neighborhoods Where Houses Shown

Racial Composition of House Location	Percent of Houses Shown to Blacks (N = 34)	Percent of Houses Shown to Whites (N = 123)
Census Tract (percent black)		
Zero	65	92
1–5	15	3
6–15	15	2
16–50	0	1
51–100	3	1
N.A.	3	2
Total	100%	100%
Mean Percent Black*	4.05	1.02
Specific Block (percent black)		
Zero	76	91
1–5	12	3
6–15	6	2
16–50	0	0
51–100	3	1
N.A.	3	2
Total	100%	100%
Mean Percent Black**	3.0	1.05

*Mean Difference = 3.03, t = 1.89, n.s.
**Mean Difference = 1.95, t = 1.15, n.s.

Table 6

Distance from Black Population Areas of Houses Shown, by Race of Homeseekers

Mean Distance in Miles	Houses Shown to Blacks (N = 34)	Houses Shown to Whites (N = 123)	Mean Difference	t-test	Level of Significance
To Nearest Census Tract, 5–49% black	1.09	1.97	.88	3.43	p < .001
To Nearest Census Tract, 50–89% black	2.22	2.94	.72	1.75	p < .10
To Nearest Census Tract, 90–100% black	2.89	4.06	1.17	2.16	p < .05

further out from these areas, other things being equal, a house that is very close to or in racially mixed or black areas may have a *lower* price, but as one gets further out, it is not likely to have a *higher* price. . . .

Location and Racial Steering

In the discussion above, we used measures of distance from black population areas on the assumption that linear distance may measure meaningful social distance. City boundaries and intra-city neighborhood boundaries create much more distance than is shown in the hundred-foot width of a street. Put another way, the likelihood of black families moving from a mixed neighborhood on one side of the street to a previously all-white neighborhood on the other side of the street is much higher in parts of northwest Detroit than it is from southwest Detroit into all-white Dearborn. For example, a BBC reporter doing a documentary on race relations in the United States was told that Eight Mile Road (the northern boundary of Detroit) was the Mason-Dixon line of Detroit. Not only the major thoroughfares, but different land uses, transportation patterns and chance factors create and divide the metropolitan area into somewhat discontinuous communities (see Suttles, 1972). To the extent that the city racial composition is a series of communities that "shade" into each other gradually, physical distance is an accurate reflection of social distance. To the extent that there are impermeable boundaries instead, which at the extreme divide a 100 percent black population on one side from a 100 percent white population on the other, a physical distance of one block does *not* reflect the social distance.

This phenomenon of social distance is reflected in the patterns of racial steering found here in two ways. First, blacks, more often than whites, were shown houses *not* located in the city where the sales agent's office was located; that is, they were steered "out of town." Second, where and whether houses were shown to black couples depended upon the location of the sales office within the suburban ring. The totals in Table 7, columns 2 and 3, show that the chances were significantly greater for whites to be shown houses in the same city as the real estate office's location (56% vs. 33%, p < .05). Moreover, when whites were "steered out," about four-fifths of the cities where they were shown houses were nearby white suburbs. In contrast, when blacks were "steered out," two-thirds of the houses shown were in the racially mixed cities of Inkster and Detroit. Detroit alone accounted for almost a third of the homes shown to blacks, although only 13 percent of the firms were located in the central city (see Table 7).

The skewed patterns of locations of houses shown blacks is even more apparent in Table 7. Not only did black couples see a disproportionate number of houses in Inkster and Detroit, they were "steered" there disproportionately by firms located in the western, southern and eastern shore suburbs. . . .

As can be seen in Table 7 the geographic subareas fall into groups, indicated here as Pattern A (Discriminatory) and Pattern B (Nondiscriminatory) suburbs. By comparing the percentage of firms located in each area (column 1) with the geographic distribution of homes shown (columns 2 and 3) these patterns become clear. While the Pattern A suburbs, in which 50 percent of the firms visited were located, accounted for approximately 50 percent of the homes shown to whites, these suburbs accounted for only about one-fifth of the homes shown to blacks; moreover, the homes shown were almost in all areas that were predominantly black. In contrast, while only a third of the firms visited were in Pattern B suburbs, 45 percent of the homes shown to blacks were in Pattern B suburbs, and their locations were scattered throughout the area.[13]

Racial Steering: Wealth, History and Ecology

The fact that black couples were more often shown homes and urged to buy homes in areas that are racially mixed is not surprising, but the distinctive geographical concentration both in the showing of homes and the steering of people "out" is an unexpected finding. Why were blacks more often shown homes in the suburbs

Table 7

Geographic Location of Homes Shown, by Geographic Location of Salesperson's Office, by Race

Geographic Location of Salesperson's Office	Percent of Firms Visited Located in Geographic Area	Percent of Homes Shown Located in Geographic Area, by Race												Percent of homes shown located in same city as salesperson's office	
		Pattern A Suburbs:						Pattern B Suburbs:				Detroit			
		Southern		Western		Eastern Shore		Northwestern		North Central		Detroit			
		Black (N=0)	White (N=10)	Black (N=6)	White (N=32)	Black (N=1)	White (N=14)	Black (N=9)	White (N=27)	Black (N=5)	White (N=9)	Black (N=10)	White (N=17)	Black	White
Pattern A Suburbs															
Southern	8	0	0	0	0	0	0	0	0	0	0	6	0	—	60
Western	31	0	0	19	29	0	0	0	0	0	0	6	5	0	62
Eastern Shore	10	0	0	0	0	0	11	0	0	0	1	0	2	0	60
Subtotal	49	0	10	19	29	0	11	0	0	0	1	12	7		
Pattern B Suburbs															
Northwestern	25	0	0	0	0	0	0	29	25	0	0	0	0	78	48
North Central	11	0	0	0	0	3	2	0	0	16	7	6	0	25	50
Subtotal	36	0	0	0	0	3	2	29	25	16	7	6	0		
Detroit	13	0	0	0	0	0	0	0	0	0	0	13	9	100	100
Total	100	0	10	19	29	3	13	29	25	16	8	32	16	100	100

north and northwest of Detroit (Pattern B suburbs) than elsewhere? We will consider three possible explanations here: wealth, historical patterns and an ecological argument.[14]

First, if one calculates the mean housing values for each of the geographic groupings,[15] their rank order is as follows: Detroit ($16,100), Southern ($19,950), Western ($24,658), North Central ($24,736), Eastern Shore ($29,970), Northwestern ($31,858). Except for the Eastern Shore suburbs, it was the areas with somewhat more expensive housing in which disproportionately more homes were shown to blacks, in spite of the fact that more of the housing shown to blacks was less expensive. Thus, not only are relative housing values not an explanation of differential steering behavior between geographic areas, but the tendency of agents in the higher housing value suburbs (northern and northwestern) to show houses more often to blacks runs counter to the overall tendency for more expensive areas to be more discriminatory on measures of discrimination other than steering, such as the amount of time spent with the couple, and amount of advice given.

The paradox of blacks being shown homes that averaged lower prices (by about $3,000) but were located in higher-priced housing areas (the north and the northwestern suburbs) does account for an anomaly noted earlier. That is, the housing shown blacks is located disproportionately not only in *more* expensive areas, but also disproportionately in *less* expensive areas; the moderately-priced communities are underrepresented as places where houses were shown to blacks, and are concentrated geographically in areas west and south of Detroit.

A second explanation of this anomaly rests on historical patterns, both of racial succession and of metropolitan growth. There has been a century long pattern of the Detroit ghetto's expansion in a northwest direction (Deskins, 1972). Historically, black expansion (especially in the middle class) followed Jewish residential movement (Wolf, 1957). Wolf, Mayer (1960) and others have documented the transition in Detroit from Jewish-dominated neighborhoods to majority black neighborhoods in the 1950's and 1960's. It may be that the pattern will re-

peat itself (on the same geographic axis) in the Northwestern suburbs and that this is the very beginning of the pattern.

Third, . . . there is only one large concentration of black population outside the Detroit ghetto, and that is the suburb of Inkster to the west of Detroit.[16] In many ways that city may be seen not as a smaller version of the Detroit ghetto, but rather as a suburb that "happens" to have a large black population.[17] Home ownership is high (72%), housing values (in 1970, $17,800) are above those of Detroit, and most of the housing is single family. Presented with would-be black suburbanites, then, it is possible for the real estate agent in the western or southern suburbs "legitimately" to show housing in Inkster, for it is suburban in character and location as well as racially mixed. North of Eight Mile Road (the northern boundary of Detroit), on the other hand, there is no concentration of black suburban population. Without an obvious place to steer would-be black suburbanites, they were shown homes in a variety of communities, although many were close to the edge of the city.

SUMMARY AND CONCLUSIONS

The patterns of racial steering examined here begin and end with the fact that most blacks did not experience racial steering simply because the majority of blacks were not shown homes on the first visit to the real estate office; the majority of whites, however, were. Not only were black homeseeker couples seldom shown homes at all, but also the manner and method used in such refusals made the detection of discrimination very difficult. The first type of gatekeeping, then, was to keep the gate closed for all but a minority of black homeseekers. Needless to say, it is difficult to purchase a home if one is not shown any.

If black couples were shown homes, they were likely to be:

1. Less expensive, averaging $3300 less than the average house shown to whites. This was apparently not because the houses shown were of relatively poorer quality, but rather due to

their location in cities with overall lower housing values and/or their location closer to black population areas.

2. Located, paradoxically, in the (more expensive) suburbs to the north and the northwest of Detroit, as well as in the (less expensive) suburb of Inkster and the city of Detroit.

Clearly, then we have found a consistent pattern of racially differentiated treatment of homeseekers, both in the showing/not showing of homes, and in the price and location of homes shown.

But is this treatment, clearly differentiated by race, aptly characterized as "institutional racism"? First of all, the data show that these are not isolated instances of individual racism. Although there are differences between communities, there is a high level of consistency across the entire metropolitan area: the clear existence of practices that exclude three-fourths of black couples from ever seeing homes, and "steers out" many of the few that do see homes, strongly suggests a strong consensus among real estate agents about the desirable demographic character that Detroit communities should assume.

Next, most real estate agents belong to real estate boards, and many belong to NAREB, the National Association of Real Estate Boards. Whether or not one is formally a member of NAREB, it exerts a powerful influence over the real estate profession as a whole, and far beyond it as well. NAREB now supports Open Housing Laws, but that support has been somewhat circumscribed (see Yinger, 1975); and it vigorously opposed such laws at the local as well as national level until about 1968. While one can only guess what NAREB's role is in the discrimination documented here, both directly and indirectly NAREB has supported policies and practices that more often than not have been discriminatory in effect.

Finally, these data do document discrimination that took place during personal interviews, whereas institutional racism is often seen as "no fault" discrimination. That is, the unequal outcomes are portrayed as the accidental byproducts of actions taken for purposes other than

racial exclusion. Certainly one cannot attribute intention solely on the basis of the sort of data we obtained on the real estate agents' actions (and inactions); but their actions are far from random and it is highly unlikely that they are done blindly or unwittingly.

I would argue, therefore, that a clear answer to the question of whether the manifest differences in treatment afforded black and white homeseekers is institutional racism, requires reconceptualization of institutional racism. As a start, I think we must first reject the image of an automaton heedlessly and helplessly grinding out differential treatment. We also should not attribute discrimination to a handful of people, anomalous individuals whose discrimination against blacks contrasts with the behavior (and perhaps norms and values) of the majority of their peers. In fact, it is precisely because the individual real estate agents are typical, both in their communities and their professions, that these practices can be characterized as institutional racism (see Pearce, 1976).[18]

The conclusion that the racially discriminatory practices described here are institutional in nature has some important implications for housing policy aimed at reducing discrimination. First, open housing laws and litigation which are based implicitly on individual racism models, are going, so to speak, to affect a few trees, but miss the forest. Nearly a decade after the passage of federal legislation and a landmark Supreme Court decision, there has not been even one large lawsuit about housing, one affecting a significant number of people.[19] In contrast, in school desegregation and employment discrimination, which have been attacked on the institutional level, laws and court decisions have had comparatively more impact. As long as it is assumed in the general legislation, and as long as lawyers and judges assume generally that the problem in housing discrimination is that of a few individual homeowners (or real estate agents who step out of line), practices such as those described here will continue to perpetuate housing segregation. As Mayhew (1968) concluded in his analysis of the Massachusetts Commission Against Discrimination, case by case litigation is inadequate and inappropriate as a means to deal with institutional practices. The use of the leverage of government power to change institutional practices, however, should be in addition to, not a substitute for, the enforcement of the law against the most blatant discrimination by individuals.

To concentrate, however, on institutional racism implies concentration on litigation and/or legislation aimed at practices of groups of real estate agents, whether or not they are associated formally. To move laws and policies in this direction is difficult, however, for it is no longer possible to find formal and/or open declaration of discriminatory regulations and rules at the institutional level. Today, the enforcement of discriminatory norms is informal, largely beyond the reach of the law. Thus, real estate boards can be forced *not* to expel a member who sells nondiscriminatorily, but they cannot be forced to compel their members to cooperate with that agent in making sales (and without cooperation few agents would sell very many houses). Indeed, much of the discrimination described here is beyond the reach of present law, for basically, it involves *inaction*, rather than actions specifically proscribable by the law—acts for which an individual or organization could be held responsible.

Government power, however, in actions such as withholding mortgage insurance (e.g., FHA), housing subsidy programs or community development block grants has never been used effectively to combat racial segregation. At times it has even promoted such segregation (Lawson, 1971). For example, H.U.D.'s requirement that grant applications include Housing Assistance Plans, i.e., plans for housing for low income people, could be made into more than unread paperwork.[20] Also, whether positive incentives or negative sanctions are used, such efforts seek to prevent the development of mini-ghettoes, such as Inkster. Even small suburban enclaves are enough, apparently, to absorb black housing demand, resulting in limited suburbanization but not desegregation of black suburbanites.[21]

Finally, the fact that discrimination in housing is institutional should not blur the responsibility for the racist practices described here.

While individual agents must be held responsible for their own actions, as well as their professional associations' implicit support of discrimination, it is also clear that white suburban community residents must recognize their role. Their tacit, if not explicit, approval of realtors' behavior is an important factor in the continued exclusion of blacks from their neighborhoods and community. And of course, although not dealt with in detail here, the role of other actors in the housing market (e.g., mortgage lenders and real estate appraisers) also contributes to the "web of racism" in the housing market (U.S. Department of Housing and Urban Development, 1977). As long as there is an implied value consensus among real estate agents, white communities and mortgage lenders—that whites' freedom to live where they want, and to leave when they want, is more important than blacks' rights to equal access to equal housing—then institutional racism in housing will remain.

Notes

1. Three *caveats* should be noted about this trend: First, the white acceptance is of Negro neighbors of similar socioeconomic status; second, the changes noted may be only in what people feel is the verbally acceptable response and not necessarily either their real feelings or related to their likely reactions if a Negro neighbor *did* move next door; third, the majority of whites are much less willing to accept more than token integration of their neighborhoods (see Farley *et al.*, 1977).

2. Legally "broker" is reserved for those who have a broker's license (obtained in Michigan after serving a three-year apprenticeship as a sales associate), and all others are "sales associates"; in this paper we will use the simple term "agent" to refer to all those who buy, sell and list real estate. It should also be noted that Realtor in its capitalized form is a copyrighted word, referring to members of the boards belonging to the National Association of Real Estate Boards. Again, in common usage, realtor is used interchangeably with broker, but real estate agent will be used here.

3. The homeseekers were forty people whose

real backgrounds reflected a great deal of diversity. About half were graduate students in sociology, social work, political science, and psychology; the rest included a librarian, a trumpet player, an actor, a dental student, and a marriage counselor. Some were real couples, and some were not. Neither student status nor being a real couple explained variation in treatment (see Pearce, 1976).

4. Although each individual filled out a form separately, for simplicity's sake we report here a combined black and a combined white observation. For a discussion of differences by sex and race, which are systematically apparent only on the subjective evaluations of the interview *in toto*, see Pearce (1976).

5. Because it would have been unrealistic *and highly artificial* for a white couple to have sought housing in areas that were all or nearly all-black in racial composition, real estate agents located in these areas were eliminated from the sample (N=7). Some were eliminated because they dealt only in commercial real estate (N=8), or because the *pair* of interviews was not successfully completed because the agent became ill, left the business or the office closed (N=14). The total of ninety-seven interviews thus represents agents in white or racially mixed areas who saw a black couple and a white couple.

6. Referrals are a source of about a third of a real estate agent's customers according to Hempel (1969), so homeseekers' explanations were not seriously questioned by the agents.

7. While it is possible that black homeseekers might have been shown homes on subsequent visits to the agent, it should be emphasized that the gatekeeping being exercised in the first visit is intrinsically important, for it is likely to discourage any but the most persistent black homeseeker from ever trying again. Also, while subsequent visits may result in seeing homes, it is likely that the homeseeker will experience steering of the kind described above.

8. Only two instances of homeowner-homeseeker contact were at all negative—one white couple and one black couple met owners who did not want to sell to them.

9. More blacks than whites were told that the price was negotiable (see Table 2). This is puz-
zling, as it implies that the blacks were being offered the possibility of a better deal; given that only a quarter of the real estate agents even showed homes to the black couples, some may have sincerely wished to enhance the likelihood that the black homeseekers buy a house. Or it may also be true, since blacks were shown homes in areas that were closer to black neighborhoods (see below), that the sales agent believed that whites would "panic" and sell at less than the stated price (believing that this black household would be followed by others). Apparently that belief has led real estate agents to encourage whites to sell at lower prices, making a belief into a self-fulfilling prophecy (see Helper, 1969; Wolf, 1957). A less sanguine approach is that the real estate agent would be able to later use the lack of the seller's price reduction as a means to prevent a sale, by suggesting that the black couple would be paying too much if they paid the stated price. Finally, it may just be a random difference; that is, the group of homes shown to blacks by chance included a few more sellers who were willing to bargain.

10. The underlying assumption in making these measurements is that racial succession between 1970 and 1975 occurred at roughly the same rate all along the edge of black population areas.

11. Note that the racial composition data is that of 1970 while the houses were seen in 1974 and 1975. To the extent that the racial composition of Detroit neighborhoods has not changed "regularly" between 1970 and 1975 (i.e., racial change has not occurred at the same rate at all edges of the ghetto), the distance figures will be inaccurate. Since more of the houses seen by blacks were in census tracts close to or contiguous to census tracts with some black population in 1970, it is probable that more of these areas have experienced an increase in the percent black between 1970 and 1975. This suggests that the percent black of the census tracts is underestimated to a greater extent for the houses shown to blacks than for the houses shown to whites.

12. Since "distance to nearest census tract with 90 to 100% black" showed both the greatest difference by race and the widest variation, it was used here.

13. Compared to ten white couples, twenty-one black couples were "steered out," frequently to racially mixed communities.

14. The reader should be reminded that it is the *showing* of homes, not their *purchase* that is being discussed. Strictly speaking, it is possible that blacks may be shown housing in these areas more than other areas precisely because the real estate agent is confident that it will not result in a purchase. That is, the agent assumes that the blacks would not be able to obtain a mortgage (because of mortgage discrimination, or lack of money, or both), or the homeowner would refuse to sell, or the couple would find it undesirable or too expensive to move to that area. On the other hand, while institutional racism in the mortgage market and other institutional barriers to black homeownership are important in the total picture of racism in the housing market, it is risky for an agent to count on such factors in any one particular situation. In addition, such an explanation is somewhat in conflict with the evidence presented above that blacks were, on the average, shown homes closer to black areas and in less expensive areas, and homes that were priced lower—all of which would enhance the chances of a black couple obtaining a mortgage.

15. These means are weighted by the number of firms in the community in the sample which in turn approximates the relative size of the suburbs (particularly their relative portion of the housing market).

16. There is a small unincorporated area on the northern edge of Detroit, contiguous with the ghetto, that is 100% black (Royal Oak Township). It seems to be an extension of the ghetto, rather than a suburb like Inkster.

17. Inkster was created to house black autoworkers separately from the white autoworkers; the latter lived, and still live, in Dearborn, an all-white suburb of Detroit.

18. The real estate agents studied were "liberal" in their racial attitudes, but tended to be the most discriminatory. Also, those who were the most business-like in orientation, and to some extent the more successful, tended to be more discriminatory. In other words, it is not the marginal members of the profession, but rather those who are well integrated into the institution, who account for more of the discrimination. For further discussion of this aspect of the study, as well as other measures of discrimination used, see Pearce, 1976.

19. This statement pertains to housing discrimination cases only, i.e., those involved in the selling or brokeraging of houses. While large real estate firms have been sued, there has not been a "class action" suit involving a large number of defendants and/or plaintiffs (with the exception of a Bergen County case). In related areas, however, such as zoning cases (alleging racially discriminatory intent in local zoning ordinances), there have been large-scale cases.

20. There have been some instances of effectively wielded local community pressure around the issues of housing discrimination, resulting in delays, modifications, and even some changes in the allocation of federal government monies. Unfortunately, these are seldom publicly announced, and have little impact from one community to another.

21. In fact, in the last year or so, one of the Northwestern suburbs has discovered the beginning of such a "mini-ghetto." Their efforts to deal with the problem, however, are exacerbated by the institutional character of the steering and the discrimination. Unlike the past, they cannot pinpoint a few "block-busting" agents or bigoted homeowners and thereby halt the process of resegregation.

References

Blauner, Robert
    1972   Racial Oppression in America. New York: Harper and Row.

Bradburn, Norman B., Seymour Sudman and Galen L. Gockel with the assistance of Joseph R. Noel
    1971   Side by Side: Integrated Neighborhoods in America. Chicago: Quadrangle Books.

Brink, William and Louis Harris
    1967   Black and White. New York: Simon and Schuster.

Campbell, Angus
1971 White Attitudes Toward Black People. Ann Arbor: Institute for Social Research.

Campbell, Angus and Howard Schuman
1968 Racial Attitudes in Fifteen American Cities. Ann Arbor: Survey Research Center–Institute for Social Research.

Carmichael, Stokely and Charles Hamilton
1967 Black Power: The Politics of Liberation. New York: Vintage.

deLeeuw, Frank, A. B. Schnare and R. J. Struyk
1976 "Housing." Pp. 119–178 in William Gorham and Nathan Glazer (eds.), The Urban Predicament. Washington, D.C.: The Urban Institute.

Deskins, Donald R., Jr.
1972 Residential Mobility of Negroes in Detroit, 1837–1965. Ann Arbor, Michigan: Michigan Geographical Publications, Department of Geography, University of Michigan.

Downs, Anthony
1968 "Alternative futures for the American ghetto." Daedalus 97 (Fall): 1331–1365.

Farley, Reynolds
1977 "Trends in racial inequalities: Have the gains of the 1960's disappeared in the 1970's?" American Sociological Review 42:189–208.

Farley, Reynolds, M. Schuman, S. Biardi, D. Colasanto and S. Hatchett
1977 "Chocolate city, vanilla suburbs: Will the trend toward racially separate communities continue?" Unpublished paper, University of Michigan.

Greeley, Andrew M. and Paul B. Sheatsley
1971 "The acceptance of desegregation continues to advance." Scientific American (December):13–19.

Helper, Rose
1969 Racial Politics and Practices of Real Estate Brokers. Minneapolis: University of Minnesota Press.

Hempel, Donald
1969 The Role of the Real Estate Broker in the Home Buying Process. Storrs, Connecticut: University of Connecticut.

Hermalin, Albert I. and Reynolds Farley
1973 "The potential for residential integration in cities and suburbs: Implications for the busing controversy." American Sociological Review 38: 595–610.

Lawson, Simpson
1971 "Seven days in June: The great housing debate." City 5:17–25.

Levitan, Sar, Willima Johnston and Robert Taggart
1975 Still a Dream: The Changing Status of Blacks Since 1960. Cambridge: Harvard University Press.

Mayer, Albert J.
1960 "Russel Woods: Change without conflict: A case study of racial transition in Detroit." Pp. 52–86 in Nathan Glazer and Davis McEntire (eds.), Studies in Housing and Minority Groups. Berkeley: University of California Press.

Mayhew, Leon M.
1968 Law and Equal Opportunity: A Study of the Massachusetts Commission Against Discrimination. Cambridge, Massachusetts: Harvard University Press.

National Advisory Commission on Civil Disorders
1968 The Kerner Commission Report. New York: Bantam Books.

Palmer, Stuart H.
1955 "The role of the real estate agent in the structuring of residential areas: A study in social control." Unpublished doctoral dissertation, Yale University.

Pearce, Diana
1976 "Black, white, and many shades of gray: Real estate brokers and their racial practices." Unpublished doctoral dissertation, University of Michigan.

Pettigrew, Thomas F.
1973 "Attitudes on race and housing: A

social psychological view." In Amos H. Hawley and Vincent Rock (eds.), Segregation in Residential Areas: Papers on Socioeconomic and Racial Factors in the Choice of Housing. Washington, D.C.: National Academy of Sciences.

Schuman, Howard
1971   "Free will and determinism in public beliefs about race." TRANS-Action (December):44–48.

Sørenson, Annemette, K. E. Taeuber and L. J. Hollingsworth, Jr.
1975   "Indexes of racial residential segregation for 109 cities in the United States, 1940 to 1970." Sociological Focus 8 (April):125–152.

Suttles, Gerald
1972   The Social Construction of Communities. Chicago: University of Chicago Press.

Taeuber, Karl and Alma F. Taeuber
1965   Negroes in Cities: Residential Segregation and Neighborhood Change. Chicago: Aldine.

Taylor, D. Garth, Paul B. Sheatsley and Andrew Greeley
1978   "Attitudes toward racial integration." Scientific American (June):42–49.

U.S. Department of Housing and Urban Development
1977   Redlining and Disinvestment as a Discriminatory Practice in Residential Mortgage Loans. Washington: Government Printing Office.

Van de Berghe, Pierre
1967   Race and Racism: A Comparative Perspective. New York: Wiley.

Van Valey, Thomas, W. C. Roof and J. E. Wilcox
1977   "Trends in residential segregation: 1960–1970". American Journal of Sociology 82 (January):826–844.

von Furstenburg et al. (eds.)
1976   Patterns of Racial Discrimination, Vol. 1: Housing. Lexington, Massachusetts: D. C. Heath and Company.

Webb, Eugene J., Donald T. Campbell, Richard O. Schwartz and Lee Sechrist
1972   Unobtrusive Measures: Nonreactive Research in the Social Sciences. Chicago: Rand McNally.

Wolf, Eleanor P.
1967   "The invasion-succession sequence as a self-fulfilling prophecy." Journal of Social Issues 13:31–39.

Yinger, John
1975   An Analysis of Discrimination by Real Estate Brokers. Madison, Wisconsin: University of Wisconsin.

14
Confessions of a Househusband

Joel Roache

Editors' Introduction

"Pink is for girls, and blue is for boys." "What a delicate little thing she is!" "Have you ever seen such a big strapping fellow?" All of these may be heard from proud parents, as they look through the hospital nursery window and see newborn babies of the same size. These comments derive from another important kind of social differentiation, that based on ideas about biological sex. Since such ideas also include notions of social ranking, they become another aspect of the caste dimension of the stratification structure. The dimension of gender includes cultural definitions of sex roles and the expectations associated with them. There is considerable confusion about the term *gender*. Sometimes it is used to refer to biological sex only and sometimes only to the "psychological, social, and cultural components" that have become attached to biological sex.[1] A simple solution is to use it to refer to both biological sex and these other components.

The social and cultural components attached to gender show clearly in the stereotypes commonly held about the attributes of men and women. Women have been considered naturally dependent, passive, nurturant, nagging, and emotional, in contrast to the societal values on independence, activity, achievement, tolerance, and intellectuality, which are believed to be characteristic of men. Each gender is assumed to have certain characteristics *by nature,* and more of the characteristics attached to men than to women are deemed to be desirable. The idea that these characteristics come from nature has been challenged through several types of research.

Some very interesting findings have resulted from studies of hermaphrodites, individuals born with both male and female genitalia and reproductive organs. While there are very few full hermaphrodites, a number of babies are born whose genitalia are ambiguous. Money and Ehrhardt have followed up such babies, especially those who were assigned one sex at birth but who later were determined to be genetically of the other sex. They report that in virtually every case the gender of rearing dominates—the boys raised as girls act like "girls," while the girls raised as boys act like "boys."[2] It is clear that *socialization* is an important influence in producing sex-typed behavior.

In the following reading Joel Roache shows another source of the kinds of behavior that people often think are produced by nature. He explores the role of the housewife—by undertaking that role himself. (Notice that this is a case of adult socialization.) He and his wife decided to share the housework and child care in their family—with some very interesting consequences. They made this decision in order to free his wife for other work she needed to do, her work outside the home.

To what extent are women working outside the home today? According to the 1980 census the wife is in the labor force in about half of all marriages. The mother is in the work force in about 54 percent of families with children under eighteen years old and in about 45 percent of the families with children under six years of age.[3] How much money do women make, in relation to the earnings of men? For full-time year-round workers in 1980, the median (middle) income of all working women was 60.5 percent of the median income of men. Translating this into dollars and cents, women earned 60.5 cents for each dollar earned by men. Professional women earned just under 66.5 cents for each dollar earned by professional men, while in sales, women earned 49 cents on the male dollar. Women with four years of high school earned just over 59 cents on the male "high school" dollar, while women with five or more years of college earned just under 65.5 cents on the dollar earned by men with this level of education.[4] Several factors are operating here: occupational segregation of women in low-paying occupations, lower pay for "female" occupations than for "male" occupations demanding similar levels of skill and responsibility, years spent out of the occupational structure in child rearing, problems women have faced in getting promotions, ideas about what occupations—and pay levels—are suitable for men and for women, and so on. (Keep in mind that these data are for median earnings of full-time year-round workers, so working part-time is not a factor here.)

What about the division of work in the home as women take a larger and larger part in the labor force outside the home? The evidence is that there are few changes in most families, whether the wife works outside the home or not.[5] Housework and child care are still primarily female responsibilities. However, in the following reading, Roache and his wife made a firm decision to share the housework equally. Through this decision and his own experiences Roache came to understand that the "female" characteristics he had seen in his wife were a function of the *role*, not of the person.

As you read, notice the stages that Roache went through in his feelings about housework. What happened to his relationships with his children? What happened to his relationship with his wife? What was the crucial event that made him realize that he was a full-fledged "househusband"? And what insights did he gain about his earlier perceptions of himself and his wife? In the last couple of paragraphs Roache extends his new insights about power relationships to any hierarchical structure. What do these insights imply about the institutions of the nuclear family and the economy?

Roache arrives at his conclusions through analysis of his personal experience. He makes sense out of this experience through the lens of the conflict model, coming to understand that the characteristics he had thought "natural" in his wife are characteristics that result from a social position of subordination. Roache explores the feelings about oneself and others that flow from positions of dominance and subordination, connecting them to societal structures of privilege based on class and race, as well as on gender.

There are some additional readings on gender and sex roles in other parts of this book. Recall LeMasters' study in Part One of life in a tavern, in which the men talk about the women and the women talk about the men. In Part Two Lever's study of sex differences in the complexity of children's play helps us understand how children learn the contents of traditional sex roles. In Part Six Freeman's studies of the origins of social movements include a discussion of the dual origins of the contemporary women's movement.

Notes

1. Laurel W. Richardson, *The Dynamics of Sex and Gender,* 2d ed. (Boston: Houghton Mifflin, 1981), p. 5. For the alternate definition, see Marie Richmond-Abbott, *Masculine and Feminine* (Cambridge, Mass.: Addison-Wesley, 1983), p. v.
2. Lenore Weitzman, "Sex-role Socialization: A Focus on Women," p. 159 in Jo Freeman, *Women: A Feminist Perspective,* 3d ed. (Palo Alto, Calif.: Mayfield, 1984).
3. Andrew Hacker, ed., *U/S: A Statistical Portrait of the American People* (New York: Viking Press and Penguin Books, 1983), p. 93.
4. Hacker, pp. 148–149.
5. Richmond-Abbott, p. 225.

Many men are coming to realize that sex-role privilege inflicts enormous damage on them, turning half of humanity into their subordinates and the other half into their rivals, isolating them and making fear and loneliness the norm of their existence. That ponderous abstraction became real for me in what many men consider a trivial realm: housework.

Every movement produces its truisms, assumptions that very soon are scarcely open to argument. The Women's Movement is no exception, and one of its truisms is that the home is a prison for women, trapping them in housework and child care, frustrating and distorting their need for fulfillment as whole persons. Whatever reality lies behind many situation comedy stereotypes—the nag, the clinging wife, the telephone gossip—is rooted in this distortion. Only after *I* had assumed the role of househusband, and was myself caught in the "trap of domesticity," did I realize that the reality behind those stereotypes is a function of the role, not the person.

Two years ago, my wife Jan and I tried to change (at least within our own lives) society's imposed pattern of dependent servant and responsible master by deciding to share equally the responsibility of housework. We made no specific arrangement (a mistake from which I was to learn a great deal); it was simply understood that I was going to take on roughly half of the domestic chores so that she could do the other work she needed to do.

There was something of a shock for me in discovering the sheer quantity of the housework, and my standards of acceptable cleanliness fell rapidly. It became much easier to see my insistence on neatness as an inherited middle-class hang-up now that I had to do so much of the work myself. One of the long-standing sources of tension between Jan and me was almost immediately understood and resolved. What's more, I enjoyed it, at first. When not interrupted by the children I could, on a good day, do the kitchen and a bedroom, a load of

Reprinted from *Ms.* Magazine, November 1972. Used with permission of the author.

laundry, and a meal in a little over two hours. Then I'd clean up after the meal and relax for a while with considerable satisfaction. So I approached the work with some enthusiasm, looking forward to seeing it all put right by my own hand, and for a while I wondered what all the fuss was about.

But within a few weeks that satisfaction and that enthusiasm began to erode a little more each time I woke up or walked into the house, only to find that it all needed to be done again. Finally, the image of the finished job, the image that encouraged me to start, was crowded out of my head by the image of the job to do all over again. I became lethargic, with the result that I worked less efficiently; so that even when I did "finish," it took longer and was done less well, rendering still less satisfaction. At first I had intellectual energy to spare, thinking about my teaching while washing dishes; pausing in the middle of a load of laundry to jot down a note. But those pauses soon became passive daydreams, fantasies from which I would have to snap myself back to the grind, until finally it was all I could do to keep going at all. I became more and more irritable and resentful.

Something similar happened even sooner and more dramatically to my relationship with our three children. I soon found myself angry with them most of the time, and I almost never enjoyed them. Then I watched myself for a couple of days and realized what was going on. They were constantly interrupting. I had tried simply to be available to them in case they needed me while I went on reading, writing, cleaning, or watching television. But of course with a six-year-old, a four-year-old, and a one-year-old, *someone* would need me every five to fifteen minutes. Just enough time to get into something, and up Jay would come with a toy to be fixed, or Matthew would spill his juice, or Eric would get stuck between the playpen bars and scream. In everything I tried to do, I was frustrated by their constant demands and soon came, quite simply, to hate them; and to hate myself for hating them; and at some level, I suspect, to hate Jan for getting me into this mess. My home life became a study in frustration and resentment.

I soon reached the conclusion that if I was going to keep house and take care of the children, I might as well give up doing anything else at the same time if I hoped to maintain any equilibrium at all. So I deliberately went through my housekeeping paces in a daze, keeping alert for the children but otherwise concentrating on whatever was before me, closing down all circuits not relevant to the work at hand. I maintained my sanity, I think, and I ceased to scream at the children so much, but neither they nor anyone else got the benefit of any creative energy; there just wasn't any. In half a day I could feel my mind turning into oatmeal, cold oatmeal, and it took the other half to get it bubbling again, and by then it was bedtime; and out of physical exhaustion I would have to go to sleep on whatever coherent ideas I might have got together in my few hours of free time.

Things went on this way for quite some time, partly because I couldn't think of an acceptable alternative, and partly because I was on a kind of guilt trip, possessed by the suicidal notion that somehow I had to pay for all those years Jan was oppressed. After a while I began to "adjust"; even cold oatmeal has a certain resilience. I began to perceive my condition as normal, and I didn't notice that my professional work was at a standstill. Then Jan became involved in community organizing, which took up more and more of her time and began to eat into mine, until finally I found myself doing housekeeping and child care from eight to sixteen hours a day, and this went on for about eight weeks. The astonishing thing now is that I let this masochistic work load go on so long. I suppose my guilt trip had become almost equivalent to a woman's normal conditioning, in reducing my ability to resist effectively the demands of Jan's organizing. And the excitement of her newly discovered self-sufficiency and independence (after eight years of her struggle to make me recognize what I was doing to her) functioned in the same way as the normal assumption of the superior importance of a male's work as provider.

I can pinpoint the place in time when we saw the necessity for a more careful adjustment of responsibilities, defining duties and scheduling hours more precisely and adhering to them more faithfully. It was at a moment when it became clear that Jan's work was beginning to pay off and her group scored a definite and apparently unqualified success. I went around the house for a full day feeling very self-satisfied, proud of her achievement, *as if it were my own,* which was fine until I realized, somewhere near the end of the day, that much of that sense of achievement resulted from the fact that I had no achievement of my own. I was getting my sense of fulfillment, of self-esteem, *through her,* while she was getting it *through her work.* It had happened: I was a full-fledged househusband.

A similar moment of illumination occurred at about the same time. Jan had spent the afternoon with a friend while I took care of the children and typed a revision of the bibliography for the book I was trying to finish at the time, the kind of drudgery more prosperous authors underpay some woman to do. By the time Jan got home I was in a state of benumbed introversion, and when she began to talk about the substance of her afternoon's conversation, I was at first bored and finally irritated. Before long I was snapping at her viciously. She sat there looking first puzzled, then bewildered, and finally withdrawn. In a kind of reflexive self-defense she cut me off emotionally and went on thinking about whatever was on her mind. As I began to run down, I realized that what she had been trying to talk about would normally be interesting and important to me, yet I had driven her away. Then I looked at her and suddenly had the really weird sensation of seeing myself, my own isolation and frustration when I used to come home and try to talk to her. I realized that I was in her traditional position and felt a much fuller understanding of what that was. In that moment, on the verge of anger, an important part of what we had been doing to each other for all those years became clearer than it had ever been to either of us.

Another problem was suddenly clear to me also. The loneliness and helplessness I had felt before we traded responsibilities had been a function of my own privilege. My socially defined and reinforced role as *the* responsible party to the marriage had cut me off from Jan's experience; had made inevitably futile our attempts to communicate with each other from two very different worlds. Since she has a strong sense of herself as a responsible adult, Jan was bound to resist the limits of her role as dependent and (though we would never have said it) subordinate. When I found myself muttering and bitching, refusing to listen, refusing to provide any positive feedback on her experience in the outside world, I realized that her preoccupation, her nagging and complaining, her virtual absence from my psychic world, had not been neurotic symptoms but expressions of resistance to my privilege and to the power over her life that it conferred.

Jan's failure to force a real change in our life together for so long is a grim tribute to the power of socialization, and to my ability to exploit that power in order to protect myself from reality. When Jan realized how really minimal were the satisfactions of housework, there was also a voice within her (as well as mine without) suggesting that perhaps she was just lazy. If she began to hate the children, she knew that it was because they were helping to prevent her meeting real and legitimate personal needs, but the voices were always there hinting that the real trouble was that she was basically a hateful person and thus a poor mother. If her mind became sluggish, she knew at some level that she was making an adaptive adjustment to her situation, but those voices whispered in a thousand ways that she might be going crazy, or perhaps she was just stupid. And when she became sullen and resentful toward me, the voices were always there to obscure her perception that I had it coming. They even encouraged her to feel guilty, finally, when she did not feel my success as her reward, the payoff for all her drudgery. They kept her from realizing that such a payoff cost her a sense of her independent selfhood; that it was at best the pittance of exploitation: shit wages for shit work.

Those voices, within and without, kept reminding us both that Jan's real destiny was to keep me comfortable and productive and to raise "our" children. The feelings I'd come to experience in a few months had for years made

Jan feel lazy, selfish, and egotistic; unable to empathize with the needs of the family (read: my need for success). Just as importantly, her knowledge that the sources of her troubles were not all within herself could not have received any reinforcement in the social world. I was her only link with that world; my affection and "respect" were her only source of assurance that she was real. To the extent that identity depends on recognition by others, she depended on me for that as surely as she depended on me for grocery money. The result was that she was afraid to share with me huge areas of her life, any areas which might threaten my regard for her. She could not afford, psychologically or economically, to challenge me overtly. And when she managed to make any suggestion that her discontent was a function of what was being done to her, it was battered down, by my recriminations, into a quagmire of guilt.

I had had some inkling of all this before I ever committed myself to cooking a meal or washing a single pair of socks (as my responsibility, rather than a favor to her). But at every stage of our experiment in role reversal (or rather our attempt to escape roles) my understanding of her position became more real. I had got a lot of domestic services but I had been denied real contact with a whole human being, and hard upon my guilt came anger, rage at what had been done to us both.

I don't have space here to go on and extend our experience into the world outside the family. It is enough to say that when someone has concrete power over your life, you are going to keep a part of yourself hidden and therefore undeveloped, or developed only in fantasy. Your identity becomes bound up in other people's expectation of you—and that is the definition of alienation. It did not take long for me to make connections between the alienating ways in which Jan had to deal with me in the early years of our marriage and the way that I was dealing with my "senior colleagues," the men and women who had power to hire me and did.

Our experience also helped me to understand the distortions of perception and personality that result from being the "superior" in a hierarchical structure. The nuclear family as we know it is one such structure, perhaps the crucial one. But the alienation which results from privilege pervades all our experience in a society which values human beings on the basis of sex, race, and class and which structures those standards into all its institutions. Housework is only a tip of that iceberg, but for Jan and me it has helped to make the need to fundamentally transform those institutions a gut reality.

15
The Ethnic Mobility Trap and Stratification Theory

Norbert F. Wiley

Editors' Introduction

The title of this selection includes the three concepts of *ethnicity, mobility,* and *stratification theory.* Wiley uses ethnicity only as a strategic area in which to exemplify two very different kinds of opportunities for social mobility, movement either up or down in the class structure. His purpose is to develop a new theoretical model of the stratification structure and the mobility processes within it.

In the keynote selection Berger and Berger define ethnicity as "those cultural traits retained by immigrant groups to this country from their original home culture" (p. 108). Ethnic ties include some sense of shared historical heritage and common cultural identity. There is a sense of group belonging that provides social support, a ready source of comfortable primary relations with others of similar background. Within this group there are opportunities for social mobility—one can become, for example, an officer in the local ethnic association or the influential editor of an ethnic newspaper. However, this group exists within the larger societal structure with its own particular avenues of mobility. If a person "moves up" within the ethnic group, what are the consequences for the same person's chances of "moving up" in the larger society? This is the question Wiley poses about ethnicity—and about a whole series of other kinds of smaller groupings within the larger stratification structure. He uses ethnic groups as one example among others of the presence of what he calls a "mobility trap."

Wiley begins by showing that chances for social mobility for members of ethnic groups are complicated by opportunities for mobility within the group itself. Moving upward within the ethnic group may prevent a person from moving upward within the society. Wiley then shows that this situation is not unique to ethnic groups but that such "traps" are found in many areas of life. This leads him to a new metaphor or picture of the stratification structure. But first he identifies two earlier metaphors—that is, viewing the opportunity structure as a ladder that people climb, one rung at a time, or as a series of brick walls against which people beat their heads. What implications for social mobility does each of these metaphors hold?

Wiley goes on to present a new metaphor, conceiving of the opportunity structure as a tree. What implications for social mobility does this metaphor hold? How does this metaphor relate to the idea of a mobility trap? Note the four types of mobility traps that Wiley identifies. How does each one work? Can you add any other examples? (Are there any examples in your college or university? Consider the situations of both students and faculty.) Wiley points out the social and psychological consequences that result from going out on a limb and from climbing up the trunk. Are the fruits of climbing up the trunk worth the cost of losing the prestige and warm social support that one has out on the limb? Is the social support out on the limb worth the cost of losing the fruits of climbing the trunk? What are the social and psychological consequences from resisting and falling into the various types of mobility traps?

Think back to Kohn's reading on social class and parental values. Do Kohn's findings alert you to any possible mobility traps? Are some social classes more subject to mobility traps than others? If so, why? Are there any possible mobility traps in traditional sex-role characteristics?

This reading represents a "think piece," in which the author sits down and thinks about what he knows about a topic from various research studies. Wiley analyzes the stratification structure and the mobility processes within it in order to clarify the relationships of the parts. He then expresses these relationships in a theoretical model, making readers more aware of the complications of mobility in modern societies that include many subgroups.

The sociology of American ethnic groups has centered on ethnic acculturation and assimilation, both as pure processes and as social problems. From the viewpoint of stratification, though, these processes are cases of large-scale social mobility, and the history of American mobility is largely the history of ethnic assimilation. In examining ethnicity and mobility together, much can be learned about both. This paper will consider ethnic mobility, not as such, but as a source of new ideas for stratification theory. Ethnic mobility has been characterized by a special form of mobility which, although found elsewhere, is most easily identified in the ethnic case. Once we have named and defined this mechanism, we will consider its explanatory value.

The mobility chances of ethnic group members are often subject to special complications, not only because of discrimination, but because of features within the ethnic structure itself; for the group is usually internally stratified to some degree and offers in-group opportunities alongside of those in the larger society. This duality of intra- versus extra-group mobility is further complicated if the group is moving upward as a bloc. The individual ethnic may have to make special decisions concerning his career plans. Not only must he choose, for example, whether to aim for a job in the professions, a bureaucracy, or small business. He also faces the question of ethnicity, whether to move with it or against it, to capitalize on it or disregard it. If he makes the wrong decision, he may find himself in a mobility trap, and these exist in abundance in all fluid stratification systems.

Briefly, a mobility trap is an opportunity for mobility which offers a good deal less than it seems to, and, once pursued, permits release only at the cost of some downward mobility. . . . This paper will be an elaboration of this definition, especially in relation to ethnic groups, and it should be regarded as an attempt to form a usable concept. . . .

Reprinted from *Social Problems*, 15, 2 (Fall 1967), 147–151. Used with permission of the Society for the Study of Social Problems and the author.

METAPHORS AND CONCEPT FORMATION

To give a clearer definition of the mobility trap it will be necessary to sketch the picture of the opportunity structure which it assumes. Such pictures are usually related to some simple metaphor, and much of the theorizing in this area is influenced, perhaps unconsciously, by half-hidden metaphors.[1] Before giving our own, mention will be made of two others in relation to which ours can be more clearly seen.

Perhaps the most common metaphor is that of the "social ladder," the "ladder of success" and kindred notions. For our purposes this metaphor has two important features. Social strata are visualized in a continuous hierarchical line; that is, the ladder is a straight one and no rungs are missing. Secondly, it can be climbed, and the means of climbing are the same at all levels. It is implicit that ability and hard work determine one's place on the ladder. This optimistic picture is favored by people who are themselves in the upper strata and feel a bit guilty about being there.

A second cluster of metaphors centers around the notion of physical restraint. People speak of "beating your head against a wall," "running down a blind alley," "being on a treadmill," and so on. This picture has implications exactly opposite to those of the previous one. Social strata are not continuous; they are clearly separated. Also, climbing into a higher stratum is impossible. This picture is favored by dissatisfied people in the lower levels of the system.

The notion of the mobility trap assumes a picture that is a compromise between the two already given.[2] The opportunity system is to be visualized as a tree and mobility as tree climbing. This image is invoked when people speak of being "out on a limb," and it is the limbs that are its distinctive part. The limbs are like strata, leading gently upward but primarily outward and away from all chance of serious ascent. Normally the climber who wants to hit the top will avoid the limbs as much as possible and concentrate on the trunk.

This metaphor has implications that parallel those of the previous ones. One is that the limbs, or strata, are both continuous and discrete. On the dimension of height the limbs overlap leaving no gaps in the structure. In physical contact, however, they are discrete, with good-sized gaps in between.[3] Secondly, mobility is, in a sense, both possible and impossible. If a person is at the top of an isolated limb, direct ascent may be impossible; but if he retreats to the trunk or can reach an overhead limb, mobility is possible, for the sole connection between limbs is often at the base, by way of the trunk. To the people who are blithely climbing the limb in pursuit of a dead-end form of mobility, the truly mobile person may be pitied or scorned, for he will appear to be moving downward. Actually he is preparing to leave the stratum at its only exit, at the bottom. *The essence of the mobility trap is this: the means of moving up within a stratum are contrary to those for moving to the next higher stratum.* In other words there is a conflict between intra- and inter-stratum mobility norms. For those on a limb this paradox is obscured, for their limited vantage point persuades them to move in the wrong direction.[4]

A few examples will make this clearer. To a boy in the slums, social advancement within a delinquent gang by accumulating tattoos, knife skills and a police record is a limb. Spending his free time in a settlement house with the social workers is the trunk. To a slum girl, sexual promiscuity with its instant popularity is a limb. Sexual restraint and a marriage to a mobile young man may be the trunk. To a bright young factory worker, the blue collar hierarchy is a limb, and becoming a foreman may be its outermost point.[5] Going back to school in pursuit of a college degree is the trunk. To a young business executive, long and faithful service to one employer may be a limb, and job-hopping the trunk.

To the mobile person the trap is the limb, especially if it is long, low and lateral. Mobility comes not only from persistent and dedicated climbing. More important is knowing how to distinguish the limbs from the trunk, and even in knowing when to climb out on a strong safe limb to avoid falling from a slippery trunk. Ultimately the trap is a state of mind, and for those without further aspirations it can be as cozy as

a nest. Nevertheless it is based solidly on the structure of the system, and its reality will become clear if an attempt is made to leave it.

Up to now we have done two things. We have presented a picture which gives metaphorical, and admittedly pre-scientific, support to certain stratification variables that are presently without such support. These variables are (a) degrees of continuity or discontinuity between adjacent strata, (b) degrees of hierarchy or subordination-superordination between adjacent strata, (c) degrees of mobility opportunity, depending on location in the structure, and (d) multi-dimensionality in the forms of equality, e.g. as they appear in Max Weber's class-status-party formulation. The second thing we have done is to draw out one concept from this metaphorical base and give it an initial definition.

I should add that the picture of the tree is deliberately overdrawn to fix it securely as a reference point. In the discussion section, I will consider which points are overdrawn and what theoretical contributions a picture of this kind could reasonably lead to.

TYPES OF MOBILITY TRAPS

Without attempting to be systematic or exhaustive, we can see at least four fairly common types of mobility traps. This listing is not meant to be a formal classification but a further attempt to sharpen a definition, by means of a rough enumeration.

1. The "age-grade trap" consists in the tendency of age groups to adopt prestige standards which conflict with those of older age groups. Too much advancement within such a stratum makes it difficult, upon leaving the group, to adjust to the standards of the next. The most marked instance occurs during adolescence, in a different version for each sex and social class.[6] In later life the woman who has responded too well to motherhood faces the "empty nest," and the man who has overadjusted to his occupation faces a vacuous retirement.

2. The "overspecialization trap" is found in highly specialized administative jobs, usually

at the lower levels, which are dead-end positions in themselves, and whose skills do not help much for the performance of higher activities. The occupant who takes his duties too seriously, treating them as an effective mobility investment, may find himself at once narrowed and indispensable, thus becoming unpromotable.[7] A special variant of this trap falls to those who are given that fake promotion called being "kicked upstairs," for they are shorn of power and come to specialize solely in ritual.

3. The "localite trap" exists in those professions which, while once pursued with one employer in one locale, are beginning to require a series of job changes within a national market loosely controlled by the major employers and top professionals. Such professions as social worker, planner, school superintendent, university professor and clergyman are in various stages of this transition. These occupations have two distinct power and prestige arenas: the local, which is diminishing in importance, and the national, which is growing. Broadly speaking, the trap consists in pursuing local prestige at the expense of national.

4. The final type is the "majority group trap," including not only ethnic and racial groups, but, under some conditions, religious, female, radical political and other relatively powerless groups which offer advancement within their ghettos. This case is a trap in the most nearly literal sense because it is often a mechanism of deliberate suppression by majority group people. The ethnic subtype has special qualities which will be given further analysis.

ETHNIC MOBILITY PATTERNS

The mobility trap is often a great pitfall for the ambitious member of an ethnic group. As long as his group exists as a visible and integrated body of people, it is a limb on which there is limited opportunity for mobility. The limb will often have immediate attraction, since in-group opportunities will be the more visible as well as being continuous with existing social bonds. The mobile ethnic can choose the relatively safe and comfortable course of pursuing whatever opportunities exist within the group; or, to the extent that the majority group permits, he can take the more adventuresome and lonely course of leaving the group to climb the trunk. The latter option is not equally open to all groups. For Negroes it is almost impossible to get off the limb, except in a limited sense. For a relatively assimilated group like the Irish, it is extremely easy. But in all groups, depending on their state of assimilation, the choice is there to be made.[8]

Once made, the choice may have social and psychological effects which make it irreversible. One who chooses the ethnic career in such fields as journalism, politics or the professions will become imbedded in a firm network of ethnic relations—in his family, religion, occupation and club memberships—from which he can almost never extricate himself. On the other hand, one who leaves his group—a Negro who passes into white society, a Jew who becomes a Christian, an Italian who changes his name or a Catholic who leaves the Church—may never be able to fully re-enter his group.

In either case something will be lost as well as gained: higher opportunities will be lost if the choice is made in the ethnic direction, and the warmth of the ethnic community if the choice is made in the "outside" direction. Also, in either case the person will gradually deepen his "commitment," in the sense that choices in other areas of life will develop as offshoots of the original choice, thereby making it too costly to change.[9] But movement out on a limb entails something more than a commitment; for, not only will it be difficult to retreat or change, it will be difficult to advance beyond a certain point. The "ethnic" choice thus limits options and maneuverability considerably more than does the "outside" choice.

It is the in-group career that is the classic ethnic trap, for while it is attractive and emotionally rewarding, it usually has a low ceiling, and there is no easy way out into the world at large.[10] This form of mobility, which is tied to a minority subculture and can go only so far, has been an important part of American social experience, and I will argue that it has contributed to several of the characteristic marks of the American stratification system.

A more complete analysis of ethnic mobility as such should take account of other forms of entrapment that can occur if there are fast changes in the balance between internal and external opportunity. Internal opportunity sometimes increases unexpectedly, from a new wave of immigration, a political breakthrough, or some other change that augments the mobility value of ethnic membership. In those cases the members who have moved outside the group (trunk-climbers) might find these new internal opportunities unavailable to them. On the other hand, assimilation sometimes increases faster than expected, and ethnic careerists find themselves stranded in a declining market. These barriers, which arise from fluctuations in the dynamics of acculturation, should be added to the major barrier we have already described; and, to return to the metaphor, one might think of the limbs as growing or dying, in a none too predictable manner. But these processes only elaborate the basic proposition that ethnic mobility has often moved somewhat off the main line of ascent, into traplike situations and this has given both mild advantages and more serious disadvantages to ethnic members.

Notes

1. The importance of metaphor as a creative instrument in science has been discussed in Max Black, "Metaphor" and "Models and Archetypes" in his *Models and Metaphors*, Ithaca, N.Y.: Cornell University Press, 1962, pp. 25–47 and 219–243. The role of metaphor in sociology is evaluated in Maurice R. Stein, "The Poetic Metaphors of Sociology," in Maurice Stein and Arthur Vidich (eds.), *Sociology on Trial*, Englewood Cliffs, N.J.: Prentice-Hall, 1963, pp. 173–182.

2. We are ignoring a third metaphor which is of the greatest historical importance, but is now generally obsolete in industrialized countries. This is the notion of a social "organism" in which each person has his indispensable part to play and does not attempt to move to another part. A current metaphor which fills a somewhat similar purpose is the notion that people are laterally distributed in "all walks of life." This is invoked on national holidays and at other times when it is useful to deny the very existence of inequality.

3. The old question of whether social strata are continuous or discrete is an oversimplification resulting partly from the use of misleading metaphors.

4. Several of my colleagues who read this paper criticized the assertion that mobility usually requires a temporary retreat or loss of prestige. They urged instead that movement directly from one limb to another is the more common reality. I have not accepted this suggestion because I think it would limit the utility of the metaphor and blur the theoretical implications I will draw from it. My concern is more with finding usable concepts than with representational accuracy.

5. A disadvantage of linear mobility conceptions is that they cannot account for the overlap between blue and white collar occupations. The top of the blue collar limb is actually higher, at least in income, than the bottom of the white collar limb.

6. See James S. Coleman, *The Adolescent Society*, New York: The Free Press of Glencoe, 1961.

7. For a related point see Merton's discussion of the overconforming bureaucrat in Robert K. Merton, *Social Theory and Social Structure*, revised and enlarged edition, Glencoe, Ill.: The Free Press, 1957, pp. 197–202.

8. In speaking of mobility as involving a choice I do not mean that anyone can achieve mobility merely by choosing to do so. The choice, rather, is in whether or not and in what way to *attempt* mobility. The chance of success is a resultant of the kind of choice and the location in the opportunity structure. Some locations are, of course, just about hopeless, regardless of choice and effort.

9. Howard S. Becker, "Notes on the Concept of Commitment," *American Journal of Sociology*, 66 (July, 1960), 32–40.

10. Jews have been somewhat of an exception in the United States, for they have been able to stay within their group while experiencing considerable mobility. Although the qualities of the Jewish limb have been favorable (high, nearly vertical, etc.), it has been, and in some ways still is, a limb. Kurt Lewin was referring especially to Jews trapped on the top of the limb in his discussion of "Self-Hatred among Jews," *Contemporary Jewish Record*, 4 (June, 1941), 219–232.

PART FOUR

Institutions and Their Interrelationships

READINGS 16–20

In the selection on basic concepts in Part One of this book, you discovered that institutions are one of the most important components of society. In that selection Alex Inkeles wrote, "Just as social acts may be aggregated into customs, and sets of such actions aggregated into roles, so a more complex structure of roles organized around some central activity or social need may be aggregated into an *institution*. . . . Institutions lie at the center of sociological attention. They constitute the main building blocks of society" (p. 39).

Inkeles goes on to sort institutions into four abstract categories: kinship institutions "focused around the problem of regulating sex and providing a stable and secure framework for the care and rearing of the young"; economic institutions "concerned with the production of goods and services"; political institutions "concerned with the exercise of power and which have a monopoly on the legitimate use of force"; and expressive-integrative institutions, "which deal with ideas, and with the transmission of received values" (pp. 39–40). In more specific terms, the first of these is the *family*, the second is the *economy*, and the third is referred to as the *polity*. Modern sociologists usually divide Inkeles' fourth category into two. The first is *education*, and the second comprises that set of ideas that give meaning and unity to the whole—often (but not always) known as *religion*. These five are usually considered to be the five major institutions in society.

In the following keynote selection Raymond Mack and Calvin Bradford work with this fivefold classification, using the language of functionalism. In discussing five functions essential for society, they use the term *function* in a new way. When you have seen this term before, it has meant consequences, as in "latent and manifest functions." Now the meaning of the term shifts slightly to mean survival needs. "Consequences" or functions have become so important that they are necessary if a society is to survive. (In the rest of the readings the context will clue you in as to which meaning the author is using for the term *function*.) Mack and Bradford suggest that societal survival rests on meeting five needs or functions: replacing personnel, teaching new members, producing and distributing goods and services, preserving order, and providing and maintaining a sense of purpose. The institutional answers to these needs translate into the structures of the family, education, the economy, the polity, and religion (or the integrative belief system)—the "big five" mentioned before. Mack and Bradford offer a case for the necessity of each of the five. Be sure to consider what happens when any one of the institutions is *not* present.

If these functions are as important as Mack and Bradford say, then you should have run across societal answers to them before in this book. And, of course, you have—in each of the parts thus far—and you will continue to meet them in the parts that follow. About the need to replace societal members, Mack and Bradford say that "elaborate cultural regulations" are involved, which you have seen in the parts of the book on socialization and stratification. Berger and Berger's discussion of Jimmy and Johnny, Roache's report on reversal of sex roles, and Lever's demonstration of how sex roles are learned are all relevant here. Mack and Bradford, in discussing the need to teach new members the ways of the group, use the example of the isolated child Isabelle, already considered in Davis's keynote reading on socialization. Also in that part of the book Gracey and Lever both demonstrate forms of answers to this need. Some particular answers to the need to produce and distribute goods and services appear in Part Three on stratification, especially in the readings by Berger and Berger, Pearce, and Murray. In their discussion of the need to preserve order—through norms and rules that organize the group—Mack and Bradford also point out that everyone does not always follow the norms and rules, saying that deviance may be a tension-releasing mechanism or may produce innovative change. The next part of this book studies the topic of deviance in some detail, describing various theories of deviance. One such theory considers the ways people may adapt when they do not feel they are a "full part" of the society. This raises the question of needing a sense of purpose and hope, the last societal function discussed in the following keynote reading.

In other words, the previous parts of this book have already included readings about the major institutions. The family is the institutional setting for LeMasters's reading on the battle of the sexes, for Kohn's reading on social class and parental values, and for Roache's experiences as a househusband. In Part Six on social change, the keynote selection includes a discussion of the changes that the family has undergone because of industrialization. Education is the institutional setting for Lever's study of children's games and Gracey's description of life in kindergarten. The economy is the institutional setting for Murray's discussion of *el cortito,* for Kohn's study of the effect of work on parental values for children, for Lever's and Gracey's readings showing how children are prepared for the world of work, and for both Smelser's and Cottrell's readings in Part Six on social change.

Sorting out the readings in this way demonstrates a very important point: institutions are interrelated. Often the same reading examines more than one institutional setting. For example, Kohn's reading concerns both the family and the economy. In fact, this reading demonstrates one of the interrelationships between these two institutions. Lever's and Gracey's readings both investigate the institutions of education and the economy, again demonstrating interrelationships. Murray's reading on the short-handled hoe shows interrelationships between the economy and the polity, as does Cottrell's selection on technological change in Part Six. Smelser's reading, also in Part Six, shows the consequences of the economic change known as industrialization on the structure of the family. While we have already included readings on most of the major institutions, many of these readings also demonstrate how one institution is related to another.

You may have noticed that in our list of readings relating to various institutional settings, we mentioned all of the major institutions except religion. This omission is rectified in the first illustrative reading of this part, following Mack and Bradford's keynote selection. In his "Religion: Opiate or Inspiration of Civil Rights Militancy?" Gary Marx considers the relationship between religious beliefs and political protest—between religion and the polity. He uses the black civil rights movement as a strategic site for this analysis. As a further exploration of the polity, Peter Dreier's "The Position of the Press in the U.S. Power Structure" shows how the power structure pervades other areas of life and how it relates to the power of the press. Next Rosabeth Kanter discusses the effect of the contemporary structure of work on life in families. She shows that policy decisions in one institution (the economy) have far-reaching implications for another institution (the family.) The part closes with the first chapter from Samuel Bowles and Herbert Gintis's *Schooling in Capitalist America*. They present a Marxian analysis of the relationship between education and the economy. Bowles and Gintis make a strong case that one institution (the economy) leads and the other institution (education) follows, explaining much of the organization of education as stemming from its support service for the economy.

When you finish this part, think about the tangled web of interrelationships among the five major institutions. (Note that all five of them are represented among the four illustrative readings, along with a number of ways in which they may be interrelated.) The configuration of any one rests on the configuration of the others at that time. While changes in any one lead to changes in the others, the economy and the polity seem to be particularly influential in contemporary industrialized societies, a point made by many of the readings here and in other sections of this book.

16
Social Organization and Survival

Raymond W. Mack
Calvin P. Bradford

Any human society, if it is to survive, must be organized to accomplish five essential functions:

1. It must replace personnel when they die, leave, or become incapacitated.

2. It must teach new recruits to participate usefully, whether they are born into the society, migrate into it, or are hired or captured.
3. It must produce and distribute goods and services to keep its personnel going.
4. It must preserve order, so that its personnel are not keeping one another from the tasks of replacement, teaching, production, and distribution and so that they are not destroyed by hostile outside groups.
5. It must provide and maintain some sense of

purpose among its members, so that they will be motivated to continue as members of the group and to satisfy the other four requirements for survival.

These five functions are necessary for the continuity not only of a society but also of any relatively permanent group. Smaller groups do not have to perform all these activities within their own boundaries. They must, however, be able to barter or otherwise arrange for the accomplishment of the same ends. A corporation, for example, does not have to supervise the biological reproduction of its executives and laborers (fortunately—it has enough problems as it is), but reproduction must take place in the larger society of which the corporation is a part, so that there is a pool of potential personnel from which the corporation can recruit its executives and laborers. An adult friendship group does not have to teach its members to walk and talk, but somebody must, or there will be no more desirable recruits for the group. Finally, while the larger society must perform all five functions, societies do not consciously set out to satisfy all of these functions in a rationally integrated fashion. Consequently, some societies may emphasize some functions more than others, and one function may actually be in competition with another. For example, concentration on the production of new members may create a crisis in a society's ability to produce and distribute goods and services to all these new members. There is no "natural" force to keep these functions in balance.

This list of universal functions appears to be a set of logical deductions, but it is more than that. Let us look at some of the evidence that each of these functions must be performed as the price of survival.

REPLACING PERSONNEL

Sexual reproduction is not, to be sure, the only method of bringing new members into a society. Annexation, the acquisition of slaves, and immigration are other means of recruiting people. (Each of these three modes of population expansion has been used by the United States

during its history.) Theoretically, it would be possible for a society to fill the positions of its dying members by recruiting replacements in one or more of these three ways from people born into other societies. The practical difficulty lies less in the recruitment than in the knowledge and loyalty required to maintain the social order. Teaching new members the basic cultural values and norms of a society is a task most readily accomplished when those new members are born into the society. Being entirely dependent for their survival on the adults in their primary group, small children are much more easily taught accepted behavior and attitudes than are adult immigrants or captives. In the days of frontier warfare, American Indians, who were aware of this fact, ordinarily took captive for induction into their society only young children, seldom adults.

For the bulk of its new members, generation after generation, therefore, a society depends primarily on sexual reproduction. The function of reproduction is so obvious that its crucial importance for societal survival is often overlooked. One is inclined simply to assume that all societies reproduce themselves.

It is generally believed also that reproductive behavior is merely a natural biological phenomenon. Actually, the behavior patterns of human beings as they propagate their own kind are shaped and modified, as is their behavior in any other area of social life, by the culture through which they have been taught. The basic act of procreation is influenced by the social norms concerning size of family, form of marriage, sexual intercourse itself (whether it is considered exalted or shameful), marriage age, and economic obligations of parents toward their children. In fact, there is no society that does not have a set of norms governing the reproduction of new members. Every culture contains some set of prohibitions, expectations, and rewards having to do with who shall have children and the circumstances under which reproduction should occur.

The cultural values patterned around reproduction are enforced by both rewards and punishments. For example, we are critical of people whose families are notably larger than the norm, who "just had another child and can't support the ones they have now." But many Americans still esteem people who have large families and hence are seen as having met their responsibility to society: "They gave two sons to the Church"; "The Beckers had four boys in the service during the war."

The emphasis that most societies place on the reproductive function and the elaborate cultural regulations with which they surround it can be related to historical circumstances, in which the power of any given group or tribe was directly related to the size of the society. When physical safety depended on the number of able-bodied warriors a tribe or nation could put into the field, every additional child was an important increment in the struggle for survival.

The Shakers (who, among other accomplishments, left their name on the Cleveland suburb of Shaker Heights) offer a striking example of the social cost of failure to replace personnel. The Shakers were a religious sect, one of whose tenets forbade sexual intercourse. So firmly were they committed to the sacredness of celibacy that male and female believers were segregated in separate dormitories. For a while, the society prospered, recruiting converts to the faith. But as their proselytizing efforts became less effective and their commitment to sexual abstinence remained unshaken, their numbers dwindled. No replacement of personnel: no more Shakers.

TEACHING NEW MEMBERS

Producing new members is not sufficient. These replacements must learn the ways of the group. They must be taught the basic values, or ethos, around which the normative system is organized. They must learn all the thousands of little behavior patterns that are accepted as normal in the society in which they are born: what to eat, how to eat it, where to eat it, when to eat it; what to wear, how to wear it, where to wear it, when to wear it; what to say, how to say it; and so on. Each new member must develop, sooner or later, a sense of self. Each child must

learn to curb his or her own desires when they interfere with the reasonable expectations of others—must learn, in short, to adjust to social living.

Learning occurs both formally and informally. Going to school is part of the socialization process, and so is going to the movies. Overhearing a conversation in which someone is criticized teaches that one can avoid similar criticism by avoiding the behavior of the person under discussion. Education is a continuous process; when, at the age of eighty-two, a person learns something new about getting along in society, that person is still being socialized. Education is cumulative: learning to recognize the letters of the alphabet lays the groundwork for learning to comprehend written words, and reading written words enables one to learn still more things. Whenever we ask someone to give us new information in terms with which we are familiar—what a thing tastes like, what it feels like, what it is similar to—we are demonstrating the cumulative nature of learning.

Again we have research evidence of the consequences of failing to teach new personnel how to participate in social life. Isabelle was an illegitimate child who was discovered in Ohio in November 1938. Isabelle's grandparents, the parents of the unwed mother, were so ashamed of their daughter's having borne a child out of wedlock that they kept the mother and her little daughter secluded in a dark room, away from the rest of the family and their friends and neighbors. Isabelle was virtually a case in a controlled experiment, for her mother was a deaf-mute. For the first six years of her life, the child lived in almost total social isolation, lacking contact with human beings who could hear her or could speak to her. When authorities learned of the situation, Isabelle was removed from this environment at six years of age and placed in the hands of child specialists. When she was found, Isabelle was rachitic (had rickets), probably from improper diet and lack of sunlight. She could not speak, but she made certain croaking sounds. Her communication with her mother had been by simple gestures. Her reaction toward strangers, especially men, was almost that of a wild animal, revealing much of her fear and hostility. At first it was thought that she was deaf. Later, when it was found that she could hear, she was given various intelligence tests and pronounced feeble-minded. Her first score on the Stanford-Binet I.Q. test was nineteen months, practically a zero point on the scale. On the Vineland Social Maturity Scale, her initial score was thirty-nine—equivalent to that of a child of two-and-a-half years.

Despite Isabelle's poor performance, the specialists who had taken charge began a systematic program of training, beginning with pantomime and dramatization. Within a week, she had progressed to her first try at verbalization. From a slow start, she picked up speed in her rate of learning and in a few weeks passed through the usual stages of learning for a normal child from ages one to six years. Within two years, she had acquired knowledge and skills that ordinarily take six years to attain. By the time she was fourteen, Isabelle was in the sixth grade, socially and emotionally well adjusted, and doing well in her school work.

As Isabelle's case history illustrates, there is only one sensible answer to the old dormitory rap-session question: "Which is more important, heredity or environment?" The answer is "Yes." In the context of what social scientists know, the question is meaningless. An imbecile will remain an imbecile, regardless of the advantages of environment. Environment cannot create the traits that must be inherited through the genes. But heredity is a limiting factor, not a determining one. A potential genius can make no use of his or her mental capacities if reared in an environment as debilitating as Isabelle's. A boy with an I.Q. comparable to Albert Einstein's who is born into an isolated tribe of illiterate Patagonians may invent a more efficient method of preserving food or discover a new use for fire, but he will not write a theory of relativity, because his social environment has not equipped him to tackle such a problem.

To participate in and contribute to the social order, a person must be taught to play a part in it. If the members of a whole generation in a society were treated as Isabelle was, that society would perish.

PRODUCING AND DISTRIBUTING GOODS AND SERVICES

Many Americans speak of the United States as a "society founded on free enterprise" or as a "capitalistic nation." In a society that is so self-conscious about its economic life, it is hardly necessary to emphasize the fact that any ongoing social organization must make some provision for the production and distribution of goods and services. In a society without economic specialization, each individual would work to satisfy his or her own wants, and no one would work to produce anything for anyone else. No such society exists. The fact that newborn members of a society are at first unable to provide for their own needs would in itself make such an arrangement impossible.

Everywhere in the world, people have established some set of norms ordering their activities so that the functions of producing goods and services and distributing them will be performed. In even the most favorable environment, such social arrangements are necessary. Even where socially defined needs are minimal and natural resources are abundant, someone must be assigned the responsibility of picking the coconuts or berries for those who are unable to pick their own.

The price of failure in economic organization is clear in the history of famine. The weakened Eskimo family, exhausted and freezing and without food, or the whitening bones of an unsuccessful Bushman hunter and his family in the South African desert are mute evidence of the necessity of production and distribution for survival.

PRESERVING ORDER

The natives of Tasmania were considered by their conquerors to be less than human, missing links half-way between apes and civilized men; British colonists organized hunting parties and shot Tasmanians out of the trees. The primitive weapons of the Tasmanians were no match for the tools of the English sportsmen; the Tasmanian aborigines have gone the way of the Shakers.

The social structure dear to the hearts of the nineteenth-century Russian nobility is as extinct as the social order of the Tasmanians. The Russian monarchy did not fall because of attackers from another society with superior weapons. It ceased to exist because it could not maintain order among the peasants, workers, sailors, and other less privileged members of its own society. Two facets of order are essential: A society must not destroy itself from within, and it must not allow itself to be destroyed by another society.

If a society were to reach the stage at which most of its members failed to abide by the basic rules, it would be doomed. If people were to kill one another wantonly, refuse to honor agreements, fail to fulfill social responsibilities, and mete out no punishment to those who ignored basic social norms, the society would cease to exist. Anarchy may be a topic for philosophical discussions, but it is not a possible condition for social life.

In the land of Ik in northeastern Uganda, an anthropologist discovered a society lacking both facets of order. The Ik tribesmen were proud hunters. But the Ugandan government made a national park of their hunting grounds. They were unable to resist the force and power of the government and its policing agents. Then they were asked to farm. But they were unwilling to adapt to farming. Since they were hunters unable to hunt, food became scarce. Like the Shakers, the threatened loss of their population did not deter their basic norms; so they continued to be hunters in a land where they could kill no game. The old order of their society collapsed. Hoarding rather than sharing became admired. Eventually, the death of children or elders was an event of joy—even to the point of laughter. When this tribe was unable to preserve its order, society—indeed even the basic traits of humanity—disappeared.

While most individuals do not abandon society's rules so completely, there is some deviance from the everyday rules in any society. Every individual breaks some rule at some time or another, and some people self-consciously work at being rule-breakers: *les apaches* in Paris, Bohemians in Greenwich Village in one era and Flower Children in another. Revolutionaries, too, are deviants from the norms of their time and place. Deviant behavior, then, can be an agent for introducing change, whether artistic fashion or political dogma. Deviance can help to preserve order, for it serves an escape-valve function. The Mardi Gras helps people tolerate the deprivations of Lent. Inventors, scientists, artists, and political and economic innovators are all deviants to some extent. By showing new pathways and providing responses to pressures for change, they can help to maintain internal order in a society.

It is equally important that a society protect itself from outside attack. This point is hardly debatable. There are many examples of societies that have perished through inability to maintain an order capable of resisting external pressures or attacks.

As ancient Carthage disappeared because of inability to withstand Roman might, so will any society or any group fail to survive if it cannot preserve internal and external order.

PROVIDING AND MAINTAINING A SENSE OF PURPOSE

Obviously, a society could not continue to exist if everyone decided that it was easier to quit than to go on. The French sociologist Émile Durkheim made a fascinating study of one category of people who decide to quit, in which he concluded that what he called "anomic suicide" occurs most frequently in situations of *anomie*, a French word best translated as "without rules." A society without definite norms to regulate morals and social conduct is called "anomic." In an anomic situation, like a sudden economic depression, when the old rules no longer seem to apply and no new ones are immediately forthcoming, people do not know what is right and wrong or what the social expectations are, and they lose their sense of purpose. At such times, suicide rates are likely to soar. The standard research techniques of the sociologist—observation, interviewing, and the questionnaire—are peculiarly unsuited to the study of people who have committed suicide. A considerable body of recent evidence suggests, however, that the lack of a sense of purpose can cause the death of a person in ways more subtle than by his or her own hand. Both human beings and animals can have their motivation to continue so damaged that the physical mechanism itself simply quits.

Wild rats (the sinking-ship cliché to the contrary) are capable of swimming for ninety hours or more. Nevertheless, if a rat in a laboratory is terrified and then plunged into water, it will die in a matter of minutes. Careful study of the rat's heart indicates that death is caused by a gradual depressive action of the nervous system. Contrary to the popular notion of being "scared to death," in the sense of a panic-induced speeding up of all the reflexes leading to excessive strain on the organism, what occurs is a gradual slowing of the heart's beat until the system quits operating. Furthermore, if the rat is removed from the water just before death, it recovers and is later able to swim as well as it did before being frightened.

Many physicians testify that they have seen inexplicable cases of death among patients who were profoundly depressed or filled with despair. Anthropologists, physiologists, and physicians who have studied cases of tribal "hexing" sometimes argue that when people believe in "black magic," a hex may notably shorten life, if not immediately kill a victim.

The eminent neurologist Harold G. Wolff reported precise information gleaned from American war records, demonstrating the impact of prolonged adversity on health and life span. Of approximately 6,000 United States prisoners of war captured by the North Koreans, about one-third died. According to medical observers, the cause of death in many cases was ill-defined; they called it "give-up-itis." Living in an environment of deprivation, a prisoner would become listless and apathetic. He would refuse to eat, to clean himself, or even to move. He would sit listless and staring and would finally die. Returned American POWs recounted more than one tale of this type of death in North Vietnam prisoner-of-war camps.

During World War II, about 94,000 American soldiers were taken prisoner in the European theater. They were imprisoned approximately ten months, on the average, and less than 1 percent of them died in prisoner-of-war camps. In the Pacific, in contrast, the Japanese took about 25,000 American prisoners. They remained in captivity four times as long as those in Europe and suffered considerably more from humiliation, threats, and abuse. More than one-third of them died before liberation.

Six years after liberation, researchers reexamined those who had survived Japanese prison camps. During the intervening six years, the total number of deaths in this group had been more than twice the expected incidence for a comparable group that had not suffered the prisoner-of-war experience. The causes of death included many diseases not directly related to imprisonment. Comparing deaths among the former prisoners with the death rate for a comparable sample of the population, nine times the expected number died of pulmonary tuberculosis. More than four times the expected number died from diseases of the gastrointestinal tract. More than twice the expected number died of cancer, and twice the expected number died of heart disease. Most impressive from the point of view of studying sense of purpose, twice the expected number committed suicide, and there were three times the expected number of deaths by accident. Among those who survived, the admission rate to veterans' hospitals was closely related to the amount of stress endured during imprisonment. Those who had "suffered greatly" had admission rates seven times as high as men who had not been prisoners.

Although no such statistical evidence exists for soldiers who returned from Southeast Asian prison camps, the sad stories of psychological problems and suicide have made their way into the press. Comments by doctors that the "POWs do not seem to be as healthy as they appeared when they first returned" are grim signals of a possible replication of the World War II experience.

As we try to comprehend the significance of maintaining a sense of purpose, it may be useful to examine the cases of a few of the survivors of the Vietnam War who have become unusually effective citizens. These men, despite the deprivation they suffered, viewed imprisonment as a temporary interruption. They had long-range goals. They remained convinced that they would come out alive, and they continued to plan for the future. They were able to get some satisfaction out of life even while living under stress. They cultivated new interests. One prisoner, for example, raised rabbits for food and became interested in breeding them. The immediate distress seemed less real to these men, because they focused their attention on life as they would live it in the future. They made elaborate plans for marriage, families, children, jobs, and they even plotted their recreation after liberation—where they would go and what they would eat. They formed cohesive groups, taught courses, had discussions, and even laughed together. Their maintenance of a sense of purpose kept the prison experience from sapping their vitality. We have learned that even under the exceptional stresses of torture and physical isolation, Americans in North Vietnamese prison camps created a means of communication in order to maintain contact and a group cohesiveness. This process alone seems to have created a kind of sense of purpose which kept these men alive, as well as sane.

Although we know of no circumstances in which an entire society has perished through lack of motivation to continue, it is clear that an individual can be destroyed by extinguishing his will to carry on. As Wolff says in his article," . . . prolonged circumstances which are perceived as dangerous, as lonely, as hopeless, may drain a man of hope and of his health; but he is capable of enduring incredible burdens and taking cruel punishment, when he has self-esteem, hope, purpose, and belief in his fellows."

17
Religion: Opiate or Inspiration of Civil Rights Militancy?

Gary T. Marx

Editors' Introduction

In Part Three you saw that although it is commonly believed that the situation of blacks has steadily improved in the United States in recent years, statistics comparing blacks with whites on a number of factors indicate this common belief is in error. Although the civil rights movement has brought about a number of changes in the laws, the overall results have been much less than equality for blacks. Another commonly held, and equally erroneous, belief is that the most deprived members of a society are most likely to en-

195

gage in protest activity. As you will see in this reading, one very important factor in approval of civil rights militancy is religion. To put it another way, the institutions of religion and the polity are interrelated even in protest activity. Religion contributes to the acceptance or rejection of "proper" channels of political activity, not only for blacks but for everyone.

Throughout the 1960s the United States experienced divisive racial conflicts. Hundreds of demonstrations and riots erupted to protest the lack of racial equality. Although these disturbances were quite common (you may have heard about the "long hot summers" of the mid 1960s), not all blacks participated, nor did they all give moral support to such activities of the civil rights movement. Who, then, among the blacks were militant? What characteristics did they have that set them apart from blacks who did not feel this same militancy?

This reading raises the question: Do people who vary in religiosity also vary in their civil rights militancy? To put it in more institutional terms: Are attitudes found in the institution of religion related to attitudes found in the institution of the polity? What is meant by *religiosity*? By *militancy*? What is the relationship Marx (Gary, that is) finds between these two variables? Does this relationship appear across all ages? Both sexes? All denominations? Those raised in the South? In the beginning and at the end of this reading Gary Marx talks about the dual functions of religion. What are these dual functions? What light does this reading shed on these dual functions in civil rights militancy? How does this reading demonstrate the interrelationships of institutions? Can Marx's findings be generalized to other groups in the society?

Marx uses the language of the functional theoretical orientation when he examines the functions of religion in civil rights militancy. But notice how the conflict perspective is implied in the reading—what are these people militant about? How are these two theoretical orientations intertwined with the dual functions of religion discussed in the article? How can religion be viewed from both orientations simultaneously? (Think back to the original discussion of theoretical orientations in Part One.)

This selection is part of a larger work, *Protest and Prejudice*. The study was done in 1964, at the height of the civil rights movement, but just before the "long hot summers" of 1965–1967. Drawn from several different samples, a total of 1,119 black adults were interviewed. About half of these were randomly sampled from metropolitan areas outside the South. The other half of the respondents were specifically selected from Chicago, New York, Atlanta, and Birmingham. These four cities were singled out because they represented important centers of black population that differed in region, history, and current black-white relations. (This second half of the sample is sometimes called a "purposive sample" since the particular cities were chosen on purpose—they differed in important recognizable characteristics.) Whenever possible, the interviews were conducted by blacks; about nine out of ten interviews were conducted in this way. When the researchers thought the white interviewer had a biasing effect, they omitted those interviews from the analysis. Why did they omit rural blacks from the study? How do you think the results would have differed had rural blacks been included? What if white interviewers had been used throughout?

Differences in the degree of militancy are what Gary Marx is trying to explain (the dependent variable), but this selection does not include his measurement scheme. He used an eight-item index (a set of questions or statements that together are used to measure some attitude) to determine the level of militancy in his respondents. The eight items (and the militant response for each) are: (1) In your opinion, is the government in Washington pushing integration too slow, too fast, or about right? (Too slow.) (2) Blacks should spend more time praying and less time demonstrating. (Disagree.) (3) To tell the truth I would be afraid to take part in civil rights demonstrations. (Disagree.) (4) Would you like to see more demonstrations or less [sic] demonstrations? (More.) (5) A restaurant owner should not have to serve blacks if he doesn't want to. (Disagree.) (6) Before blacks are given equal rights, they have to show that they deserve them. (Disagree.) (7) Blacks who want to work hard can get ahead just as easily as anyone else. (Disagree.) (8) An owner of property should not have to sell to blacks if he doesn't want to. (Disagree.) Each respondent was given one point for each militant response, and these points were added together to obtain a total militancy score. With these scores Marx was able to rank order his respondents, putting them in order of their degree of militancy. Anyone with a score of 6 or more was considered a *militant*; persons scoring 3, 4, or 5 were *moderates*; *conservatives* had scores of 2 or less. Go back to the actual questions and think about what each of these scores means in concrete terms. What does a militant think about civil rights? A conservative? It is very important for you to relate these numerical scores to some concrete meaning the scores represent. Numbers, per se, do not tell anything about the social world.

As has been pointed out several times before, institutions form a basic part of what sociologists call social structure. But process plays a big part in this reading as well. Civil rights militancy is very much involved with social change—it has been a relatively (although not totally) effective mechanism pushing the processes of change in this society. But once again, you can see the interaction of structure and process. Structures set limits on process (religious institutions may limit political activity), while process attempts to change structure (political activity, in turn, is aimed at changing the stratification structure). Incidentally, you will find a short history of the civil rights movement in Jo Freeman's reading on social movements in Part Six. Freeman discusses the important role played by religion in the civil rights movement, but she focuses only on those who did become involved.

Let justice roll down like waters, and righteousness like a mighty stream.

—*Amos 5:24*

The white folks like for us to be religious, then they can do what they want to with us.

—*Bigger Thomas*

Did we not straitly command that ye should not teach in this name? And behold, ye have filled Jerusalem with your doctrine. . . . Then Peter and the other apostles answered and said, We ought to obey God rather than men.

—*Acts 5:28*

But God . . . is white. And if his love was so great, and if he loved all his children, why were we the blacks, cast down so far?

—*James Baldwin*

The relation between religion and political radicalism is a confusing one. On the one hand, established religious institutions have generally had a stake in the *status quo* and hence have fostered conservatism. The otherworldly orientation of the masses, particularly as expressed in the more fundamentalist branches of Christianity, has been seen as an alternative to the development of political radicalism. On the other hand, as the source of both universal hu-

manistic values and the strength that can come from believing one is carrying out God's will in political matters, religion has occasionally played a positive role in movements for radical social change.

This dual role of religion is clearly indicated in the case of the black American and race protest. Slaves are said to have been first brought to this country on the ship *Jesus Christ*. Despite occasional controversy over religion's effect, most slave owners eventually came to view supervised religion as an effective means of social control. Stampp, in commenting on the effect of religion, notes:

Through religious instruction the bondsmen learned that slavery had divine sanction, that insolence was as much an offense against God as against the temporal master. They received the Biblical command that servants should obey their masters, and they heard of the punishments awaiting the disobedient slave in the hereafter. They heard, too, that eternal salvation would be their reward for faithful service. . . .[1]

In discussing the period after the Civil War, Myrdal states: "Under the pressure of political reaction, the Negro church in the South came to have much the same role as it did before the Civil War. Negro frustration was sublimated into emotionalism, and Negro hopes were fixed on the afterworld."[2] A large number of other analysts, in considering the consequences of black religion after slavery until the early 1950s, reached similar conclusions about its conservative effect.

However, the effect of religion on race protest throughout American history has by no means been exclusively in one direction. While many blacks were no doubt seriously singing about chariots in the sky, black preachers such as Denmark Vesey and Nat Turner and the religiously inspired abolitionists were actively fighting slavery in their own way. All-black churches first came into being as protest organizations, and later some served as meeting places where protest strategy was planned or as stations on the underground railroad. The richness of protest symbolism in black spirituals and sermons has often been noted. Beyond this symbolic role, the all-black church brought together in privacy people with a shared problem. It was in the church that many leaders were exposed to a broad range of ideas legitimizing protest and obtained the *savoir faire*, self-confidence, and organizational experience needed to challenge an oppressive system. A recent commentator states that the slave churches were "the nucleus of the Negro protest."[3] And another, that "in religion, Negro leaders had begun to find sanction and support for their movements of protest more than 150 years ago."[4]

Differing perceptions of the varied consequences religion may have on protest have continued to the present time. While there has been very little in the way of empirical research on the effect of the black church on protest, the literature on race relations is rich with impressionistic statements which generally contradict each other about how the church either encourages and is the source of race protest or inhibits and retards its development. For example, two observers note: "As primitive evangelism gave way to a more sophisticated social consciousness, the church became the spearhead of Negro protest in the Deep South,"[5] while another indicates that "the Negro church is a sleeping giant. In civil rights participation its feet are hardly wet."[6] A civil rights activist, himself a clergyman, states: "The church today is central to the movement. . . . If there had been no Negro church, there would have been no civil rights movement today."[7] On the other hand, a sociologist, commenting on the more

involved higher-status ministers, notes: "Middle class Negro clergymen in the cities of the South generally advocated cautious gradualism in race activities until the mid-1950's when there was an upsurge of protest sentiment among urban Negroes . . . but most of them [ministers] did not embrace the most vigorous techniques of protest until other leaders took the initiative and gained widespread support."[8] Another sociologist states: "Whatever their previous conservative stance has been, the churches have now become 'spearheads of reform.' "[9] Still another suggests that "the Negro church is particularly culpable for its general lack of concern for the moral and social problems of the community . . . it has been accommodatory. Fostering indulgence in religious sentimentality, and riveting the attention of the masses on the bounties of a hereafter, the Negro church remains a refuge, an escape from the cruel realities of the here and now."[10]

Thus one faces opposing views, or at best, ambiguity in contemplating the current effect of religion. The quietistic consequences of religion are all too well known, as is the fact that only a relatively small segment of the black church is actively involved. On the other hand, the prominent role of the black church in supplying much of the ideology of the movement, many of its foremost leaders, and a place where protest can be organized, can hardly be denied. It would appear from the bombings of churches and the writing of Martin Luther King and other religiously inspired activists that, for many, religion and protest are linked.

DENOMINATION

It has been long known that the more fundamental sects, such as the Holiness groups and the Jehovah's Witnesses, are relatively uninterested in movements for concrete, secular, political or social change. Such transvaluational movements, with their otherworldly orientations and their promise that the last shall be first in the great beyond, are said to solace the individual for his lowly status in this world and to direct attention away from efforts at collec-

Table 1

Militancy by Religious Denomination

	Religious Denomination[a]						
	Episcopalian	United Church of Christ	Presbyterian	Catholic	Methodist	Baptist	Sects and Cults
Militant	43%	42%	36%	36%	28%	25%	15%
Number	(23)	(12)	(25)	(107)	(141)	(657)	(106)

[a]Twenty-five respondents are not shown in this table because they did not specify a denomination or belonged to non-Christian religious groups or other smaller Christian groups.

tive social change. While only a minority of blacks actually belong to such groups, the relative percentage belonging is higher than among whites. Black literature is rich in descriptions of these churches and their position on race protest.

Table 1 shows data on civil rights militancy which are consistent with past research on political radicalism among sects. The percentage of respondents scored as militant is about twice as high among members of the more conventional religious groups than among those who belong to sects. The percentage militant increases from only 15 percent for the sects to 43 percent for Episcopalians. It is perhaps ironic that those individuals in largely white denominations (Episcopalian, Presbyterian, and Catholic) appear somewhat higher in militancy than those in black denominations, in spite of the greater civil rights activism of the latter. This was true even when social class was held constant.

In their comments, some of which were noted earlier, members of the less conventional religious groups clearly expressed the classical attitudes of sects toward participation in the politics of the secular world. An automobile serviceman in Philadelphia stated, "I, as a Jehovah's Witness, cannot express things involving the race issue." A housewife in the Far West ventured, "In my religion we do not approve of anything except living like it says in the Bible.

Demonstrations mean calling attention to you, and it's sinful."

The finding that persons who belong to sects are among the least likely to be militant was to be expected. Clearly, for most people, this type of religious involvement rules out the development of radicalism. But what of religious blacks in the more conventional churches, which may put relatively less stress on the after-life and encourage various forms of secular participation? Are the more religiously inclined within these groups also less likely to be militant?

RELIGIOSITY

The study measured several dimensions of religious involvement: the importance of religion to the respondent, the orthodoxy of his religious belief, and the frequency of his attendance at worship service. Even with the sects excluded, irrespective of the dimension of religiosity considered, the greater the religiosity, the lower the percentage militant (Table 2). Militancy increases consistently from a low of 22 percent among those who said religion was "extremely important" to a high of 62 percent for those who indicated that religion was "not at all important" to them. For those high in orthodoxy (having no doubt about the existence of God, the devil, or an after-life), only 20 percent were militant, while for those totally rejecting

Table 2

Militancy by Subjective Importance
of Religion to Respondent[a]

	Percent Militant	Number
Religion is:		
Extremely important	22	(664)
Quite important	34	(194)
Fairly important	44	(96)
Not too important	56	(18)
Not at all important	62	(13)

[a]Members of sects are excluded here and in all
subsequent tables in this [reading].

these ideas 57 percent indicated concern over
civil rights (Table 3). Militancy is also inversely
related to frequency of attendance at worship
service. As seen in Table 4, while 18 percent of
those who attend church more than once a week
are high on militancy, 32 percent who attend
less than once a year are high in militancy.

These items were strongly interrelated and
have been combined into an over-all measure
of religiosity. Those scored as very religious in
terms of this index attended church at least
once a week, felt that religion was extremely
important to them, and had no doubts about

the existence of God and the devil. As one
moves down the index, frequency of church
attendance, the importance of religion, and acceptance of the belief items decline consistently
until for those scored not at all religious church
is rarely if ever attended, religion is not considered personally important, and the belief items
are rejected.

Observing the effect of this measure on civil
rights concern, it can be seen that militancy
increases from a low of 19 percent for those
labeled very religious to a high of 49 percent
for those considered not at all religious (Table 5).

Religiosity and militancy are both related to
age, sex, region of the country raised in, and
denomination. Older people, women, those
raised in the South, and those in black denominations were more likely to be scored as religious and to have lower percentages scoring as
militant. Thus it is possible that the relation of
religiosity to militancy is simply a consequence
of the relation of both religiosity and militancy
to some third factor. However, it can be seen
that even controlling for these factors the finding remains the same (Table 6). Even among
older people, women, those raised in the South,
and those in black denominations, the greater
the religiosity the less the militancy. . . .

The incompatibility of piety and protest that
these data show is evident in comments offered
by respondents. Many religious people hold beliefs that clearly inhibit race protest. For a few,

Table 3

Militancy by Religious Orthodoxy

	Score on Index of Religious Orthodoxy[a]						
	High 6	5	4	3	2	1	Low 0
Militant	20%	26%	25%	24%	42%	41%	57%
Number	(284)	(158)	(210)	(129)	(110)	(51)	(42)

[a]Having no doubt about the existence of God, the devil, and the after-life were
each scored two, being fairly certain in acceptance of these beliefs was scored
one, while having some doubts was scored zero.

Table 4

Militancy by Frequency of Attendance at Worship Service

	Percent Militant	Number
Attend church:		
More than once a week	18	(79)
Once a week	26	(309)
Once to several times a month	28	(354)
Less than once a month to once a year	34	(178)
Less than once a year	32	(61)

Table 5

As Religiosity Increases Militancy Decreases

	Score on Index of Religiosity[a]			
	Very Religious (11, 12)	Quite Religious (7–10)	Not Very Religious (3–6)	Not at all Religious (0–2)
Militant	19%	24%	33%	49%
Number	(209)	(485)	(166)	(124)

[a]Those for whom religion was extremely, quite, fairly, not too, and not at all important were scored 4, 3, 2, 1, and 0, respectively. Those with scores of 6, 5 and 4, 3, 2 and 1, and 0 on the Orthodoxy Index were scored 4, 3, 2, 1, and 0, respectively. Those attending worship services more than once a week, once a week, once to several times a month, less than once a month to once a year, and less than once a year were scored 4, 3, 2, 1, and 0, respectively.

segregation and a lowly status for blacks are somehow God's will and not for men to question. Thus a housewife in South Bend, Indiana, in saying that civil rights demonstrations had hurt blacks, added, "God is the Creator of everything. We don't know why we all dark-skinned. We should try to put forth the effort to do what God wants and not question." A black spiritual contains the lines, "I'm gonna wait upon the Lord till my change comes." Rather than seeing segregation as God's will, our respondents more frequently stressed that God, as absolute controller of the universe, would bring about change in his own way and at his own time. In indicating her unwillingness to take part in a civil rights demonstration, a Detroit housewife said, "I don't go for demonstrations. I believe that God created all men equal and at his appointed time he will give every man his portion; no one can hinder it." And in response to the question about whether or not the government in Washington was pushing integration too slowly, a clerk in Atlanta said, "You can't hurry God. He has a certain time for this to take place. I don't know about Washington."

Others who desired integration and immediate social change felt that, since God was on their side, man need not do anything to help bring it about. Thus a worker in Cleveland gave as his reason for desiring fewer civil rights demonstrations: "With God helping to fight our battle, I believe we can do with less demonstrations." And in saying that blacks should spend more time praying and less time demonstrating, an Atlanta clergyman added, "Praying is demonstrating."

Although the net effect of religion is clearly to inhibit attitudes of protest, many religious people are nevertheless militant. A religious orientation and a concern with racial protest are

certainly not mutually exclusive. Given the active involvement of some churches, the singing of protest spirituals, and the ideology of the movement as it relates to Christian principles of love, equality, passive suffering, and the appeal to a higher moral law, it would be surprising if there were only a few religious people among the militants. A study of Southern black CORE activists indicates that less than one person in ten never attends church while almost six out of ten attended church weekly. A religious orientation and a concern with racial protest are certainly not mutually exclusive, and some of

Table 6

Militancy Related to Religiosity by Age, Sex, Place of Upbringing, and Denomination (percent militant; number of respondents shown in parentheses)

	Index of Religiosity			
	Very Religious	Quite Religious	Not Very Religious	Not at All Religious
Age:				
18–29	20% (25)	28% (110)	35% (55)	43% (37)
30–44	22 (54)	31 (161)	37 (59)	53 (58)
45–59	21 (63)	21 (117)	24 (33)	52 (21)
60+	13 (67)	11 (96)	26 (19)	—[a]
Sex:				
Women	18 (133)	21 (286)	32 (76)	42 (38)
Men	20 (76)	28 (199)	33 (90)	52 (86)
Where raised:				
Deep South	16 (122)	19 (255)	25 (61)	38 (29)
Border states	29 (49)	28 (104)	31 (42)	54 (35)
Non-South	16 (38)	32 (126)	41 (63)	60 (52)
Denomination:				
Episcopalian, Presbyterian, or Congregationalist	17 (12)	39 (23)	46 (13)	58 (12)
Catholic	10 (10)	31 (49)	40 (20)	54 (28)
Methodist	35 (23)	20 (76)	36 (28)	50 (12)
Baptist	17 (161)	23 (325)	30 (101)	46 (68)

[a]Three out of six respondents scored as militant.

those in our study would no doubt agree with Thomas Jefferson that "resistance to tyranny is obedience to God."

However, what determines whether religion leads to an active concern with racial matters or results in quietism?

The classical indictment of religion from the Marxist perspective is that, by focusing concern on an after-life, the evils of this life are ignored. However, there are important differences among religious institutions and among individuals in the importance they give to other-worldly concerns. Like most ideologies, both religious and secular, Christianity contains many themes, which, if not in contradiction, are certainly in tension with one another. Here, no doubt, lies part of the explanation of religion's varied consequences for protest. One important strand of Christianity stresses acceptance of one's lot and glorifies the after-life. However, another is more concerned with the realization of Judaeo-Christian values in the current life. Martin Luther King clearly represents this "social gospel" tradition. When one's religious involvement includes temporal concerns and acceptance of the belief that men as well as God have a role in the structuring of human affairs, then, rather than serving to inhibit protest, religion can serve to inspire and sustain it. This religious inspiration is clearly present in the writings of King and others.

However, among sect members and the religious with an otherworldly orientation, religion and race protest, if not mutually exclusive, are certainly what one observer has referred to as "mutually corrosive kinds of commitments."[11] Until such time as religion loosens its hold over these people, or comes to embody to a greater extent the belief that man as well as God can bring about secular change, and focuses more on the here and now, religion would seem to be an important factor working against the widespread radicalization of the black public.

Notes

1. Kenneth Stampp, *The Peculiar Institution*, New York, Alfred Knopf, 1956, p. 158.

2. Gunnar Myrdal *et al.*, *An American Dilemma*, New York, Harper & Row, 1944, pp. 861–863.

3. Daniel Thompson, "The Rise of Negro Protest," *Annals of the American Academy of Political and Social Science*, January 1965, p. 26.

4. Liston Pope, "The Negro and Religion in America," *Review of Religious Research*, Spring 1964, p. 145.

5. Jane Record and Wilson Record, "Ideological Forces and the Negro Protest," *Annals of the American Academy of Political and Social Science*, January 1965, p. 92.

6. G. Booker, *Black Man's America*, Englewood Cliffs, N.J., Prentice-Hall, 1964, p. 111.

7. Rev. W. T. Walker, as quoted in William Brink and Louis Harris, *The Negro Revolution in America*, New York, Simon and Schuster, 1964, p. 103.

8. N. Glenn, "Negro Religion in the United States," in L. Schneider, ed., *Religion, Culture and Society*, New York, J. Wiley, 1964.

9. J. Fichter, "American Religion and the Negro," *Daedalus*, Fall 1965, p. 1087.

10. E. U. Essien-Udom, *Black Nationalism*, New York, Dell, 1962, pp. 357–358.

11. Rodney Stark, "Class, Radicalism, and Religious Involvement," *American Sociological Review*, October 1964.

18
The Position of the Press in the U.S. Power Structure

Peter Dreier

Editors' Introduction

In the introduction to the keynote reading we discussed the complex web of institutional interrelationships. You may have asked yourself as you read the selections up to this point, "How do these interrelationships come about and how are they maintained?" In the first illustrative reading, "Religion: Opiate or Inspiration for Civil Rights Militancy?" you saw that the way religion and the polity are interrelated is a result of particular religious beliefs and practices. In the following reading, Peter Dreier offers another explanation for institutional interrelationships.

Although Dreier is dealing with the press, institutions are very much a part of his analysis. Think about the broad impact of the press in the United States. It pervades the polity, the economy, education, religion, and sometimes the family. The press is itself a part of the economy (it produces and distributes a product) and of education (it teaches "new recruits" and old ones, too). But *how* has this happened and how is this interrelationship maintained? Dreier looks at what are called "corporate interlocks" to discover if the same people are sitting at the tops of the major U.S. institutions. Are members of the boards of directors of the major newspapers in this country also in influential positions in the economy and in the political structure? If they are, can one assume that these persons will "coordinate" (in their favor) the different sectors of the society? Can this set of influential people, then, be an answer to the question of how institutions are interrelated and remain so? This is a popular explanation, as you will see.

In the early 1950s C. Wright Mills, an influential sociologist, wrote *The Power Elite*. In it he argues that there exists in America a small group of people made up of key corporate leaders, top military personnel, and high government officials who together direct many of the crucial decisions made in this country. The "power elite," as Mills calls this group of people, is the real source of power. These people have their interests served by the rest of society. Although others before Mills had made similar arguments, his book touched off a debate that is still going on, although with less energy than in the past. The other side of the debate, the pluralist side, states that influential people operate within issue areas but do not operate across them to any great degree. In other words, a person who is influential in the area of decisions about taxes will have little to do with decisions on education. Therefore, pluralists envision not a pyramid of power with an elite on top, but a much more diffuse power structure made up of many small pyramids intersecting only rarely and randomly.

One of the issues Mills raises is that of interconnections among the elite. In recent years sociologists have investigated this by examining the degree to which the members of boards of directors interconnect or interlock across major corporations, universities, financial institutions, and nonprofit organizations. Peter Dreier is working in this "power elite" tradition, as he searches for interlocking directorates, this time in the newspaper business. Why are corporate interlocks involving the newspaper business so crucial? Do these interlocks have implications far beyond, say, an interlock between a steel company and an auto manufacturer? Dreier says he is most interested in the interrelationships involving the "inner group" within the capitalist class. What is this inner group? Dreier looks at three dimensions of the web of institutional affiliations of this inner group: "the extent of the press' affiliations with other institutions," "the distribution of affiliations," and "the different patterns of affiliations between newspaper firms." What evidence does he offer for each of these? Dreier presents lots of numbers, but if you examine each of these three dimensions, one at a time, you will be able to sort out his arguments. One of the most important points Dreier makes is his explanation of the "corporate liberal" ideology as it appears in the *Washington Post,* the *New York Times,* the *Wall Street Journal,* and the *Los Angeles Times*—the four most influential papers in the United States. How does he explain this liberalism? When these papers expose "bad guys" or criticize policies, what are they supporting? Also, note the degree to which these papers are controlled by the inner circle. How do the interlocks found by Dreier contribute to overall interrelationships among the institutions in the society?

This reading is a classic example of a conflict theoretical orientation. In the tradition of C. Wright Mills, the argument is that a small group of people run this country. The capitalist class acts through this small group to pursue its own interests, often at the expense of other groups in this society.

Carefully read the section on Dreier's methods. You will find that much of his information came from standard reference sources probably available in your college library. Dreier has combined these available data with questionnaire and interview data collected directly from the newspaper companies. He also has interviewed "more than 20 newspaper company directors and many journalists." Would his data have been improved if he had talked with more directors? What might he have asked them? What would *you* ask them?

A great deal has been written about the "power of the press," but little is known about the position of the press within the power structure of the United States. This paper examines the relationship between the U.S. business elite and the mass media elite. The mass media play two critical roles in society. First, they are profit-seeking firms; their owners, directors, suppliers, and advertisers are interested in the economic health of these firms. Second, they are ideological institutions. The media set the agenda of political, social, and economic debate. They shape public opinion on crucial issues; socialize individuals to social roles and behavior; and can legitimate or undermine powerful institutions, individuals, and ideas. Who controls these organizations is an important area for research.

Observers of and spokespersons for the mass media both view it as unique among U.S. industries. They view the media as a "fourth estate," standing apart from other institutions and segments of society, putting its public role and its social responsibility above the unfettered pursuit of profits. Publishers, editors, and journalists alike claim that their organizations are not beholden to any special interests except the pursuit of truth. The prime function of the press, according to the canons of the American Society of Newspaper Editors, is "to satisfy the public's need to know" (Udell, 1978:24). Because of their unique function in society, the mass media are, alone among U.S. industries, protected by the Constitution through First

Reprinted from *Social Problems*, 29, 3 (February 1982). Used with permission of the author and the Society for the Study of Social Problems.

Amendment guarantees of "freedom of the press" (Bagdikian, 1971).

The media's special status is codified in an ideology extolling objectivity and impartiality. According to this ideology, the media should not reflect the views of any particular segment of society, but should try to provide a balance of all perspectives and points of view (Schudson, 1978; Tuchman, 1978). These norms are institutionalized in the daily practice of journalism. To guarantee that journalists' judgments are not colored by their own affiliations, newspapers encourage, and often require, that journalists avoid potentially conflicting commitments. The code of ethics of Sigma Delta Chi, the Society of Professional Journalists (whose officers are usually high-level editors of influential newspapers) states: "Journalists and their employers should conduct their personal lives in a manner which protects them from conflicts of interest, real or apparent. Their responsibilities to the public are paramount." Most journalists espouse these professional norms (Johnstone *et al.*, 1976).

While the Sigma Delta Chi statement includes employers (media executives) as well as journalists in its proscription against conflicts of interest, interviews with and letters from newspaper board directors, as well as their statements in various articles, reveal contradictory norms and practices among newspaper firms regarding executives' institutional affiliations (Dreier and Weinberg, 1979; Ingrassia, 1979; Morgenthaler, 1970; Rockmore, 1977). Some believe that all such affiliations compromise the credibility of the press and thus should be prohibited or discouraged. For example, the chairman of one of the nation's largest newspaper firms (who requested anonymity) said: "I have turned down directorships of major banks, saving-fund societies, life insurance companies, fire insurance companies, graduate business schools, hospitals, art museums, orchestra, and Port Authority, to avoid conflict of interest and the mere appearance of conflict of interest, direct or indirect (as in news coverage of strikes against such institutions)" (personal letter to author). Ben Bradlee, editor of the *Washington Post,* believes that newspaper company editors and executives should not join "any civic groups, clubs, or institutions" (personal interview). Otis Chandler, publisher of the *Los Angeles Times,* has resigned from all his corporate directorships, citing the desire to avoid conflict of interest, although fellow board members at the parent Times-Mirror Company have not followed suit. Some firms prohibit affiliations only with profit-seeking corporations. Even among those who prohibit or discourage outside involvements, some apply such standards only to "inside" directors (employees of the firm) and not "outside" directors. Others view such involvements as part of a newspaper's role as an active "citizen" of the community, even suggesting that such involvements improve news coverage by allowing executives to feel the community's pulse. Still others suggest that affiliations related to the media's business operations, such as corporate directorships or business policy groups, are entirely separate from its journalistic activities and thus do not reflect potential conflicts of interest. Allen Neuharth, chairman of Gannett (the largest chain in terms of number of newspapers), explained that "I accepted the Marine Midland (bank) directorship because it has branches in all our communities in New York State. . . . It's a good way for our company, through me, to be in touch with the business communities in the cities where we publish. You learn a lot of things about business developments that you might not otherwise know about" (personal interview).

During the past decade, sociologists have developed a growing interest in the upper echelons of business and political power, but they have not focused on the press as a special segment. At the same time, interest in the mass media and its inner workings has also grown. Research, however, has centered on the day-to-day activities of the newsroom itself and the processes of identifying, gathering, writing and editing the news. This has provided a wealth of insight into the social construction of news and the pressures on news media personnel (Dreier, 1978; Epstein, 1973; Fishman, 1980; Gans, 1979; Tuchman, 1972, 1978). But this research has not penetrated the upper echelons of the newspaper hierarchy, the top decision-makers or the boards of directors of newspaper-owning corporations. Much of what we know about these individuals comes from official and unofficial biographies of publishers, histories of particular newspapers and journalistic accounts of the "lords of the press" (Gottlieb and Wolt, 1977; Halberstam, 1979; Lundberg, 1936; Roberts, 1977; Talese, 1969). While these studies suggest that publishers and board members can have an influence on the general tone of a paper as well as upon specific stories, there has been little systematic research on the characteristics of these individuals and how (or if) they are connected to other sectors of the U.S. power structure.

In the most recent and comprehensive survey of media management, Bogart (1974:170) notes that "the people who run such major media organizations are super-elites, notoriously difficult for social scientists to study first-hand." In this paper, I systematically examine the media elites' position in the web of institution affiliations that comprise the U.S. power structure. First, I examine the *extent* of the press' affiliations with other institutions. Despite their occupational code and ideology, the press is deeply involved in the power structure network. Second, I describe the *distribution* of affiliations, particularly between inside and outside directors, a distinction mentioned by several executives as the critical difference in terms of outside involvements. Third, I look at the different *patterns* of affiliation between newspaper firms. Some companies are more closely linked to the power structure than others. There is a small subset of influential papers whose affiliations are significantly greater than the others. This distinctive pattern corresponds to the ideological outlook of the pinnacle of the corporate elite, an outlook termed "corporate liberalism."

THE U.S. POWER STRUCTURE

Following Domhoff (1970, 1979), Dye (1976), Useem (1978, 1979) and others, I defined the U.S. power structure as the top positions in the institutional structure of the society, especially the elite institutions in four major sectors—corporations, business policy groups, non-profit civic organizations, and social clubs. Research has found that, despite divisions among the members of the power structure, overlapping memberships in these elite institutions form a network, or web, of inter-relationships that allows a high degree of cohesiveness within the capitalist class. At the pinnacle of this network is what Useem (1978, 1979), Zeitlin *et al.* (1974), and others call the "inner group" within the capitalist class. This inner group includes those individuals connected to several major corporations who seek to protect the general welfare of large corporations as a class rather than the narrower interests of particular corporations, industries or regions. This inner group is the general voice of big business. Members of the inner group are disproportionately represented in institutions that promote class cohesiveness and integration, such as civic organizations, business policy groups, clubs, and high-level government posts (Useem, 1979, 1980). This paper examines the press' position within the U.S. power structure and its links with this inner group.

METHODS

I defined the newspaper elite as the directors of the 25 largest newspaper companies in the United States (in terms of daily circulation) during 1978 and 1979 (Morton, 1980). The top 25 companies accounted for over one-half (53.5 percent) of the total daily circulation in 1979. In that year there were 1,764 papers in the United States with a combined circulation of 62.2 million (Compaine, 1979:13). The top 25 companies owned 425 daily papers with a total circulation of 33.3 million. These included most of the major metropolitan papers (including 20 of the 25 largest dailies) and many small- and medium-sized papers as well. The top 25 newspaper companies dominate the industry. This reflects the long-term trend, accelerated in the postwar period, toward concentration, conglomeration, and centralization within the newspaper industry (Bagdikian, 1978; *Business Week,* 1977; Compaine, 1979). While many of these companies are diversifying, they are still primarily engaged in newspaper publishing (Compaine, 1979:32). Of the top 25 companies, all except Newhouse (the third-largest chain) provided me with a list of its board of directors for 1978 and 1979. I checked the lists of directors against information from annual reports (for those that publish them) and public references such as Standard and Poor's *Register of Corporations*. Because the list of Newhouse's board could not be obtained directly or indirectly (*Business Week,* 1976a, noted the company's exceptional secrecy), this research focuses on 24 of the top 25 chains.

This method netted a total of 290 individuals. Their names and affiliations (revised and updated here) appear in Dreier and Weinberg (1979). I examined affiliations with elite institutions, as defined by Bonacich and Domhoff (1977), Domhoff (1970), Dye (1976), and Useem (1978, 1979).[1] I obtained information on the affiliations of these 290 individuals from the following sources: Standard biographical data on 60 percent of the directors was obtained from *Who's Who in America*, the regional edition of *Who's Who, Who's Who in Business and Finance*, and several other similar reference books on ethnic and minority group members, educators, government officials, and lawyers. The reference books were consulted for 1975 to 1979. While the individuals listed in these public reference books provided their own, often incomplete, biographical information, what information that is there is generally considered reliable. G. William Domhoff provided recent membership lists of the major business policy groups and of eight nationally prominent social clubs. Many of the directors listed membership in these (and other) business policy groups and social clubs in their *Who's Who* biographies, but some affiliations missing from official biographies were added using the complete membership lists. I checked each individual in the *Business Periodical Index,* which indexes all major business periodicals from 1975 to 1979; articles about or mentioning them were consulted. Finally, I sent each newspaper company a questionnaire requesting biographical information (including institutional affiliations) on their board members. The questionnaire included all information already obtained on each individual and asked that errors be corrected. Mailed questionnaires were followed up by phone calls to public relations directors (or their closest counterparts) in each company. This elicited additional information from some chains and individuals. The data may overlook non-elite affiliations (which are least likely to be caught in this research net), but this is not a significant problem for this research. In addition, I interviewed more than 20 newspaper company directors and many journalists.

TOTAL ELITE AFFILIATIONS

Dreier and Weinberg (1979) found that newspaper firms are actively involved in their local communities. This confirms Molotch's (1976: 315) view of the newspaper as one of the key actors in local affairs, its interests "anchored in the aggregate growth of the locality." Social science and journalistic case studies have also revealed the involvement of local papers and their executives in community affairs (Banfield, 1961; Burd, 1977; Devereux, 1976; Hayes, 1972). But as the newspaper industry has shifted from local to chain ownership, and as parent corporations have become large diversified enterprises, those who control these corporations wield power and influence across local and regional boundaries. One would expect these media elites to become more integrated into the web of affiliations that form the national power structure, if they follow the pattern of other industries.

In fact, the data indicate that the nation's major newspaper firms *are* heavily linked with the nation's power structure. As Table 1 shows, the 24 newspaper companies have 447 ties with elite organizations, including 196 with *Fortune's* 1,300 largest corporations, 97 with the 15 major business policy groups, 24 with the 12 major private universities, and 130 with the 47 elite social clubs. Banks and other financial institutions account for the largest number of corporate interlocks compared with other industries, a pattern found in other interlock studies (Palmer, 1981:7). This is not surprising, given the newspaper industry's rapid growth and expansion in the postwar period and these firms' need for capital (Halberstam, 1979:811).

The power elite influences government policy not only through lobbying, campaign contributions, and policy groups and think tanks, but also by placing representatives (drawn disproportionately from the inner group) in high-level appointed positions in government (Domhoff, 1970, 1979; Dye, 1976; Mintz, 1975; Salzman and Domhoff, 1980; Shoup and Minter, 1977). Table 2 shows that the newspaper industry shares in this pattern of "revolving door" links between the private sector and government. Thirty-six directors have been appointed to at least one (past or present) high-level federal government position. These posts include cabinet posts, presidential advisory commissions, advisory committees to federal agencies (U.S. Congress: Senate, 1977), and regional boards of the Federal Reserve Bank. Individuals with extensive and high-level experience in the federal government provide useful resources for newspaper companies, because these companies engage in activities (such as broadcasting and mergers) that are closely regulated by government. For example, Allen Neuharth, Gannett's chairman, explained:

(William) Bill Rogers is in a position to make major contributions to Gannett in its dealings with government, on anti-trust matters, with the FCC (Federal Communications Commission), whatever. He's been on the inside and can help top management understand what can be done and what can't be done (personal interview).

Table 1

Elite Affiliations by Newspaper Company

	No. of Inside Directors (No. of Affiliations)	No. of Outside Directors (No. of Affiliations)	Fortune Interlocks	Business Policy Groups	Elite University Trusteeships	Elite Clubs	Total Affiliations
Dow Jones	11(3)	9(54)	24	19	2	12	57
N.Y. Times	6(12)	5(35)	23	14	3	7	47
Washington Post	8(17)	4(24)	12	17	3	9	41
Times-Mirror	9(18)	6(22)	24	7	0	9	40
Field Enterprises	4(16)	8(20)	15	4	5	12	36
Gannett	14(5)	7(25)	17	4	1	8	30
Knight-Ridder	14(14)	4(15)	12	2	2	13	29
Minn. Star and Tribune	9(23)	3(3)	6	7	1	12	26
Media General	4(3)	5(19)	9	7	1	5	22
Hearst	19(20)	0(0)	3	2	0	15	20
[Chicago] Tribune	9(2)	2(17)	12	1	3	3	19
Thomson	6(1)	4(15)	9	4	1	2	16
Harte Hanks	7(1)	3(14)	13	2	0	0	15
Capital Cities	10(10)	2(3)	8	2	0	3	13
Affiliated	7(5)	3(3)	0	1	1	6	8
Scripps	10(8)	0(0)	1	1	0	6	8
Cox	8(5)	0(0)	2	1	0	2	5
Copley	11(4)	0(0)	1	2	0	1	4
Lee	8(0)	3(4)	3	0	0	1	4
Independent	11(3)	0(0)	1	0	0	2	3
Central	6(2)	1(1)	1	0	1	1	3
Evening News	9(1)	0(0)	0	0	0	1	1
News America	7(0)	1(0)	0	0	0	0	0
Freedom	12(0)	0(0)	0	0	0	0	0
Total	220(173)	70(274)	196	97	24	130	447

Table 2

Individual Affiliations with High-Level Positions in the Federal
Government (Past and Present)*

| | Number of Individuals Appointed | | |
Newspaper Company**	Inside Directors	Outside Directors	Total
N.Y. Times	2	4	6
Field Enterprises	1	3	4
Minn. Star and Tribune	3	1	4
Times-Mirror	2	2	4
Washington Post	0	3	3
Dow Jones	0	3	3
Media General	1	2	3
Gannett	0	2	2
Cox	2	0	2
Knight-Ridder	0	1	1
Capital Cities	1	0	1
[Chicago] Tribune	0	1	1
Thomson	0	1	1
Evening News	1	0	1
Total	13	23	36

* High-level federal government positions include: first- or second-level cabinet
  secretary, ambassador, presidential advisory commission, advisory committee
  to federal agency, and regional Federal Reserve Bank board.
** The other companies have no high-level federal government affiliations.

Distribution of Affiliations

Affiliations with power structure institutions are
not equally distributed among the 290 directors. As Table 3 indicates, some directors are
highly integrated into the network, others are
marginally integrated, while others are not integrated at all. Indeed, 157 directors have absolutely no ties to any of the elite institutions of
the national power structure; 108 have one to
five affiliations; 20 have six to nine affiliations;
and five have 10 or more (13 being the highest)
affiliations. In other words, 25 of the 290 directors (8.6 percent) account for 204 of the 447
(45.6 percent) elite affiliations.

Moreover, as Table 3 shows, the newspaper
companies' outside directors account for a disproportionate share of the linkages with the

national power structure. Although outside directors account for only 70 of the 290 (24.1
percent) newspaper company directors, they account for 274 of the 447 (61.2 percent) total
elite affiliations. Of the five directors with 10 or
more elite affiliations, all are outside directors;
of the 20 directors with six to nine affiliations,
15 are outside directors. In addition, as Table
2 shows, 23 of the 70 outside directors (32.8
percent), compared with only 13 of the 220
inside directors (5.9 percent) have been appointed to high-level positions in the federal
government.

These data indicate that the newspaper companies' ties with the U.S. power structure come
primarily from outside directors brought onto
their boards for a variety of reasons, and that a
relatively small group of these outside directors

Table 3

Distribution of Elite Affiliations

No. of Elite Affiliations	No. of Inside Directors	No. of Outside Directors	Total No. of Directors
0	146 (0)	11 (0)	157 (0)
1–5	69 (138)	39 (105)	108 (243)
6–9	5 (35)	15 (113)	20 (148)
10–13	0 (0)	5 (56)	5 (56)
Total	220 (173)	70 (274)	290 (447)

Note: Numbers in parentheses give the total number of elite affiliations for each cell.

account for a disproportionate share of these elite affiliations. This pattern suggests that a division of labor may exist within the boards of these newspaper firms. The inside directors, with some exceptions, run the day-to-day operations of the newspaper-owning firms (or simply benefit through trusts as beneficiaries). Their affiliations, also with some exceptions, are with industry-related activities—boards of the Associated Press, or newspaper executives' organizations, press clubs, awards committees, and so on—and reflect an industry-oriented outlook. These are mainly professional managers who either climbed the newspaper corporate ladder or were brought in from outside to provide specific kinds of expertise. The exceptions to this rule are those inside directors who are part of the owning families—Katherine Graham of the *Washington Post,* Arthur Sulzberger of the *New York Times,* John Cowles and John Cowles, Jr., of the *Minneapolis Star and Tribune,* Marshall Field of Field Enterprises, Helen Copley of Copley Press, William Taylor of Affiliated Publications, and William R. Hearst, Jr., of Hearst Corporation, for example. Members of owning families tend to be part of

both the social aristocracy of the nation (Baltzell, 1964; Domhoff, 1970; Roberts, 1977; Swanberg, 1961) and the network of the U.S. power structure. Thus, they share more in common with the outside directors than with the professional executives hired to run the newspaper companies on a day-to-day basis. With few exceptions, even the members of the owning families are not as heavily involved as the outside directors; they are less likely, for example, to have directorships on major corporations (Roberts, 1977:460). As members of "old wealth" families, however, many are likely to retain memberships in the exclusive social clubs and civic groups that form an important part of the power structure (Baltzell, 1964; *Business Week,* 1980; Domhoff, 1974; Lundberg, 1968). There are also professional executives— inside directors are part of the owning families—who are heavily involved with the elite institutions, but as a proportion of affiliations they take a back seat to the outside directors.

The outside directors provide a bridge between the newspaper companies and the capitalist class and its institutions. Some, as bank directors, may oversee their banks' investment in newspaper firms. Some, as former government officials, may provide expertise on government matters. But beyond these specific roles, these outside directors—many of them members of the inner group at the pinnacle of the capitalist class—provide a link to the broader interests of the business community with which the newspaper companies' future is tied. They provide important links to the major corporate decision-makers and the larger corporate world. Thus, while they may represent stockholders' interests (*Business Week,* 1979), or banks, or other institutions in the narrow sense, they also provide a link to the central decision-making networks within the capitalist class.

DIFFERENCES AMONG NEWSPAPER COMPANIES

As Table 1 indicates, not all newspaper companies are equally linked with the power structure. Four companies—Dow Jones Company (57 affiliations), the New York Times Company (47), the Washington Post Company (41), and the Times-Mirror Corporation (40)—together account for 185 (41.6 percent) of all elite affiliations. The next four companies account for 27.1 percent, the next four 17.2 percent, the next four 9.8 percent, the next four 3.5 percent, and the final four less than one percent. How can this disproportionate share at the top be explained? What distinguishes the companies with the most elite affiliations, and therefore the strongest institutional integration within the national power structure, from the other companies?

The literature on interlocking directorates suggests that interlocks are relationships between corporations and that directors are agents of these relationships. Organizations seek such ties in pursuit of their interests. Indeed, there is evidence that different interlocks perform different functions, including access to general information about corporations' environments, specific information about corporate plans and procedures, and explicit coordination between interlocked firms (Allen, 1974 and 1978; Burt, 1980; Levine, 1972; Mariolis, 1975;

Palmer, 1981; Ratcliff *et al.,* 1979). Interviews with and statements by the newspaper directors under study indicate that all of these factors help to explain specific interlocks for each firm. But these do not explain why the Dow Jones Company, New York Times Company, Washington Post Company, and the Times-Mirror Corporation have a significantly greater share of elite affiliations, of which corporate interlocks are only one type. Alternative hypotheses drawn from the literature do not explain this pattern. These four companies are not the largest in terms of sales or profitability, which are found to be correlated with interlocks (Bunting, 1977; Pennings, 1980), as found in the Dun and Bradstreet *Million Market Directory* and as found in Morton's (1981) analysis of newspaper firms' average after-tax profit margins over a five-year period. (See also *Business Week,* 1976b and 1978.) Neither are these four companies the largest in terms of total daily circulation, number of newspapers, or number of market areas in which their newspapers circulate, as indicated by the 1980 *Editor and Publisher Yearbook.*

What is clear, however, is that these four companies own the four most prestigious and politically influential newspapers in the United States, the *Washington Post,* the *Wall Street Journal* (Dow Jones), the *Los Angeles Times* (Times-Mirror Corporation), and the *New York Times* (Bagdikian, 1971; Emery and Emery, 1978; Gans, 1979; Merrill, 1968; Merrill and Fisher, 1980; Tebbel, 1961).

Journalistic influence and prestige probably accounts for the pattern of elite affiliations. There is a perfect correlation between the four newspaper companies with the most elite affiliations and the four most influential newspapers. The data do not explain the causal relationship. Outside directors may be co-opted onto the boards of newspapers seeking access to capital or decision-making elites. Then too, the most powerful corporations and other elite institutions may be co-opting these four powerful papers to ensure their conformity with the power structure's long-term views (Rockmore, 1979). In fact, both of these processes are plausible. Moreover, some individuals may be motivated to join the boards largely for the prestige of affiliating with a highly visible and powerful institution.

Voices of the Inner Group

The four firms/papers with the closest ties to the U.S. power structure—the *New York Times,* the *Washington Post,* the *Wall Street Journal* and the *Los Angeles Times*—are distinguished from most other daily newspapers by their ideological outlook. These four papers reflect a "corporate liberal" perspective. This is the outlook identified with the inner group of the capitalist class (Block, 1977, 1980; Domhoff, 1970; Weinstein, 1968). While leaders of small and medium size businesses have characteristically opposed unions, social welfare, foreign aid, and government regulation in all forms, leaders of the major corporations (the inner group) have sought to forestall challenges from below and stabilize the long-term foundations of capitalism by implementing strategic reforms to co-opt dissent. Concerned with the stability of the entire system rather than the narrow interests of any one industry, corporation, or region, the leaders of the major corporations have conceded the need for some government regulation of business, as well as trade unionism, civil rights and social welfare legislation, foreign aid to promote free trade and stability, and other related policies. Corporate-sponsored think tanks and business policy groups generally adhere to this "corporate liberal" outlook.[2]

Most U.S. newspapers are relatively narrow and parochial in outlook. Few have offices in Washington, D.C., or in foreign capitals. They emphasize local or regional news and economic development and growth (Molotch, 1976). Newspaper publishers traditionally have been politically conservative, reflecting a small-business outlook of government intervention in the marketplace, foreign aid and trade, defense policy, labor relations, and other policies. For the past 40 years, the overwhelming number of daily papers have supported the Republican party. In every presidential election since 1940, with the exception of 1964, most U.S. newspapers (between 57.7 percent in 1960 and 71.4 percent in 1972) endorsed the Republican candidate. This parochialism continues to this day (Emery and Emery, 1978).

There is evidence, however, that as newspapers and newspaper companies grow as corporate entities (and as competition between papers declines, leaving most dailies without any direct competition), they begin to broaden their political outlook. Today there are few independent, locally owned dailies. Gradually, chains have purchased independent papers and large chains have purchased smaller chains (Bagdikian, 1978; *Business Week,* 1977; Compaine, 1979; Louis, 1978; Rosse *et al.,* 1975). As the chains grow, their high-level employees and executives make links outside the local community. They are no longer under the strong personal control of individuals such as William R. Hearst (Lundberg, 1936; Swanberg, 1961) or Col. Robert McCormick (Waldrop, 1966). Moreover, as newspaper competition declines, monopoloy or near-monopoly newspapers must appeal to a broader audience. These reasons are clearly responsible for the increasingly corporate liberal outlook of both the *Chicago Tribune* and the *Los Angeles Times,* once bastions of extreme conservatism (Dreier, 1976; Gottlieb and Wolt, 1977; Halberstam, 1979). Many papers, especially the *Wall Street Journal,* the *New York Times,* and the *Washington Post,* wish to appeal to the "upscale," affluent readers, the target for both advertisers and opinion-leaders. One indication of newspapers' increasingly "statesman-like" role is the steady increase in papers making no presidential endorsements at all—from only 13.4 percent in 1940 to 25.6 percent in 1976 (Emery and Emery, 1978:483).

Although daily newspapers are moving away from narrow parochialism, the four papers with the closest links to the power structure best reflect the corporate liberal viewpoint. They have taken the lead, among major daily papers, in exposing corporate wrongdoing and government corruption. They regularly investigate corporations and government actions that violate what Gans (1979) calls "responsible capitalism." The *New York Times* published the Pentagon Papers, the *Washington Post* and the *Los Angeles Times* took the lead in the Watergate exposé, and the *Wall Street Journal* was the first major paper to investigate the foreign policy views and business ethics of Reagan advisor Richard Allen, to question the State Department's view of the ties between El Salvador's insurgents and both Cuba and the Soviet Union, and to expose many corporate scandals that corporate officers would have preferred to remain secret. These papers were among the first to reflect the disenchantment with the Vietnam War among the inner group of the business community (Joseph, 1981). Other papers also do such investigations and reporting, but none as consistently and with such national influence as these four papers. What this suggests is that these papers' corporate liberal outlook transcends the narrow interests of any one industry, corporation, or region. The corporate liberal press may criticize or expose *particular* corporate or government practices as harmful to the legitimacy and thus long-term stability of the entire system, or *particular* corporations or elected officials for the same reason. They take the long view. Thus, while at first it may seem paradoxical that the papers and firms with the *most* elite connections are the most likely to expose corporate and government practices, from the standpoint of their role as corporate liberal spokesmen for the inner group, it makes perfect sense.

In examining how the mass media functions, sociologists have usually explained the tendency of newspapers to reflect the outlook of the powerful in terms of the routines of newsgathering and the ability of powerful institutions and individuals to gain regular access to journalists. Or, they point to the attitude of journalists that those in positions of power and influence are more "responsible" news sources (Dreier, 1978; Epstein, 1973; Fishman, 1980; Gans, 1979; Molotch and Lester, 1974; Sigal, 1973; Tuchman, 1972, 1978). Certainly these factors help explain why newspapers in general reflect the world view of the powerful, but they cannot explain *variations* in ideology and world view, between newspapers, since the routines of news gathering are similar on most papers. That is

why factors external to the newsroom, including the social, political, and corporate ties of newspaper directors, must be considered in explaining why some newspapers are different than others.

Our data confirm that the nation's leading newspaper companies are all linked to outside institutions. Of the 24 firms, 22 are linked to at least one elite institution of the *national* power structure. Moreover, these links are primarily through outside directors, who serve as the major link to the business community. The patterns of affiliations also suggest that four companies—those that publish the *New York Times,* the *Washington Post,* the *Los Angeles Times,* and the *Wall Street Journal*—represent the newspaper industry's part of the national power structure. These four papers speak not only for the directors and owners, but also for the inner group of the larger capitalist class. This is not to deny that they have a degree of autonomy and independence; they are not mere "tools" of this class (Dreier, 1982). But the structural links help to maintain and reinforce the ideology of corporate liberalism that these papers share with the inner group.

Notes

1. In terms of *corporations,* the elite institutions are defined as the 1,000 largest industrial corporations and 50 of each of the largest banks, insurance companies, financial companies, utilities, retail companies, and transportation companies in 1979, as listed by *Fortune* magazine. In a society in which economic power is highly concentrated, these 1,300 corporations control the overwhelming share of the nation's economic assets, and thus its economic power. In terms of *business policy groups,* the elite institutions are defined as the 15 major groups that prior research indicates play a critical role in establishing a common position among the major corporations on major issues. These 15 organizations were established to provide a forum for the discussion, articulation and promotion of policies that affect most major companies, regardless of industrial sector or geographic region. They draw their members from the top ranks of a broad range of corporations and include, in some cases, academics, attorneys and other professionals involved with and sympathetic to the business community (Eakins, 1969; Domhoff, 1970, 1979; Hirsch, 1975; Shoup and Minter, 1977). In terms of *non-profit civic organizations,* elite institutions are defined as the 12 private colleges and universities with the largest endowments. There are two reasons for isolating colleges and universities to represent this sector. First, among this sector, college and university board members are the largest sub-category (compared with cultural organizations, research and scientific institutions, philanthropic foundations, health-related organizations, charitable groups) and thus make it easier to see variations by newspaper companies. Second, identifying the "elite" institutions in the other sub-categories of the civic sector is more problematic. For example, it is difficult to determine which cultural institutions in the world of art, music, theater and related activities are the most powerful and prestigious. These 12 colleges and universities control over half (54 percent) of the resources available to private higher education and these institutions (although some of the more prestigious public universities such as Michigan and California and small private colleges such as Amherst and Reed are not included). The trustees of these 12 institutions "exercise a significant influence over higher education and thus over the quality of life in America" (Dye, 1976:133). A disproportionate number of the nation's top leaders attended one of these institutions, which attract a disproportionate number of the inner group members to their boards (Useem, 1979). In terms of *social clubs,* elite institutions are defined in terms of the 47 exclusive clubs identified by Domhoff (1970) and Bonacich and Domhoff (1977) as those that draw their membership from a nation-wide pool of elites, linking together individuals from across the country, disproportionately from the inner group. The author will supply lists of the specific institutions upon request.

2. Corporate liberal ideology and policy—which is most evident during periods of social unrest, such as the Progressive era, the Depression, and the 1960s—can also be seen as a product of the steady expansion of U.S. corporate and political power in the first three-quarters of this century. Although proponents of corporate liberalism were ascendant within the capitalist class during much of that period, they did meet resistance from other segments of the class. The success of corporate liberalism, moreover, rested on continued corporate and political expansion, a trend that was challenged in the 1970s, both domestically and abroad. The decline of U.S. power in the world economy (Kolko, 1974) and the domestic fiscal crisis of the state (O'Connor, 1973) created difficulties for proponents of corporate liberalism.

References

Allen, Michael
1974   "The structure of interorganizational elite cooptation: Interlocking corporate directorates." American Sociological Review 39:393–406.
1978   "Economic interest groups and the corporate elite structure." Social Science Quarterly 58:597–615.
Bagdikian, Ben
1971   The Information Machines. New York: Harper.
1978   "Conglomeration, concentration and the flow of information." Proceedings of the Symposium on Media Concentration. Federal Trade Commission, Bureau of Competition. Washington, D.C.: U.S. Government Printing Office.
Baltzell, E. Digby
1964   The Protestant Establishment: Aristocracy and Caste in America. New York: Random House.
Banfield, Edward
1961   Political Influence. New York: Free Press.
Block, Fred
1977   "Beyond corporate liberalism." Social Problems 24:252–261.
1980   "Beyond relative autonomy." Socialist Register: 227–242.

Bogart, Leo
    1974   "The management of mass media."
            Pp. 143–170 in W. Phillips Davidson
            and Frederick Yu (eds.), Mass Com-
            munication Research. New York:
            Praeger.
Bonacich, Phillip and G. William Domhoff
    1977   "Overlapping memberships among
            clubs and policy groups of the Amer-
            ican ruling class." Paper presented at
            the meetings of the American Socio-
            logical Association, Chicago. August.
Bunting, David
    1977   "Corporate interlocking, part III: In-
            terlocks and return on investment."
            Directors and Boards 1:4–11.
Burd, Gene
    1977   "The selling of the sunbelt: Civic
            boosterism in the media." Pp. 129–
            150 in David Perry and Alfred Wat-
            kins (eds.), The Rise of the Sunbelt
            Cities. Beverly Hills: Sage Publica-
            tions.
Burt, Ronald
    1980   "Testing a structural theory of cor-
            porate cooptation." American Socio-
            logical Review 45:821–841.
Business Week
    1976a   "America's most profitable pub-
            lisher." Jan. 26:56–69.
    1976b   "Behind the profit squeeze at the
            New York Times." August 30:42–49.
    1977   "The big money hunts for indepen-
            dent newspapers." Feb. 21:56–62.
    1978   "Dow Jones joins the media conglom-
            erates." Nov. 13:60–72.
    1979   "End of the directors' rubber stamp."
            Sept. 10:72–83.
    1980   "The all-male club: Threatened on
            all sides." August 11:90–91.
Compaine, Benjamin M. (ed.)
    1979   Who Owns the Media? White Plains,
            N.Y.: Knowledge Industry Publica-
            tions.
Devereux, Sean
    1976   "Boosters in the newsroom: The
            Jacksonville case." Columbia Jour-
            nalism Review (January/February):
            38–47.

Domhoff, G. William
    1970   The Higher Circles. New York: Vin-
            tage Books.
    1974   The Bohemian Grove and Other Re-
            treats. New York: Harper & Row.
    1979   The Powers That Be. New York:
            Random House .
Dreier, Peter
    1976   "The Urban Press in Transition: The
            Political Economy of Newswork."
            Unpublished Ph.D. dissertation, Uni-
            versity of Chicago.
    1978   "Newsroom democracy and media
            monopoly: Dilemmas of workplace
            reform among professional journal-
            ists." Insurgent Sociologist 7:70–86.
    1982   "Capitalists vs. the media: An analysis
            of an ideological mobilization among
            business leaders." Media, Culture,
            and Society 4(2):111–132.
Dreier, Peter and Steven Weinberg
    1979   "The ties that blind: Interlocking di-
            rectorates." Columbia Journalism
            Review 18:(November/December):
            51–68.
Dye, Thomas
    1976   Who's Running America? Institu-
            tional Leadership in the United
            States. Englewood Cliffs, N.J.: Pren-
            tice-Hall.
Eakins, David
    1969   "Business planners and America's
            postwar expansion." Pp. 143–171 in
            David Horowitz (ed.), Corporations
            and the Cold War. New York:
            Monthly Review Press.
Emery, Edwin and Michael Emery
    1978   The Press and America. Englewood
            Cliffs, N.J.: Prentice-Hall.
Epstein, Edward Jay
    1973   News from Nowhere. New York:
            Random House.
Fishman, Mark
    1980   Manufacturing the News. Austin:
            University of Texas Press.
Gans, Herbert
    1979   Deciding What's News. New York:
            Pantheon.

Gottlieb, Robert and Irene Wolt
  1977   Thinking Big: The Story of the *Los Angeles Times,* Its Publishers and Their Influence on Southern California. New York: G. P. Putnam's Sons.
Halberstam, David
  1979   The Powers That Be. New York: Knopf.
Hayes, Edward C.
  1972   Power Structure and Urban Policy: Who Rules in Oakland? New York: McGraw-Hill.
Hirsch, Glen
  1975   "Only you can prevent ideological hegemony: The Advertising Council and its place in the American power structure." Insurgent Sociologist 5: 64–82.
Ingrassia, Lawrence
  1979   "Owners of newspapers stir debate by taking a role in public affairs." Wall Street Journal, Aug. 24:1, 26.
Johnstone, John W., Edward Slawski and William Bowman
  1976   The Newspeople. Urbana: University of Illinois Press.
Joseph, Paul
  1981   Cracks in the Empire. Boston: South End Press.
Kolko, Joyce
  1974   America and the Crisis of World Capitalism. Boston: Beacon Press.
Levine, Joel
  1972   "The sphere of influence." American Sociological Review 37:14–27.
Louis, Arthur M.
  1978   "Independent dailies are an endangered species." Fortune, June 19: 160–166.
  1981   "Growth gets harder at Gannett." Fortune, April 20:118–129.
Lundberg, Ferdinand
  1936   Imperial Hearst: A Social Biography. New York. The Modern Library.
  1968   The Rich and the Super-Rich. New York: Lyle Stuart.
Mariolis, Peter
  1975   "Interlocking directorates and the control of corporations." Social Science Quarterly 56:425–439.
Merrill, John C.
  1968   The Elite Press. New York: Pitman.
Merrill, John C., and Harold A. Fisher
  1980   The World's Great Dailies. New York: Hastings House.
Mintz, Beth
  1975   "The president's cabinet, 1897–1972: A contribution to the power structure debate." Insurgent Sociologist 5:131–148.
Molotch, Harvey
  1976   "The city as a growth machine: Toward a political economy of place." American Journal of Sociology 82:309–332.
Molotch, Harvey and Marilyn Lester
  1974   "News and purposive behavior." American Sociological Review 39: 101–112.
Morgenthaler, Eric
  1970   "Some question ethics of putting a newsman on a corporate board." Wall Street Journal, Sept. 4:1, 15.
Morton, John
  1980   Financial Profile of the Newspaper Industry. Washington, D.C.: John Muir and Company.
  1981   Newsletter. Washington, D.C.: John Muir and Company, Jan. 31.
O'Connor, James
  1973   The Fiscal Crisis of the State. New York: St. Martin's Press.
Palmer, Donald
  1981   "Broken ties: Interlocking directorates, the interorganizational paradigm and intercorporate coordination." Unpublished research paper No. 595. Stanford University Graduate School of Business. Stanford, California.
Pennings, Johannes M.
  1980   Interlocking Directorates. San Francisco: Jossey-Bass.
Ratcliff, Richard, Mary Gallagher, and Kathryn Ratcliff.
  1979   "The civic involvement of bankers:

An analysis of the influence of economic power and social prominence in the command of civic policy positions." Social Problems 26:298–313.

Roberts, Chalmers M.
1977   The Washington Post: The First 100 Years. Boston: Houghton Mifflin.

Rockmore, Milton
1977   "How activist should a publisher be?" Editor and Publisher, Nov. 12:74–75.
1979   "How does an outside director contribute?" Editor and Publisher, April 21:24–37, 44.

Rosse, James N., Bruce M. Owen and James Dertouzos
1975   Trends in the Daily Newspaper Industry, 1923–73. Studies in Industry Economics, No. 55. Stanford, Calif.: Department of Economics, Stanford University.

Salzman, Harold and G. William Domhoff
1980   "Corporations, non-profit groups and government: Do they interlock?" Insurgent Sociologist 9:121–135.

Schudson, Michael
1978   Discovering the News: A Social History of American Newspapers. New York: Basic Books.

Shoup, Laurence H. and William Minter
1977   Imperial Brain Trust: The Council on Foreign Relations and United States Foreign Policy. New York: Monthly Review Press.

Sigal, Leon V.
1973   Reporters and Officials. Lexington, Mass.: D.C. Heath.

Standard and Poor's Corporation.
1975–   Standard and Poor's Register of
79   Corporations, Directors and Executives. New York: Standard and Poor's Corporation.

Swanberg, W. A.
1961   Citizen Hearst. New York: Scribner's.

Talese, Gay
1969   The Kingdom and the Power. New York: World.

Tebbel, John
1961   "Rating the American newspaper."

Saturday Review, May 13, 44(19):59–62; June 10, 44(23):54–56.

Tuchman, Gaye
1972   "Objectivity as strategic ritual." American Journal of Sociology 77:660–679.
1978   Making News. New York: Free Press.

Udell, Jon G.
1978   The Economics of the American Newspaper. New York: Hastings House.

U.S. Congress: Senate
1977   Federal Advisory Committees. Committee on Governmental Affairs, Subcommittee on Reports, Accounting and Management. Washington, D.C.: U.S. Government Printing Office.

Useem, Michael
1978   "The inner group of the American capitalist class." Social Problems 25:225–240.
1979   "The social organization of the American business elite and participation of corporate directors in the governance of American institutions." American Sociological Review 44:553–572.
1980   "Which business leaders help govern?" Insurgent Sociologist 9:107–120.

Waldrop, Frank C.
1966   McCormick of Chicago. Englewood Cliffs, N.J.: Prentice-Hall.

Weinstein, James
1968   The Corporate Ideal in the Liberal State. Boston: Beacon Press.

Zeitlin, Maurice
1974   "Corporate ownership and control: The large corporation and the capitalist class." American Journal of Sociology 79:1073–1119.

Zeitlin, Maurice, Richard Ratcliff and Linda Ewen
1974   "The 'inner group.'" Paper presented at meetings of the American Sociological Association, Montreal. August.

19
Jobs and Families: Impact of Working Roles on Family Life

Rosabeth Moss Kanter

Editors' Introduction

In the keynote reading Mack and Bradford identify five essential functions, each tied to an institution. However, this whole part has concentrated attention not on single institutions but on their inter-relationships. In this next reading Rosabeth Moss Kanter focuses on the interrelationships of two institutions that seem especially important at a personal level. On a day-to-day basis little in life receives more personal attention than families and jobs. In institutional terms, of course, these are the family and the economy. Regardless of what you call them, they are very important concerns on both the personal and the societal levels. But how are they inter-related?

In Part Six Neil Smelser points out the changes in work relations and family relations during the period of transition from a tradi-tional agricultural society to a modernizing industrial society. Smel-ser's basic argument is that this transition separated economic activ-ities from family activities. Prior to the transformation families were usually producing *and* consuming units, but these activities became separated in industrial society. The family no longer consumed what it produced; it consumed what someone else had produced. Taking production out of the family unit had another important result: It took one or more members of the family out of the family unit for long periods of time each day, since someone had to *go to work*. The family, in turn, became more specialized, concentrating on socialization, along with emotional support and gratification. The nuclear family (husband, wife, kids, and dog) became more important in the newly mobile society—people had to travel far from the old home town to find jobs in cities. All of this was accom-panied by changing relationships between parents and children. The father began to play a lesser role in the rearing of children since he was at work much of the time. Add to this the fact that children started leaving home earlier to set up their own households, and the result is a dramatically different family structure under industrialization than under an agricultural economy. This is only a brief sketch of the changes that took place in these important institutions.

It has been a long time since these transformations took place. Although it is easy to see how the changes may have caused problems during the nineteenth century, we have now lived with them for so long that any problems should long since have been ironed out. Right? Rosabeth Moss Kanter picks up the interrelationships between these family and work roles in modern times. Why is this a very important topic today? What events or changes have taken place in the society that brought the work-family mix into the limelight? Kanter focuses on four ways in which work constrains family life: time and timing of work-related activities, material and/or "psychic" rewards associated with work, occupational cultures, and the emotional climate of work. All of these, Kanter argues, have direct impacts on the family. As you read about these constraints, look at the differences in impact on women and men and the differences across types of work (most notably in white-collar versus blue-collar work). Also note the social policy implications that Kanter outlines and other implications that are only suggested by her discussion.

As you read this selection, think back to two of the readings in Part Three of this book. Kanter makes direct and lengthy reference to Melvin Kohn's important work on social class and parental values. You recall that he related values parents hold for children to the nature of work done by parents. The reading by Joel Roache is less directly tied to Kanter's article but is nevertheless quite relevant. Roache's discussion of the trials and tribulations of a househusband grew out of his attempt to blend work and family chores, as he tried to free his wife from some of the household work. His new house*work* can be seen as another example of the constraints work places on family life.

Kanter's analysis of the important interrelationships between family and work is another example of the melding of structure and process. The structure of work directly influences both the structure and the process of family roles. Kanter does not directly address the impacts on the process but it should be relatively easy for you to construct some of them. The process side of sociology is also seen when Kanter talks about the importance of jobs in developing one's world view and orientation to self. But note that when it is time to make policy recommendations, Kanter says, "Major changes in the world of work and the structure of work organizations may, indeed, turn out to have more profound effects on the quality of family life than all the attempts to influence individual behavior."

Kanter is attempting to pull together a great deal of information from several sources. Because of this "summary and synthesis" approach, you will find no discussion of research methods in her article. You also will not be able to identify a particular theoretical orientation. Each of the separate works she talks about has its own orientation and method of investigation. This type of synthesizing is very important in sociology. From time to time sociologists need to step back and see exactly how far sociology has come and where it currently stands. It is especially important to do this when the audience is not made up of sociologists, but of lay people who are interested in solving the dilemmas of contemporary society. Kanter is speaking to just such an audience.

I come at the issue of families from a roundabout direction: the factory, the office, the boardroom, the hospital, the shop. It is in these work settings that, to a large, virtually unexamined and often unacknowledged extent, the quality of American family life is decided. If this assertion was true for the past, for the somewhat mythical pairing of breadwinner-husbands and secondary-worker wives, it will be even more apropos in the future, as ever large numbers of young women enter the labor force with the expectation of successfully combining marriage and a career. Thus, an understanding of work settings and occupations, or organizations and public policies may offer as much insight into the stresses, strains and challenges that families of the future will face as all the private decisions made by individuals about their relationships and households.

This is a particularly appropriate time to be looking at the dynamic intersections of work and family life, for many converging trends call

attention to the nature of work and work organizations as determinants of the quality of life for individuals and families. In their concern for the increased well-being of citizens, national policymakers have recently focused attention on the impact of the structure and availability of work on the quality of life. At the same time [1978], Vice President Walter Mondale, while in the Senate, and others have turned attention to dilemmas and changes in family structure, arguing for the creation of a national family policy which would, in turn, consider the effects on family life of governmental legislation and organizational decisions. And a far-reaching investigation of the feasibility of attaching "family impact" statements to legislation is now under way in Washington, D.C.[1]

Such concerns derive from specific recent social changes as well as from a general interest in the quality of life. The women's movement and the increase of women in the paid labor force (especially married women with children) have focused policy attention on the work-family link for women and on the extent to which work systems make it possible to maintain effective participation in both worlds. A rise in the number of single-parent families has similarly directed attention to the question of bridging the two worlds of work and family. And these issues, of course, are of critical interest to those individuals who find themselves bearing major responsibilities in both domains—working mothers or single-parent fathers.

The late 1960s also brought a number of social movements that challenged the usual patterns of middle-class work and family life. There were groups concerned with some of the unfortunate human effects of contemporary economic organization such as pollution, blue-collar occupational diseases, executive ulcers and heart disease. Meanwhile, the development of the "human potential" movement with its focus on personal fulfillment and growth led to a variety of experiments—communes and work cooperatives—in which people tried to connect work and private life in very different ways, giving priority to leisure, personal expression and relationships rather than to career mobility. Indeed, the movements of the past decade gave rise to the common use of the term lifestyle and to awareness of the plurality of American lifestyles.[2]

Other public discussions have tried to promote a turning away from career striving as the dominant measure of individual success, although this is difficult in times of job scarcity and slow economic growth. Similarly, there appears to have been a revaluing of private family life on the part of professionals inside organizations as well as by younger people, particularly as the personal "costs" of overly work-absorbed careers have been made clear. Whether institutional patterns are actually changing in response, which is still unlikely, at least some relevant questions are being asked, and with increasing public legitimacy.

Several recent intellectual trends have also highlighted the importance of studying work and family life together. In sociology and economics, a revival of interest in Marxist theory and research has taken as a first premise that no part of modern life goes uninfluenced by the structure of capitalist institutions. Families as well as schools, in this view, take their own shape from the demands of capitalism for producers and consumers. Thus the family is one of the critical links in the capitalist economy, since it both produces "labor power" and con-

sumer goods and services. Secondly, in psychology, sociology and psychohistory, a concern with the total life cycle has also led to interest in the variety of settings in which adults as well as children spend their lives as both family members and workers. (School is the workplace for children.)

Furthermore, a growing interest in adult development, in the stages of adult as well as childhood growth, naturally leads to questions about the ways in which people are shaped by and manage their multiple involvements in their private and organizational lives. The timing of events in both the work and family worlds has also begun to receive attention in the developmental perspective. (It has also been argued that historical studies of family structure also need to add this developmental focus on the family as "process," unfolding and changing during the life cycle.)

Developments in certain applied fields also pave the way for the examination of work-family linkages. In both organizational and social psychology (applied behavioral science and industrial psychology) and the growing field of family therapy, "open systems theory" has provided a useful perspective. Organization development has concerned itself with integrating social and technical aspects of work, and family therapy has taken as its central premise the notion that the problems of an individual must be seen and treated in the context of the total family system. The "open systems" perspective makes it possible to consider the inputs into each system from others in its environment.

Finally, the evolving character of society as a whole has made this a particularly good time to consider the relationships between work and family life. Growth in the numbers of people employed in white-collar jobs and service institutions and other changes signalling the "postindustrial society" have led such scholars as Daniel Bell to conclude that future economic enterprises will pay more attention to their "sociologizing" (human welfare) functions than to their "economizing" (profit-making) functions. But, of course, people come to work in organizations not just as individuals but also as members of private systems, such as families, that are themselves constrained by the policies and practices of organizations.

It may be that organizations of the future will have to pay attention to their effects on people other than those who work for them— on spouses and children of employees—and allow the needs of families to influence the decisions and shape the policies of the organization. Questions about day care, part-time work, maternity and paternity leave, executive transfers, spousal involvement in career planning and treatment of family dysfunctions—all difficult to raise at present—may become primary considerations for organizations in the future.

HOW WORK CONSTRAINS FAMILIES

One set of themes relating to the constraints work places on families revolves around time and timing—the scheduling of work and the timing of major demands. Especially in highly absorptive occupations, such as upper-level management, politics or certain professions, which make time demands well beyond the 40-hour week and even draw other family members in as vital players in the occupational world, the limited amount of time left for personal or familial pursuits is a source of strain. Indeed, recent literature has focused on the corporate or political wife as "victim"—drawn into the public arena in a visible way but left to handle family affairs as virtually alone as a single parent.

But even in less absorptive pursuits, the timing of work events can have profound impact on families. The most egalitarian or "companionate" marriages seem to be found among lower-middle-class, white-collar workers, perhaps as a function of the greater temporal availability of husbands to share chores and act as companions to their wives. In other occupational groups, such as professors or executives the spillover of work into leisure time can generate irritability and lack of attention at home.

Shift workers have other work-family issues to contend with, due to the way their hours affect the expected synchrony between work and nonwork events.[3] One study discovered that each shift carried its own characteristic family problems. There was more friction between husband and wife for night-shift workers and more trouble with the father role for afternoon-shift workers.[4] Shift work, in a study of a large midwestern company, produced added psychological burdens, in that workers could not establish regular eating and sleeping patterns. But for those preferring isolation, shift work relieved them of community and family responsibilities.

Night workers have not been carefully researched, but journalistic accounts and recent research suggest some of the family issues they face. For one night manager of a grocery store, for example, the major cost was the stress engendered by the limited time the family had to spend together and problems with his wife because of their limited social life, especially on Saturday nights when her friends were all going out. On the other hand, night workers may also be able to help with housework, errands and greeting the children when they come home from school. But when night work fosters a strong occupational community, as among craft printers, the family may lose importance as a focus of primary ties. In any case, such families have to organize their lives around the schedule of the night worker.

The examples of shift and night workers make clear that it is not only the *amount* of time available for family and leisure that is an issue but its *timing*. Since other family members have their own priorities and schedules, and since society makes certain events possible only at certain times, timing becomes important in determining the effects of working hours. Two-worker families, especially, must work out their scheduling issues. Husbands who are home during the day can more easily help with child care, even though wives who do the housework may feel they lose their "job autonomy." In one study, fathers with preschool children were reported to prefer the night shift, hoping to change to a day shift when their children began to attend school.[5]

One striking example of issues created by schedule problems is the failure of some experiments with a 4-day week. In 1958 an aircraft parts plant in California provided workers with one 3-day weekend a month, without a reduction in the total hours worked—once a month the workers had a free Monday. Despite initial enthusiasm, the workers voted to discontinue the system after less than a year. Some of their complaints make clear how much the *timing* of free time may have been at fault: the time was used for home chores that could as easily have been done on Saturdays, it was lonely at home on Mondays with everyone else at work or at school, and daytime television was designed for women and children. In other words, a lump of free time out of synchrony with the rhythms of the rest of the family and society may not improve the quality of family life at all.[6] As David Riesman suggested after reporting a 1957 Roper poll indicating some negative feelings about the 4-day week, housewives may not be eager to have their husbands underfoot on one of *their* working days.[7]

A different kind of time experiment, however, also makes apparent the intertwining of work hours and family life, but with more positive effects. The practice of flexible working hours or *flextime* (a word coined by Willi Haller in Germany) is now in widespread operation throughout Europe and is gradually being introduced in some United States companies. Within specified limits, employees choose their own hours. There is already evidence of its positive effects. (Among other benefits, when enough organizations in a community institute flextime, it lessens traffic congestion and cuts down on commuting time.)

In one survey of workers in a Swiss company, 35 percent (including more men than women) used the flextime hours for spending more time with their families. Married women tended to use their flextime hours to provide more time for domestic chores (in keeping with the highly traditional sex role allocation in Switzerland). Almost 95 percent of the 1,500 employees surveyed were in favor of flextime—45 percent because of the way it improved the organization of private life. Not surprisingly, married women

with children were the most enthusiastic of all groups.[8]

For working women in traditional kinds of families, single parents with sole responsibility for children, or men who expect to share family tasks, flextime seems to permit a more comfortable synchrony of work and family responsibilities. Social policy as well as scientific knowledge would benefit from further research on the use and effects of flextime.

Work-related travel poses another time issue for families. If executive husbands and fathers have little time left over after their very long working days to be helpers to wives and companions to children, they are available *none* of the time when they travel. One researcher studied 128 managers and wives in a large multinational corporation for which extensive travel was a job requirement.[9] All felt burdened and stressed by the travel except two people—a single female manager and a man who used travel to escape from his family. The problems of the others included disconnected social relations, especially for the men; increasing responsibility for the wives, since virtually no areas of family life could be assigned to the husbands who were away so frequently; guilt on the part of the husbands for "deserting" their families; fatigue stemming from the travel itself; wives' fears of being alone; and extra worry for one another while the spouses were apart.

Other scholars have mentioned additional travel-related problems: infidelity and a growing gap in the knowledge and life experiences of husbands and wives. If fathers are often absent, the family system may begin to close itself off to them, making re-entry difficult. Important events may occur without them, and the person who has been family leader in their absence may not want to give up their role.

One solution to the travel problem would be to increase the work-family connection and find ways for traveling workers to bring their families along.

Another theme involving work and families relates to jobs as sources of reward—material and/or psychic. The rhythm and setting of work may affect its rewardingness, but these are not the variables considered important in linking work to family life. Instead, the important variables have to do with the prestige, money or exchangeable resources generated by the job. This line of reasoning lies behind the large number of studies of income or, even more frequently, of occupational prestige as correlates of lifestyle and family patterns. It is clear, for example, that income levels and unemployment affect marital stability.

Many social class analyses assign a rank or level to the husband-father's occupation and indicate what proportion of people or families in each group exhibits the predicted private behavior and attitudes. (While the groupings tend to be called "classes," the assignment of ranks in prestige as determinants of consumption style is actually closer to the Weberian definition of "status" than the Marxist notion of class as stemming from relationship to the means of production.) Research in this area remains compelling because of the large number of variables that show predictable patterning when gross occupational and income levels are differentiated, even though there is also a striking amount of variation within income classes.

In a dynamic extension of the reward framework, John Scanzoni has developed and tested an exchange theory of the effects on family cohesiveness of income and general location in the economic structure.[10] He argued that economic and psychic income from a job affects the presence or absence of marital tension. The more a man is integrated into the economic opportunity structure (as measured objectively by his occupational status, education and income and subjectively by his alienation or lack of alienation) the greater the cohesiveness of the family and of satisfaction with the husband-wife relationship, since the husband brings status and income into the family to exchange for services and positive feelings. Lack of integration, however, may cause the displacement of economic discontents onto personal relations.

A third way to approach work-family linkages concerns the cultures within occupations, cultures that are brought home to varying degrees. The assumption here is that jobs shape one's outlook on the world and orientation to self and others, that jobs are important socializers and teachers of values. For example, Melvin Kohn differentiated the nature of white-collar and blue-collar work as it might affect one's world view.[11] White-collar work involves the manipulation of ideas, symbols and interpersonal relations and blue-collar work, the manipulation of physical objects, which requires less interpersonal skill. White-collar work may be more complex and require greater flexibility, thought and judgment, with less supervision, while blue-collar work may be more standardized and supervised.

Kohn then predicted that these differences would be associated with childrearing values and practices—that is, white-collar parents would value creativity, self-direction and initiative in children while blue-collar parents would stress conformity and obedience. Many of Kohn's findings have been replicated, although class-based differences in socialization seem to have diminished during the last decades. The difference between fathers in the white- and blue-collar categories seems greater, in some research reports, than the difference between mothers.

The degree to which the gap between blue-collar and white-collar parents is closing is a function of changes in work, with much white-collar work becoming more routinized and machine-oriented, while blue-collar workers are growing into an affluent working class. Other influences outside of working conditions, such as those of the media, also play a role in closing this gap.

How parental values are influenced by jobs is only one question that can be raised about occupational cultures. How people change as they are exposed to occupational outlooks, and what happens when that change is not congruent with those undergone by other family members, are others. What happens when occupational cultures are esoteric or mysterious and so help exclude family members from important parts of each other's experiences? Here work organizations play a part in determining the quality and ease of communication in the family, according to the extent to which companies close their doors against the family or attempt to create bridges between the language, technology and culture of work and that of the home.

The extent to which jobs and work form a culture, cultural outlook—and vocabulary—is seldom recognized. When a group of executives' wives at a workshop were asked to list words which their husbands used, and which they did not understand, more than 100 words were cited by the 12 wives present.

A fourth theme is related: the emotional climate of work. This is the way workers come to feel about themselves and their day, the degree of self-esteem or self-doubt they feel and the sense of well-being or tension which they bring home. There is some evidence, for example, that workers in low autonomy jobs are more severe and hostile as parents. There is also evidence of variation in preferences for leisure "release" among men in different occupations: advertising men, for example, need to "blow off steam" from their high pressure, competitive work. Yet, other people also argue that the emotional climate of work is *not* brought home, that people can behave very differently in the two settings.

Clearly the nature of the links between work experience and family life still needs to be explored. Many important questions remain. Does the family world serve *compensatory* functions for emotional deprivations suffered at work, or *displacement-of-aggression* functions? Does the family get the best parts of a working member's energy or commitment when these are not called for at work, as some research hints, or does it get only the parts left over from an emotionally draining job? Do people orient themselves to the family emotionally in the same way they come to approach their work?

The overwhelming tendency in social theory has been to assume that experiences of alienation at work result in negative consequences in personal life. Melvin Seeman has recently challenged this perspective, presenting Swedish data indicating that work alienation has few of the unpleasant personal consequences imagined.[12] Yet other evidence does make a case for the spillover from the emotional connection with work to other areas of life. People with boring work tend to have boring leisure, and people with involving work tend to have higher levels of both leisure and family involvement, even though the latter may work longer hours and bring home more work than the former. Blue-collar workers in similar occupations at the same pay level tend to be more democratic in their politics and more creative in their leisure when their jobs permit more control, participation and self-direction.

Too often in the past we have viewed families in a vacuum, as a realm unto themselves. Only now are we beginning to consider how public policy and such institutions as employing organizations may be responsible for what happens, or does not happen, in private life.

Structural rearrangements that provide people with more flexibility and options may be a first step in helping families. These would include the use of flextime; more flexible leaves and sabbaticals; greater availability of day care; income supports; explicit focus on communication about work events and work culture to workers' families; and reduction in the number of low autonomy low opportunity jobs that create emotional tensions at home. Major changes in the world of work and the structure of work organizations may, indeed, turn out to have more profound effects on the quality of family life than all the attempts to influence individual behavior.

Let us—the professionals—leave people alone to make their own decisions about their relationships. But let us also do what we can do effectively: work to reduce the constraints brought to them by other institutions that bind them to less satisfying, less relationship-enhancing ways of being.

Notes

1. Information of the Family Impact Seminar, a program of the National Center for Family Studies, the Catholic University of America, is available from Theodora Ooms, Director, St. John's Hall, Suite 200, the Catholic University of America, Washington, D.C. 20064.

2. Benjamin Zablocki and Rosabeth Kanter, "Differentiation of Life Styles," *Annual Review of Sociology*, 2, 1976.

3. Joan Aldous, "Occupational Characteristics and Males' Role Performance in the Family," *Journal of Marriage and the Family*, November 1969.

4. Paul E. Mott et al., *Shift Work: The Social, Psychological, and Physical Consequences*, Ann Arbor, University of Michigan Press, 1965.

5. Laura Lein et al., *Work and Family Life*, Final Report to the National Institute of Education, Cambridge, Mass., Center for the Study of Public Policy, 1974.

6. Rolf Meyersohn, "Changing Work and Leisure Routines," in E. Swigel (ed.), *Work and Leisure: A Contemporary Social Problem*, New Haven, Conn., College and University Press, 1963.

7. David Riesman, "Work and Leisure in Post-Industrial Society," in E. Larrabee and R. Meyersohn (eds.), *Mass Leisure*, Glencoe, Ill., Free Press, 1958.

8. Georg H. E. M. Racki, "The Effects of Flexible Working Hours," Ph.D. dissertation, University of Lausanne, 1975.

9. Jean R. Renshaw, "An Exploration of the Dynamics of the Overlapping Worlds of Work and Family," *Family Process* 15, March 1976.

10. John H. Scanzoni, *Opportunity and the Family: A Study of the Conjugal Family in Relation to the Economic Opportunity Structure*, New York, Free Press, 1970.

11. See Melvin L. Kohn, "Social Class and Parental Values," *American Journal of Sociology*, January 1959; Melvin L. Kohn, "Social Class and Parent-Child Relationships: An Interpretation," *American Journal of Sociology*, January 1963; and Melvin L. Kohn, *Class and Conformity*, Homewood, Ill., Dorsey Press, 1969.

12. Melvin Seeman, "On the Personal Consequences of Alienation in Work," *American Sociological Review*, April 1967.

20
Beyond the Educational Frontier:
The Great American Dream Freeze

Samuel Bowles
Herbert Gintis

Editors' Introduction

In the keynote selection Mack and Bradford say, "To participate in and contribute to the social order, a person must be taught to play a part in it" (p. 192). This implies that the social order comes first and the institution of education is structured to fulfill its needs rather than playing a decisive role in creating that order. This is another way in which institutions may be interrelated. In the following selection from *Schooling in Capitalist America*, Bowles and Gintis explore this implication in some depth. They present a Marxian analysis of the relationship between education and the economy, showing that schools are structured to produce workers who have certain technical skills, to be sure, but who also have the social skills and proper motivation to participate as subordinates in hierarchical and repressive work structures. (It probably would be a good idea to refresh your memory about Marx's main ideas by referring back to the Berger and Berger keynote reading in Part Three.)

Bowles and Gintis begin by comparing the role of education in this society to the role played by the frontier. What do they see as the role of each? In what ways have these roles been similar? How have they been related to the American Dream, as the authors call it? In what ways has the American Dream faded? Trace with the authors the "boom and bust" of ideas about economic opportunity and the relationship of education to such opportunity—including some fairly recent efforts at reform. Bowles and Gintis then set out to destroy some myths commonly held about education and its role in fostering equality of opportunity. What are these myths and what are the facts of the case? They say that the educational institution "serves to perpetuate the social relationships of economic life through which these patterns are set. . . ." How does economic life set the patterns found in schools? How do schools echo and maintain the social relationships of economic life? In other words, how does the structure of the economy affect the processes of schooling? The last question is the crucial one in Bowles and Gintis's analysis. Notice that this is the same question considered by Gracey in his article on kindergarten in Part Two. However, Gracey is operating at a far different level. He describes the *processes* of daily life within the institution of education, while Bowles and Gintis stress the *structure* of the economy with its consequences for educational process. Together the two readings provide a comprehensive view of both structure and process in education.

Bowles and Gintis ask, "How can we best understand the evidently critical relationship beween education and the capitalist economy?" From this point on they make extensive use of Marxian concepts. They describe wage workers who have only their labor power to sell, opposed by employers who control the means of production. They discuss the creation of "surplus value," in which the price of an article is considerably more than the cost of materials and tools along with what is paid to the people who actually produce it. This surplus value goes to those who control production, and it is in their interest to ensure that the workers do not question it. Bowles and Gintis say that education serves to "defuse" these class relations and produce workers who simply go along with the system. However, it is not quite that simple—since the authors also show some contradictory outcomes from the educational institution. What are these outcomes and how do they arise?

Bowles and Gintis end the selection with some suggestions for action—suggestions that involve a radical restructuring of the economic institution and the class structure that reflects it. This is certainly in the Marxian tradition. Marx said, "The philosophers have only *interpreted* the world in different ways; the point is to *change* it."[1] Bowles and Gintis are following this dictum from Marx, trying to fulfill their responsibility as scholars and scientists.

The book from which this reading comes is an example of historical analysis and use of available data. The authors use a wide variety of sources on the history of education in the United States. They also provide statistical evidence from analysis of data collected mostly by the U.S. Bureau of the Census, as they set out to destroy the common myths about education and equality.

Note

1. T. B. Bottomore and M. Rubel, eds., *Karl Marx: Selected Writings in Sociology and Social Philosophy* (New York: McGraw-Hill, 1956), p. 69.

Those who take the meat from the table
Preach contentment. . . .
Those who eat their fill speak to the hungry
Of wonderful times to come. . . .
Those who lead the country into the abyss
Call ruling too difficult
For the ordinary.

—*Bertolt Brecht, 1937*

"Go West, young man!" advised Horace Greeley in 1851. A century later, he might have said: "Go to college!"

The Western frontier was the nineteenth-century land of opportunity. In open competition with nature, venturesome white settlers found their own levels, unfettered by birth or

Reprinted from *Schooling in Capitalist America* by Samuel Bowles and Herbert Gintis. © 1976 by Basic Books, Inc. Used with permission of the publisher.

creed. The frontier was a way out—out of poverty, out of dismal factories, out of the crowded Eastern cities. The frontier was the Great Escape.

Few escaped. Railroad companies, mine owners, and, before long, an elite of successful farmers and ranchers soon captured both land and opportunity. The rest were left with the adventure of making ends meet. But throughout the nineteenth century, the image of the frontier sustained the vision of economic opportunity and unfettered personal freedom in an emerging industrial system offering little of either.

With the closing of the Western frontier in the latter part of the nineteenth century and with the growing conflicts accompanying the spread of the now established "factory system," a new ideology of opportunity became the order of the day. The folklore of capitalism was revitalized: Education became the new frontier. Rapidly expanding educational opportunity in the twentieth century has met many of the functions served earlier by the Western frontier. Physical escape? Out of the question. But in school, an objective competition—as the story goes—provides an arena for discovering the limits of one's talents and, thence, the boundaries of one's life pursuit. Educational reformers have proposed an end run on economic strife by offering all children an equal opportunity to make it. Those who have failed to measure up have only themselves to blame.

For half a century or more, the educational system provided an admirable safety valve for the economic pressure cooker. Larger numbers of children completed high school and continued on to college every year. Most thought they were getting ahead, and many were. But by the late 1950s, the educational frontier was pressing its limits. Already a third of the age group was entering college; over the next decade, the fraction would rise to almost half. College graduates were driving cabs; others were collecting unemployment checks. Some were on welfare. The once relatively homogeneous appearance of the system of higher education was rapidly giving way to a hierarchy of colleges, dominated at the top by the elite Ivy League schools and descending through a fine gradation of private schools, state universities, and community colleges. Not surprisingly, a decade later, the expansion of education was slowed to a crawl. Between 1968 and 1973, the percentage of high-school graduates going on to college fell from 55 percent to 47 percent.[1] Public support for education began to wane. The fraction of all municipal school bond issues voted down in referenda doubled—from about a quarter in the mid-1960s to about a half in the early 1970s.[2] The percentage of national output devoted to educational expenditures, having more than doubled in the thirty years since 1940, fell slightly.[3]

Like the nineteenth-century prairie settler, the late twentieth-century student has come to realize the fancy of flight. The school system has been increasingly unable to support the myth of equal opportunity and full personal development. And the fading of the American Dream, hardly confined to education, has been a persistent theme of recent years.

The decade of the 1960s burst upon a complacent public in successive waves of political and cultural conflict. Their formative years untouched by depression, mobilization, and total world war, youth of the emerging generation were afforded more than a glimpse of the future of the American Dream. Large numbers were less than enthusiastic. Discontent often took the form of sporadic, but intense, political assaults against economic inequality in the United States. Minorities, women, welfare recipients, students, and working people have periodically brought the issue of inequality into the streets, forced it onto the front pages, and thrown it into the legislature and the courts. The dominant response of the privileged has been concern, tempered by a hardy optimism that social programs can be devised to alleviate social distress and restore a modicum of social harmony. Not exempt from this optimism has been modern academic economics and sociology. At the core of this conventional wisdom has rested the conviction that, within the "free enterprise" system of the United States, significant social progress can be achieved through a combination of enlightened persuasion and governmental initiative, particularly in the spheres of education and vocational training.

The social movements of the sixties and seventies did not limit their attack to inequality. The period witnessed a growing reaction against authoritarian and repressive social relationships. Wildcat strikes, worker insubordination, and especially, absenteeism became a serious problem for union bosses and for employers. Black people in open revolt against centuries of discrimination demanded control of their communities. Armed students seized administration buildings, general strikes swept the colleges, and police patrolled high-school study halls. What appeared to many as the cornerstone of social stability—the family itself—was rocked by a women's movement which challenged the sexual division of labor and the monopolization of personal and social power by males.

While the "law-and-order" forces gathered guns and adherents, the liberal community sought a more flexible answer. The "soft" human relations school of labor management enjoyed a boom. Civil rights legislation was passed. Some of the more oppressive laws defining women's place were repealed. But the key response to the movement against repressive social relations appeared in education. A free-school movement, reflecting the highest ideals of progressive students and parents, was welcomed by major foundations and supported by the U.S. Office of Education. The "open classroom" was quickly perceived by liberal educators as a means of accommodating and circumscribing the growing antiauthoritarianism of young people and keeping things from getting out of hand. Free schools proliferated.

The educational system, perhaps more than any other contemporary social institution, has become the laboratory in which competing solutions to the problems of personal liberation and social equality are tested and the arena in which social struggles are fought out. The school system is a monument to the capacity of the advanced corporate economy to accommodate and deflect thrusts away from its foundations. Yet at the same time, the educational system mirrors the growing contradictions of the larger society, most dramatically in the disappointing results of reform efforts.

By now, it is clear to many that the liberal school-reform balloon has burst. The social scientists and reformers who provided the intellectual impetus and rationale for compensatory education, for school integration, for the open classroom, for Project Headstart and Title I, are in retreat. In political as much as in intellectual circles, the current mood is one of retrenchment. In less than a decade, liberal preeminence in the field of educational theory and policy has been shattered. How did it happen?

The disappointing results of the War on Poverty and, in a larger sense, the persistence of poverty and discrimination in the United States have decisively discredited liberal social policy. The record of educational reform in the War on Poverty has been just short of catastrophic.

A major Rand Corporation study, assessing the efficacy of educational programs, concluded that ". . . virtually without exception all of the large surveys of the large national compensatory educational programs have shown no beneficial results on the average."[4] The dissemination of the results of the Office of Education's Survey of Educational Opportunity—the Coleman Report—did nothing to bolster the fading optimism of the school reformers.[5] Coleman's massive 1966 study of 600,000 students in over 4,000 schools had been mandated by the Civil Rights Act of 1964; ostensibly, it was designed to provide statistical support for a policy of financial redistribution that would correct educational inequality. But while Coleman and his associates did identify positive effects of a few aspects of the school—such as teacher quality—the weight of the evidence seemed to point to the virtual irrelevance of educational resources or quality as a determinant of educational outcomes. Studies by economists in the latter 1960s revealed an unexpectedly tenuous relationship of schooling to economic success for blacks.[6] By the early 1970s, a broad spectrum of social-science opinion was ready to accept the view put forward by Jencks et al. in their highly publicized study, *Inequality*: that a more egalitarian school system would do little to create a more equal distribution of income or opportunity.[7]

The barrage of statistical studies in the late 1960s and early 1970s—the Coleman Report, Jencks' study, the evaluations of compensatory education, and others—cleared the ground for a conservative counterattack. Most notably, there has been a revival of the genetic interpretation of IQ. Thus Arthur Jensen—sensing the opportunity afforded by the liberal debacle—began his celebrated article on the heritability of IQ with: "Compensatory education has been tried and apparently it has failed."[8] In the ensuing debate, an interpretation of the role of IQ in the structure of inequality has been elaborated: The poor are poor because they are intellectually incompetent; their incompetence is particularly intractable because it is inherited from their poor, and also intellectually deficient, parents.[9] An explanation of the failure of egalitarian reform is thus found in the immutability of genetic structure. (This idea is not new: An earlier wave of genetic interpretations of economic inequality among ethnic groups followed the avowedly egalitarian, but largely unsuccessful, educational reforms of the Progressive Era.[10]) Others—Edward C. Banfield and Daniel P. Moynihan prominent among them—have found a ready audience for their view that the failure of liberal reform is to be located not in the genes, but in the attitudes, time perspectives, family patterns, and values of the poor.[11]

Free schools have fared better than egalitarian school reform. But not much—the boom peaked in the early 1970s. Today, much of the free-school rhetoric has been absorbed into the mainstream of educational thinking as a new wrinkle on how to get kids to work harder. Surviving free schools have not developed as their originators had hoped. The do-your-own-thing perspective found little favor with the majority of parents. Financial support has become harder to locate. Critics of the free-school movement increasingly raise the time-honored question: Are the majority of youth—or their elders—capable of making good use of freedom? Minus some of the more petty regulations and anachronistic dress codes, perhaps the schools are about all that can be expected—human nature being what it is, the complexity of modern life, and so forth.

These times, then, project a mood of inertial pessimism. Not a healthy conservatism founded on the affirmation of traditional values, but a rheumy loss of nerve, a product of the dashed hopes of the past decades. Even the new widespread search for individual solutions to social ills is not rooted in any celebration of individuality. Rather, to many people—viewing the failure of progressive social movements—the private pursuit of pleasure through consumption, drugs, and sexual experimentation is seen as the only show in town. Liberal social reform has been reduced to a program of Band-Aid remedies whose most eloquent vision is making do with the inevitable. In the camp of the optimists, there remain only two groups: One, those who mouth old truths and trot out tired formulas for social betterment in the vain hope

that the past decade has been a quirk, a perverse and incomprehensible tangle in the history of progress which will—equally incomprehensibly—shake itself out. The other group, like ourselves, have been driven to explore the very foundation of our social order and have found there both a deeper understanding of our common situation and a conviction that our future is indeed a hopeful one.

We began our joint work together in 1968 when, actively involved in campus political movements, and facing the mass of contradictory evidence on educational reform, we became committed to comprehensive intellectual reconstruction of the role of education in economic life. Setting out to bring the total theoretical, empirical, and historical evidence of the social sciences to bear on the problem of rendering education a potent instrument of progressive social reform, we fully expected the results of this analysis to take novel and even radical forms. Moreover, we approached this task with a single overarching preconception: the vision of schools which promote economic equality and positive human development. Beyond this, we have questioned everything; we have found the social changes required to bring about what we would call a good educational system to be—while eminently feasible—quite far-reaching.

Some of the statistical results of this investigation . . . shed light on what are and are not reasons for the faltering of reform efforts. First, liberal strategies for achieving economic equality have been based on a fundamental misconception of the historical evolution of the educational system. Education over the years has never been a potent force for economic equality. Since World War I, there has been a dramatic increase in the general level of education in the United States, as well as considerable equalization of its distribution among individuals. Yet economic mobility—i.e., the degree to which economic success (income or occupational status) is independent of family background of individuals—has not changed measurably. And the total effect of family background on educational attainment (years of schooling) has remained substantially constant.

Thus the evidence indicates that, despite the vast increase in college enrollments, the probability of a high-school graduate attending college is just as dependent on parental socioeconomic status as it was thirty years ago. Moreover, despite the important contribution of education to an individual's economic chances, the substantial equalization of educational attainments over the years has not led measurably to an equalization in income among individuals.

Second, the failure of reform efforts as well as the feeble contribution of education to economic equality cannot be attributed to inequalities among individuals in IQ or other measured cognitive capacities, whether of genetic or environmental origin. Thus while one's race and the socioeconomic status of one's family have substantial effect on the amount of schooling one receives, these racial and family background effects are practically unrelated to socioeconomic or racial differences in measured IQ. Similarly, while family background has an important effect on an individual's chances of economic success, this effect is not attributable to the genetic or environmental transmission of measured IQ. Thus the bitter debate of recent years over the "heritability of intelligence" would seem to be quite misplaced. Indeed, the salience of these issues in educational circles appears to be part of a widespread overestimation of the importance of mental performance in understanding education in the United States and its relationship to economic life. The intensive effort to investigate the effect of educational resources on the cognitive attainments of different races and social classes loses much of its rationale given the wide variety of statistical sources which indicate that the association of income and occupational status with an individual's educational attainment is not due to measured mental skills. More surprising, perhaps, for the bulk of the population, the dollar payoff to increased education—while strongly dependent on race and sex—is related to IQ only tenuously, if at all. Thus the standard educational practice of using IQ and test scores as a criterion for access to higher educational levels has little merit in terms of economic (not to mention educational) rationality and efficiency, except perhaps for the extremes of the IQ-distribution curve.

These results suggest that it is a mistake to think of the educational system in relation to the economy simply in "technical" terms of the mental skills it supplies students and for which employers pay in the labor market. To capture the economic import of education, we must relate its social structure to the forms of consciousness, interpersonal behavior, and personality it fosters and reinforces in students. This method gives rise to our third comment on the reform process. The free-school movement and related efforts to make education more conducive to full human development have assumed that the present school system is the product of irrationality, mindlessness, and social backwardness on the part of teachers, administrators, school boards, and parents. On the contrary, we believe the available evidence indicates that the pattern of social relationships fostered in schools is hardly irrational or accidental. Rather, the structure of the educational experience is admirably suited to nurturing attitudes and behavior consonant with participation in the labor force. Particularly dramatic is the statistically verifiable congruence between the personality traits conducive to proper work performance on the job and those which are rewarded with high grades in the classroom. Like the egalitarian reformers, the free-school movement seems to have run afoul of social logic rather than reaction, apathy, inertia, or the deficiencies of human nature.

As long as one does not question the structure of the economy itself, the current structure of schools seems eminently rational. Reform efforts must therefore go beyond the application of logical or moral argument to a public who probably understand these social realities far better than most advocates of the liberated classroom. Indeed, an impressive statistical study by Melvin Kohn indicates that parents are significantly affected by their job experiences—particularly those of dominance and subordinacy in work—and that these, in turn, are realistically reflected in the attitudes they exhibit toward the rearing and training of their children. Moreover, our historical investigations suggest that, for the past century and a half at least, employers have been similarly aware of the function of the schools in preparing youth psychologically for work. They have applied their considerable political influence accordingly.

How can we best understand the evidently critical relationship between education and the capitalist economy? Any adequate explanation must begin with the fact that schools produce workers. The traditional theory explains the increased value of an educated worker by treating the worker as a machine.[12] According to this view, workers have certain technical specifications (skills and motivational patterns) which in any given production situation determine their economic productivity. Productive traits are enhanced through schooling. We believe this worker-as-machine analogy is essentially incorrect, and we shall develop an alternative. . . .

The motivating force in the capitalist economy is the employer's quest for profit. Profits are made through hiring workers and organizing production in such a way that the price paid for the worker's time—the wage—is less than the value of the goods produced by labor. The difference between the wage and the value of goods produced is profit, or surplus value. The production of surplus value requires as a precondition the existence of a body of wage workers whose sole source of livelihood is the sale of their capacity to work, their labor power. Opposing these wage workers is the employer, whose control of the tools, structures, and goods required in production constitutes both the immediate basis of his power over labor and his legal claim on the surplus value generated in production.

Capitalist production, in our view, is not simply a technical process; it is also a social process. Workers are neither machines nor commodities but, rather, active human beings who participate in production with the aim of satisfying their personal and social needs. The central problem of the employer is to erect a set of social relationships and organizational forms, both within the enterprise and, if possible, in society at large, that will channel these aims into

the production and expropriation of surplus value.[13] Thus as a social process, capitalist production is inherently antagonistic and always potentially explosive. Though class conflicts take many forms, the most basic occurs in this struggle over the creation and expropriation of surplus value.

It is immediately evident that profits will be greater, the lower is the total wage bill paid by the employer and the greater is the productivity and intensity of labor. Education in the United States plays a dual role in the social process whereby surplus value, i.e., profit, is created and expropriated. On the one hand, by imparting technical and social skills and appropriate motivations, education increases the productive capacity of workers. On the other hand, education helps defuse and depoliticize the potentially explosive class relations of the production process, and thus serves to perpetuate the social, political, and economic conditions through which a portion of the product of labor is expropriated in the form of profits.

This simple model, reflecting the undemocratic and class-based character of economic life in the United States, bears a number of central implications which will be elaborated upon and empirically supported in the sequel.

First, we find that prevailing degrees of economic inequality and types of personal development are defined primarily by the market, property, and power relationships which define the capitalist system. Moreover, basic changes in the degree of inequality and in socially directed forms of personal development occur almost exclusively—if sometimes indirectly—through the normal process of capital accumulation and economic growth, and through shifts in the power among groups engaged in economic activity.

Second, the educational system does not add to or subtract from the overall degree of inequality and repressive personal development. Rather, it is best understood as an institution which serves to perpetuate the social relationships of economic life through which these patterns are set, by facilitating a smooth integration of youth into the labor force. This role takes a variety of forms. Schools legitimate inequality through the ostensibly meritocratic manner by which they reward and promote students, and allocate them to distinct positions in the occupational hierarchy. They create and reinforce patterns of social class, racial and sexual identification among students which allow them to relate "properly" to their eventual standing in the hierarchy of authority and status in the production process. Schools foster types of personal development compatible with the relationships of dominance and subordinacy in the economic sphere, and finally, schools create surpluses of skilled labor sufficiently extensive to render effective the prime weapon of the employer in disciplining labor—the power to hire and fire.

Third, the educational system operates in this manner not so much through the conscious intentions of teachers and administrators in their day-to-day activities, but through a close correspondence between the social relationships which govern personal interaction in the work place and the social relationships of the educational system. Specifically, the relationships of authority and control between administrators and teachers, teachers and students, students and students, and students and their work replicate the hierarchical division of labor which dominates the work place. Power is organized along vertical lines of authority from administration to faculty to student body; students have a degree of control over their curriculum comparable to that of the worker over the content of his job. The motivational system of the school, involving as it does grades and other external rewards and the threat of failure rather than the intrinsic social benefits of the process of education (learning) or its tangible outcome (knowledge), mirrors closely the role of wages and the specter of unemployment in the motivation of workers. The fragmented nature of jobs is reflected in the institutionalized and rarely constructive competition among students and in the specialization and compartmentalization of academic knowledge. Finally, the relationships of dominance and subordinacy in education differ by level. The rule orientation of the high school reflects the close supervision of low-level workers; the internalization

of norms and freedom from continual supervision in elite colleges reflect the social relationships of upper-level white-collar work. Most state universities and community colleges, which fall in between, conform to the behavioral requisites of low-level technical, service, and supervisory personnel.

Fourth, though the school system has effectively served the interests of profit and political stability, it has hardly been a finely tuned instrument of manipulation in the hands of socially dominant groups. Schools and colleges do indeed help to justify inequality, but they also have become arenas in which a highly politicized egalitarian consciousness has developed among some parents, teachers, and students. The authoritarian classroom does produce docile workers, but it also produces misfits and rebels. The university trains the elite in the skills of domination, but it has also given birth to a powerful radical movement and critique of capitalist society. The contradictory nature of U.S. education stems in part from the fact that the imperatives of profit often pull the school system in opposite directions. The types of training required to develop productive workers are often ill suited to the perpetuation of those ideas and institutions which facilitate the profitable employment of labor. Furthermore, contradictory forces external to the school system continually impinge upon its operations. Students, working people, parents, and others have attempted to use education to attain a greater share of the social wealth, to develop genuinely critical capacities, to gain material security, in short to pursue objectives different—and often diametrically opposed—to those of capital. Education in the United States is as contradictory and complex as the larger society; no simplistic or mechanical theory can help us understand it.

Lastly, the organization of education—in particular the correspondence between school structure and job structure—has taken distinct and characteristic forms in different periods of U.S. history, and has evolved in response to political and economic struggles associated with the process of capital accumulation, the extension of the wage-labor system, and the transition from an entrepreneurial to a corporate economy.

We believe that current educational reform movements reflect these dynamics of the larger society. Thus the free-school movement and, more generally, youth culture are diffuse reactions to the reduced status and personal control of white-collar labor and its expression in repressive schooling. The extent to which the educational establishment will embrace free schooling depends to some extent on the political power of the parents and children pressing these objectives. But the long-run survival of the free school as anything but an isolated haven for the overprivileged will depend on the extent to which the interpersonal relationships it fosters can be brought into line with the realities of economic life. The increasing complexity of work, the growing difficulty of supervising labor and the rampant dissatisfaction of workers with their lack of power may foretell a sustained effort by employers to redesign jobs to allow limited worker participation in production decisions. Experiments with job enlargement and team work are manifestations of what may become a trend in the soft human relations school of personnel management. A co-opted free-school movement, shorn of its radical rhetoric, could play an important role in providing employers with young workers with a "built-in" supervisor. In this, it would follow the Progressive Movement of an earlier era. This much, at least, is clear: the possibility of schooling which promotes truly self-initiated and self-conscious personal development will await a change in the work place more fundamental than any proposed by even the softest of the soft human relations experts. For only when work processes are self-initiated and controlled by workers themselves will free schooling be an integral part of the necessary process of growing up and getting a job. Nor, we suggest, are these necessary changes limited to the work place alone; they entail a radical transformation of the very class structure of U.S. society.

The impact of the current movement for equalization of schooling—through resource transfers, open enrollment, and similar programs—likewise hinges on the future of economic institutions. Education plays a major role in hiding or justifying the exploitative nature of the U.S. economy. Equal access to educational credentials, of course, could not arise by accident. But were egalitarian education reformers to win spectacular victories—the social relationships of economic life remaining untouched—we can confidently predict that employers would quickly resort to other means of labeling and segmenting working people so as to fortify the structure of power and privilege within the capitalist enterprise.

In short, our approach to U.S. education suggests that movements for educational reform have faltered through refusing to call into question the basic structure of property and power in economic life. We are optimistic indeed concerning the feasibility of achieving a society fostering economic equality and full personal development. But we understand that the prerequisite is a far-reaching economic transformation. An educational system can be egalitarian and liberating only when it prepares youth for life and an equal claim to the fruits of fully economic democratic participation in social activity. In the United States, democratic forms in the electoral sphere of political life are paralleled by highly dictatorial forms in the economic sphere. Thus we believe that the key to reform is the democratization of economic relationships: social ownership, democratic and participatory control of the production process by workers, equal sharing of socially necessary labor by all, and progressive equalization of incomes and destruction of hierarchical economic relationships. This is, of course, socialism, conceived of as an extension of democracy from the narrowly political to the economic realm.

In this conception, educational strategy is part of a revolutionary transformation of economic life. Under what conditions and by what means such a movement might be successful is discussed toward the end of our investigation. But the broad outlines of such an educational strategy are clear. We must press for an educational environment in which youth can develop the capacity and commitment collectively to control their lives and regulate their social interactions with a sense of equality, reciprocity, and communality. Not that such an environment will of itself alter the quality of social life. Rather, that it will nurture a new generation of workers—white and blue collar, male and female, black, white, brown, and red—unwilling to submit to the fragmented relationships of dominance and subordinacy prevailing in economic life.

It will not have escaped the reader that the economic transformation which we envision, and which is the basis for our optimism, is so far-reaching and total in its impact on social life as to betoken a new stage in the development of U.S. society. Moreover, it requires an historical consciousness on the part of citizens of a type uncommon in our history. Perhaps only at the time of the American Revolution and the Civil War have any significant numbers of people been aware of the need consciously to remake the institutions which govern their everyday lives and structure the quality of their social development. Yet to attain the social prerequisites for equality and full human development as a natural byproduct of economic life requires no less than this in the contemporary United States. Even the most sympathetic reader will understandably ask what view of the dynamics of historical change leads us to believe such a period might be at hand. In a word, we are impressed by Karl Marx's observation that fundamental social change occurs only when evident possibilities for progress are held in check by a set of anachronistic social arrangements. In such periods, basic social institutions lose their appearance of normality and inevitability; they take on the air of increasing irrationality and dispensability. In these conditions individuals, and especially those groups and classes most likely to benefit from progress, consciously seek alternative social arrangements. It is for this reason that the history of the human race, despite its tortuous path and periodic retrogression, has been basically progressive.

In short, history in the long run seems to progress through a blending of reason and struggle. We take strong exception to such voguish historical pessimisms as Konrad Lorenz's view that:

The ever-recurrent phenomena of history do not have reasonable causes. . . . Most of us fail to realize how abjectly stupid and undesirable the historical mass behavior of humanity actually is.[14]

United States society offers all the material, technical, and organizational preconditions for a new stage in human liberation, but its economic institutions prevent progress from taking place. While there is nothing inevitable about a democratic socialist movement bursting through the fabric of irrational social relationships, the possibility grows yearly. More and more frequently and in ever-wider spheres of social life—of which education is merely one—the anachronism of our social institutions is impressed upon us.

But is an egalitarian and humanistic socialism even technically possible? Some have suggested that inequality and dehumanized social relationships are imposed upon us by the very nature of modern technology. In the words of Jacques Ellul, a well-known critic of modern life:

Technique has become autonomous; it has fashioned an omnivorous world which obeys its own laws and which has renounced all tradition. . . . Man himself is overpowered by technique and becomes its object.[15]

This common view, we believe, is quite unfounded. Technology, we shall argue, can only increase the set of alternatives open to society toward the satisfaction of its needs. Harmful social outcomes are the product of irrational power relationships in the dynamic of social choice, not the inevitable product of scientific rationality or technological necessity. Even the modern organization of work in the corporate enterprise, we suggest, is not technically rational but, rather, is geared toward the reproduction of contemporary patterns of property and power. Democratic and participatory work is not only more human, it is also more in line with modern technology.

Another common objection to the possibility of an egalitarian society must be squarely faced: the seeming inevitability of bureaucracies controlling our lives. According to this view, aptly expressed by Robert Michels in his classic *Political Parties*:

It is organization which gives birth to the domination of the elected over the electors, of the mandatories over the mandates, of the delegates over the delegators. Who says organization says oligarchy.[16]

Indeed, the ossification of the Russian Revolution and the souring of innumerable reform movements has convinced many that, to use Seymour Martin Lipset's words, ". . . the objective of the mass-based elite is to replace the power of one minority with that of another."[17] The problem with this view is that all of the historical examples on which it is based involve economic systems whose power relations are formally undemocratic. While governmental bureaucracies have not been terribly responsive to the needs of the masses, it is fair to say they have been responsive to groups in proportion to their economic power. Thus economic democracy should be a precondition—though hardly a guarantee—to truly representative government. With its appearance, Michels' "iron law of oligarchy" can be relegated to the proverbial trash bin of history.

Finally, it might be objected that the types of changes we envision are incompatible with basic human nature. The view we expound in this [article] is that the antagonisms, insecurities, provincialisms, egotisms, competitiveness, greed, and chauvinism which we observe in U.S. society do not derive from innate biological needs or instincts or infirmities. Rather, these are reasonable responses to the exigencies and experiences of daily life. Just as slavery, feudalism, and political autocracies have been viewed in their time as the only systems compatible with the Natural Order, so it is with U.S. capitalism. Yet in the contemporary United States, we perceive a nearly universal striving among people

for control over their lives, free space to grow, and social relationships conducive to the satisfaction of group needs. The concept which infuses our vision of educational reform and social transformation is that of an irrepressible need for individuality and community. Most likely, this is a result of an interaction between innate characteristics and concrete historical circumstances. A proper organization of educational and economic life, we believe, can unleash a people's creative powers without recreating the oppressive poles of domination and subordinacy, self-esteem and self-hatred, affluence and deprivation.

A revolutionary transformation of social life will not simply happen through piecemeal change. Rather, we believe it will occur only as the result of a prolonged struggle based on hope and a total vision of a qualitatively new society, waged by those social classes and groups who stand to benefit from the new era. . . .

Notes

1. U.S. Department of Labor, *Monthly Labor Review*, September 1974, p. 50.

2. Irene A. King, *Bond Sales for Public School Purposes*, U.S. Department of Health, Education and Welfare, 1974, Publication No. (OE)-73-11406.

3. U.S. Department of Labor (1974), *op. cit.*

4. Harvey Averech *et al.*, *How Effective Is Schooling: A Critical Review and Synthesis of Research Findings* (Santa Monica: The Rand Corporation, 1972), p. 125.

5. James S. Coleman *et al.*, *Equality of Educational Opportunity* (Washington, D.C.: U.S. Government Printing Office, 1966). For a discussion of some of the shortcomings of the Coleman Report, see Samuel Bowles and Henry Levin, "The Determinants of Scholastic Achievement: An Appraisal of Some Recent Evidence," *Journal of Human Resources*, Winter 1968; and "More on Multicollinearity and the Effectiveness of Schools," *Journal of Human Resources*, Summer 1968.

6. Giora Hanoch, "An Economic Analysis of Earnings and Schooling," in *Journal of Human*

Resources, No. 2, Summer 1967; Randall Weiss, "The Effects of Education on the Earnings of Blacks and Whites," in *Review of Economics and Statistics*, No. 52, May 1970; Bennett Harrison, *Education, Training, and the Urban Ghetto* (Baltimore: Johns Hopkins University Press, 1972).

7. Jencks, Smith, Ackland, Bane, Cohen, Gintis, Heyns, Michelson, *Inequality: A Reassessment of the Effects of Family and Schooling in America* (New York: Basic Books, 1972).

8. Arthur A. Jensen, "How Much Can We Boost IQ and Scholastic Achievement?" *Harvard Educational Review*, Vol. 39, No. 1, 1969, p. 1.

9. Jensen (1969), *op. cit.*; Richard Herrnstein, "IQ," *Atlantic Monthly*, Vol. 228, No. 3, September 1971; J. Eysenck, *The IQ Argument* (New York: Library Press, 1971); Arthur A. Jensen, *Educability and Group Differences* (New York: Harper & Row, 1975).

10. Clarence Karier, "Testing for Order and Control in the Corporate Liberal State," in *Education Theory*, Vol. 22, Spring 1972; Leon

Kamin, *The Science and Politics of IQ* (Potomac, Maryland: Erlbaum Associates, 1974).

11. Edward Banfield, *The Unheavenly City* (Boston: Little, Brown and Company, 1968); Daniel Patrick Moynihan, *The Negro Family* (Cambridge, Mass.: MIT Press, 1967).

12. We have confined our attention to education in the United States. For an excellent treatment of education on a world-wide basis, see Martin Carnoy, *Education as Cultural Imperialism* (New York: McKay, 1974).

13. For a more extensive treatment, see Samuel Bowles and Herbert Gintis, "The Problem with Human Capital . . . A Marxian Critique," *American Economic Review*, May 1975.

14. Konrad Lorenz, *On Aggression* (New York: Bantam Books, 1963), p. 228.

15. Jacques Ellul, *The Technological Society* (New York: Alfred Knopf, 1964), pp. 14, 227.

16. Robert Michels, *Political Parties* (New York: Free Press, 1962), p. 365.

17. Seymour Martin Lipset, "Introduction," in Robert Michels, *Political Parties, op. cit.*, p. 68.

PART FIVE

Social Deviance

READINGS 21–23

This book has focused on patterns of social organization, along with the social processes producing these patterns and going on within them. While no one has said that *everyone* follows them, the patterns are clearly there, with some degree of stability and thus predictability of behavior. Human behavior generally varies somewhere in the vicinity of normative expectations. However, some behavior is so far away from important norms that it is considered "deviant." In the selection on basic concepts, Inkeles says, "*Social deviance* arises when the departure from accepted norms involves action about which the community feels strongly, so strongly as to adopt sanctions to prevent or otherwise control the deviant behavior" (p. 47). Deviance, then, is not only behavior that violates normative expectations but also behavior about which someone becomes upset. This raises some interesting issues: Who is it that becomes upset? Who can decide that certain behavior is so far out of line that it is deviant? And who has the power to make such definitions of deviance stick?

There is another interesting issue to consider: *Why* do some people engage in behavior so far out of line with important normative expectations that they are considered deviant? Are they somehow just defective people? That has been a popular answer over the years. However, the sociological perspective on social organization provides a different view, as Reece McGee demonstrates in the following keynote selection. McGee shows us that deviance often is produced by social patterns themselves. In this view, both conformity and deviance can be the results of social patterns.

In this selection from *Points of Departure* McGee begins by comparing the conventional "wisdom" about the nature and causes of deviance to more recent social science ideas on the subject. Be sure to locate the various elements in the conventional view. How do sociologists respond to each of these elements? McGee then presents in some detail two of the major sociological theories of deviance, one dealing with societal pressures and the other dealing with interaction processes.

Robert K. Merton's anomie theory is a *structural* theory, locating deviance as a possible response to one's position in the stratification structure. Merton includes two major variables: the general knowledge on the part of practically everybody as to the "proper" goals in the society (whether they are one's own goals or not) and the differential availability of the means considered proper to use in attaining these goals. It is general knowledge that our society values material goods, but not everyone has the same chance to obtain the education and good jobs that yield material success. It is one's position in the stratification structure that counts.

Howard S. Becker's labeling theory is a *process* theory, locating deviance as the product of a transaction between rule makers and rule breakers. This theory sets out to answer the kinds of questions raised in the first paragraph of this introduction—who decides what is deviant, and who is able to make such definitions stick? Becker maintains there is no behavior that is inherently deviant, since deviance is created by the label placed upon it. While Merton's theory focuses on societal structures, Becker's labeling theory examines interaction processes.

Another major theory of deviance takes a position somewhere between these two. According to Edwin Sutherland's differential association theory, deviance is learned through interaction processes with others in the subculture in which one lives. People living in a subculture that legitimates lawbreaking will learn that it is all right to break laws, while those living in another subculture will not. These differing subcultures are often located at different levels in the stratification structure; subcultures legitimating lawbreaking are more frequently found at the lower levels. Sutherland's theory includes both structural and process dimensions. Whether a sociological theory focuses on structure, process, or some combination of the two, sociologists typically treat deviance as a product of social patterns rather than as a characteristic of pathological individuals. Be sure to note McGee's four concluding points in which he sums up the purposes of this reading.

Think about how the theories of deviance developed by Merton and Becker are related to the larger theoretical orientations in sociology. Can you see that Merton's theory develops from a general functionalist concern with the interrelated parts of a social system? Becker, of course, is applying the symbolic interactionist orientation to the study of deviance.

The illustrative reading following the keynote selection is "The Saints and the Roughnecks," by William Chambliss. In this interesting illustration of labeling theory, you will meet two gangs of young men, both engaged in delinquent activities. But the members of one of these gangs are considered to be fine upstanding citizens—

the Saints of the title—while the members of the other gang are the Roughnecks, considered to be young, tough criminals. Why are their similar activities viewed so differently? That is the question Chambliss sets out to answer.

The second illustrative reading in this part comes from Charles Silberman's book *Criminal Violence, Criminal Justice*. Drawing from Merton's theory, Silberman treats violent crime as a result of opportunities *not* available in ghettos and central cities. With many other occupations blocked, crime becomes a realistic occupational choice for some people.

21
Deviance as Variance from Norms

Reece McGee

In every society there are people and behaviors which are considered socially deviant because they vary in undesirable ways from what the society defines as proper. Deviation, then, implicitly refers to a departure from ideal norms, from what "ought to be." Deviant behavior is activity which differs from what the norms prescribe or prohibit. Deviant people are those who exhibit sufficient amounts of deviant behavior or a few deviant behaviors of such severity that they are seen as being different from other people. Thus, deviation is popularly understood to mean a departure from some standard; that is, deviant behavior is perceived as a failure to observe social norms.

Reprinted from *Points of Departure: Basic Concepts in Sociology*, 1st ed., by Reece McGee. Copyright © 1972, 1973 by the Dryden Press, a division of Holt, Reinhart and Winston, Inc. Used with permission of the publisher. Footnotes have been renumbered.

Deviation also is popularly seen as being pathological in character; that is, deviants are supposed to be pathological individuals and deviant behavior is supposed to be either sick or vicious. People usually believe that there is "something wrong" with people who violate popular standards, who do not do what they are supposed to do, who choose to defy conventional norms. To define a behavior or an individual as deviant, then, is to make a moral judgment as well as an empirical one. It is necessary to judge that a norm has been violated and that it was wrong to do so. In both ways the judgment reflects the normative structure of the society.

Despite this popular view of deviance, sociologists have reason to doubt both the pathological character of much deviation and its departure from social norms.[1] One of the problems of understanding deviant behavior, at least in large, complex societies, is that the society is likely to have more than one set of norms for judging deviation. Probably every society has a popular culture whose norms are known to most members of the society, and the people will more or less conform to many of them. But in heterogeneous societies such as the United States we also find subcultures of region, race, class, occupation, and ethnicity. Such subcultures typically develop some norms of their own which differ from those of the larger society. Thus, what is deviant by the norms of the larger society may be conforming by the norms of the subculture, and vice versa. These norm conflicts are relatively rare only in simple societies. . . .

In practice there is a range of permissible variation about most norms. Thus, deviation is not just any departure from an ideal norm but rather one which exceeds the amount of permissible variation. Strictly speaking, most people probably deviate from most ideal norms most of the time. As long as they do not depart from them *too far*, they are not perceived as being deviant (different, pathological), because in statistical facts they are not; that is, everyone else behaves the same way. Someone who gets drunk occasionally is not viewed as being an alcoholic; but someone who never violates a speed limit is looked on as being a "nut" (deviant) for observing the norm too rigidly.

DEVIANCE AS A FAILURE OF SOCIAL CONTROL

In Western societies deviance is popularly understood as resulting from a failure of the mechanisms of socialization and social control. That is, deviants are perceived to be individuals who for some reason are not inhibited by the same considerations that inhibit the rest of us. This understanding is the basis of the American and British penal systems. If people who perform "bad" or socially disapproved actions are punished for them, they will fear the punishment more than they will desire to again commit the prohibited acts. Also, other people will see them as examples and will be deterred from doing the same kinds of things. Originally this theory substituted the contemporary type of

prison for torture and capital punishment; it was conceived as a humane reform of Western penal systems. Freud's belief that human behavior is a function of socialization and of a lack of control over elemental processes (the "drives") fits into this theory of punishment. If socialization is adequate, people will conform to the norms of their society; if they do not conform, the social control mechanisms have failed in those particular cases. Deviation is explained by failure in the individual deviant, an inadequacy of his history, psychology, or even constitutional makeup. It can be understood, then, by studying the characteristics of deviants in order to determine "where they went wrong," and it can be deterred by making its costs too high.

Since about the time of the Second World War this theory of deviation and punishment has come under increasing criticism from social scientists. Approximately two centuries of penal treatment of criminals, for example, has failed to greatly alter either the frequency or the nature of crime. The American public is just beginning to understand what sociologists have known for almost fifty years: The prison system, far from deterring crime or rehabilitating criminals, serves as advanced education in criminal activity for most of its inmates. No concrete evidence has yet been developed to support the belief that most types of behavior popularly understood as deviant are much different from other kinds of behavior. Nor is there any evidence that many "deviant" actions are performed by persons who differ in any significant way from the so-called law-abiding (purportedly nondeviant) population. Furthermore, there seems to be no evidence that most people who are defined as deviant have had upbringings significantly different from those of other people. In fact, on most psychological and biological measures, such "deviant" populations as institutionalized criminals or delinquents do not differ for the most part in any important ways from the population beyond their prison walls. A number of the patients in mental hospitals also seem to be no different in important ways from the population of a prison or of a typical town.[2]

The idea, then, that deviant behavior is a characteristic of special kinds of individuals and is itself significantly different from "normal" behavior seems inadequate as a description of the way the world really works. Most people who are considered deviant cannot be distinguished from other people in any way that would explain their behavior. Indeed, much of the behavior popularly called deviant turns out to be pretty much the same as what most people do most of the time anyway. Popular understanding of this, however, has lagged far behind scientific recognition. Only in the last thirty years or so have social scientists even begun to develop new ideas and theories to replace those still enshrined in the law and the public mind. . . .

DEVIATION AND SOCIAL STRUCTURE

As we suggested earlier, social science in recent years has begun to cast doubt upon the propositions underlying the popular understanding of deviation and to develop new theories which seem to fit the observable facts more adequately. These theories explain deviance in the following way.

1. There are circumstances in which the nature of the society itself can generate definite pressures upon individuals or social groups which lead them to nonconforming behavior; that is, there are circumstances in which nonconformity is a reasonable and entirely normal response to the demands of the society.
2. "Deviation" is a characteristic of neither acts nor persons. It is a label which gets applied to some people as the result of a long social transaction.

These explanations are partially congruent with one another. The first is offered by Robert K. Merton, a sociologist who attempts to explain why high rates of certain kinds of deviant behavior (for example, crime and suicide) characterize some groups more than others. He seeks to answer the fundamental question: "How does deviant behavior persist in the face of social disapproval?"[3] The second explanation, referred to as labeling theory, is offered by Howard S. Becker, a sociologist who attempts to explain how individuals come to be identified as deviants by the societies in which they live.[4]

Merton's work largely concerns itself with group phenomena, while Becker's work is aimed mainly at individuals. In this they are complementary. Using Merton's theory we can begin to understand why some social groups have a greater incidence of deviant behavior than others; using Becker's theory we can learn how groups may come to be labeled as deviant in themselves and how some individuals in such groups may not be defined as deviant while others are. The primary difference between the two theories is that Merton accepts the idea that some kinds of behavior really are deviant, even though the individuals engaging in them may be responding positively to social pressure from their culture rather than in an antisocial manner. Becker, on the other hand, questions if there is any such thing as deviant behavior (as distinguished from nondeviant behavior) in the first place, or if deviation is something that is defined after the fact.

Merton's argument is contained in his famous theory of anomie.[5] This theory explains that social structures can sometimes generate pressures on certain individuals or social groups to engage in nonconforming behavior. When this occurs, the individual must violate some norms in order to conform to certain social pressures. If we can locate groups in society which are particularly subject to such pressures, we might expect rates of deviant or nonconforming behavior among them to be relatively high, regardless of the characteristics of the individuals who make up such groups.

Through socialization, all societies teach their members two important particulars of their culture—cultural goals (the things that are worth striving for) and cultural means (the norms which are considered appropriate for seeking and attaining the goals). Under most circumstances, the members of a society are able to use the means they have learned are legitimate in order to attain the ends they have been taught to desire. It is important that this should be true, for a failure to attain the goals we have internalized results in a loss of self-esteem (a lowered judgment of ourselves by ourselves) and a "pain that only human beings can experience."[6] This loss of self-esteem is not only extremely painful but may also be psychologically damaging, and people will do almost anything to avoid it. Most of the time they do not have to do anything. However, there are some individuals and groups who, although they have been taught to seek the same cultural goals as the rest of us and to utilize the same norms in the search, are denied access to the means for their goal attainment. In the United States material success is defined as a cultural goal; and competition is defined as the cultural means to that goal. But there are some groups (for example, black or other nonwhite Americans) whose members are not permitted to compete, or who are permitted to do so only under conditions of considerable disadvantage, although the demand that they be successful is maintained. Using Merton's argument, we would expect higher degrees of deviant behavior among the members of such groups than among members of other groups which had no roadblocks set in their path by the social structure.

Merton proposes five possible combinations of access to or acceptance of means and ends (goals), four of which represent social situations that can produce anomic, or deviant, reactions among persons subjected to them. These reactions may occur when "the system doesn't work," when people, because of their position in society, are denied access either to the means for reward or to the rewards (goals) which their legitimate use of the means ought to bring. They may occur also when the lowered self-esteem experienced as a result of either condition leads these people to socially unacceptable attempts to escape their plight. The five combinations are conformity, innovation, ritualism, retreatism, and rebellion. With the exception of conformity, all the other combinations are anomic, or deviant, reactions.

The reader might find it easier to comprehend Merton's model for predicting deviant behavior if he observes [Table 1]. The pluses represent acceptance of and access to the cultural phenomenon in question, and the minuses represent rejection and/or lack of access.

Conformity. The individual accepts and internalizes both the cultural goals and the cultural means which he has been taught, and his social position gives him adequate access to both. This is what most people do most of the time.

Innovation. The individual accepts the cultural goals he has been taught; but because of a social position which denies him access to those means which his society defines as legitimate, he "innovates" (invents new means of attaining the socially desired ends). The most common example of this kind of innovation is crime. In the United States crime can often be explained as a response to excessive cultural emphasis on material success with a corresponding lack of

Table 1

Methods of Adaptation to Societal Means-Ends	Culturally Prescribed Means to Social Goals	Culturally Prescribed Goals
Conformity	I	I
Innovation	−	+
Ritualism	+	−
Retreatism	−	−
Rebellion	∓	∓

emphasis on the legitimacy of the means used to attain this goal.

Ritualism. The individual accepts and internalizes both the cultural goals and the means which he has been taught. However, if he fails to attain the goals he has learned to want (perhaps because of inadequate access to the means for their attainment), he psychologically diminishes the importance of attaining the goal and exaggerates the significance of the socially approved means. An example of this is the losing coach who tells his team how important it is that they played fairly while their winning opponents cheated. Another example is the "radical right" in the United States, which seems to be composed mainly of persons who in one way or another have already lost the status game but who make up for it by accentuating one legitimate means to status by perverting patriotism into superpatriotism.[7]

Retreatism. The individual rejects the claims to legitimacy of both the socially defined means and ends and withdraws from the painful situation entirely. He does this because he has failed to attain the rewards which he has been taught to pursue in order to maintain an adequate self-image. He stops trying to be successful and rejects the value of the goals which success presumably would have offered. The conventional forms of retreatism in American society are alcoholism, suicide, drug addiction, and some forms of mental illness. Retreatism also is a prominent theme in some facets of the contemporary American youth culture. More than the other anomic reactions, retreatism is a response for "losers."

Rebellion. The individual either accepts the cultural means while rejecting the goals or vice versa. This anomic adaptation is characterized by the individual's attempt to substitute forcefully new means or goals for the societal ones he rejects. Rebellion differs from innovation by virtue of the rebel's attempt to substitute the new goals for the society as well as for himself. When rejecting means rather than goals, it differs from ritualism in that new means for attaining societal goals are again proposed for everyone. Rebellion may result either from lack of access to means or their failure to produce expected rewards, or from the frustration of self-esteem which the latter may create. Familiar examples of the two types of rebellion are the secession of the southern states, which led to the Civil War (rejection of societal means but acceptance of societal ends) and the new counter culture developing among some segments of American youth (rejection of societal goals but acceptance of conventional means to the attainment of new goals). Examples of this are ecological actions, the return to rural life, and so on.

The key to understanding Merton's views on anomie and how they contradict the idea of deviation as being some form of personal pathology is to remember that in the four anomic adaptations (or reactions) the individuals are behaving as they have been taught by their societies. They are not sinful or weak individuals who choose to deviate. They are, in fact, doing what they have learned they are supposed to do in order to earn the rewards which their society purports to offer its members. But either because their positions in the social structure do not permit them access to the means through which to seek the rewards they have learned to want, or because the means do not in fact guarantee goal attainment, they become frustrated and experience loss of self-esteem. In a final attempt to do and be what they have been taught they must, they engage in what is called deviant behavior. Such behavior is simply an attempt to gain the self-esteem which others are presumed to have and which the society has made it intolerable to be without. In the case of crime in the United States, material success is the desired goal. Thus, deviant behavior may be seen as an understandable social response on the part of normal people to situations where they cannot do or be what their society has claimed is necessary. It is the behavior of people so thoroughly socialized in the means-ends mechanism of their society that even when the system is out of balance due to an inappropriate assignment of weight on goals or means they are unable to do anything but attempt to work out their destinies and suffer the consequences. As we have seen, such "deviant" responses are particularly prevalent among social groups who are peculiarly subject to societal imbalances—the poor, nonwhite, immigrants, women (under some circumstances), children, and so on.

Becker's work also supports the sociological perception that deviant behavior is the product of social interaction rather than an attribute of deviant persons themselves. As we indicated earlier, Becker has founded a new school of thought on deviant behavior which has come to be known as labeling theory. The basic position from which Becker argues may be seen in the following extract from his work.

Social groups create deviance by making the rules whose infraction constitutes deviance, and by applying the rules to particular people and labeling them as outsiders [deviants]. From this point of view, deviance is *not* a quality of the act the person commits, but rather a consequence of the application by others of rules and sanctions to an "offender." The deviant is one to whom that label has successfully been applied; deviant behavior is behavior that people so label.[8]

If we accept this idea of the nature of deviance, then certain other conclusions must logically follow. The point of the excerpt is that groups make the rules which are used to define deviance for them, but the rules are not enforced universally and identically. Some people are punished for doing something, while others are not punished for doing the same thing; some actions are defined as deviant only because they occur in a particular time, place, or context. What constitutes deviation, then, is something other than particular people or particular behaviors. Deviance is a label, and in order to understand it we must understand the social process through which labels are successfully applied and why and how they are applied to some people and not to others.

Becker points out that if deviance consists of the responses of other people to an act by an individual, then we cannot assume the existence of a homogeneous category of deviant persons. That is, the "deviance" of those who have acquired a particular deviant label is only the response of others to something they did, and their actions may not have been identical or even similar. Not all people who have killed are defined as murderers, and not all who have committed the act called murder are known to have done so; some murderers escape the label. As a matter of fact, not only can we not assume that everyone who is labeled as deviant in some particular way has committed the same act in order to get labeled that way, but we cannot even be sure that every "deviant" has committed a "deviant" act at all, since labels are sometimes misapplied.

Then, according to Becker's labeling theory, the key to understanding deviant behavior is to understand that the application of the label "deviant" is simply the last stage of a social transaction between an individual and some social group. In order to learn how and why the label is applied, we must know the "natural history" of the transaction, that is, the series of interactions which resulted in the person being publicly identified as a deviant (nut, fairy, Red, and so on). The rules which govern the interaction between the individual and the social group and which determine whether or not the label will be successfully applied seem reasonably clear.

1. The only thing which we can be sure people who have been labeled deviant share in common is the experience of being so labeled. Beyond that, we cannot be certain. (This is not an attempt to deny that most people convicted of larceny have in all probability stolen something. But so have all of us. The key question is why some thieves become known as criminals and others—the rest of us—do not).[9]
2. This being the case, whether a given act is deviant depends not upon the nature of the act but upon how other people react to it. The degree to which others respond to a

given act is variable, and a number of factors seem to influence their responses. Among these are the following.

Time. The same acts may be punished at one time and ignored at others (as in recurrent "law enforcement drives" directed against gambling or prostitution in big cities). Or time itself may be the only variable defining a given act as deviant. The example of statutory rape is particularly instructive. Statutory rape is defined simply as sexual intercourse with a girl who is under "the age of consent" (whatever that may be in a given state). It is independent of the consent or nonconsent of the girl. Similarly, the use of LSD was not illegal anywhere in the United States until about [twenty] years ago. On the day in which the law forbidding it came into effect in a particular state, an act that had the day before been legal became felonious.

Social Roles and Statuses of the "Deviant" and the Person or Persons Supposedly Harmed by the "Deviant" Act. Whether certain behaviors are defined as deviant is a function of who commits them against whom. In many southern or southwestern towns a Mexican American or a Negro who assaults an Anglo with a knife would be accused of attempted murder or assault with a deadly weapon and would probably be severely punished for the action. The same person attacking a member of his own ethnic group might be defined simply as a participant in a "cutting scrape" and would probably get off with a bash on the head from a policeman's nightstick. Similarly, an attack by a white on a person defined as nonwhite might simply be referred to as a "good old boy who got likkered up too much one night and went out nigger bashin'." Obviously, rules tend to get applied more to some people than to others.[10]

Specific Consequences. Some rules are enforced only when the behavior they forbid has a particular set of consequences and are largely ignored at other times. The conventional rules forbidding premarital sexual relations, for example, are traditionally applied only when the female partner becomes pregnant—and then only against her. Who has ever heard of an unmarried father being expelled from his high school.

Becker summarizes the labeling theory position on the nature of deviance as follows.

Deviance is not a simple quality, present in some kinds of behavior and absent in others. Rather, it is the product of a process which involves the responses of other people to the behavior. The same behavior may be an infraction of the rules at one time and not at another; may be an infraction when committed by one person, but not when committed by another; some rules are broken with impunity, others are not. In short, whether a given act is deviant or not depends in part on the nature of the act (that is, whether or not it violates some rule) and in part on what other people do about it. . . . We must recognize that we cannot know whether a given act will be categorized as deviant until the response of others has occurred. Deviance is not a quality that lies in behavior itself, but in the interaction between the person who commits an act and those who respond to it.[11]

We can see from the preceding discussion that contrary to centuries of popular understanding, to conventional law, and to a considerable body of contemporary psychiatry, deviation may be understood as a normal social process in which people pretty much like everyone else, acting in ways not particularly unique, come to have special social identities as a consequence of their relations with others in their society. These identities, as identities, are like conventional roles and statuses which other people share, except that they are defined by others as unconventional.

The purpose of the detailed treatment which deviation has been given in this [reading] is multiple. It has sought to establish at least four concepts for the reader's satisfaction.

1. What "everybody knows" about human behavior is not necessarily true; the conventional wisdom of a society is nothing more than conventional.

2. Even very individualistic kinds of behavior have social components and can be subjected usefully to sociological analysis.

3. The individualistic-psychologistic perspective which is so much a part of the cultural understanding and outlook of contemporary Americans is not adequate to explain and understand even rather personal and subjective phenomena.

4. Much human behavior cannot be understood only in terms of motive but must also be analyzed in the light of social process.

Beyond this, we have tried to suggest that a great deal of what we regard as everyday reality is, in fact, a matter of social consensus (agreement among the members of a society) and that the "ultimate reality" of events in society is based on definition. We said much earlier that man is the most symbolic of animals, that he lives his life submerged in a sea of symbols.

Notes

1. The belief that deviant behavior is pathological is an old one in Western thought. It accepts a medical-organic analogy of society in which the society is viewed as a living body and normative violation is defined as a sickness which must be cured for the sake of the health of the body politic. The analogy may have been developed to replace an essentially spiritualistic or demonological theory of deviance at a time when the breakdown of the church and the onslaught of science was casting doubt on medieval understanding of human behavior. Needless to say, the medical-organic analogy is a poor one. A society is not an organic system; we have neither a germ theory of deviant behavior nor any medicine with which to "treat" it. This analogy is, however, more humane than the spiritual theory of deviation, for it implies that if a deviant is "sick," he should be treated for his illness, rather than tortured in order to drive out the evil spirits possessing him or burned at the stake as a punishment for having sold his soul to the devil.

2. In fact, it is quite probable that significant proportions of the populations of state prisons, state mental hospitals, and, say, local Army posts could be physically exchanged for one another without causing any changes in either the conduct of the three institutions or the behavior outcomes of those switched.

3. Robert K. Merton, "Social Structure and Anomie," *Social Theory and Social Structure* (Glencoe: The Free Press, 1949).

4. Howard S. Becker, *Outsiders: Studies in the Sociology of Deviance* (New York: The Free Press of Glencoe, 1963).

5. *Anomie* is a term invented by the French sociologist Durkheim. It means literally "normlessness" and is used to describe a mental condition in which the individual is unsure of how he is expected to behave, due to lack of understanding or knowledge of the social rules. Durkheim used the word to explain the relatively higher suicide rates among the widowed and single than among the married and among noncommissioned as opposed to commissioned officers in the army, that is, among people whose bonds holding them to others were, for one reason or another, weak.

6. I am indebted for the phrase and some of my argument to an excellent social problems textbook which utilizes the Merton theory as its theoretical framework. Although old enough now that some of its illustrations may strike modern students as quaint, it remains, in my opinion, the best social problems text ever written. See Harry C. Bredemeier and Jackson Toby, *Social Problems in America* (New York: John Wiley & Sons, Inc., 1960).

7. See Ira S. Rohter, "The Righteous Rightists," *Transaction* 4, No. 6 (May 1967): 27–35.

8. Becker, p. 9.

9. I do not mean to imply that all larceny is the same or that most people engage in serious theft throughout their lives. However, it does seem to be a fact (as Porterfield's research on university students and my own questioning of college classes demonstrates) that practically everyone has stolen something at some time in his life, if only pennies from his mother's purse or stamps from his employer. But we do not normally regard ourselves or others as thieves. That is, the act of committing a theft is not what defines a person as a thief. As a matter of fact,

a great many so-called law-abiding people habitually engage in various larcenies such as stealing tools, materials, merchandise, or time from
an employer, falsifying expense accounts, and
shoplifting.

10. In college towns it is not uncommon for
professors who are found driving while intoxicated to be driven home by the police with a
quiet—or even humorously condescending—
lecture as their total punishment, while students
found in the same condition can expect at least
to spend the rest of the night in the drunk tank
and might be reported to the school and expelled.

11. Becker, p. 14

22
The Saints and the Roughnecks

William J. Chambliss

Editors' Introduction

In the keynote reading McGee says, "Some people are punished for
doing something, while others are not punished for doing the same
thing . . ." (p. 251). William Chambliss describes an extreme case
of this in the following reading. He compares the activities of a
group of upper-middle-class high school students with the activities
of a group of lower-class students. Both sets of activities include
delinquent behavior, yet one set of students is labeled delinquent
while the other set is not. Chambliss illustrates this situation by calling one gang the Roughnecks and the other gang the Saints. He
raises the issue of why the community became upset about the activities of the Roughnecks but did not question the very similar activities of the Saints.

Note the various activities of the Saints. How do they manage to
get away with such behavior? How do their activities compare to
the activities of the Roughnecks? Chambliss says that the Roughnecks were both more and less delinquent than they were thought
to be. How is this so? Which group actually was "more delinquent"?
What factors does Chambliss identify in trying to make this assessment? Can you explain the selective perceptions of parents, teachers, and police regarding these two groups? Why could one gang

254

manage people's impressions of them so well, while the other gang could not? How did the police and the community *reinforce* deviance? What effects did the definitions of being "fine, upstanding young men" or "delinquents" have on the later lives of these youths? To what extent was the development of self-image involved?

This article is an empirical demonstration of Becker's labeling theory, using the symbolic interactionist theoretical orientation. Chambliss shows how meanings are developed and definitions are maintained through the processes of symbolic interaction, in which different labels are attached to very similar behavior. Chambliss also uses the conflict orientation when he points out that the differing definitions stem from control of the legal institutions by those at the top of the class structure. He says that police pay attention to influential upper-middle-class parents and ignore powerless lower-class parents.

This study rests on two years of observation of eight white upper-middle-class male high school students and six white lower-class male students—a case study of two gangs. What is Chambliss's purpose in this study? Can he meet this particular purpose in a study of only two gangs? What are the limitations in a study of only two gangs? From the information Chambliss gives, it is clear that he observed the gang members in school as well as out in the community. He also followed up their activities for about ten years after high school. He does not give the details of how he was able to observe these young men in their "private" activities. Possibly Chambliss encountered the general problems of doing research on deviance.

Imagine trying to study deviant behavior through observation, as Chambliss did. If the behavior is deviant, then some people with the power to make a label stick are upset about that behavior. Since it is in the self-interest of the deviants not to be exposed to whatever legal, psychological, or social sanctions are laid on the behavior, they will be very careful about nosy strangers, as researchers must appear. The researchers must first locate the deviant behavior, which is likely to be well hidden. Then they must somehow get into a position from which they can observe the behavior. Can they manage to observe it from "the outside"? (Chambliss seems to have managed this, but he keeps to himself how he did it.) If this is impossible—and it often is—then the researchers must somehow become a part of the deviant group. This is considerably easier to say than it is to do. Suppose, however, that the researchers manage to earn the trust of the deviants and become accepted into the group. What then? When researchers enter a setting where deviance exists, they may have special obligations to those who have accepted them. What should the researchers do when they learn about illegal activities? Should they "blow the whistle" on violations of the law—and lose their research setting in the process? If they do not, aren't they also guilty?

Eight promising young men—children of good, stable, white upper-middle-class families, active in school affairs, good pre-college students—were some of the most delinquent boys at Hanibal High School. While community residents and parents knew that these boys occasionally sowed a few wild oats, they were totally unaware that sowing wild oats completely occupied the daily routine of these young men. The Saints were constantly occupied with truancy, drinking, wild driving, petty theft and vandalism. Yet not one was officially arrested for any misdeed during the two years I observed them.

This record was particularly surprising in light of my observations during the same two years of another gang of Hanibal High School students, six lower-class white boys known as the Roughnecks. The Roughnecks were constantly in trouble with police and community even though their rate of delinquency was about equal with that of the Saints. What was the cause of this disparity? the result? The following consideration of the activities, social class and community perceptions of both gangs may provide some answers.

THE SAINTS FROM MONDAY TO FRIDAY

The Saints' principal daily concern was with getting out of school as early as possible. The boys managed to get out of school with minimum danger that they would be accused of playing hookey through an elaborate procedure for obtaining "legitimate" release from class. The most common procedure was for one boy to obtain the release of another by fabricating

Published by permission of Transaction, Inc. from *Society*, Vol. 11, No. 1. Copyright © Nov./Dec. 1981 by Transaction, Inc.

a meeting of some committee, program or recognized club. Charles might raise his hand in his 9:00 chemistry class and ask to be excused—a euphemism for going to the bathroom. Charles would go to Ed's math class and inform the teacher that Ed was needed for a 9:30 rehearsal of the drama club play. The math teacher would recognize Ed and Charles as "good students" involved in numerous school activities and would permit Ed to leave at 9:30. Charles would return to his class, and Ed would go to Tom's English class to obtain his release. Tom would engineer Charles' escape. The strategy would continue until as many of the Saints as possible were freed. After a stealthy trip to the car (which had been parked in a strategic spot), the boys were off for a day of fun.

Over the two years I observed the Saints, this pattern was repeated nearly every day. There were variations on the theme, but in one form or another, the boys used this procedure for getting out of class and then off the school grounds. Rarely did all eight of the Saints manage to leave school at the same time. The average number avoiding school on the days I observed them was five.

Having escaped from the concrete corridors the boys usually went either to a pool hall on the other (lower-class) side of town or to a cafe in the suburbs. Both places were out of the way of people the boys were likely to know (family or school officials), and both provided a source of entertainment. The pool hall entertainment was the generally rough atmosphere, the occasional hustler, the sometimes drunk proprietor and, of course, the game of pool. The cafe's entertainment was provided by the owner. The boys would "accidentally" knock a glass on the floor or spill cola on the counter—not all the time, but enough to be sporting. They would also bend spoons, put salt in sugar bowls and generally tease whoever was working in the cafe. The owner had opened the cafe recently and was dependent on the boys' business which was, in fact, substantial since between the horsing around and the teasing they bought food and drinks.

THE SAINTS ON WEEKENDS

On weekends, the automobile was even more critical than during the week, for on weekends the Saints went to Big Town—a large city with a population of over a million 25 miles from Hanibal. Every Friday and Saturday night most of the Saints would meet between 8:00 and 8:30 and would go into Big Town. Big Town activities included drinking heavily in taverns or nightclubs, driving drunkenly through the streets, and committing acts of vandalism and playing pranks.

By midnight on Fridays and Saturdays the Saints were usually thoroughly high, and one or two of them were often so drunk they had to be carried to the cars. Then the boys drove around town, calling obscenities to women and girls; occasionally trying (unsuccessfully so far as I could tell) to pick girls up; and driving recklessly through red lights and at high speeds with their lights out. Occasionally they played "chicken." One boy would climb out the back window of the car and across the roof to the driver's side of the car while the car was moving at high speed (between 40 and 50 miles an hour); then the driver would move over and the boy who had just crawled across the car roof would take the driver's seat.

Searching for "fair game" for a prank was the boys' principal activity after they left the tavern. The boys would drive alongside a foot patrolman and ask directions to some street. If the policeman leaned on the car in the course of answering the question, the driver would speed away, causing him to lose his balance. The Saints were careful to play this prank only in an area where they were not going to spend much time and where they could quickly disappear around a corner to avoid having their license plate number taken.

Construction sites and road repair areas were the special province of the Saints' mischief. A soon-to-be-repaired hole in the road inevitably invited the Saints to remove lanterns and wooden barricades and put them in the car, leaving the hole unprotected. The boys would find a safe vantage point and wait for an unsuspecting motorist to drive into the hole. Often, though not always, the boys would go up to the motorist and commiserate with him about the dreadful way the city protected its citizenry.

Leaving the scene of the open hole and the motorist, the boys would then go searching for an appropriate place to erect the stolen barricade. An "appropriate place" was often a spot on a highway near a curve in the road where the barricade would not be seen by an oncoming motorist. The boys would wait to watch an unsuspecting motorist attempt to stop and (usually) crash into the wooden barricade. With saintly bearing the boys might offer help and understanding.

A stolen lantern might well find its way onto the back of a police car or hang from a street lamp. Once a lantern served as a prop for a reenactment of the "midnight ride of Paul Revere" until the "play," which was taking place at 2:00 A.M. in the center of a main street of Big Town, was interrupted by a police car several blocks away. The boys ran, leaving the lanterns on the street, and managed to avoid being apprehended.

Abandoned houses, especially if they were located in out-of-the-way places, were fair game for destruction and spontaneous vandalism. The boys would break windows, remove furniture to the yard and tear it apart, urinate on the walls and scrawl obscenities inside.

Through all the pranks, drinking and reckless driving the boys managed miraculously to avoid being stopped by police. Only twice in two years was I aware that they had been stopped by a Big City policeman. Once was for speeding (which they did every time they drove whether they were drunk or sober), and the driver managed to convince the policeman that it was simply an error. The second time they were stopped they had just left a nightclub and were walking through an alley. Aaron stopped to urinate and the boys began making obscene remarks. A foot patrolman came into the alley, lectured the boys and sent them home. Before the boys got to the car one began talking in a loud voice again. The policeman, who had followed them down the alley, arrested this boy for disturbing the peace and took him to the police station where the other Saints gathered. After paying a $5.00 fine, and with the assurance that there would be no permanent record of the arrest, the boy was released.

The boys had a spirit of frivolity and fun about their escapades. They did not view what they were engaged in as "delinquency," though it surely was by any reasonable definition of that word. They simply viewed themselves as having a little fun and who, they would ask, was really hurt by it? The answer had to be no one, although this fact remains one of the most difficult things to explain about the gang's behavior. Unlikely though it seems, in two years of drinking, driving, carousing and vandalism no one was seriously injured as a result of the Saints' activities.

THE SAINTS IN SCHOOL

The Saints were highly successful in school. The average grade for the group was "B," with two of the boys having close to a straight "A" average. Almost all of the boys were popular and many of them held offices in the school. One of the boys was vice-president of the student body one year. Six of the boys played on athletic teams.

At the end of their senior year, the student body selected ten seniors for special recognition as the "school wheels"; four of the ten were Saints. Teachers and school officials saw no problem with any of these boys and anticipated that they would all "make something of themselves."

How the boys managed to maintain this impression is surprising in view of their actual behavior while in school. Their technique for covering truancy was so successful that teachers did not even realize that the boys were absent from school much of the time. Occasionally, of

course, the system would backfire and then the boy was on his own. A boy who was caught would be most contrite, would plead guilty and ask for mercy. He inevitably got the mercy he sought.

Cheating on examinations was rampant, even to the point of orally communicating answers to exams as well as looking at one another's papers. Since none of the group studied, and since they were primarily dependent on one another for help, it is surprising that grades were so high. Teachers contributed to the deception in their admitted inclination to give these boys (and presumably others like them) the benefit of the doubt. When asked how the boys did in school, and when pressed on specific examinations, teachers might admit that they were disappointed in John's performance, but would quickly add that they "knew he was capable of doing better," so John was given a higher grade than he had actually earned. How often this happened is impossible to know. During the time that I observed the group, I never saw any of the boys take homework home. Teachers may have been "understanding" very regularly.

One exception to the gang's generally good performance was Jerry, who had a "C" average in his junior year, experienced disaster the next year and failed to graduate. Jerry had always been a little more nonchalant than the others about the liberties he took in school. Rather than wait for someone to come get him from class, he would offer his own excuse and leave. Although he probably did not miss any more classes than most of the others in the group, he did not take the requisite pains to cover his absences. Jerry was the only Saint whom I ever heard talk back to a teacher. Although teachers often called him a "cut up" or a "smart kid," they never referred to him as a troublemaker or as a kid headed for trouble. It seems likely, then, that Jerry's failure his senior year and his mediocre performance his junior year were consequences of his not playing the game the proper way (possibly because he was disturbed by his parents' divorce). His teachers regarded him as "immature" and not quite ready to get out of high school.

THE POLICE AND THE SAINTS

The local police saw the Saints as good boys who were among the leaders of the youth in the community. Rarely, the boys might be stopped in town for speeding or for running a stop sign. When this happened the boys were always polite, contrite and pled for mercy. As in school, they received the mercy they asked for. None ever received a ticket or was taken into the precinct by the local police.

The situation in Big City, where the boys engaged in most of their delinquency, was only slightly different. The police there did not know the boys at all, although occasionally the boys were stopped by a patrolman. Once they were caught taking a lantern from a construction site. Another time they were stopped for running a stop sign, and on several occasions they were stopped for speeding. Their behavior was as before: contrite, polite and penitent. The urban police, like the local police, accepted their demeanor as sincere. More important, the urban police were convinced that these were good boys just out for a lark.

THE ROUGHNECKS

Hanibal townspeople never perceived the Saints' high level of delinquency. The Saints were good boys who just went in for an occasional prank. After all, they were well dressed, well mannered and had nice cars. The Roughnecks were a different story. Although the two gangs of boys were the same age, and both groups engaged in an equal amount of wild-oat sowing, everyone agreed that the not-so-well-dressed, not-so-well-mannered, not-so-rich boys were heading for trouble. Townspeople would say, "You can see the gang members at the drugstore night after night, leaning against the storefront (sometimes drunk) or slouching around inside buying cokes, reading magazines, and probably stealing old Mr. Wall blind. When they are outside and girls walk by, even respectable girls, these boys make suggestive remarks. Sometimes their remarks are downright lewd."

From the community's viewpoint, the real indication that these kids were in for trouble was that they were constantly involved with the police. Some of them had been picked up for stealing, mostly small stuff, of course, "but still it's stealing small stuff that leads to big time crimes." "Too bad," people said. "Too bad that these boys couldn't behave like the other kids in town; stay out of trouble, be polite to adults, and look to their future."

The community's impression of the degree to which this group of six boys (ranging in age from 16 to 19) engaged in delinquency was somewhat distorted. In some ways the gang was more delinquent than the community thought; in other ways they were less.

The fighting activities of the group were fairly readily and accurately perceived by almost everyone. At least once a month, the boys would get into some sort of fight, although most fights were scraps between members of the group or involved only one member of the group and some peripheral hanger-on. Only three times in the period of observation did the group fight together: once against a gang from across town, once against two blacks and once against a group of boys from another school. For the first two fights the group went out "looking for trouble"—and they found it both times. The third fight followed a football game and began spontaneously with an argument on the football field between one of the Roughnecks and a member of the opposition's football team.

Jack had a particular propensity for fighting and was involved in most of the brawls. He was a prime mover of the escalation of arguments into fights.

More serious than fighting, had the community been aware of it, was theft. Although almost everyone was aware that the boys occasionally stole things, they did not realize the extent of the activity. Petty stealing was a frequent event for the Roughnecks. Sometimes they stole as a group and coordinated their efforts; other times they stole in pairs. Rarely did they steal alone.

The thefts ranged from very small things like paperback books, comics and ballpoint pens to expensive items like watches. The nature of the thefts varied from time to time. The gang would go through a period of systematically lifting items from automobiles or school lockers. Types of thievery varied with the whim of the gang. Some forms of thievery were more profitable than others, but all thefts were for profit, not just thrills.

Roughnecks siphoned gasoline from cars as often as they had access to an automobile, which was not very often. Unlike the Saints, who owned their own cars, the Roughnecks would have to borrow their parents' cars, an event which occurred only eight or nine times a year. The boys claimed to have stolen cars for joy rides from time to time.

Ron committed the most serious of the group's offenses. With an unidentified associate the boy attempted to burglarize a gasoline station. Although this station had been robbed twice previously in the same month, Ron denied any involvement in either of the other thefts. When Ron and his accomplice approached the station, the owner was hiding in the bushes beside the station. He fired both barrels of a double-barreled shotgun at the boys. Ron was severely injured; the other boy ran away and was never caught. Though he remained in critical condition for several months, Ron finally recovered and served six months of the following year in reform school. Upon release from reform school, Ron was put back a grade in school, and began running around with a different gang of boys. The Roughnecks considered the new gang less delinquent than themselves, and during the following year Ron had no more trouble with the police.

The Roughnecks, then, engaged mainly in three types of delinquency: theft, drinking and fighting. Although community members perceived that this gang of kids was delinquent, they mistakenly believed that their illegal activities were primarily drinking, fighting and being a nuisance to passersby. Drinking was limited among the gang members, although it did occur, and theft was much more prevalent than anyone realized.

Drinking would doubtless have been more prevalent had the boys had ready access to liquor. Since they rarely had automobiles at their disposal, they could not travel very far, and the bars in town would not serve them. Most of the boys had little money, and this, too, inhibited their purchase of alcohol. Their major source of liquor was a local drunk who would buy them a fifth if they would give him enough extra to buy himself a pint of whiskey or a bottle of wine.

The community's perception of drinking as prevalent stemmed from the fact that it was the most obvious delinquency the boys engaged in. When one of the boys had been drinking, even a casual observer seeing him on the corner would suspect that he was high.

There was a high level of mutual distrust and dislike between the Roughnecks and the police. The boys felt very strongly that the police were unfair and corrupt. Some evidence existed that the boys were correct in their perception.

The main source of the boys' dislike for the police undoubtedly stemmed from the fact that the police would sporadically harass the group. From the standpoint of the boys, these acts of occasional enforcement of the law were whimsical and uncalled for. It made no sense to them, for example, that the police would come to the corner occasionally and threaten them with arrest for loitering when the night before the boys had been out siphoning gasoline from cars and the police had been nowhere in sight. To the boys, the police were stupid on the one hand, for not being where they should have been and catching the boys in a serious offense, and unfair on the other hand, for trumping up "loitering" charges against them.

From the viewpoint of the police, the situation was quite different. They knew, with all the confidence necessary to be a policeman, that these boys were engaged in criminal activities. They knew this partly from occasionally catching them, mostly from circumstantial evidence ("the boys were around when those tires were slashed"), and partly because the police shared the view of the community in general that this was a bad bunch of boys. The best the police could hope to do was to be sensitive to the fact that these boys were engaged in illegal acts and arrest them whenever there was some evidence that they had been involved. Whether or not the boys had in fact committed a particular act in a particular way was not especially important. The police had a broader view: their job was to stamp out these kids' crimes; the tactics were not as important as the end result.

Over the period that the group was under observation, each member was arrested at least once. Several of the boys were arrested a number of times and spent at least one night in jail. While most were never taken to court, two of the boys were sentenced to six months' incarceration in boys' schools.

THE ROUGHNECKS IN SCHOOL

The Roughnecks' behavior in school was not particularly disruptive. During school hours they did not all hang around together, but tended instead to spend most of their time with one or two other members of the gang who were their special buddies. Although every member of the gang attempted to avoid school as much as possible, they were not particularly successful and most of them attended school with surprising regularity. They considered school a burden—something to be gotten through with a minimum of conflict. If they were "bugged" by a particular teacher, it could lead to trouble. One of the boys, Al, once threatened to beat up a teacher and, according to the other boys, the teacher hid under a desk to escape him.

Teachers saw the boys the way the general community did, as heading for trouble, as being uninterested in making something of themselves. Some were also seen as being incapable of meeting the academic standards of the school. Most of the teachers expressed concern for this group of boys and were willing to pass them despite poor performance, in the belief that failing them would only aggravate the problem.

The group of boys had a grade point average just slightly above "C." No one in the group failed either grade, and no one had better than a "C" average. They were very consistent in their achievement or, at least, the teachers were consistent in their perception of the boys' achievement.

Two of the boys were good football players. Herb was acknowledged to be the best player in the school and Jack was almost as good. Both boys were criticized for their failure to abide by training rules, for refusing to come to practice as often as they should, and for not playing their best during practice. What they lacked in sportsmanship they made up for in skill, apparently, and played every game no matter how poorly they had performed in practice or how many practice sessions they had missed.

TWO QUESTIONS

Why did the community, the school and the police react to the Saints as though they were good, upstanding, nondelinquent youths with bright futures but to the Roughnecks as though they were tough, young criminals who were headed for trouble? Why did the Roughnecks and the Saints in fact have quite different careers after high school—careers which, by and large, lived up to the expectations of the community?

The most obvious explanation for the differences in the community's and law enforcement agencies' reactions to the two gangs is that one group of boys was "more delinquent" than the other. Which group *was* more delinquent? The answer to this question will determine in part how we explain the differential responses to these groups by the members of the community and, particularly, by law enforcement and school officials.

In sheer number of illegal acts, the Saints were the more delinquent. They were truant from school for at least part of the day almost every day of the week. In addition, their drinking and vandalism occurred with surprising regularity. The Roughnecks, in contrast, engaged sporadically in delinquent episodes. While these episodes were frequent, they certainly did not occur on a daily or even a weekly basis.

The difference in frequency of offenses was probably caused by the Roughnecks' inability to obtain liquor and to manipulate legitimate excuses from school. Since the Roughnecks had less money than the Saints, and teachers carefully supervised their school activities, the Roughnecks' hearts may have been as black as the Saints', but their misdeeds were not nearly as frequent.

There are really no clear-cut criteria by which to measure qualitative differences in antisocial behavior. The most important dimension of the difference is generally referred to as the "seriousness" of the offenses.

If seriousness encompasses the relative economic costs of delinquent acts, then some assessment can be made. The Roughnecks probably stole an average of about $5.00 worth of goods a week. Some weeks the figure was considerably higher, but these times must be balanced against long periods when almost nothing was stolen.

The Saints were more continuously engaged in delinquency but their acts were not for the most part costly to property. Only their vandalism and occasional theft of gasoline would so qualify. Perhaps once or twice a month they would siphon a tankful of gas. The other costly items were street signs, construction lanterns and the like. All of these acts combined probably did not quite average $5.00 a week, partly because much of the stolen equipment was abandoned and presumably could be recovered. The difference in cost of the stolen property between the two groups was trivial, but the Roughnecks probably had a slightly more expensive set of activities than did the Saints.

Another meaning of seriousness is the potential threat of physical harm to members of the community and to the boys themselves. The Roughnecks were more prone to physical violence; they not only welcomed an opportunity to fight, they went seeking it. In addition, they fought among themselves frequently. Although the fighting never included deadly weapons, it was still a menace, however minor, to the physical safety of those involved.

The Saints never fought. They avoided physical conflict both inside and outside the group. At the same time, though, the Saints frequently endangered their own and other people's lives. They did so almost every time they drove a car, especially if they had been drinking. Sober, their driving was risky; under the influence of alcohol it was horrendous. In addition, the

Saints endangered the lives of others with their pranks. Street excavations left unmarked were a very serious hazard.

Evaluating the relative seriousness of the two gangs' activities is difficult. The community reacted as though the behavior of the Roughnecks was a problem, and they reacted as though the behavior of the Saints was not. But the members of the community were ignorant of the array of delinquent acts that characterized the Saints' behavior. Although concerned citizens were unaware of much of the Roughnecks' behavior as well, they were much better informed about the Roughnecks' involvement in delinquency than they were about the Saints'.

VISIBILITY

Differential treatment of the two gangs resulted in part because one gang was infinitely more visible than the other. This differential visibility was a direct function of the economic standing of the families. The Saints had access to automobiles and were able to remove themselves from the sight of the community. In as routine a decision as to where to go to have a milkshake after school, the Saints stayed away from the mainstream of community life. Lacking transportation, the Roughnecks could not make it to the edge of town. The center of town was the only practical place for them to meet since their homes were scattered throughout the town and any noncentral meeting place put an undue hardship on some members. Through necessity the Roughnecks congregated in a crowded area where everyone in the community passed frequently, including teachers and law enforcement officers. They could easily see the Roughnecks hanging around the drugstore.

The Roughnecks, of course, made themselves even more visible by making remarks to passersby and by occasionally getting into fights on the corner. Meanwhile, just as regularly, the Saints were either at the cafe on one edge of town or in the pool hall at the other edge of town. Without any particular realization that they were making themselves inconspicuous, the Saints were able to hide their time-wasting. Not only were they removed from the mainstream of traffic, but they were almost always inside a building.

On their escapades the Saints were also relatively invisible, since they left Hanibal and travelled to Big City. Here, too, they were mobile, roaming the city, rarely going to the same area twice.

DEMEANOR

To the notion of visibility must be added the difference in the responses of group members to outside intervention with their activities. If one of the Saints was confronted with an accusing policeman, even if he felt he was truly innocent of a wrongdoing, his demeanor was apologetic and penitent. A Roughneck's attitude was almost the polar opposite. When confronted with a threatening adult authority, even one who tried to be pleasant, the Roughneck's hostility and disdain were clearly observable. Sometimes he might attempt to put up a veneer of respect, but it was thin and was not accepted as sincere by the authority.

School was no different from the community at large. The Saints could manipulate the system by feigning compliance with the school norms. The availability of cars at school meant that once free from the immediate sight of the teacher, the boys could disappear rapidly. And this escape was well enough planned that no administrator or teacher was nearby when the boys left. A Roughneck who wished to escape for a few hours was in a bind. If it were possible to get free from class, downtown was still a mile away, and even if he arrived there, he was still very visible. Truancy for the Roughnecks meant almost certain detection, while the Saints enjoyed almost complete immunity from sanctions.

BIAS

Community members were not aware of the transgressions of the Saints. Even if the Saints had been less discreet, their favorite delinquencies would have been perceived as less serious than those of the Roughnecks.

In the eyes of the police and school officials, a boy who drinks in an alley and stands intoxicated on the street corner is committing a more serious offense than is a boy who drinks to inebriation in a nightclub or a tavern and drives around afterwards in a car. Similarly, a boy who steals a wallet from a store will be viewed as having committed a more serious offense than a boy who steals a lantern from a construction site.

Perceptual bias also operates with respect to the demeanor of the boys in the two groups when they are confronted by adults. It is not simply that adults dislike the posture affected by boys of the Roughneck ilk; more important is the conviction that the posture adopted by the Roughnecks is an indication of their devotion and commitment to deviance as a way of life. The posture becomes a cue, just as the type of the offense is a cue, to the degree to which the known transgressions are indicators of the youths' potential for other problems.

Visibility, demeanor and bias are surface variables which explain the day-to-day operations of the police. Why do these surface variables operate as they do? Why did the police choose to disregard the Saints' delinquencies while breathing down the backs of the Roughnecks?

The answer lies in the class structure of American society and the control of legal institutions by those at the top of the class structure. Obviously, no representative of the upper class drew up the operational chart for the police which led them to look in the ghettoes and on streetcorners—which led them to see the demeanor of lower-class youth as troublesome and that of upper-middle-class youth as tolerable. Rather, the procedures simply developed from experience—experience with irate and influential upper-middle-class parents insisting that their son's vandalism was simply a prank and his drunkenness only a momentary "sowing of wild oats"—experience with cooperative or indifferent, powerless, lower-class parents who acquiesced to the laws' definition of their son's behavior.

ADULT CAREERS OF THE SAINTS AND THE ROUGHNECKS

The community's confidence in the potential of the Saints and the Roughnecks apparently was justified. If anything, the community members underestimated the degree to which these youngsters would turn out "good" or "bad."

Seven of the eight members of the Saints went on to college immediately after high school. Five of the boys graduated from college in four years. The sixth one finished college after two years in the army, and the seventh spent four years in the air force before returning to college and receiving a B.A. degree. Of these seven college graduates, three went on for advanced degrees. One finished law school and is now active in state politics, one finished medical school and is practicing near Hanibal, and one boy is now working for a Ph.D. The other four college graduates entered submanagerial, managerial or executive training positions with larger firms.

The only Saint who did not complete college was Jerry. Jerry had failed to graduate from high school with the other Saints. During his second senior year, after the other Saints had gone on to college, Jerry began to hang around with what several teachers described as a "rough crowd"—the gang that was heir apparent to the Roughnecks. At the end of his second senior year, when he did graduate from high school, Jerry took a job as a used-car salesman, got married and quickly had a child. Although he made several abortive attempts to go to college by attending night school, when I last saw him (ten years after high school) Jerry was unemployed and had been living on unemployment for almost a year. His wife worked as a waitress.

Some of the Roughnecks have lived up to community expectations. A number of them were headed for trouble. A few were not.

Jack and Herb were the athletes among the Roughnecks and their athletic prowess paid off handsomely. Both boys received unsolicited athletic scholarships to college. After Herb received his scholarship (near the end of his senior year), he apparently did an about-face. His demeanor became very similar to that of the Saints. Although he remained a member in good standing of the Roughnecks, he stopped participating in most activities and did not hang on the corner as often.

Jack did not change. If anything, he became more prone to fighting. He even made excuses for accepting the scholarship. He told the other gang members that the school had guaranteed him a "C" average if he would come to play football—an idea that seems far-fetched, even in this day of highly competitive recruiting.

During the summer after graduation from high school, Jack attempted suicide by jumping from a tall building. The jump would certainly have killed most people trying it, but Jack survived. He entered college in the fall and played four years of football. He and Herb graduated in four years, and both are teaching and coaching in high schools. They are married and have stable families. If anything, Jack appears to have a more prestigious position in the community than does Herb, though both are well respected and secure in their positions.

Two of the boys never finished high school. Tommy left at the end of his junior year and went to another state. That summer he was arrested and placed on probation on a manslaughter charge. Three years later he was arrested for murder; he pleaded guilty to second degree murder and is serving a 30-year sentence in the state penitentiary.

Al, the other boy who did not finish high school, also left the state in his senior year. He is serving a life sentence in a state penitentiary for first degree murder.

Wes is a small-time gambler. He finished high school and "bummed around." After several years he made contact with a bookmaker who employed him as a runner. Later he acquired his own area and has been working it ever since. His position among the bookmakers is almost identical to the position he had in the gang; he is always around but no one is really aware of him. He makes no trouble and he does not get into any. Steady, reliable, capable of keeping his mouth closed, he plays the game by the rules, even though the game is an illegal one.

That leaves only Ron. Some of his former

friends reported that they had heard he was "driving a truck up north," but no one could provide any concrete information.

REINFORCEMENT

The community responded to the Roughnecks as boys in trouble, and the boys agreed with that perception. Their pattern of deviancy was reinforced, and breaking away from it became increasingly unlikely. Once the boys acquired an image of themselves as deviants, they selected new friends who affirmed that self-image. As that self-conception became more firmly entrenched, they also became willing to try new and more extreme deviances. With their growing alienation came freer expression of disrespect and hostility for representatives of the legitimate society. This disrespect increased the community's negativism, perpetuating the entire process of commitment to deviance. Lack of a commitment to deviance works the same way. In either case, the process will perpetuate itself unless some event (like a scholarship to college or a sudden failure) external to the established relationship intervenes. For two of the Roughnecks (Herb and Jack), receiving college athletic scholarships created new relations and culminated in a break with the established pattern of deviance. In the case of one of the Saints (Jerry), his parents' divorce and his failing to graduate from high school changed some of his other relations. Being held back in school for a year and losing his place among the Saints had sufficient impact on Jerry to alter his self-image and virtually to assure that he would not go on to college as his peers did. Although the experiments of life can rarely be reversed, it seems likely in view of the behavior of the other boys who did not enjoy this special treatment by the school that Jerry, too, would have "become something" had he graduated as anticipated. For Herb and Jack outside intervention worked to their advantage; for Jerry it was his undoing.

Selective perception and labelling—finding, processing and punishing some kinds of criminality and not others—means that visible, poor, nonmobile, outspoken, undiplomatic "tough" kids will be noticed, whether their actions are seriously delinquent or not. Other kids, who have established a reputation for being bright (even though underachieving), disciplined and involved in respectable activities, who are mobile and monied, will be invisible when they deviate from sanctioned activities. They'll sow their wild oats—perhaps even wider and thicker than their lower-class cohorts—but they won't be noticed. When it's time to leave adolescence most will follow the expected path, settling into the ways of the middle class, remembering fondly the delinquent but unnoticed fling of their youth. The Roughnecks and others like them may turn around, too. It is more likely that their noticeable deviance will have been so reinforced by police and community that their lives will be effectively channelled into careers consistent with their adolescent background.

23
Poverty and Crime

Charles E. Silberman

Editors' Introduction

This selection from the best-selling book *Criminal Violence, Criminal Justice* begins with quotations from three people: an armed robber, a sociologist, and a "numbers" operator. Note that the sociologist is Robert Merton, whose anomie theory you met in the keynote reading. The author of this selection, Charles E. Silberman, says, "The close association of violent crime with urban lower-class life is a direct result of opportunities that are *not* available." This statement flows directly from Merton's theory—and from the three quotations that begin the selection.

After the three quotations Silberman poses a question: "Why are violent criminals drawn so heavily from the ranks of the poor?" He quickly elaborates on the question. It is not "why particular individuals choose a life of crime and violence; it is why the people who make that choice are concentrated more heavily in the lower class than in the middle or working class." This is an excellent example of how sociologists handle individual characteristics. In the discussion of the sociological perspective in Part One, Alan Bates says, "In its purest form the sociological frame of reference does not take into account the idiosyncracies of single persons or of separate historical occurrences. . . . Looking at an individual case from this perspective, it will be seen as a single instance of a more general class of similar instances . . ." (p. 6). And this is exactly what Silberman is doing.

Silberman goes on to show that the opportunities that *are* available to lower-class urban residents include crime as a viable occupational choice. In considering the opportunities that are and are not available, Silberman maintains that the ways people think and act are, in large part, responses they make to the conditions under which they live. This point is crucial to a sociological interpretation of deviance as well as of conforming behavior. Look again at the nature-nurture argument presented in the Davis keynote reading in Part Two to review this fundamental sociological position.

Pay particular attention to the way in which Silberman uses Merton's anomie theory in explaining the occurrence of much violent crime among urban lower classes. What are the opportunities for achieving success in your own particular social class background? (The fact that you are now involved in higher education says something about your access to opportunities for success.) From what you know about the stratification structure, would you say that opportunities for success are distributed evenly across social classes? Silberman illustrates some of the major points in Merton's theory by considering questions such as these relative to the urban poor.

One very important factor in making opportunities for crime available is the presence of a support network. In central cities there are plenty of sources of information about crime and how to get away with it, there are role models in abundance, and there are professionals such as fences to make crime lucrative. Silberman demonstrates the presence of a subculture in which people can readily learn crime. This is the crucial idea in Edwin Sutherland's differential association theory, presented in the introduction to the keynote reading. (Together the two illustrative readings in this part provide concrete applications of all three major theories of deviance: labeling theory, anomie theory, and differential association.) However, there are people outside the subculture who also become part of the support network. Who are these people?

Silberman takes into consideration both structure and process. Not every lower-class person is a criminal, nor does every lower-class neighborhood have a high crime rate. Criminal behavior is learned behavior—learned from someone else. Thus, people become criminals when structural conditions are right (or wrong) and when interaction with others presents them with the needed information, incentive, and skills. Within the structure of classes and subcultures, education for crime is a social process in which people learn to become criminals from friends and intermediaries such as fences. These ideas represent a symbolic interactionist orientation without the labeling aspect.

In the last part of the reading Silberman considers the "stolen property system." He shows the positive consequences of this system for the poor—and its negative consequences for them. What are these consequences? How are middle-class people involved in this system—and what are the consequences for them? What does Silberman mean when he says that supply and demand feed on each other in the stolen property system? Notice that Silberman deals with this system by applying the concepts of a functionalist orientation.

I really think there's a lot of similarity between the people who live out in the middle-class neighborhoods and the people I know.... Everybody wants to have their own joint, own their own home, and have two cars. It's just that we are going about it in a different way. I think keeping up with the Joneses is important everywhere.

—*John Allen, armed robber*

... vice and crime constitute a "normal" response to a situation where the cultural emphasis upon pecuniary success has been absorbed, but where there is little access to conventional and legitimate means for becoming successful.... In this setting, a cardinal American virtue, "ambition," produces a cardinal American vice, "deviant behavior."

—*Robert K. Merton, sociologist*

"Sounds like you've got to have a master's degree in math to understand all that."
"Nope. You just gotta be poor to understand."
—*Conversation between a* Washington Post *reporter and a "numbers" operator*

Why are violent criminals drawn so heavily from the ranks of the poor? The answer lies not in the genes, but in the nature of the lives poor people lead and of the communities in which they reside. The close association of violent crime with urban lower-class life is a direct result of the opportunities that are *not* available. Psychological factors may help explain why some individuals turn to street crime and others do not. But the question posed in this [reading] is not why particular individuals choose a life of crime and violence; it is why the people who make that choice are concentrated more heavily in the lower class than in the middle or working class.

Children growing up in urban slums and ghettos face a different set of choices than do

youngsters growing up in middle-class neighborhoods, and they have a radically different sense of what life offers. By the time children are six or eight years old, their view of the world has been shaped by their surroundings and by their parents' as well as their own experiences. Children of the upper class and upper-middle class develop what the psychiatrist Robert Coles calls a sense of "entitlement." "Wealth does not corrupt nor does it ennoble," Coles writes. "But wealth does govern the minds of privileged children, gives them a peculiar kind of identity which they never lose, whether they grow up to be stockbrokers or communards." That identity grows out of the wide range of choices with which privileged children live—choices about toys and games, food and clothing, vacations and careers. Their identity grows out of their sense of competence as well, for they (and, to a lesser degree, ordinary middle-class children) live in a world in which their parents and, by reflection, they themselves exercise authority, in which they influence and often control their environment. They are, in a phrase, the masters of their fate; their world, as an eleven-year-old boy told Coles, is one in which "If you really work for the rewards, you'll get them." This view is confirmed in school. "Those who want something badly enough get it," the boy's fourth-grade teacher wrote on the blackboard, "provided they are willing to wait and work."[1]

To the "children of poverty," those who want something badly enough usually do *not* get it, no matter how hard they work or how long they wait. Nothing about their own lives or the lives of their parents (or relatives or friends) suggests that "If you really work for the rewards, you'll get them." Quite the contrary: poor children grow up in a world in which people work hard and long, for painfully meager rewards. It is a world, too, in which parents and relatives are at the mercy of forces they cannot control—a world in which illness, an accident, a recession, an employer's business reverses, or a foreman's whim can mean the loss of a job and a long period of unemployment, and in which a bureaucrat's arbitrary ruling can mean denial or loss of welfare benefits and, thereby, of food, clothing, fuel, or shelter.

Understandably, poor children come to see themselves as the servants, not the masters, of their fate. When I was doing research on secondary education in the late 1960s, I attended a number of high school graduations. In schools with a predominantly middle-class population, the valedictorians typically spoke of how they and their classmates would affect and change American society. In schools with a lower-class student body, the student speakers sounded a different theme. In one such school, the valedictorian read a long Edgar Guest–type poem that began, "Sometimes you win, and sometimes you lose; here's luck." The poem continued in the same vein, with the refrain "Here's luck" repeated at the end of each stanza. For lower-class adolescents, this is an all too accurate assessment of the world they inhabit.

It is hard to be poor; it is harder to be poor in the United States than in most other countries, for American culture has always placed a heavy premium on "success." ("Winning is not the main thing; it is the only thing.") It is not the success ethic alone that causes problems, the sociologist Robert K. Merton observes, but the fact that the emphasis on success is coupled with an equally heavy emphasis on ambition, on maintaining lofty goals whatever one's station in life. "Americans are admonished 'not to be a quitter,'" Merton writes, "for in the dictionary of American culture, as in the lexicon of youth, 'there is no such word as "fail." ' "[2]

Crime and violence are more frequent among the poor than among members of the middle class, Merton argues, because American culture imbues everyone with the importance of ambition and success without providing everyone with the opportunity to achieve success through conventional means. And the cultural emphasis on success is greater now than it used to be: Every day of the week, in the films they see, the television programs they watch, and the public schools they attend, poor people are bombarded with messages about success— vivid images of the life style of the middle class. Television, in particular, drives home the idea that one is not a full-fledged American unless one can afford the goods and services portrayed in the commercials and in the programs themselves. To poor people, the TV screen provides a daily reminder, if any is needed, of the contrast between their own poverty and the affluence enjoyed by the rest of society.

It should not be surprising that many poor people choose the routes to success that seem open to them. To youngsters growing up in lower-class neighborhoods, crime is available as an occupational choice, much as law, medicine, or business management is for adolescents raised in Palo Alto or Scarsdale—except that lower-class youngsters often know a good deal more about the criminal occupations available to them than middle-class youngsters do about their options. In my conversations with young offenders, I was struck by the depth of their knowledge about robbery, burglary, "fencing," the sale and use of hard and soft drugs, prostitution and pimping, the "numbers" business, loan-sharking, and other crimes and rackets. In a great many cities, I was impressed, too, by their detailed knowledge of which fences, numbers operators, and other criminals were paying off which police officers, as well as by their cynicism about governmental corruption in general.

Thus the fabric and texture of life in urban slums and ghettos provide an environment in which opportunities for criminal activity are manifold, and in which the rewards for engaging in crime appear to be high—higher than the penalties for crime, and higher than the rewards for avoiding it. "It seems to me that the kind of neighborhood you come up in may make all the difference in which way you go and where you end up," John Allen suggests. In his neighborhood, most people earned their living from illegitimate activity. "Hustling was their thing: number running, bootlegging, selling narcotics, selling stolen goods, prostitution," he continues. "There's so many things that go on—it's a whole system that operates inside itself."

Say I was to take you by it. You want some junk, then I would take you to the dude that handles drugs. You want some clothes, I could take you somewhere that handles that. You want some liquor, I could take you someplace other than a liquor store. Of course, it's all outside the law.[3]

It is not simply a matter of opportunity; role models are important as well. "When I think about who's got the power in my neighborhood," John Allen says, "I mostly think about people who've got to the top in strictly illegal ways." As a child, his hero was a successful numbers operator: "he was about the biggest because everybody respected him, he always had plenty of money, he always dressed nice, and everybody always done what he wanted them to do. I dug the respect that he gave and that he got. . . ." "The ones you see are the ones who interest you," an ex-offender says, recalling his childhood. "If it had been doctors and lawyers who drove up and parked in front of the bars in their catylacks, I'd be a doctor today. But it wasn't; it was the men who were into things, the pimps, the hustlers and the numbers guys."[4]

In some lower-class neighborhoods, youngsters learn to become criminals almost as a matter of course. "Education for crime must be looked upon as habituation to a way of life," the late Frank Tannenbaum wrote in 1938, in his neglected classic, *Crime and the Community.* "As such, it partakes of the nature of all education. It is a gradual adaptation to, and a gradual absorption of, certain elements in the environment." Since it would be hard to improve upon Tannenbaum's description, I shall quote from it at length.

The development of a criminal career has "elements of curiosity, wonder, knowledge, adventure," Tannenbaum wrote. "Like all true education, it has its beginnings in play, it starts in more or less random movements, and builds up toward techniques, insights, judgments, attitudes." Like all true education, it also uses whatever is available in the environment, including "such humble things as junk heaps, alley ways, abandoned houses, pushcarts, railroad tracks, coal cars." Children begin with things that can be easily picked up and carried away, and easily used or sold.

Education for crime is a social process as well—"part of the adventure of living in a certain way in a certain environment," Tannen-

baum continued. "But both the environment and the way of using it must already be there." If his career is to develop, the young criminal must have encouragement, support, and instruction from his friends and elders, particularly from what Tannenbaum calls "the intermediary," i.e., the fence. Even if he is nothing more than a junk dealer or peddler, the fence will "purchase bottles, copper wire, lead pipes, bicycles, and trinkets. He will not only pay cash which can be used to continue the play life of the growing children, for movies, candies, sweets, harmonicas, baseball bats, gloves, and other paraphernalia, but if he is a friendly and enterprising fence he will throw out suggestions, indicate where things can be found, will even supply the tools with which to rip and tear down lead pipes or other marketable materials. And the young gang will accept the suggestions and carry out the enterprise as a part of a game, each act providing a new experience, new knowledge, new ways of seeing the world, new interests."

Other factors are needed, too. There must be a cynical attitude toward the police and toward property belonging to business firms and government agencies. There must be older criminals who use adolescents as messengers or lookouts, and to whom the youngsters look for approval. And there must be a conflict between delinquent youngsters and older, more settled people who are their victims, and who call for police protection. "All these elements are part of the atmosphere, of the environment" within which education for crime proceeds.[5]

The "slow, persistent habituation of an individual to a criminal way of life" occurs frequently and naturally in lower-class neighborhoods because so many criminal opportunities are available: numbers operations, bookmaking, and other illegal gambling enterprises; selling heroin, cocaine, marijuana, "uppers," "downers," and other drugs; loan-sharking; male and female prostitution; pimping; bootlegging and after-hours sales of alcoholic beverages; and hustling and theft in all their manifold forms.

Theft is in the very air that lower-class youngsters breathe. It is visible not just because of its frequency, but because crimes such as burglary, boosting, "clouting" (taking merchandise from a delivery truck while the driver is occupied), and stealing from parked cars are not isolated acts by isolated individuals. On the contrary, the individual act of theft is just the beginning of an elaborate process whereby "stolen merchandise is acquired, converted, redistributed and reintegrated into the legitimate property stream."[6] This "stolen property system," as the criminologists Marilyn Walsh and Duncan Chappell call it, is an integral part of the economy of urban lower-class neighborhoods. "About 95 percent of the people around here will buy hot goods," one of William West's Toronto informants told him. "It's a bargain, they're not going to turn it down."

Reluctance to turn down a bargain is not unique to the lower class. Many middle-class people knowingly buy stolen merchandise, and some respectable merchants increase their profits by selling stolen goods unbeknownst to their customers. It is not just coincidence that a particularly good bargain is referred to colloquially as a "steal." "Everybody's looking for a bargain," the professional fence whom the criminologist Carl Klockars calls Vincent Swaggi observed. "If the price is right and a man can use the merchandise, he's gonna buy. No question about it."

Swaggi had reason to know; he was speaking from the vantage point of more than twenty-five years' experience as a fence, selling to judges, prosecutors, policemen (high officials as well as patrolmen), independent businessmen, and buyers for department stores and retailing chains, in addition to ordinary consumers. He did a booming retail business in merchandise acquired through manufacturers' close-outs and other legitimate channels; his reputation as a fence cast an aura of "bargain" over his entire inventory. "See, most people figure all of the stuff in my store is hot, which you know it ain't," Swaggi told Klockars. "But if they figure it's hot you can't keep 'em away from it. . . . People figurin' they're gonna get something for nothing. You think I'm gonna tell 'em it ain't hot? Not on your life."[7]

For lower-class people, buying stolen merchandise is more than just a matter of picking up a bargain or accommodating the larceny that confidence men, as well as fences, tell us is in almost everyone's heart. Buying from a "peddler" at the back door may be the only way impoverished parents can afford to serve meat to their families, and patronizing a "bargain store" the only way they can afford shoes for their children's growing feet or name-brand sneakers so that teenagers do not lose face among their friends. For many poor people, too, buying stolen property is a way of buying into the American Dream, of being able to afford those consumption items—Stacy Adams shoes, Johnny Walker Black Label Scotch, a stereo or color television set, a motorcycle or ten-speed bike, a sporty-looking car—that the mass media tell them are the mark of a "successful" American. Because they lack the job titles and other devices that shore up middle-class people's sense of self, members of the lower class feel an even greater need than members of the middle class to define themselves through consumption.

Buying stolen property also provides a way of getting back at "them."[8] "Many people on Clay Street had had problems resulting in what they called 'getting screwed,'" Joseph T. Howell writes about the lower-class, mainly Southern white neighborhood in Washington, D.C., in which he lived for a year as a participant-observer. "For this reason, few people thought twice about 'getting back.'"

For instance, hot merchandise was plentiful on Clay Street. At Christmas, June and Sam gave Sammy a five-speed chopper bike, listing at seventy-five dollars but for which they paid a "friend" thirty dollars. Les gave Phyllis a twenty-one inch color TV in exchange for a new high-powered automatic rifle, both of which were hot. Les said about half of everything in their house was stolen. . . . Although few disclosed how they came upon the hot merchandise, they would usually take pride in getting an especially good deal. Having this merchandise was in no way considered dishonest.[9]

Far from being considered dishonest, patronizing the stolen property system is a way of evening the score, of getting one's fair share in an unfair world. From a lower-class perspective, buying a name-brand item at 50 percent or more below list price is a means of correcting a social imbalance, of redressing the maldistribution of income from which they suffer. Their sense of the rightness of the enterprise is enhanced by their conviction—often right, sometimes wrong—that local merchants and local outlets of national chains sell shoddy merchandise at premium prices. Since "hot" merchandise often is stolen from "downtown" retailers as well as from factories, warehouses, trucking firms, and middle-class residences, the stolen property system (like the progressive income tax) is a means of redistributing income from rich to poor. It may also serve to expand the overall consumer market and hence total production and employment; without the large "discounts" the stolen property system provides, Leroy Gould and his colleagues speculate, poor people might not be able to buy certain kinds of merchandise at all.[10]

At the same time, poor people's readiness to buy stolen merchandise contributes significantly to their own poverty. Thieves do not limit their scores to middle-class targets; juveniles, addicts, and other impulsive and semiprofessional thieves tend to prey on their own communities, where apprehension is less likely. The result is a vicious circle: normally law-abiding people who have been victimized by burglary or some other form of theft feel justified in buying hot merchandise to recoup their losses as cheaply as possible; but their patronage, in turn, makes it easier for thieves and fences to dispose of their wares and encourages further theft.

Thus the stolen property system develops its own dynamic, with supply and demand feeding on one another. Because lower-class people feel aggrieved, and because they are persuaded that American society is little more than one gigantic "hustle," there is no more opprobrium attached to selling stolen merchandise than to buying it. "That's the only way to make a living up here," a deliveryman who supplemented his salary by selling merchandise he stole from his own truck told Joseph Howell. "You earn half and you steal half." The man learned his illegal trade

through on-the-job training given him by a more experienced driver. "You work hard, don't you?" the older man had pointed out. "Why not take out your cut?" Why not, indeed, when the cops are known—or, what amounts to the same thing, are believed—to be taking *their* cut from the local fences, as well as from numbers runners and bankers, bootleggers, after-hours clubs, gambling joints, prostitutes, pimps, and heroin dealers.

Corruption aside, lower-class people's readiness to support the stolen property system is upheld by the benign view the rest of society takes toward fencing. Judges, prosecutors, police, and the public at large share a myopic legal tradition that focuses on individual acts of theft rather than on the stolen property system as a whole. One consequence is that judges rarely give prison sentences to fences, preferring to reserve the harsh penalty of incarceration for people they deem dangerous. Prosecutors and police administrators, in turn, are reluctant to proceed against fences. Building a strong case against a fence requires the investment of a great deal of prosecutorial and/or police time and effort, and the investment appears to be a poor allocation of resources when the end result is likely to be no more than probation or a fine for the convicted fence. From a police perspective, therefore, it often makes more sense to offer a fence protection in exchange for information. But from the perspective of people living in lower-class neighborhoods, the fact that fences go free, while burglars go to prison, serves to reinforce their cynicism about the law and law enforcement.

Be that as it may, fencing is a relatively low-risk criminal "industry" with great ease of entry. Some thieves act as their own fences, peddling their stolen wares themselves; most prefer to sell to a professional fence, who may retail the merchandise himself or sell to other "retailers."[11] Although thieves receive less money from a fence than they might earn if they sold direct to the consumer, they are relieved of the burden of carrying a retail "inventory" which constitutes incriminating evidence that can be used to tie them to their crime. The sooner a thief disposes of his loot, the better he likes it—

a fact that fences take into account in deciding what price to offer.

For residents of lower-class neighborhoods, stolen merchandise is likely to be available wherever they turn: in beauty parlors, barbershops, restaurants and bars, newsstands, after-hours clubs, gambling joints, appliance stores and repair shops, jewelry stores, pawnshops, liquor stores, junkyards, dry-cleaning stores, auto-repair and body shops, auto accessory stores, used-car lots, lumber yards, and retail clothing stores, as well as from cabdrivers, truckdrivers, delivery and "route" men, and so on.

Some of these outlets are primarily sellers of stolen merchandise, with the legitimate business serving only or mainly as a front. Most are more or less legitimate businesses whose owners supplement their incomes by selling stolen merchandise on the side. Such firms may be quite prosperous; or they may be small, often marginal, enterprises for whom the trade in stolen merchandise means the difference between losing money and making a small profit. Moonlighting as a fence may also mean the difference between earning a decent living and just scraping by for bartenders, waiters, beauticians, and other employees.[12]

For safety's safe, professional thieves prefer to deal with the same fence or fences on a regular basis; a fence is far more likely to "finger" an unknown or occasional thief than one on whom he depends for his inventory. When thieves know beforehand what their take will be, they may negotiate a price in advance; or they may simply know what the market price is for stolen merchandise of a particular sort and plan their scores accordingly. For their part, professional fences may have their own thieves whom they employ on a regular basis, or to whom they turn when they need merchandise of a particular variety.

Notes

1. Robert Coles, "The Children of Affluence," *The Atlantic Monthly,* Vol. 240, No. 3 (September, 1977), pp. 52–66.

2. Robert K. Merton, "Social Structure and Anomie," in Merton, *Social Theory and Social Structure,* enlarged ed. (New York: The Free Press, 1968), pp. 192–93.

3. John Allen, *Assault with a Deadly Weapon: The Autobiography of a Street Criminal,* Dianne Hall Kelly and Philip Heymann, eds. (New York: Pantheon Books, 1977), p. 1.

4. Allen, *Assault with a Deadly Weapon,* pp. 37, 5; Francis A. J. Ianni, *Black Mafia* (New York: Simon & Schuster, 1974), p. 285.

5. Frank Tannenbaum, *Crime and the Community* (New York: Columbia University Press, 1938), pp. 51–52.

6. Marilyn Walsh and Duncan Chappell, "Operational Parameters in the Stolen Property System," Hearings before the Select Committee on Small Business, U.S. Senate, on *Criminal Redistribution (Fencing) of Goods Stolen from Legitimate Business Activities and Their Effect on Commerce,* Part 3 (April 30 and May 2, 1974), pp. 765–66. A briefer version of the paper appears in *Journal of Criminal Justice,* Vol. 2, No. 2 (1974), pp. 113–29.

The discussion that follows relies also on the following sources, as well as on research by Richard D. Van Wagenen: Carl B. Klockars, *The Professional Fence* (New York: The Free Press, 1974); Marilyn Walsh, *The Fence* (Westport, Conn.: Greenwood Press, 1977); Duncan Chappell and Marilyn Walsh, "Receiving Stolen Property," *Criminology,* Vol. 11, No. 4 (February, 1974), pp. 484–97; Chappell and Walsh, "'No Questions Asked': A Consideration of the History of Criminal Receiving," *An Analysis of Criminal Redistribution Systems and Their Economic Impact on Small Business,* A Staff Report prepared for the Select Committee on Small Business, U.S. Senate (Washington, D.C.: U.S. Government Printing Office, 1972); Ianni, *Black Mafia,* pp. 37–47, 230–39, 246–75; Daniel Jack Chasan, "Good Fences Make Bad Neighbors," *New York Times Magazine* (December 29, 1974); Desmond Cartey, "How Black Enterprisers Do Their Thing: An Odyssey Through Ghetto Capitalism," in Glenn Jacobs, eds., *The Participant Observer* (New York: George Braziller, 1970), Ch. 1; William Gordon West, *Serious Thieves: Lower-Class Adolescent Males in a Short-Term Deviant Occupation,* Ph.D. dissertation, Northeastern University (Ann Arbor, Mich.:

University Microfilms, 1974), pp. 156–66; Julian B. Roebuck and Wolfgang Frese, *The Rendezvous* (New York: The Free Press, 1972), pp. 181–201; Leroy C. Gould et al., *Crime as a Profession,* Final Report to the Office of Law Enforcement Assistance and President's Commission on Law Enforcement and Administration of Justice, 1967, mimeo.

7. Klockars, *Professional Fence,* p. 50, note 8, and pp. 62, 77–79.

8. Frequent use of the pronoun "them" reflects both the way poor people see the rest of society and their conception of how the rest of society sees them.

9. Joseph T. Howell, *Hard Living on Clay Street* (Garden City, N.Y.: Anchor Books, 1973), p. 322.

10. Gould et al., *Crime as a Profession,* p. 42, note 1.

11. For an analysis of fences' other occupations, see Walsh, *The Fence,* Chs. 2–4.

12. Marilyn Walsh has analyzed the occupations of a group of 110 fences in a northeastern city. Seventy owned their own business; 11 worked for others; and 14 ran a fencing operation as an adjunct to some other illegal enterprise, such as loan-sharking or the numbers. Most of the remainder were burglars who did their own fencing. Walsh, *The Fence,* pp. 43–47. For an analysis of the different ways in which fences use their "front," see Walsh, *The Fence,* Ch. 4, and Klockars, *The Professional Fence,* Chs. 4, 5.

PART SIX

Social Change

READINGS 24–26

As you have read many of the selections in this book, you have probably wondered, "But isn't it all changing?" If so, you have already begun to think about our last topic, social change. In the very first reading in this book, Alan Bates identifies social change as one of the primary concerns of sociology. While not always obvious, social change has been represented throughout this book. Many of the readings in earlier parts are descriptions or analyses of slices taken from the social world. However, as Bates pointed out, these static slices are but a part of an ongoing, ever-changing social reality. What brings about this ever-present changing? What do some of the changes look like? As you read the selections in this part, look back and consider the other readings in the book from the standpoint of social change. This section will provide you with some necessary analytical tools for investigating social change.

The following keynote selection by Neil Smelser will give you some of the tools for analyzing social change. Smelser begins by identifying four dependent and four independent variables that together form the important components of a theory of social change. (Be sure you understand what is meant by dependent and independent variables. If you are unsure, go back to Jerry Rose's reading in Part One.) What does Smelser identify as the major dependent variables in social change? What are some current examples of change in each of these four categories? Note that for each, Smelser always asks, "Under what conditions can we expect change in this category?" These categories are what sociologists try to explain. They attempt such explanation by using the set of independent variables or determinants that Smelser discusses. Unlike the dependent variables where the focus may be on only one or a combination of factors, the independent variables work as a set. As you read through them, notice how each of the first three increases the possibility that social change will occur while narrowing the possibilities as to what this change may be. The fourth independent variable operates at all levels of the first three, always resisting those instigating the change.

This cumulative approach to social change is called "value-added." To illustrate this approach let's look at an example from the economy. Think about today's automobile. It is made from steel, aluminum, glass, and plastic. The average American car sells for about $10,000. Do you know how much steel, aluminum, glass, and plastic that amount of money will buy? So why does a car cost so much? Well, at each step in the production process, from digging the ore to hanging the last bit of trim on the finished car, value has been added to that car. A fender, all shaped and painted, costs considerably more than the raw material in that fender because value has been added to it as it took on its "fenderness." This can also be seen as a narrowing process. The moment a fender is stamped out of a sheet of steel, it is increasingly difficult to make a stove out of that same sheet of steel. The moment that fender is painted blue, it is difficult to put it on a new red car. All of this applies to Smelser's theory of social change as well. Each step in the process "adds value" to the social change and makes it more difficult for some other form of change to take place. Look carefully at the list of independent variables and notice how they work together *as a set.*

In the second part of this reading Smelser turns to a specific sweeping social change: modernization, or economic development. He examines only a small part of modernization since a complete job would require a rather large volume. He concentrates on work, family, and community relations in modernizing societies. As in Part Four dealing with the interrelationships of institutions, the focus of this reading is on how the different institutions act upon one another, but here Smelser focuses on *changing* relations. What are the more general changes that might take place in the basic institutions as modernization occurs? What specific changes does Smelser identify in work relations, family relations, and community life? To what degree are these specific changes interrelated?

Is social change best characterized as a smooth transition from "old" to "new"? Well, perhaps. But most often "discontinuities" are created, which may lead to social unrest released in many ways. When Smelser speaks of "discontinuities," what does he mean? Why do these discontinuities occur? Can you think of examples beyond those offered by Smelser? How are the feelings of unrest generated by modernization released? What role do agents of social control play in the release of this unrest? These are all important questions raised by Smelser in the last section of the reading. They reveal an important point about social change and the theoretical orientations we have used throughout this book. Structural-functionalists are concerned with the integration of parts of the system. Conflict theorists look at disintegration and dominance. How would each of these deal with social change? Would they differ in their identification of the causes of discontinuity and unrest? Would they differ in their analyses of the role of agents of social control?

One word of caution as you read the last section of the reading. Smelser makes an unfortunate choice of words when discussing "underground" cults and clubs. He speaks of them developing ". . . fantasies and ideologies of social regeneration." Although it is quite possible to find "fantasies" among groups agitating for social change, it is probably more fair to call them "visions" or "dreams."

Following the keynote selection, two illustrative readings round out this part on social change. The first, "Death by Dieselization: A Case Study in the Reaction to Technological Change," by W. F. Cottrell, is, on the surface, a dated piece. But as you read about the changes that took place in Caliente, you will see that the lessons taught are not dated in the least. In the second illustrative reading, "On the Origins of Social Movements," Jo Freeman lays out the history of several social movements, including the civil rights and the women's movements. These movements, important sources of social change in our society, have been especially influential since the 1950s. The keynote reading gives only brief treatment to these movements. As you read the selections on social change, you should try to determine how the dependent and independent variables introduced by Smelser worked in each case.

24
The Processes of Social Change

Neil Smelser

By one index, the study of social change is a solidly established subdivision of sociology. Almost all introductory textbooks . . . include a chapter toward the end on change. In addition, many texts and symposia are titled *Social Change* or some variation of it. Almost all undergraduate curricula have an upper-division course on the subject. And doctoral candidates are frequently examined on social change as one of their specialized fields of interest. All of this indicates that social change is a definite thing, with tangible subject matter to be taught and learned.

Yet, if we move behind the apparent reality bestowed on the subject by its fixed place in institutions of higher learning, we find that the topic is very difficult to define. Its core is evasive, and its boundaries are fuzzy. It occupies a kind of no-man's land between sociology and history and, depending on how we define it, is forever threatening to absorb—or be absorbed by—one or both of these fields. Insofar as social change is defined as the systematic study of variations in social life, it does not seem to differ from sociology in general; insofar as it is defined as the study of the unfolding of man's social arrangements through time, it appears to be indistinguishable from social history. . . .

THE COMPONENTS OF A THEORY OF SOCIAL CHANGE

. . . The first task facing any investigator [studying social change] is to specify *what he wishes to*

Reprinted from *Sociology*, 1st ed., by Neil Smelser (New York: John Wiley, 1967). Used with permission of the author. Footnotes have been renumbered.

explain. To put it another way, he must raise a problem about a *dependent variable.* Moving from specific to general examples, the following are sample problems: . . . Why has the divorce rate in America showed a steady upward climb during the past century? What social conditions are associated with the rise of totalitarian social movements? In these questions the dependent variables—changes for which we wish to account—are . . . the divorce rate, and totalitarian movements. The first component of a theory of change, then, is a scientific problem, or a "why" question about some variation in a dependent variable. Furthermore, if an investigator of change fails to specify a scientific problem, his approach may be legitimately criticized as being scientifically inadequate.

Analysts of social change focus their interest on temporal variations of one or more of the following types of dependent variables.

1. Changes in *aggregated attributes* of the population of a social unit. Examples of these attributes are the proportions of persons of different ages in a population, persons holding various occupations, persons professing various religious beliefs, and illiterate persons. To pose scientific questions is to ask under what conditions changes in these aggregated attributes may be expected.
2. Changes in *rates of behavior* in a population over time. Here I have in mind changes such as variations in rates of voting, religious attendance, crime, suicide, and collective protest. To pose scientific questions is to ask under what conditions changes in these rates may be expected. . . .

3. Changes in *social structure,* or patterns of interaction among individuals. To pose scientific questions is to ask under what conditions changes in structure may be expected. . . .
4. Changes in *cultural patterns.* Cultural patterns—including, for instance, values, world views, knowledge, and expressive symbols—supply systems of meaning and legitimacy for patterned social interaction. Examples of cultural patterns are the Judaic-Christian religious heritage, the values of democratic constitutional government, and the baroque musical style. To pose scientific questions is to ask under what conditions changes in these kinds of patterns may be expected.

These dependent variables are constituent parts of any theory of change. Without specifying some question about a dependent variable, the investigator is in the embarrassing position of not knowing what he wishes to explain. . . . To learn about the dynamics of change we must ask about the determinants (causes) of change. . . . The determinants of processes of change can be divided conveniently into the following four broad classes.

1. *The structural setting for change.* What implications does the existing structure of a social unit have for future changes of the unit? The concept of structural setting includes both an opportunity and an obstacle aspect. Suppose we wish to estimate the probabilities of a speculative boom and collapse on the stock market. If 90% of the securities are possessed by individual holders who can dispose of them quickly, the opportunities for rapid changes in the market are great. If, however, 90% of the securities are held by trust companies, whose managers must clear big transactions with their boards of directors before undertaking them, the obstacles to wild buying and selling sprees are considerable. To take another example, suppose we wish to estimate the probabilities of orderly change through reform in a society. If, like contemporary Great Britain, the society possesses numerous channels for the effective expression of grievances—channels such as elections, petitions,

and demonstrations—the probabilities for this kind of change are high. If, like contemporary South Africa, the society possesses few channels of this kind, the probabilities of repressive perpetuation or violent revolutionary overthrow of the status quo are higher. In considering the structural opportunities for and obstacles to change, it is also important to consider the power balance among different social groups (including vested interests) in the society.
2. *The impetus to change.* A conducive structural setting alone does not guarantee that change will occur. The social unit must be under some kind of pressure (which is called by many names, such as strain, tension, imbalance, and disequilibrium) that provides a more definite push toward change. The origins of these pressures for change are numerous. Pressure may accumulate as people go about their business in normal ways. For example, the fact that thousands of commuters pour in and out of a metropolis every day may create such problems of highway congestion that changes in public transport policy may result. Or pressures to change may result from events external to the society itself, such as foreign wars and natural catastrophes, which influence the internal balance of the society. Or a social system may generate pressure through different rates of change in its different parts. For example, the fact that an underdeveloped country, upon achieving national independence, institutes some version of universal suffrage tends to create a crisis in education—a need to create a responsible mass electorate—in these countries.
3. *Mobilization for change.* If the structural setting is conducive and pressures have accumulated, the probability that *some* sort of social change will occur is high. But these two determinants by themselves are too general to indicate what specific direction change will take. This direction depends on the ways in which resources are mobilized and are brought to bear on modifying the elements of social action. For some kinds of change, this mobilization may involve only a very routine operation. For example, suppose the ex-

ecutives of a business firm perceive that a potential demand exists for some new product. After a period of planning, they decide to invest some financial reserves in the manufacturing and marketing of the product, to hire a number of new employees, and perhaps to create a new subdivision of the research branch to develop the product. As these decisions are implemented, the firm undergoes a number of changes in finance, personnel, and social structure. For other kinds of change the agents may not be so well "programmed" regarding the direction of change, and may not have such immediate access to resources. Consider, for example, how an inchoate demand for social reform comes to be translated into a concrete, effective proposal for change. Before change can be effected, it is necessary for some sort of belief in a specific kind of reform to crystallize and disseminate; for leaders to form an organization or pressure group; and for workers to collect funds, publish propaganda, and organize demonstrations. As these examples show, leadership plays a very important role in the processes of mobilization for change.

4. *The operation of social controls.* As leaders of reform movements well know, their efforts to mobilize do not automatically result in change, but encounter a variety of resistances. Various authorities—for instance, government officials, courts, community leaders, religious agencies, and the press— are not indifferent to efforts of groups to change society. They may be hostile to the aims of the reform movement, or they may be exposed to countermovements to the proposed change. Moreover, the behavior of these agents of social control determines, in part, the direction of change. For example, if governmental authorities are persistently hostile and repressive toward modest demands for reform, the persons desiring reform may be driven into underground organizations, may become more extreme in their demands for change, and may even begin to challenge the legitimacy of the political authorities. If this happens, the agents of so-

cial control themselves have been influential in transforming a reform movement into a revolutionary movement. . . .

INTERRELATIONS AMONG DIFFERENT PROCESSES OF CHANGE: THE EXAMPLE OF MODERNIZATION

If I were writing a whole book rather than a single chapter on social change, I would now develop several chapters, each devoted to a type of social change. Representative types might be (1) social cycles, including, for instance, business cycles, cycles of fashions, and alterations of liberalism and conservatism in public policy; (2) the breakdown and reconstitution of the social order under the impact of crises, such as wars, natural disasters, and famines; (3) the creation of new value systems, which would include analyses of the growth of religions and of revolutionary movements and revolutionary regimes; and (4) the integration of smaller social units into large ones, which would include the study of customs unions and other international federations and organizations. I would review the literature to indicate what we know and do not know about each type of change. Toward the end of the book I would attempt to show how the various types are related to one another.

Because there is not space for such a comprehensive approach, I must rely on a substitute. I shall choose a single type of change— economic development or modernization— specify some of the processes that typically enter this type of change, and indicate some of the ways that these processes are related to one another.[1] I cannot be exhaustive, but I do hope to give an idea of the complexity of modernization, and to show the theoretical and empirical challenges that confront the analyst attempting to fathom whole societies in flux.

The riddles of the development of industrial society have perplexed sociologists since the very inception of the field. The great classical figures—Spencer, Marx, Weber, and Durkheim, for example[2]—were preoccupied in different ways with the causes and consequences of what we now call economic development. The ideas of these men still dominate much sociological thinking about change. In addition, interest in development has been heightened in recent decades by a profound world revolution that has forced itself on the attention of social scientists. This revolution is the dissolution of the Western countries' colonial empires, the emergence of the former colonies as new nations, and the attempts of these nations to introduce marked and rapid economic social changes in their societies. Since World War II, many sociologists, economists, anthropologists, and political scientists have applied their skills to an understanding of the changes shaking these developing areas of the world.

Because the idea of economic development has become such an everyday notion in our mid-twentieth-century outlook, we are likely to be tempted to think of it as a simple, unitary type of process. But economic development is neither simple nor unitary. When we employ the term, we usually have at least four distinct but interrelated processes implicitly in mind:

1. In the realm of technology, a developing society is changing *from* simple and traditionalized techniques *toward* the application of scientific knowledge.
2. In agriculture, the developing society evolves *from* subsistence farming *toward* the commercial production of agricultural goods. This means specialization in cash crops, purchase of nonagricultural products in the market, and often agricultural wage-labor.
3. In industry, the developing society undergoes a transition *from* the use of human and animal power *toward* industrialization proper, or men working for wages at power-driven machines, which produce commodities marketed outside the community of production.
4. In ecological arrangements, the developing society moves *from* the farm and village *toward* urban concentrations.

Furthermore, while these four processes often occur simultaneously during development, they need not necessarily do so. Agricul-

ture may become commercialized without any appreciable changes in the industrial sector, as was the case in the colonial countries in which the dominant powers strove to increase production of primary products. Industrialization may occur in villages, as was the case in early British industrialization and in some Southeast Asian societies. And cities may proliferate even where there is no significant industrialization, as had happened in some Asian and African societies. The conclusion to be drawn from these observations is that the causes, courses, and consequences of economic development must be expected to vary widely from nation to nation.

Economic development, moreover, is only one aspect of the complex of social change experienced by the emerging nations. The term "modernization"—a conceptual cousin of the term "economic development" but more comprehensive in scope—refers to the fact that technical, economic, and ecological changes ramify through the whole social and cultural fabric. In an emerging nation we may expect profound changes in these spheres: in the *political* sphere as simple tribal or village authority systems give way to systems of suffrage, political parties, representation, and civil-service bureaucracies; in the *educational* sphere as the society strives to reduce illiteracy and increase economically productive skills; in the *religious* sphere as secularized belief systems begin to replace traditionalistic religions; in the *familial* sphere as extended kinship units lose their pervasiveness; and in the *stratificational* sphere, as geographical and social mobility tend to loosen fixed, ascriptive hierarchical systems. Furthermore, these various changes begin at different times and proceed at different rates in a developing nation. A modernizing country, then, displays a multiplicity of institutional changes; and no matter how carefully social change is planned, some institutional changes will always lead the way, while others will always lag behind. Thus a developing society, if it could be depicted graphically, would resemble a large, awkward animal lumbering forward by moving each of its parts, sometimes in partial coordination and sometimes in opposition to one another.

I shall begin by describing some of the typical institutional changes and discontinuities that are part of the modernizing process, limiting my attention to three areas—work relations, family relations, and community relations. I shall necessarily deal with generalities, thus doing some injustice to national differences in the developmental process. Then I shall note some relations among the various institutional changes and discontinuities, and suggest some of the reasons for a high potential for social and political unrest in the developing nations. Finally, I shall explore the reasons why unrest is manifested sometimes in withdrawal behavior, sometimes in modest reform movements, and sometimes in violent revolutionary movements.

Changing Work Relations

In preindustrial societies, production is typically located in kinship units. Subsistence farming predominates; other industry, such as domestic manufacture, is supplementary to farming but still attached to kin and village. In some cases, occupational position is determined by an extended group, such as the caste. Exchange relations are also determined by traditional kinship and community obligations. In short, economic activities are relatively undifferentiated from the traditional family-community setting.

Economic development means, above all, the segregation of economic activities from this traditional setting. In agriculture, the introduction of money crops means that—unlike subsistence farming—the goods are consumed in households different from those in which they are produced. Agricultural wage labor, in which individuals rather than families are likely to be hired, often undermines the family production unit. In industry, handicraft production and cottage industry—like commercial farming—means that individual families do not produce for themselves but for other, unknown families somewhere in the market. And when manufac-

turing and factory systems arise, the worker is segregated not only from the control of his capital but also from other members of his family, since he is placed side by side with individual workers recruited in the labor market. In these ways, modernization separates economic activities from family and community activities.

As a result of these changes, the worker's relations to economic life are greatly altered. He now receives cash for services performed and spends this cash for goods and services in the market. More and more of his income and welfare comes to depend on the pay envelope, and less and less on the traditional rights and obligations expected from and owed to kinspeople and neighbors. This means that the worker in a modernizing market faces a number of problems of adjustment.

First, he finds that a new basis of calculation is foisted upon him. From the standpoint of allocating his productive time, he may no longer work at his own pace; he must adjust to the notion of a work day and a work week and, on the job, he must adjust to the rhythm of the machine rather than the rhythm of his own mind and body. From the standpoint of allocating his wealth, he must think in terms of budgeting a weekly bundle of cash; on the face of it, this would not appear to be much of an adjustment, but when we contrast the requisite level of calculation required with the day-by-day flow of economic activities in the traditional setting—in which cash payments scarcely figure—it is possible to appreciate the significant changes in outlook required of the new urban industrial worker.

Second, he finds the definition of his economic security greatly changed. In a traditional system of agriculture or domestic manufacture, a worker is likely to be underemployed rather than unemployed as a result of market fluctuations. In this case he works somewhat less, and turns to kinsmen, tribesmen, and neighbors for help. In the urban industrial setting, however, the worker is likely to be laid off and totally unemployed when economic activity is slack. In the new setting, then, the worker is subject to sharper, more severe changes in welfare and security, even though his average income may be higher than it was in the traditional setting.

Third, with respect to consumption, the worker in the modernizing market is faced with continuously changing standards. The urban market provides a veritable flood of new items—sweets, beer, gadgets, bicycles, transistor radios, and the like. As the worker is simultaneously drifting away from traditional expenditures—such as the dowry—and being exposed to new forms of gratification, he is likely to experience confusions and disorientations. Obviously, opportunities abound for merchants to market shabby products and to swindle inexperienced and uncertain consumers.

A fourth need for adjustment is imposed on the traditional sector. Many urban industrial workers visit or migrate back to the countryside. When in the urban industrial setting they are probably ambivalent about its demands and opportunities; but they surely often paint a beautiful picture of city life to their kinsmen and former neighbors who have remained in the countryside. Insofar as this occurs, it is likely to prove unsettling to the traditional way of life—especially if conditions are not good in the countryside—and to augment social conflicts between urban and rural sectors, as well as between younger migrating generations and older generations who remain in the country.

I do not mean to exaggerate the differences and discontinuities between the traditional and modern sectors. Many halfway arrangements between the two sectors are worked out in the modernizing process. Migratory labor, for instance, is a kind of compromise between full membership in a wage-labor force and attachment to an old community life. Cottage industry introduces extended markets but retains the family-production fusion. The employment of families in factories—which is a more frequent phenomenon than is commonly appreciated—maintains a version of family production. The expenditure of wages on traditional items also manifests the half-entry into the full urban industrial structure. The social and psychological reasons for these halfway houses are many; but no matter what the reasons are, the adjustments

and discontinuities just discussed are lessened accordingly in the compromise arrangements.

Changing Family Relations

One consequence of the removal of economic activities from the family-community setting is that the family itself loses some of its previous functions and becomes a more specialized agency. As the family ceases to be an economic unit of production, one or more members leave the household to seek employment in the labor market. The family's activities become more concentrated on emotional gratification and socialization.

The social implications of these changes in family life are enormous. The most fundamental of these implications—imposed mainly by the demands for mobility of the family—is the individuation and isolation of the nuclear family. If the family has to move about through the labor market, it cannot afford to carry all of its relatives with it, or even to maintain close, diffuse ties with extended kin. Thus the ties with collateral kinsmen begin to erode; few generations live in the same household; newly married couples set up new households, and leave the elders behind. One of the social problems that arise as a consequence of these kinship changes concerns the place of the aged. No longer cushioned by a protective kinship unit, the aged are thrown onto the community or the state as "charges" in greater numbers than before. Because of the social isolation of the aged, new institutional arrangements, such as pensions and social security programs, become imperative.

I do not want to oversimplify the process of decline of the extended kinship unit. In many cases—Japan is a good example—it survives intact for quite a long period of industrialization; in other cases, some features of extended kinship (for example, reciprocal working) erode, but other features (for example, mutual visiting) survive. Even the most advanced industrial societies still show some viable extended kinship structures. Despite these qualifications, however, it must be remembered that advanced urban industrial market conditions and full-scale extended kinship systems are inimical to one another in many respects.

Simultaneously the relations between parents and children undergo a transformation. The father, who now has to leave the household for employment in a separate establishment, necessarily loses many of the economic training functions that he previously enjoyed over his children. Correspondingly, apprenticeship systems which require the continuous presence of father and son decline as specialized factory production arises. Often, it is claimed, this decline in economic authority spreads to a decline in *general* paternal authority, although these claims have proved difficult to substantiate empirically. The mother, often being the only adult in the presence of young children during most of the day, develops a more intensive emotional relationship with them. Her role in socialization thus becomes more crucial, since she has almost sole responsibility for shaping the early emotional life of the children.

No matter how concentrated the relations are between mother and children in the early years, this period is short-lived. An advancing urban industrial society demands more complex technical skills than the family is able to provide. Hence the family tends to surrender many of its training functions to formal educational systems. The nuclear family very early loses control of its children to primary school (or even nursery school); by adolescence the child has outside contacts not only with education but also with some parts of the labor market. Furthermore, children may have married by their late teens or early 20's, may have set up a new household of their own, and may have become even more independent of their parents.

One ramification of these changing relations between parents and children is the "gap of adolescence," when the youth has been freed from the intensive parental ties of his early years but has not yet become fully engaged in adult occupational, marital, and civic roles. He thereby experiences a few years of loose role involvements. Psychologically, this is a period of

uncertainty for the young person; and this uncertainty usually produces a number of symptoms of disturbance, such as random protest, compulsive search for love and security, faddism and experimentation, and lethargy and apathy. Many commentators have noted the historical fact that urban industrial societies invariably witness a growth of adolescent protest and delinquency. The explanation for this historical fact cannot be appreciated, however, until we grasp the simultaneous and interrelated changes that occur among the economic, educational, and familial structures in a modernizing society.

A further ramification of the revolution in kinship relations in the urban industrial setting concerns the formation of new families. In many traditional settings, marriage is closely regulated by elders; the tastes and sentiments of the couple to be married are relatively unimportant. The basis for marriage, then, lies not in love, but rather in more practical arrangements, such as the availability of a substantial dowry or the promise of marrying into a choice parcel of land. With the decay of extended kinship ties and the redefinition of parental authority, youth becomes emancipated with respect to choosing a spouse. This emancipation, however, simultaneously produces a "vacuum." If some variety of arranged marriage is not available as an institutional mechanism for forming new families, what criteria are available? Having posed the question in this way, we may better appreciate the social importance of "romantic love" as the dominant basis for marriage in urban industrial societies. The feeling of being in love provides an alternative criterion for choice in an uncertain situation in which other institutional arrangements are lacking.

In sum, modernization tends to foster the rise of a family unit that is formed on emotional attraction and built on a limited sexual-emotional basis. The family has been removed from other major social spheres except for the segmental, external ties of individual family members. The family, being thus isolated and specialized, impinges less on these other social spheres; nepotism as a basis for recruitment into other social roles tends to become at most corrupt and at least suspect, whereas in traditional society it was the legitimate basis for recruitment into roles. Finally, within the family the complex and multifunctional relations of family members to one another tend to be pared down to more exclusively emotional ties.

Changes in Community and Associational Life

In the simplified model of traditional society that we have been using, community and associational life are closely knit with the ascribed bases of social existence—kinship, clanship, tribal, and caste affiliations. Formal organizations such as trade unions, social clubs, voluntary associations, and special interest groups seldom develop. Most of social life and its problems are worked through in the multifunctional ascribed groupings themselves.

These traditional bases for community and associational life retain much vitality even as the urban and industrial complex begins to emerge. When industrialization occurs in villages, for example, or when villages are built around paternalistic industrial enterprises, many ties of community and kinship can be maintained under industrial conditions. Furthermore, some evidence shows that migrants to cities display what might be called the "brother-in-law" syndrome; they seek out relatives or tribesmen, reside with them while searching for employment and sometimes after finding it, and limit their social life primarily to them. The invariable development of racial, tribal, and ethnic "ghettos" in the growing cities of the world is probably the result of both outright residential discrimination and a search for community in cities.

The persistence of exclusively traditional ties in the urban industrial setting, however, appears not to be a sufficient basis for community and associational life. After a time, these traditional ties come to be supplemented by more specialized organizations, football clubs, and chapel or church societies. The names of these groups—which would suggest special purposes

for each—should not obscure the fact, however, that especially in the early days of their formation, they are frequently multifunctional organizations. The friendly societies of eighteenth-century England, for example, were simultaneously trade unions, insurance societies, and drinking clubs. Many of the loose formal organizations among African urban migrants are simultaneously tribal associations, trade unions, football clubs, and social centers. Furthermore, these organizations tend to be quite unstable in their early days. They may begin as a tribal association, turn next into a saving association, and then take an interest in nationalism. As time passes, however, the fluidity of these organizations diminishes, and more "functional" groupings, based on economic or political interest, begin to replace them.

Discontinuities in Modernization and the Genesis of Social Unrest

The various economic and social changes that I have described are disruptive to the social order for several reasons.

First, structural change is, above all, uneven during periods of modernization, as I stressed at the beginning. In colonial societies, for instance, the European powers frequently revolutionized the economic and political framework by exploiting economic resources and establishing colonial administrations, but at the same time encouraged or imposed a conservatism in traditional religious, class, and family systems. In a society undergoing postcolonial modernization, similar discontinuities appear. Within the economy itself, rapid industrialization bites unevenly into established social and economic structures. Social institutions also display a pattern of growth that produces leads, lags, and bottlenecks. For example, most of the colonial nations, upon attaining independence, more or less immediately established some form of universal suffrage, thus entering instantaneously into the modern era. This action promptly created a crisis in education, since a mass electorate rests upon the assumption of a literate electorate with a sense of citizenship and an ability to participate in the polity. Social change thus moves ahead by a complicated leapfrog process, creating recurrent crises of adjustment. The first paradox of development, then, is that a developing society must change in all ways at once, but cannot conceivably plan such a regular, coordinated pattern of growth. A certain amount of social unrest inevitably is created.

Second, the development of new kinds of social and economic activities creates conflicts with traditional ways of life. For example, when factories begin to mass-produce items that compete with the same items produced domestically, the market is flooded with cheap goods, depriving the domestic workers of their means of livelihood. In theory, this should drive domestic workers into more remunerative lines of wage labor. In practice, however, the process of converting domestic labor into wage labor is a very slow and painful one, sometimes taking several generations to complete. To take another example, the growth of a class of highly trained doctors poses a threat to traditional medicine men and magicians, as well as to many revered domestic cures. The second paradox of modernization then, is that when economic and social advances take place, many people in the society turn out to be at least ambivalent and possibly openly hostile toward these advances. This continuing conflict between modern and traditional ways is a further source of social unrest.

Third, efforts on the part of governments of the new nations to contain and handle social unrest often creates the conditions for even further unrest. Most of the effective efforts to integrate and to develop societies rest with the centralized governments. In view of the severe and pervasive problems of integration faced by these nations, it could scarcely be otherwise. But insofar as central authorities establish themselves as viable governments, they simultaneously become threats to local, caste, regional, and other traditional types of authority. These threats underlie the apparent tendencies toward Balkanization in some of the developing countries. The third paradox of development, then, is that even the effective exercise of authority creates unrest and conflict with competing authority systems.

The conclusion to be drawn is that developing nations face a danger if they conceive of economic development simply in terms of developing as fast as possible. To focus unduly on this criterion is likely to create social costs—expressed in terms of unmanageable levels of social unrest and political instability—that may in the end defeat the effort to develop, itself. If speed is the only criterion, the developing nation may destroy too rapidly various forms of integration and unleash explosive levels of unrest. Furthermore, if too much speed is fostered in any one institutional sphere—for example, the economic—the society is likely to create an unbalanced pattern of growth, which is also a source of social unrest. It seems to me that the key problem in successful development is not to focus on a single criterion of growth, but rather to balance and measure development according to several different economic and social criteria.

Different Manifestations of Social Unrest

Modernization, then, no matter how much a society may desire to achieve it, is a trying thing, and generally is accompanied by much social unrest. But this fact alone does not reveal very much about the specific forms that this unrest may take. Will it be expressed in individual form—crime, alcohol and drug addiction, suicide, and mental illness? Or will it be collective? And if collective, will it be religious or political? If political, will it be manifested in peaceful and modest movements for reform or in revolutionary threats to the legitimacy of the existing government?

The answers to these questions are bound to be complicated, since so many factors influence the channeling of social unrest. Foreign influence on social unrest plays a part. For example, the strategy and tactics of Communist youth movements in a Latin American country differ according to whether they are under the influence of the Soviet, Chinese, or Cuban model, or under the influence of no specific foreign party. The character of leadership of protest also plays a part. If a country is still essentially tribal and illiterate, leaders who can provide an articulate ideological base for organized protest are in short supply. (In this connection, notice that many of the leaders of African and Asian movements for independence from the colonial powers were not strictly "from the land," but were intellectuals educated in the universities of Oxford, London, and Paris, where they were exposed to the ideas and ideologies of the West.) Instead of attempting to catalogue all of the factors influencing protest in developing countries, however, I shall concentrate on the part played by the governing authorities themselves in determining the form of protest.

The agencies of social control, especially political leaders, are seldom neutral toward social unrest in their societies, since unrest is always potentially disruptive of the social order and is threatening to the political regime itself. Consequently, part of the legal and constitutional structure of a society is related to the management of unrest. The important point is that the very posture taken by the governing authorities will itself influence the direction of protest. Consider the following examples.

If the political authorities do not enjoy legitimacy, and if they do not have control over the police and the military, unrest will tend to take the forms of uncontrolled violence, successful defiance of governmental action, and periodic *coups d'etat*. These reactions occur mainly because the government itself is incapable of preventing them. This pattern of constitutionally unviable, politically ineffective authority, on the one hand, and simple, nonideological defiance of political authorities, on the other, is best illustrated in many of the Latin American republics in the nineteenth and early twentieth centuries.

Suppose, however, that political leaders have the constitutional and military means to prevent outright defiance of their authority. The way in which they use these means also influences the form of protest. If the society has institutionalized a variety of meaningful channels for expressing protest—for instance, democratic elec-

tions, the opportunity for petition and demonstration, a free press, and a court system to check political invasions of citizens' rights—protest will probably take the form of peaceful and lawful agitation designed to influence the policies of the governing authorities. (If, however, a group feels that it has been consistently excluded from the political decision-making process, it may adopt more militant means such as civil disobedience or outright subversive activity.) The combination of a constitutionally viable but flexible government, on the one hand, and peaceful protest and agitation for reform, on the other, is illustrated by some of the long-established Western democracies.

If a society lacks these channels to express protest, and if the political leaders are repressive toward its expression, social unrest is likely to take another form. Because of harassment by the authorities, it is frequently driven underground. In addition, being frustrated in action, it tends to develop elaborate fantasies and ideologies of social regeneration. Many of these fantasies and ideologies are hostile to the political system but, because of the strength and repressiveness of the regime, they remain latent. Such underground organizations often develop elaborate rituals and initiation ceremonies. The pattern of a strong and repressive government, on the one hand, and protest through withdrawal and fantasy, on the other, is illustrated by the cults and clubs that appear in societies under colonial rule or totalitarian dictatorship.

Finally, if a period of harsh repression is followed by a period of increasingly ineffective government, still another type of protest is manifested. The source of the ineffectiveness need not concern us here; it may, for example, result from the government's involvement in a losing war, or from the accession of a weak leader to power. During the first period, we would expect the pattern just discussed—protest through withdrawal and fantasy. As the authorities lose their power to repress, however, the hostile and potentially revolutionary fantasies emerge from underground and become the basis for outright attacks on the government. If this protest goes far, it develops into a full-scale

ideological revolutionary movement. If successful, this kind of revolution is different from the
simple *coup d'etat* mentioned above, which is
often little more than a changeover in governing personnel; an ideological revolution involves the overthrow of a government, but it
does so in the name of a fantasy of national and
perhaps even world regeneration. Consequently its motivation to reconstruct the social
order and rid itself of its enemies is very great.

Without building a full theory of modernization, I have attempted in this final section to
indicate some of the interrelations among different types of social change—change in various
quantitative indices such as per capita production and literacy rates; change in social structures such as the family and community; and
change in the level and kinds of social unrest.
In the present state of social-scientific knowledge, it is not possible to formalize these interrelations into a theory that will meet effectively
all of the requirements that I laid out earlier.
But perhaps I have indicated some directions
that the persons who eventually construct such
a theory might take.

Notes

1. Much of the material in this last section
was originally prepared as a lecture for broad-
cast in the Voice of America's Forum Series on
Modernization, recorded in the spring of 1965.
My lecture was entitled "The Modernization of
Social Relations." It subsequently appeared in a
volume entitled *Modernization: The Dynamics of
Growth,* edited by Myron Weiner (New York:
Basic Books, 1966), pp. 110–121.

2. Herbert Spencer, *The Principles of Sociology*
(London: Williams and Norgate, 1897), Vol.
III; Karl Marx, *Capital,* translated by Samuel
Moore and Edward Aveling and edited by
Friedrich Engels (London: George Allen and
Unwin, 1946); Max Weber, *The Theory of Social
and Economic Organization,* translated by A. M.
Henderson and Talcott Parsons (New York:
Oxford University Press, 1947); Max Weber,
The Protestant Ethic and the Spirit of Capitalism,
translated by Talcott Parsons (London: George
Allen and Unwin, 1935); and Émile Durkheim,
The Division of Labor in Society, translated by
George Simpson (Glencoe, Ill.: The Free Press,
1949).

25

Death by Dieselization: A Case Study in the Reaction to Technological Change

W. F. Cottrell

Editors' Introduction

We live in an age of head-spinning technological advancements, some of which are changing the way in which we live our daily lives. Over the past several decades numerous inventions have altered our culture and the ways in which people interact. Several examples come easily to mind: the automobile, the airplane, the television, the computer, and the atomic bomb. Each of these has had a deep impact throughout the society. Sometimes, however, to see the impact of a new development it is necessary not to view broad societal consequences, but rather to focus on some small segment of the society to see how it is influenced by technological change. In this reading, W. F. Cottrell looks at such an example, as the diesel locomotive is introduced into the town of Caliente in the late 1940s. Although you may think such subject matter is quite dated, the relevance of the plight of Caliente to today's world will become apparent as you read through this selection.

The development of the diesel locomotive, like most technological advances, is commonly considered progress. People's lives are improved by such developments. Travel is less time-consuming, shipping costs are reduced, employment is increased, and so on. In this reading Cottrell reveals the other side of progress—the unplanned negative consequences suffered by the residents of this small desert town. Cottrell raises the important question in social change, "Who benefits, and at whose expense?" Think about the dependent and independent variables Smelser set forth in the keynote reading. What is changing in Caliente? Are many changes taking place? Are they interrelated? Smelser laid out a set of four independent variables: the structural setting for change, the impetus for change, mobilization for change, and the operation of social controls. As you read, think about how these variables progressively limit the chances for Caliente's future.

The people of Caliente did not accept this change passively.

They expressed the unrest that results from modernization. How did they express their discontent? How did outsiders react to their protest? What role was the government called upon to play? Think of other examples of progress that are similar to Cottrell's discussion of dieselization and its consequences. Are the positive outcomes inevitably accompanied by social costs? Do those affected usually react the way the displaced railroaders did? (Today they would be called the "technologically unemployed.")

This article illustrates elements from both the functional and conflict theoretical orientations. The functional model views social change as gradual and adjustive, with the parts of a social system adjusting to forces impinging from the outside or to rather small changes in one of its own parts. The conflict model views social change as rapid and revolutionary, coming from internal tensions among groups with dissimilar goals and interests, such as owners of production and workers or the politically powerful and the powerless.

Cottrell shows how a change in the economic structure of the social system known as Caliente affected (destroyed?) the rest of the system. He shows how initial technological changes actually aided Caliente, but with the arrival of the diesel, the town was doomed. He points out that dieselization would have occurred much more slowly and gradually, had it not been for World War II. He talks the language of functionalism when he notes that the people of Caliente demanded a shift of the regulating function of one institution (the economic) to another (the political), calling for government intervention in the "normal processes of supply and demand to protect the basis of their community and daily lives."

At the same time Cottrell shows how the railroad, controlling the economic production of the town, pursued its own best interests, even though those interests were contrary to the interests of the people who had invested their lives in Caliente. He shows the wrenching disruptions of this new manifestation of the Industrial Revolution and talks the language of "conflict" when he asks who benefits at whose expense. Who benefited most? Who benefited least? Who paid most? Who paid least?

"Death by Dieselization" is another example of the use of historical records for sociological analysis. Cottrell used information on the technological changes in the railroad industry to trace the dramatic shifts in the life of Caliente. Although this form of analysis has been used since the early days of sociology, it is becoming increasingly important as sociologists try to understand the organization of the modern world. One criticism of the methods used in the study should be made. Cottrell never tells exactly *where* he got his data. This leaves open the questions of validity and reliability. Did he go to Caliente and talk to people? He mentions using a newspaper at one point in the study, but did he use newspapers extensively? Did he get information from the railroad company? From former and current employees? These kinds of questions should be asked of any study and should have been answered by Cottrell.

One final point about this reading. As you finish it, you will notice that Cottrell takes a not-so-subtle political stand on the actions that should have been taken in this case. This introduces the question of the value-free nature of any scientific discipline, a point raised by Jerry Rose in Part One. Should science remain neutral? If scientists create knowledge, should they also pass judgment on that knowledge by spelling out not only the implications of their findings but also recommendations for social policy? While these are questions that will not be answered here, they have been central concerns in sociology, as well as in many other sciences.

In the following instance it is proposed that we examine a community confronted with radical change in its basic economic institution and to trace the effects of this change throughout the social structure. From these facts it may be possible in some degree to anticipate the resultant changing attitudes and values of the people in the community, particularly as they reveal whether or not there is a demand for modification of the social structure or a shift in function from one institution to another. Some of the implications of the facts discovered may be valuable in anticipating future social change.

The community chosen for examination has been disrupted by the dieselization of the railroads. Since the railroad is among the oldest of those industries organized around steam, and since therefore the social structure of railroad communities is a product of long-continued processes of adaptation to the technology of steam, the sharp contrast between the technological requirements of the steam engine and those of the diesel should clearly reveal the changes in social structure required. Any one of a great many railroad towns might have been chosen for examination. However, many railroad towns are only partly dependent upon the railroad for their existence. In them many of the effects which take place are blurred and not easily distinguishable by the observer. Thus, the "normal" railroad town may not be the best place to see the consequences of dieselization. For this reason a one-industry town was chosen for examination.

In a sense it is an "ideal type" railroad town, and hence not complicated by other extraneous economic factors. It lies in the desert and is here given the name "Caliente" which is the Spanish adjective for "hot." Caliente was built in a break in an eighty-mile canyon traversing the desert. Its reason for existence was to service the steam locomotive. There are few resources in the area to support it on any other basis, and such as they are they would contribute more to the growth and maintenance of other little settlements in the vicinity than to that of Caliente. So long as the steam locomotive was in use, Caliente was a necessity. With the adoption of the diesel it became obsolescent.

This stark fact was not, however, part of the expectations of the residents of Caliente. Based upon the "certainty" of the railroad's need for Caliente, men built their homes there, frequently of concrete and brick, at the cost, in many cases, of their life savings. The water system was laid in cast iron which will last for

Reprinted from *American Sociological Review*, 1951, Vol. 16, No. 3 (June): 358–365, by permission of the American Sociological Association.

centuries. Business men erected substantial buildings which could be paid for only by profits gained through many years of business. Four churches evidence the faith of Caliente people in the future of their community. A twenty-seven bed hospital serves the town. Those who built it thought that their investment was as well warranted as the fact of birth, sickness, accident and death. They believed in education. Their school buildings represent the investment of savings guaranteed by bonds and future taxes. There is a combined park and play field which, together with a recently modernized theater, has been serving recreational needs. All these physical structures are material evidence of the expectations, morally and legally sanctioned and financially funded, of the people of Caliente. This is a normal and rational aspect of the culture of all "solid" and "sound" communities.

Similarly normal are the social organizations. These include Rotary, Chamber of Commerce, Masons, Odd Fellows, American Legion and the Veterans of Foreign Wars. There are the usual unions, churches, and myriad little clubs to which the women belong. In short, here is the average American community with normal social life, subscribing to normal American codes. Nothing its members had been taught would indicate that the whole pattern of this normal existence depended completely upon a few elements of technology which were themselves in flux. For them the continued use of the steam engine was as "natural" a phenomenon as any other element in their physical environment. Yet suddenly their life pattern was destroyed by the announcement that the railroad was moving its division point, and with it destroying the economic basis of Caliente's existence.

Turning from this specific community for a moment, let us examine the technical changes which took place and the reasons for the change. Division points on a railroad are established by the frequency with which the rolling stock must be serviced and the operating crews changed. At the turn of the century when this particular road was built, the engines produced wet steam at low temperatures. The steel in the boilers was of comparatively low tensile strength

and could not withstand the high temperatures and pressures required for the efficient use of coal and water. At intervals of roughly a hundred miles the engine had to be disconnected from the train for service. At these points the cars also were inspected and if they were found to be defective they were either removed from the train or repaired while it was standing and the new engine being coupled on. Thus the location of Caliente, as far as the railroad was concerned, was a function of boiler temperature and pressure and the resultant service requirements of the locomotive.

Following World War II, the high tensile steels developed to create superior artillery and armor were used for locomotives. As a consequence it was possible to utilize steam at higher temperatures and pressure. Speed, power, and efficiency were increased and the distance between service intervals was increased.

The "ideal distance" between freight divisions became approximately 150 to 200 miles whereas it had formerly been 100 to 150. Wherever possible, freight divisions were increased in length to that formerly used by passenger trains, and passenger divisions were lengthened from two old freight divisions to three. Thus towns located at 100 miles from a terminal became obsolescent, those at 200 became freight points only, and those at three hundred miles became passenger division points.

The increase in speed permitted the train crews to make the greater distance in the time previously required for the lesser trip, and roughly a third of the train and engine crews, car inspectors, boilermakers and machinists and other service men were dropped. The towns thus abandoned were crossed off the social record of the nation in the adjustment to these technological changes in the use of the steam locomotive. Caliente, located midway between terminals about six hundred miles apart, survived. In fact it gained, since the less frequent stops caused an increase in the service required of the maintenance crews at those points where it took place. However, the introduction of the change to diesel engines projected a very different future.

In its demands for service the diesel engine

differs almost completely from a steam loco-motive. It requires infrequent, highly skilled service, carried on within very close limits, in contrast to the frequent, crude adjustments required by the steam locomotive. Diesels operate at about 35 percent efficiency, in contrast to the approximately 4 percent efficiency of the steam locomotives in use after World War II in the United States. Hence diesels require much less frequent stops for fuel and water. These facts reduce their operating costs sufficiently to compensate for their much higher initial cost.

In spite of these reductions in operating costs the introduction of diesels ordinarily would have taken a good deal of time. The change-over would have been slowed by the high capital costs of retooling the locomotive works, the long period required to recapture the costs of existing steam locomotives, and the effective resistance of the workers. World War II altered each of these factors. The locomotive works were required to make the change in order to provide marine engines, and the costs of the change were assumed by the government. Steam engines were used up by the tremendous demand placed upon the railroads by war traffic. The costs were recaptured by shipping charges. Labor shortages were such that labor resistance was less formidable and much less acceptable to the public than it would have been in peace time. Hence the shift to diesels was greatly facilitated by the war. In consequence, every third and sometimes every second division point suddenly became technologically obsolescent.

Caliente, like all other towns in similar plight, is supposed to accept its fate in the name of "progress." The general public, as shippers and consumers of shipped goods, reaps the harvest in better, faster service and eventually perhaps in lower charges. A few of the workers in Caliente will also share the gains, as they move to other division points, through higher wages. They will share in the higher pay, though whether this will be adequate to compensate for the costs of moving no one can say. Certain it is that their pay will not be adjusted to compensate for their specific losses. They will gain only as their seniority gives them the opportunity to

work. These are those who gain. What are the losses, and who bears them?

The railroad company can figure its losses at Caliente fairly accurately. It owns 39 private dwellings, a modern clubhouse with 116 single rooms, and a twelve-room hotel with dining-room and lunch-counter facilities. These now become useless, as does much of the fixed physical equipment used for servicing trains. Some of the machinery can be used elsewhere. Some part of the roundhouse can be used to store unused locomotives and standby equipment. The rest will be torn down to save taxes. All of these costs can be entered as capital losses on the statement which the company draws up for its stockholders and for the government. Presumably they will be recovered by the use of the more efficient engines.

What are the losses that may not be entered on the company books? The total tax assessment in Caliente was $9,946.80 for the year 1948, of which $6,103.39 represented taxes assessed on the railroad. Thus the railroad valuation was about three-fifths that of the town. This does not take into account tax-free property belonging to the churches, the schools, the hospital, or the municipality itself which included all the public utilities. Some idea of the losses sustained by the railroad in comparison with the losses of others can be surmised by reflecting on these figures for real estate alone. The story is an old one and often repeated in the economic history of America. It represents the "loss" side of a profit and loss system of adjusting to technological change. Perhaps for sociological purposes we need an answer to the question "just who pays?"

Probably the greatest losses are suffered by the older "non-operating" employees. Seniority among these men extends only within the local shop and craft. A man with twenty-five years' seniority at Caliente has no claim on the job of a similar craftsman at another point who has only twenty-five days' seniority. Moreover, some of the skills formerly valuable are no longer needed. The boilermaker, for example, knows that jobs for his kind are disappearing and he must enter the ranks of the unskilled. The protection and status offered by the union while he was employed have become meaningless now that he is no longer needed. The cost of this is high both in loss of income and in personal demoralization.

Operating employees also pay. Their seniority extends over a division, which in this case includes three division points. The older members can move from Caliente and claim another job at another point, but in many cases they move leaving a good portion of their life savings behind. The younger men must abandon their stake in railroad employment. The loss may mean a new apprenticeship in another occupation, at a time in life when apprenticeship wages are not adequate to meet the obligations of mature men with families. A steam engine hauled 2,000 tons up the hill out of Caliente with the aid of two helpers. The four-unit diesel in command of one crew handles a train of 5,000 tons alone. Thus, to handle the same amount of tonnage required only about a fourth the manpower it formerly took. Three out of four men must start out anew at something else.

The local merchants pay. The boarded windows, half-empty shelves, and abandoned store buildings bear mute evidence of these costs. The older merchants stay, and pay; the younger ones, and those with no stake in the community will move; but the value of their property will in both cases largely be gone.

The bondholders will pay. They can't foreclose on a dead town. If the town were wiped out altogether, that which would remain for salvage would be too little to satisfy their claims. Should the town continue there is little hope that taxes adequate to carry the overhead of bonds and day-to-day expenses could be secured by taxing the diminished number of property owners or employed persons.

The church will pay. The smaller congregations cannot support services as in the past. As the church men leave, the buildings will be abandoned.

Homeowners will pay. A hundred and thirty-five men owned homes in Caliente. They must accept the available means of support or rent

to those who do. In either case the income available will be far less than that on which the houses were built. The least desirable homes will stand unoccupied, their value completely lost. The others must be revalued at a figure far below that at which they were formerly held.

In a word, those pay who are, by traditional American standards, *most moral.* Those who have raised children see friendships broken and neighborhoods disintegrated. The childless more freely shake the dust of Caliente from their feet. Those who built their personalities into the structure of the community watch their work destroyed. Those too wise or too selfish to have entangled themselves in community affairs suffer no such qualms. The chain store can pull down its sign, move its equipment and charge the costs off against more profitable and better located units, and against taxes. The local owner has no such alternatives. In short, "good citizens" who assumed family and community responsibility are the greatest losers. Nomads suffer least.

The people of Caliente are asked to accept as "normal" this strange inversion of their expectations. It is assumed that they will, without protest or change in sentiment, accept the dictum of the "law of supply and demand." Certainly they must comply in part with this dictum. While their behavior in part reflects this compliance, there are also other changes perhaps equally important in their attitudes and values.

The first reaction took the form of an effort at community self-preservation. Caliente became visible to its inhabitants as a real entity, as meaningful as the individual personalities which they had hitherto been taught to see as atomistic or nomadic elements. Community survival was seen as prerequisite to many of the individual values that had been given precedence in the past. The organized community made a search for new industry, citing elements of community organization themselves as reasons why industry should move to Caliente. But the conditions that led the railroad to abandon the point made the place even less attractive to new industry than it had hitherto been. Yet the effort to keep the community a going concern persisted.

There was also a change in sentiment. In the past the glib assertion that progress spelled sacrifice could be offered when some distant group was a victim of technological change. There was no such reaction when the event struck home. The change can probably be as well revealed as in any other way by quoting from the Caliente *Herald:*

. . . (over the) years . . . (this) . . . railroad and its affiliates . . . became to this writer his ideal of a railroad empire. The (company) . . . appeared to take much more than the ordinary interest of big railroads in the development of areas adjacent to its lines, all the while doing a great deal for the communities large and small through which the lines passed.

Those were the days creative of (its) enviable reputation as one of the finest, most progressive—and most human—of American railroads, enjoying the confidence and respect of employees, investors, and communities alike!

One of the factors bringing about this confidence and respect was the consideration shown communities which otherwise would have suffered serious blows when division and other changes were effected. A notable example was . . . (a town) . . . where the shock of division change was made almost unnoticed by installation of a rolling stock reclamation point, which gave (that town) an opportunity to hold its community intact until tourist traffic and other industries could get better established—with the result that . . . (it) . . . is now on a firm foundation. And through this display of consideration for a community, the railroad gained friends—not only among the people of . . . (that town) . . . who were perhaps more vocal than others, but also among thousands of others throughout the country on whom this action made an indelible impression.

But things seem to have changed materially during the last few years, the . . . (company) . . . seems to this writer to have gone all out for glamor and the dollars which glamorous

people have to spend, sadly neglecting one of the principal factors which helped to make . . . (it) . . . great: that fine consideration of communities and individuals, as well as employees, who have been happy in cooperating steadfastly with the railroad in times of stress as well as prosperity. The loyalty of these people and communities seems to count for little with the . . . (company) . . . of this day, though other "Big Business" corporations do not hesitate to expend huge sums to encourage the loyalty of community and people which old friends of . . . (the company) . . . have been happy to give voluntarily.

Ever since the . . . railroad was constructed . . . Caliente has been a key town on the railroad. It is true, the town owed its inception to the railroad, but it has paid this back in becoming one of the most attractive communities on the system. With nice homes, streets and parks, good school . . . good city government . . . Caliente offers advantages that most big corporations would be gratified to have for their employees—a homey spot where they could live their lives of contentment, happiness and security.

Caliente's strategic location, midway of some of the toughest road on the entire system has been a lifesaver for the road several times when floods have wrecked havoc on the roadbed in the canyon above and below Caliente. This has been possible through storage in Caliente of large stocks of repair material and equipment—and not overlooking manpower—which has thus become available on short notice.

. . . But (the railroad) or at least one of its big officials appearing to be almost completely divorced from policies which made this railroad great, has ordered changes which are about as inconsiderate as anything of which "Big Business" has ever been accused! Employees who have given the best years of their lives to this railroad are cut off without anything to which they can turn, many of them with homes in which they have taken much pride; while others, similarly with nice homes, are told to move elsewhere and are given runs that only a few will be able to endure from a physical standpoint, according to common opinion.

Smart big corporations the country over encourage their employees to own their own homes—and loud are their boasts when the percentage of such employees is favorable! But in contrast, a high (company) official is reported to have said only recently that "a railroad man has no business owning a home!" Quite a departure from what has appeared to be (company) tradition.

It is difficult for the Herald to believe that this official however "big" he is, speaks for the . . . (company) . . . when he enunciates a policy that, carried to the [letter], would make tramps of (company) employees and their families!

No thinking person wants to stand in the way of progress, but true progress is not made when it is overshadowed by cold-blooded disregard for the loyalty of employees, their families, and the communities which have developed in the good American way through the decades of loyal service and good citizenship.

This editorial, written by a member of all the service clubs, approved by Caliente business men, and quoted with approbation by the most conservative members of the community, is significant of changing sentiment.

The people of Caliente continually profess their belief in "The American Way," but like the editor of the Herald they criticize decisions made solely in pursuit of profit, even though these decisions grow out of a clear-cut case of technological "progress." They feel that the company should have based its decision upon consideration for loyalty, citizenship, and community morale. They assume that the company should regard the seniority rights of workers as important considerations, and that it should consider significant the effect of permanent unemployment upon old and faithful employees. They look upon community integrity as an important community asset. Caught between the support of a "rational" system of "economic" forces and laws, and sentiments

which they accept as significant values, they seek a solution to their dilemma which will at once permit them to retain their expected rewards for continued adherence to past norms and to defend the social system which they have been taught to revere but which now offers them a stone instead of bread.

IMPLICATIONS

We have shown that those in Caliente whose behavior most nearly approached the ideal taught are hardest hit by change. On the other hand, those seemingly farthest removed in conduct from that ideal are either rewarded or pay less of the costs of change than do those who follow the ideal more closely. Absentee owners, completely anonymous, and consumers who are not expected to cooperate to make the gains possible are rewarded most highly, while the local people who must cooperate to raise productivity pay dearly for having contributed.

In a society run through sacred mysteries whose rationale it is not man's privilege to criticize, such incongruities may be explained away. Such a society may even provide some "explanation" which makes them seem rational. In a secular society, supposedly defended rationally upon scientific facts, in which the pragmatic test "Does it work?" is continually applied, such discrepancy between expectation and realization is difficult to reconcile.

Defense of our traditional system of assessing the costs of technological change is made on the theory that the costs of such change are more than offset by the benefits to "society as a whole." However, it is difficult to show the people of Caliente just why *they* should pay for advances made to benefit others whom they have never known and who, in their judgment, have done nothing to justify such rewards. Any action that will permit the people of Caliente to levy the costs of change upon those who will benefit from them will be morally justifiable to the people of Caliente. Appeals to the general welfare leave them cold and the compulsions of the price system are not felt to be self-justifying "natural laws" but are regarded as being the specific consequence of specific bookkeeping decisions as to what should be included in the costs of change. They seek to change these decisions through social action. They do not consider that the "American Way" consists primarily of acceptance of the market as the final arbiter of their destiny. Rather they conceive that the system as a whole exists to render "justice," and if the consequences of the price system are such as to produce what they consider to be "injustice" they proceed to use some other institution as a means to reverse or offset the effects of the price system. Like other groups faced with the same situation, those in Caliente seize upon the means available to them. The operating employees had in their unions a device to secure what they consider to be their rights. Union practices developed over the years make it possible for the organized workers to avoid some of the costs of change which they would otherwise have had to bear. Feather-bed rules, make-work practices, restricted work weeks, train length legislation and other similar devices were designed to permit union members to continue work even when "efficiency" dictated that they be disemployed. Members of the "Big Four" in Caliente joined with their fellows in demanding not only the retention of previously existing rules, but the imposition of new ones such as that requiring the presence of a third man in the diesel cab. For other groups there was available only the appeal to the company that it establish some other facility at Caliente, or alternatively a demand that "government" do something. One such demand took the form of a request to the Interstate Commerce Commission that it require inspection of rolling stock at Caliente. This request was denied.

It rapidly became apparent to the people of Caliente that they could not gain their objectives by organized community action nor individual endeavor but there was hope that by adding their voices to those of others similarly injured there might be hope of solution. They began to look to the activities of the whole labor movement for succor. Union strategy which forced the transfer of control from the market to government mediation or to legislation and oper-

ation was widely approved on all sides. This was not confined to those only who were currently seeking rule changes but was equally approved by the great bulk of those in the community who had been hit by the change. Cries of public outrage at their demands for make-work rules were looked upon as coming from those at best ignorant, ill-informed or stupid, and at worst as being the hypocritical efforts of others to gain at the workers' expense. When the union threat of a national strike for rule changes was met by government seizure, Caliente workers like most of their compatriots across the country welcomed this shift in control, secure in their belief that if "justice" were done they could only be gainers by government intervention. These attitudes are not "class" phenomena purely nor are they merely occupational sentiments. They result from the fact that modern life, with the interdependence that it creates, particularly in one-industry communities, imposes penalties far beyond the membership of the groups presumably involved in industry. When make-work rules contributed to the livelihood of the community, the support of the churches, and the taxes which maintain the schools; when feather-bed practices determine the standard of living, the profits of the business man and the circulation of the press; when they contribute to the salary of the teacher and the preacher; they can no longer be treated as accidental, immoral, deviant or temporary. Rather they are elevated into the position of emergent morality and law. Such practices generate a morality which serves them just as the practices in turn nourish those who participate in and preserve them. They are as firmly a part of what one "has a right to expect" from industry as are parity payments to the farmer, bonuses and pensions to the veterans, assistance to the aged, tariffs to the industrialist, or the sanctity of property to those who inherit. On the other hand, all these practices conceivably help create a structure that is particularly vulnerable to changes such as that described here.

Practices which force the company to spend in Caliente part of what has been saved through technological change, or failing that, to reward those who are forced to move by increased income for the same service, are not, by the people of Caliente, considered to be unjustifiable. Confronted by a choice between the old means and resultant "injustice" which their use entails, and the acceptance of new means which they believe will secure them the "justice" they hold to be their right, they are willing to abandon (in so far as this particular area is concerned) the liberal state and the omnicompetent market in favor of something that works to provide "justice."

The study of the politics of pressure groups will show how widely the reactions of Caliente people are paralled by those of other groups. Amongst them it is in politics that the decisions as to who will pay and who will profit are made. Through organized political force railroaders maintain the continuance of rules which operate to their benefit rather than for "the public good" or "the general welfare." Their defense of these practices is found in the argument that only so can their rights be protected against the power of other groups who hope to gain at their expense by functioning through the corporation and the market.

We should expect that where there are other groups similarly affected by technological change, there will be similar efforts to change the operation of our institutions. The case cited is not unique. Not only is it duplicated in hundreds of railroad division points but also in other towns abandoned by management for similar reasons. Changes in the location of markets or in the method of calculating transportation costs, changes in technology making necessary the use of new materials, changes due to the exhaustion of old sources of materials, changes to avoid labor costs such as the shift of the textile industry from New England to the South, changes to expedite decentralization to avoid the consequences of bombing, or those of congested living, all give rise to the question, "Who benefits, and at whose expense?"

The accounting practices of the corporation permit the entry only of those costs which have become "legitimate" claims upon the company. But the tremendous risks borne by the workers and frequently all the members of the community in an era of technological change are real phenomena. Rapid shifts in technology which destroy the "legitimate" expectations derived from past experience force the recognition of new obligations. Such recognition may be made voluntarily as management foresees the necessity, or it may be thrust upon it by political or other action. Rigidity of property concepts, the legal structure controlling directors in what they may admit to be costs, and the stereotyped nature of the "economics" used by management make rapid change within the corporation itself difficult even in a "free democratic society." Hence while management is likely to be permitted or required to initiate technological change in the interest of profits, it may and probably will be barred from compensating for the social consequences certain to arise from those changes. Management thus shuts out the rising flood of demands in its cost-accounting only to have them reappear in its tax accounts, in legal regulations or in new insistent union demands. If economics fails to provide an answer to social demands then politics will be tried.

It is clear that while traditional morality provides a means of protecting some groups from the consequences of technological change, or some method of meliorating the effects of change upon them, other large segments of the population are left unprotected. It should be equally clear that rather than a quiet acquiescence in the finality and justice of such arrangements, there is an active effort to force new devices into being which will extend protection to those hitherto expected to bear the brunt of these costs. A good proportion of these inventions increasingly call for the intervention of the state. To call such arrangements immoral, unpatriotic, socialistic or to hurl other epithets at them is not to deal effectively with them. They are as "natural" as are the "normal" reactions for which we have "rational" explanations based upon some pre-scientific generalization about human nature such as "the law of supply and demand" or "the inevitability of progress." To be dealt with effectively they will have to be understood and treated as such.

26
On the Origins of Social Movements

Jo Freeman

Editors' Introduction

In the keynote selection, Neil Smelser points out that discontinuities created by modernization can lead to social unrest. He then goes on to discuss the different forms this unrest may take: uncontrolled violence, peaceful and lawful agitation, or protests of other kinds. Although his lists of dependent and independent variables aid understanding, Smelser does not go "behind the scenes" to show *how* such unrest occurs. It is as if discontinuities lead to spontaneous generation of social unrest; that is, when structural conditions are right, unrest occurs. In this reading, Jo Freeman goes beyond Smelser, and takes us behind the scenes of four social movements to show how they got started.

A social movement is a group of people who have banded together with some degree of organization in order to initiate (or stop) social change. Reacting to some source of strain or dissatisfaction, these people often use spontaneous and nonroutine activities in their unrest, rather than relying on the regularized channels of political processes (party participation, petitions, and voting). What conditions breed such social movements and how are the movements mobilized?

Jo Freeman identifies a number of conditions necessary for the formation of any social movement, derived from her study of the origins of several different movements. Take special note of the three propositions Freeman presents at the end of the first section of the reading. (Propositions are statements of *expected* relationships between two or more variables; for example, as amount of education increases, income is likely to increase.) How do these propositions conform to Smelser's set of independent variables (structural setting, impetus for change, mobilization for change, and operation of social control)? Freeman then uses the events leading into the civil rights movement, the student protest movement, the welfare rights movement, and the contemporary women's movement to illustrate these principles. Since the civil rights movement and the women's movement each had two sources, they provide additional illustrations of Freeman's propositions. Do Smelser's variables seem to apply to the movements Freeman describes?

Why were there two origins for the civil rights movement? How did organizations stemming from these origins "fit" with those founded considerably earlier (the Urban League, NAACP, and CORE)? As you read the section dealing with the civil rights movement, think back to the Gary Marx reading on the relationship between religion and politics (in Part Four). Do Marx's arguments about the role of religion in civil rights militancy agree with Freeman's description of the civil rights movement? How was the civil rights movement related to the New Left student movement? To the contemporary women's movement? How did the welfare rights movement *differ* from the civil rights and student movements? In her discussion of the contemporary women's movement, Freeman calls one of the sources the "older" branch and the other the "younger" branch. In what ways do these branches differ? Why do they differ in these ways? How are they related? For each of the four movements that Freeman discusses, identify the source of the preexisting communication network, the reason why it could be co-opted, and the crises or organizing efforts that resulted in a full-blown social movement.

Although Freeman gives a detailed account of the contemporary women's movement, she does not tell of earlier efforts to win equal rights for women. This is an old battle that, according to the readings on gender stratification in Part Three, is not over yet. Here is a bit of history on the early women's movement; look for parallels between it and the contemporary movement. In the period just prior to the Civil War a number of men and women worked together to call to public attention the plight of the slaves. In this endeavor women gained some experience in organizing groups and speaking in public. Some of these women became more and more convinced that the position of women in society bore some resemblance to the position of slaves; they started to write and speak about this issue too. In 1840 a number of delegates, both men and women, went to the World Anti-Slavery Conference in London. However, the women delegates were denied access to their seats as delegates and were relegated to the balcony to listen without participating. Elizabeth Cady Stanton and Lucretia Mott, two of the women suffering this humiliation, later organized the first Women's Rights Convention, meeting in Seneca Falls, New York, in 1848. This was the start of the early women's movement that culminated in 1920 in gaining the right for women to vote. How do the events of this earlier movement fit with the propositions that Freeman gives for the origins of social movements?

Freeman draws on historical data for her analyses of the civil rights movement, the student movement, and the welfare rights movement. In gaining her firsthand information about the contemporary women's movement, Freeman used a variety of research methods and sources. She was a participant-observer in the younger branch in Chicago for three years in the late sixties and also was a member of NOW (National Organization for Women). She did extensive interviewing, both formal and informal, and attended various conventions. She read large numbers of documents, publications, dissertations, and other historical materials. One of the strengths of her study of the women's movement comes from this combination of research methods and data sources. This is the same type of multiple data collection technique that you saw earlier in Janet Lever's reading on the complexity of children's play and games. Why is this combination of techniques a strength in this, or any other, study?

Most movements have inconspicuous beginnings. The significant elements of their origins are usually forgotten or distorted by the time a trained observer seeks to trace them out. Perhaps this is why the theoretical literature on social movements usually concentrates on causes (Gurr 1970, Davis 1962, Oberschall 1973) and motivations (Toch 1965, Cantril 1941, Hoffer 1951, Adorno et al. 1950), while the "spark of life" by which the "mass is to cross the threshold of organizational life" (Lowi 1971, p. 41) has received scant attention.

From the implicit assumptions in the literature one would postulate either a "spontaneous generation" theory or an "outside agitator" theory of movement formation. The first asserts that if grievances exist and the social structure is conducive to movement activity, a movement will automatically occur. Conversely, if movement activity does not occur, it is because the political system provides adequate channels to pursue solutions or because grievances are insufficient. The second theory assumes that there are always grievances; outsiders translate

them into action. Remove the outsiders, or their outside funding sources, and movements will cease (Kornhauser 1959, McCarthy and Zald 1973).

All these assumptions contain grains of truth, but they must be separated out, subject to microsociological analysis, and reformulated into testable propositions. This in turn requires that we identify the phenomena to be analyzed.

Recognizing with Heberle (1951, p. 8) that "movements as such are not organized groups," it is still the structured aspects that are more amenable to study, if not always the most salient. Turner and Killian (1957, p. 307) have argued that it is when "members of a public who share a common position concerning the issue at hand supplement their informal person-to-person discussion with some organization to promote their convictions more effectively and insure more sustained activity, a social movement is incipient" (see also Killian 1964, p. 426). Such organization(s) and other core groups of a movement not only determine much of its conscious policy but serve as foci for its values and activities. Just as it has been argued that society as a whole has a cultural and structural "center" about which most members of the society are more or less "peripheral" (Shils 1970), so, too, can a social movement be conceived of as having a center and a periphery. An investigation into

Reprinted from *Social Movements of the Sixties and Seventies,* edited by Jo Freeman (New York: Longman, 1983). Copyright 1983 by Jo Freeman. Used with permission of the author. Footnotes have been renumbered.

a movement's origins must be concerned with the microstructural preconditions for the emergence of such a movement center. From where do the people come who make up the initial, organizing cadre of a movement? How do they come together, and how do they come to share a similar view of the world in circumstances that compel them to political action? In what ways does the nature of the original center affect the future development of the movement?

Before answering these questions, let us first look at data on the origins of four social movements prominent in the sixties and seventies: civil rights, student protest, welfare rights, and women's liberation. These data identify recurrent elements involved in movement formation. The ways in which these elements interact, given a sufficient level of strain, would support the following propositions:

Proposition 1: The need for a *preexisting communications network* or infrastructure within the social base of a movement is a primary prerequisite for "spontaneous" activity. Masses alone do not form movements, however discontented they may be. Groups of previously unorganized individuals may spontaneously form into small local associations—usually along the lines of informal social networks—in response to a specific strain or crisis. If they are not linked in some manner, however, the protest does not become generalized but remains a local irritant or dissolves completely. If a movement is to spread rapidly, the communications network must already exist. If only the rudiments of a network exist, movement formation requires a high input of "organizing" activity.

Proposition 2: Not just any communications network will do. It must be a network that is *co-optable* to the new ideas of the incipient movement.[1] To be co-optable, it must be composed of like-minded people whose backgrounds, experiences, or location in the social structure make them receptive to the ideas of a specific new movement.

Proposition 3: Given the existence of a co-optable communications network, or at least the rudimentary development of a potential one, and a situation of strain, one or more precipi-

tants are required. Here, two distinct patterns emerge that often overlap. In one, a *crisis* galvanizes the network into spontaneous action in a new direction. In the other, one or more persons begin *organizing* a new organization or disseminating a new idea. For spontaneous action to occur, the communications network must be well formed or the initial protest will not survive the incipient stage. If it is not well formed, organizing efforts must occur; that is, one or more persons must specifically attempt to construct a movement. To be successful, organizers must be skilled and must have a fertile field in which to work. If no communications network already exists, there must at least be emerging spontaneous groups that are acutely attuned to the issue, albeit uncoordinated. To sum up, if a co-optable communications network is already established, a crisis is all that is necessary to galvanize it. If it is rudimentary, an organizing cadre of one or more persons is necessary. Such a cadre is superfluous if the former conditions fully exist, but it is essential if they do not.

THE CIVIL RIGHTS MOVEMENT

The civil rights movement has two origins, although one contributed significantly to the other. The first can be dated from December 7, 1955, when the arrest of Rosa Parks for occupying a "white" seat on a bus stimulated both the Montgomery Bus Boycott and the formation of the Montgomery Improvement Association. The second can be dated either from February 1, 1960, when four freshmen at A & T College in Greensboro, North Carolina, sat-in at a white lunch counter, or from April 15–17, when a conference at Shaw University in Raleigh, North Carolina, resulted in the formation of the Student Non-Violent Co-ordinating Committee. To understand why there were two origins one has to understand the social structure of the southern black community, as an incipient generation gap alone is inadequate to explain it.

Within this community the two most important institutions, often the only institutions, were the church and the black college. They provided the primary networks through which most southern blacks interacted and communicated with one another on a regular basis. In turn, the colleges and churches were linked in a regional communications network. These institutions were also the source of black leadership, for being a "preacher or a teacher" were the main status positions in black society. Of the two, the church was by far the more important; it touched on more people's lives and was the largest and oldest institution in the black community. Even during slavery there had been an "invisible church." After emancipation, "organized religious life became the chief means by which a structured or organized social life came into existence among the Negro masses" (Frazier 1963, p. 17). Furthermore, preachers were more economically independent of white society than were teachers.

Neither of these institutions represented all the segments of black society, but the segments they did represent eventually formed the main social base for supplying civil rights activists. The church was composed of a male leadership and a largely middle-aged, lower-class female followership. The black colleges were the homes of black intellectuals and middle-class youth, male and female.

Both origins of the civil rights movement resulted in the formation of new organizations, despite the fact that at least three seemingly potential social movement organizations already existed. The wealthiest of these was the Urban League, founded in 1910. It, however, was not only largely restricted to a small portion of the black and white bourgeoisie but, until 1961, felt itself to be "essentially a social service agency" (Clark 1966, p. 245).

Founded in 1909, the National Association for the Advancement of Colored People (NAACP) pursued channels of legal change until it finally persuaded the Supreme Court to abolish educational segregation in *Brown* v. *Board of Education*. More than any other single event, this decision created the atmosphere of rising expectations that helped precipitate the movement. The NAACP suffered from its own success, however. Having organized itself primarily to support court cases and utilize other "respectable" means, it "either was not able or

did not desire to modify its program in response to new demands. It believed it should continue its important work by using those techniques it had already perfected" (Blumer 1951, p. 199).

The Congress of Racial Equality, like the other two organizations, was founded in the North. It began "in 1942 as the Chicago Committee of Racial Equality, which was composed primarily of students at the University of Chicago. An off-shoot of the pacifist Fellowship of Reconciliation, its leaders were middle-class intellectual reformers, less prominent and more alienated from the mainstream of American society than the founders of the NAACP. They regarded the NAACP's legalism as too gradualist and ineffective, and aimed to apply Gandhian techniques of non-violent direct action to the problem of race relations in the United States. A year later, the Chicago Committee joined with a half dozen other groups that had emerged across the country, mostly under the encouragement of the F.O.R. to form a federation known as the Congress of Racial Equality" (Rudwick and Meier 1970, p. 10).

CORE's activities anticipated many of the main forms of protest of the civil rights movement, and its attitudes certainly seemed to fit CORE for the role of a major civil rights organization. But though it became quite influential, at the time the movement actually began, CORE had declined almost to the point of extinction. Its failure reflects the historical reality that organizations are less likely to create social movements than be created by them. More important, CORE was poorly situated to lead a movement of southern blacks. Northern-based and composed primarily of pacifist intellectuals, it had no roots in any of the existing structures of the black community, and in the North these structures were themselves weak. CORE could be a source of ideas, but not of coordination.

The coordination of a new movement required the creation of a new organization. But that was not apparent until after the Montgomery bus boycott began. That boycott was organized through institutions already existing in the black community of Montgomery.

Rosa Parks's refusal to give up her seat on

the bus to a white man was not the first time such defiance of segregation laws had occurred. There had been talk of a boycott the previous time, but after local black leaders had a congenial meeting with the city commissioners, nothing happened—on either side (King 1958, pp. 37–41). When Parks, a former secretary of the local NAACP, was arrested, she immediately called E. D. Nixon, at that time the president of the local chapter. He not only bailed her out but informed a few influential women in the city, most of whom were members of the Women's Political Council. After numerous phone calls between their members, it was the WPC that actually suggested the boycott, and E. D. Nixon who initially organized it (ibid., pp. 44–45).

The Montgomery Improvement Association (MIA) was formed at a meeting of eighteen ministers and civic leaders the Monday after Parks's conviction and a day of successful boycotting, to provide ongoing coordination. No one then suspected that coordination would be necessary for over a year, with car pools organized to provide alternative transportation for seventeen thousand riders a day. During this time the MIA grew slowly to a staff of ten in order to handle the voluminous correspondence, as well as to provide rides and keep the movement's momentum going. The organization, and the car pools, were financed by $250,000 in donations that poured in from all over the world in response to heavy press publicity about the boycott. But the organizational framework for the boycott and the MIA was the church. Most, although not all, of the officers were ministers, and Sunday meetings with congregations continued to be the main means of communicating with members of the black community and encouraging them to continue the protest.

The boycott did not end until the federal courts ruled Alabama's bus segregation laws unconstitutional late in 1956—at the same time that state courts ruled the boycott illegal. In the meantime, black leaders throughout the South had visited Montgomery, and out of the discussions came agreement to continue antisegregation protests regularly and systematically under the aegis of a new organization, the Southern Christian Leadership Conference. The NAACP could not lead the protests because, according to an SCLC pamphlet, "during the late 50s, the NAACP had been driven out of some Southern states. Its branches were outlawed as foreign corporations and its lawyers were charged with barratry, that is, persistently inciting litigation."

On January 10, 1957, over one hundred people gathered in Atlanta at a meeting called by four ministers, including Martin Luther King. Bayard Rustin drew up the "working papers." Initially called the Southern Leadership Conference on Transportation and Nonviolent Integration, the SCLC never developed a mass base even when it changed its name. It established numerous "affiliates" but did most of its work through the churches in the communities to which it sent its fieldworkers.

The church was not just the only institution available for a movement to work through; in many ways it was ideal. It performed "the central organizing function in the Negro community" (Holloway 1969, p. 22), providing both access to large masses of people on a regular basis and a natural leadership. As Wyatt Tee Walker, former executive director of SCLC, commented, "The Church today is central to the movement. If a Negro's going to have a meeting, where's he going to have it? Mostly he doesn't have a Masonic lodge, and he's not going to get the public schools. And the church is the primary means of communication" (Brink and Harris 1964, p. 103). Thus the church eventually came to be the center of the voter registration drives as well as many of the other activities of the civil rights movement.

Even the young men and women of SNCC had to use the church, though they had trouble doing so because, unlike most of the officers of SCLC, they were not themselves ministers and thus did not have a "fraternal" connection. Instead they tended to draw many of their resources and people from outside the particular town in which they were working by utilizing their natural organizational base, the college.

SNCC did not begin the sit-ins, but came out of them. Once begun, the idea of the sit-in spread initially by means of the mass media.

But such sit-ins almost always took place in towns where there were Negro colleges, and groups on these campuses essentially organized the sit-in activities of their communities. Nonetheless, "CORE, with its long emphasis of nonviolent direct action, played an important part, once the sit-ins began, as an educational and organizing agent" (Zinn 1964, p. 23). CORE had very few staff in the South, but there were enough to at least hold classes and practice sessions in nonviolence.

It was SCLC, however, that was actually responsible for the formation of SNCC; though it might well have organized itself eventually. Ella Baker, then executive secretary of SCLC, thought something should be done to coordinate the rapidly spreading sit-ins in 1960, and many members of SCLC thought it might be appropriate to organize a youth group. With SCLC money, Baker persuaded her alma mater, Shaw University, to provide facilities to contact the groups at centers of sit-in activity. Some two hundred people showed up for the meeting, decided to have no official connection with SCLC beyond a "friendly relationship," and formed the Student Non-Violent Co-ordinating Committee (Zinn 1964, pp. 32–34). It had no members, and its fieldworkers numbered two hundred at their highest point, but it was from the campuses, especially the southern black colleges, that it drew its sustenance and upon which its organizational base rested.

THE MOVEMENT

The term "the Movement" was originally applied to the civil rights movement by those participating in it, but as this activity expanded into a general radical critique of American society and concomitant action, the term broadened with it. To white youth throughout most of the sixties, "the Movement" referred to the plethora of youth and/or radical activities that started from the campus and eventually enveloped a large segment of middle-class youth.

The imprecise use of the term is illustrative of the imprecise definitions of the Movement. In some ways, it was several movements operating under the same rubric with a certain affinity, if not always agreement. In other ways, it was an ill-matched pairing of a social base in search of an ideology and an ideology in search of a social base. The Movement is also referred to as "the student movement" and "the New Left," reflecting the respective social base and ideology.

It has been argued that students have good reason to feel estranged from American society *in their role as students*; that they have specific complaints of inequities to them upon which they could build a powerful movement. But the demand for "student power" that should have represented this drive was a short-lived one and in fact was aborted by the very organization that was seeking to use students as its social base. Conversely, the New Left is essentially an intellectual movement whose analyses were not always welcomed or adopted by the students who marched under its banners. Consequently, the New Left became a home for all who called themselves radicals, without ever having to direct itself to the mobilization of a specific body of people to make gains for themselves. Instead, its more general framework of political analysis led students, and ex-students, to provide the troops for many other movements while often denying they had the right to make demands for themselves.

Because of its diverse nature, the "core groups" of the Movement are more plentiful and less significant than core groups of other movements discussed here. Although it did work through organizations, the Movement was much more spontaneous and undirected than any of the others. Many an investigating committee tried to pin a "conspiracy" theory on the rapidly spreading campus sit-ins, failing to realize that the mass media were really the culprits. Students so readily recognized the community of interests they shared with other students on other campuses that mere awareness that something was happening could be enough to prompt imitation.

Nonetheless, there were "core groups," and the most important of them, the Students for a Democratic Society, played a significant enough role to allow its origin to speak for much of the movement. And its formation illustrates another interesting twist on the pattern we have been observing so far.

In some ways a student movement didn't need to develop the intricate communications network that preceded movement formation among other groups. Like southern blacks, students had a natural network. The campus was the place they shared their concerns. It was the natural focal point of organizing. But it was a large place, for the most part, so at least at the beginning the basic units had to be smaller and the ties between them more definitive than was necessary once the movement was more developed.

In the late 1950s several things happened that presaged a new intellectual and/or campus movement. With the abatement of the McCarthy scare, liberal and socialist groups of students on different campuses formed new organizations. SLATE appeared at Berkeley, POLIT at Chicago, and VOICE at Michigan. Student journals, such as *New University Thought* and *Studies on the Left*, modeled after the *New Left Review* in London, also emerged. After the Bay of Pigs fiasco, Fair Play for Cuba chapters were started on several campuses. The groundwork was laid for a campus peace movement after the Berlin crisis in the summer of 1961, the resumption of nuclear testing, and the push for a massive civil defense program. As a result, the Student Peace Union and the student branch of SANE sprouted many campus chapters (O'Brien 1969, pp. 4–5).

Yet these groups were not themselves a student movement, merely the student branches of "adult" organizations. As one early leader commented, "We must not be led into the popular characterizations of our activity as a 'spontaneous new mass movement.' . . . In many of the protests—civil defense, capital punishment, the Uphaus conviction—what students did was to translate the undramatic campaigns of various adult organizations into dramatic student demonstrations. The direct action of the great peace movement has been similarly under adult auspices: The Committee for Non-Violent Action, the War Resisters' League, and the American Friends Service Committee. These movements were thus neither spontaneous nor strictly a student movement; the new thing is that students are involved at all" (Haber 1966, pp. 35–36).

What focused these isolated groups on different campuses was the southern sit-ins of 1960. "These actions had a powerfully inspiring effect on many socially concerned, intellectually sensitive white students, who were galvanized almost immediately into a variety of activities in support of the Southern civil rights struggle. Aside from their inspirational effect, the sit-ins served as a mechanism for bringing such students together for the first time for practical interaction over political issues. It did not take long for a mood of activism to take root among significant pockets of students on many campuses, once the prevailing pattern of political apathy had been disrupted" (Flacks 1970, p. 1).

In 1960 SDS was just one of several "national" student political groups. It had recently changed its name from the Student League for Industrial Democracy (SLID), but still remained the relatively insignificant youth affiliate of an aging social democratic clearinghouse for liberal, prolabor, anticommunist ideas. What put life into this moribund group were two University of Michigan students, Al Haber and Tom Hayden. In the late spring of 1960 Al Haber organized a conference at U.M. on "Human Rights in the North." "This conference began SDS's long association with SNCC and recruited some of the young people who subsequently became the 'old guard' SDS leadership" (Kissinger and Ross 1968, p. 16).

Shortly after the conference, the United Auto Workers donated $10,000 to SDS, which used the money to hire Haber as an organizer. He corresponded widely, mimeographed and mailed pamphlets, gave speeches, and generally made contacts with and between others (Sale 1973, p. 35). Both Hayden and Haber argued that the different issues on which activists were working were interconnected, that a movement had to be created to work for broad social change, that the university was a potential base and agency in a movement for social change, and that SDS could play an important role in this movement (O'Brien 1969, p. 6).

Despite this potential, SDS "remained practically non-existent as an organization in the late 1960-to-1961 school year. Then, in the summer of 1961, the 14th Congress of the National Student Association was held in Madison, Wisconsin. . . . It was regional and national meetings of NSA which first brought together Northern white radicals" (Kissinger and Ross 1968, p. 16).

What followed were years of hard organizing effort, stimulated by civil rights activity and campus protests (Sale 1973). In the early years SDS had many competitors for the affections of students, but none in the form of organizations claiming to represent students as students. The others were largely youth groups of national liberal and socialist organizations. SDS's activities were never confined solely to the campus, and usually sought to channel student activity to the support of other movement efforts. But its formation does illustrate once again the pattern found elsewhere.

The campus provided one form of communications network, but it was an unrefined one. The development of local radical activities and the southern sit-ins selected out of the mass of students those most likely to be receptive to organizing efforts. Hayden and Haber had access to resources from LID and organized labor to finance an office and embryonic staff until SDS eventually broke away in 1962 to stand by itself. More than SDS, the multitudinous events of the sixties served to goad students into political activity, but SDS provided them with a structure in which to engage in it. And an assist in all this, in the beginning, was the "established" student organization, the NSA, its "University Press Service . . . the press work of CORE, the NAACP and other adult groups . . . [which] combined to tell the world about student actions, and so to spread the movement" (Haber 1966, p. 35).

THE NATIONAL WELFARE RIGHTS ORGANIZATION

The welfare rights movement is an excellent example of movement entrepreneurship and government involvement in movement forma-tion. If ever a movement was *constructed*, this one was. The building blocks of its construction were the Great Society antipoverty programs and the plethora of black and especially white civil rights workers who were left "unemployed" with that movement's alternation and decline (Piven and Cloward 1971, p. 321). Many local welfare protest groups originated in antipoverty agencies in order to get more money for the poor. Many others came out of community organizations formed by liberal church groups and urban civil rights activitists a few years before. These groups were widely scattered throughout the country and not linked by any communications mechanism.

The entrepreneur who linked them in order to create a movement was George Wiley, a former chemistry professor and civil rights activist who left CORE after losing his bid to become national director. Attracted to the idea of organizing welfare recipients by a pamphlet written by Columbia social work professor Richard Cloward, later published in the *Nation*, Wiley organized the Poverty/Rights Action Center in Washington in May 1966. Shortly before the P/RAC office opened on a $15,000 budget, a conference on the guaranteed annual income had been held at the University of Chicago. Organized by three social work students, it brought together organizers and representatives of welfare groups, community organizations, and poverty workers. Although not specifically invited, Wiley came and was given a place on the conference program. When the participants seemed receptive to his ideas, Wiley announced to the press that there would be national demonstrations on June 30 in support of an Ohio march for adequate welfare already being organized by the Cleveland Council of Churches (Piven and Cloward 1977, pp. 288–91).

Wiley volunteered his new organization to coordinate the national support actions. Drawing upon his contacts from the civil rights movement and those he met at the conference, his "support activities" were highly successful. "On the morning of June 30, when they finally reached Columbus, the forty marchers were joined by two thousand recipients and sympathizers from other towns in Ohio. On the same day in New York two thousand recipients massed in front of City Hall to picket in the hot sun. . . . Groups of recipients in fifteen other cities . . . also joined demonstrations against 'the welfare' " (Piven and Cloward 1971, p. 323).

This action was followed by a national conference of a hundred people in August that elected a Co-ordinating Committee to plan a founding conference for the National Welfare Rights Organization. "The organizers were members of Students for a Democratic Society, church people, and most prominently, VISTA and other antipoverty program workers" (Piven and Cloward 1977, pp. 291–92).

VISTA volunteers continued to be the NWRO's "chief organizing resource" (Piven and Cloward 1971, p. 329). But they were not the only resource supplied by the government. "If the NWRO developed as a by-product of federal intervention in the cities, it later came to have quite direct relations with the national government. In 1968, the outgoing Johnson Administration granted NWRO more than $400,000 through the Department of Labor, a sum roughly equivalent to the total amount raised from private sources after the organization was formed. . . . Federal officials were aware that the money would go toward strengthening local relief groups" (Piven and Cloward 1971, pp. 329–30). In effect, the federal government was supporting a social movement organization whose purpose was to extract more money from state and local governments.

This intimate connection between the federal government, the NWRO, and recipient groups lasted only a few years. The NWRO eventually faced organizational problems it was unable to surmount, and antipoverty programs were dismantled by the Nixon administration (Piven and Cloward 1977). But while they lasted, local recipient groups were forged into a movement by experienced civil rights activists and government-funded volunteers under the direction of a single well-trained organizer with an entrepreneurial instinct.

THE WOMEN'S LIBERATION MOVEMENT[2]

Women are not well organized. Historically tied to the family and isolated from their own kind, only in the nineteenth century did women in this country have the opportunity to develop independent associations of their own. These associations took years and years of careful organizational work to build. Eventually they formed the basis for the suffrage movement of the early twentieth century. The associations took less time to die. Today the Women's Trade Union League, the General Federation of Women's Clubs, the Women's Christian Temperance Union, not to mention the powerful National Women's Suffrage Association, are all either dead or a pale shadow of their former selves.

As of 1960, not one organization of women had the potential to become a social movement organization, nor was there any form of "neutral" structure of interaction to provide the base for such an organization. The closest exception to the former was the National Women's Party, which has remained dedicated to feminist concerns since its inception in 1916. However, the NWP has been essentially a lobbying group for the Equal Rights Amendment since 1923. From the beginning, the NWP believed that a small group of women concentrating their efforts in the right places was more effective than a mass appeal, and so was not appalled by the fact that as late as 1969 even the majority of avowed feminists in this country had never heard of the ERA or the NWP.

The one large women's organization that might have provided a base for a social movement was the 180,000-member Federation of Business and Professional Women's Clubs. Yet, while it has steadily lobbied for legislation of importance to women, as late as "1966 BPW rejected a number of suggestions that it redefine . . . goals and tactics and become a kind of 'NAACP for women' . . . out of fear of being labeled 'feminist' " (Hole and Levine 1971, p. 89).

Before any social movement could develop

among women, there had to be created a structure to bring potential feminist sympathizers together. To be sure, groups such as the BPW, and institutions such as the women's colleges, might be a good source of adherents for such a movement. But they were determined not to be the source of leadership.

What happened in the 1960s was the development of two new communications networks in which women played prominent roles that allowed, even forced, an awakened interest in the old feminist ideas. As a result, the movement actually has two origins, from two different strata of society, with two different styles, orientations, values, and forms of organization. The first of these will be referred to as the "older branch" of the movement, partially because it began first and partially because it was on the older side of the "generation gap" that pervaded the sixties. Its most prominent organization is the National Organization for Women (NOW), which was also the first to be formed. The style of its movement organizations tends to be traditional with elected officers, boards of directors, bylaws, and the other trappings of democratic procedure. Conversely, the "younger branch" consisted of innumerable small groups engaged in a variety of activities whose contact with one another was always tenuous (Freeman 1975, p. 50).

The forces that led to NOW's formation were set in motion in 1961 when President Kennedy established the President's Commission on the Status of Women at the behest of Esther Petersen, then director of the Women's Bureau. Its 1963 report, American Women, and subsequent committee publications documented just how thoroughly women were denied many rights and opportunities. The most significant response to the activity of the President's commission was the establishment of some fifty state commissions to do similar research on a state level. The Presidential and State Commission activity laid the groundwork for the future movement in two significant ways: (1) It unearthed ample evidence of women's unequal status and in the process convinced many previously uninterested women that something should be done; (2) it created a climate of ex-

pectations that something would be done. The women of the Presidential and State Commissions who were exposed to these influences exchanged visits, correspondence, and staff, and met with one another at an annual commission convention. They were in a position to share and mutually reinforce their growing awareness and concern over women's issues. These commissions thus provided an embryonic communications network.

During this time, two other events of significance occurred. The first was the publication of Betty Friedan's The Feminine Mystique in 1963. A quick bestseller, the book stimulated many women to question the status quo and some women to suggest to Friedan that an organization be formed to do something about it. The second event was the addition of "sex" to the 1964 Civil Rights Act.

Many thought the "sex" provision was a joke, and the Equal Employment Opportunity Commission treated it as one, refusing to enforce it seriously. But a rapidly growing feminist coterie within the EEOC argued that "sex" would be taken more seriously if there were "some sort of NAACP for women" to put pressure on the government.

On June 30, 1966, these three strands of incipient feminism came together, and NOW was tied from the knot. At that time, government officials running the Third National Conference of Commissions on the Status of Women, ironically titled "Targets for Action," forbade the presentation of a suggested resolution calling for the EEOC to treat sex discrimination with the same consideration as race discrimination. The officials said one government agency could not be allowed to pressure another, despite the fact that the state commissions were not federal agencies. The small group of women who desired such a resolution had met the night before in Friedan's hotel room to discuss the possibility of a civil rights organization for women. Not convinced of its need, they chose instead to propose the resolution. When conference officials vetoed it, they held a whispered conversation over lunch and agreed to form an action organization "to bring women into full participation in the mainstream of American society now, assuming all the privileges and responsibilities thereof in truly equal partnership with men." The name NOW was coined by Friedan who was at the conference doing research on a book. When word leaked out, twenty-eight women paid five dollars each to join before the day was over (Friedan 1967, p. 4).

By the time the organizing conference was held the following October 29 through 30, over three hundred men and women had become charter members. It is impossible to do a breakdown on the composition of the charter membership, but one of the officers and board is possible. Such a breakdown accurately reflected NOW's origins. Friedan was president, two former EEOC commissioners were vice presidents, a representative of the United Auto Workers Women's Committee was secretary-treasurer, and there were seven past and present members of the State Commissions on the Status of Women on the twenty member board. One hundred twenty-six of the charter members were Wisconsin residents—and Wisconsin had the most active state Commission. Occupationally, the board and officers were primarily from the professions, labor, government, and communications fields. Of these, only those from labor had any experience in organizing, and they resigned a year later in a dispute over support of the Equal Rights Amendment. Instead of organizational experience, what the early NOW members had was experience in working with and in the media, and it was here that their early efforts were aimed.

As a result, NOW often gave the impression of being larger than it was. It was highly successful in getting in the press; much less successful in either bringing about concrete changes or forming an organization. Thus it was not until 1970, when the national press simultaneously did major stories on the women's liberation movement, that NOW's membership increased significantly.

In the meantime, unaware of and unknown to NOW, the EEOC, or the State Commissions, younger women began forming their own movement. Here, too, the groundwork had been laid some years before. The different so-

cial action projects of the sixties had attracted many women, who were quickly shunted into traditional roles and faced with the self-evident contradiction of working in a "freedom movement" but not being very free. No single "youth movement" activity or organization is responsible for forming the younger branch of the women's liberation movement, but together they created a "radical community" in which like-minded people continually interacted or were made aware of one another. This community provided the necessary network of communication and its radical ideas the framework of analysis that "explained" the dismal situation in which radical women found themselves.

Papers had been circulated on women and individual temporary women's caucuses had been held as early as 1964 (see Hayden and King 1966). But it was not until 1967 and 1968 that the groups developed a determined, if cautious, continuity and began to consciously expand themselves. At least five groups in five different cities (Chicago, Toronto, Detroit, Seattle, and Gainesville, Florida) formed spontaneously, independently of one another. They came at an auspicious moment, for 1967 was the year in which the blacks kicked the whites out of the civil rights movement, student power was discredited by SDS, and the New Left was on the wane. Only draft resistance activities were on the increase, and this movement more than any other exemplified the social inequities of the sexes. Men could resist the draft. Women could only counsel resistance.

At this point, there were few opportunities available for political work. Some women fit well into the secondary role of draft counseling. Many didn't. For years their complaints of unfair treatment had been forestalled by movement men with the dictum that those things could wait until after the Revolution. Now these political women found time on their hands, but still the men would not listen.

A typical example was the event that precipitated the formation of the Chicago group, the first independent group in this country. At the August 1967 National Conference for New Politics convention a women's caucus met for days, but was told its resolution wasn't significant enough to merit a floor discussion. By threatening to tie up the convention with procedural motions the women succeeded in having their statement tacked to the end of the agenda. It was never discussed. The chair refused to recognize any of the many women standing by the microphone, their hands straining upwards. When he instead called on someone to speak on "the forgotten American, the American Indian," five women rushed the podium to demand an explanation. But the chairman just patted one of them on the head (literally) and told her, "Cool down, little girl. We have more important things to talk about than women's problems."

The "little girl" was Shulamith Firestone, future author of *The Dialectic of Sex*, and she didn't cool down. Instead she joined with another Chicago woman she met there who had unsuccessfully tried to organize a women's group that summer, to call a meeting of the women who had halfheartedly attended those summer meetings. Telling their stories to those women, they stimulated sufficient rage to carry the group for three months, and by that time it was a permanent institution.

Another somewhat similar event occurred in Seattle the following winter. At the University of Washington an SDS organizer was explaining to a large meeting how white college youth established rapport with the poor whites with whom they were working. "He noted that sometimes after analyzing societal ills, the men shared leisure time by 'balling a chick together.' He pointed out that such activities did much to enhance the political consciousness of the poor white youth. A woman in the audience asked, 'And what did it do for the consciousness of the chick?' " (Hole and Levine 1971, p. 120). After the meeting, a handful of enraged women formed Seattle's first group.

Subsequent groups to the initial five were largely organized rather than formed spontaneously out of recent events. In particular, the Chicago group was responsible for the formation of many new groups in Chicago and in other cities. Unlike NOW, the women in the first groups had had years of experience as trained organizers. They knew how to utilize

the infrastructure of the radical community, the underground press, and the free universities to disseminate women's liberation ideas. Chicago, as a center of New Left activity, had the largest number of politically conscious organizers. Many traveled widely to left conferences and demonstrations, and most used the opportunity to talk with other women about the new movement. In spite of public derision by radical men, or perhaps because of it, young women steadily formed new groups around the country.

ANALYSIS

From these data there appear to be four essential elements involved in movement formation: (1) the growth of a preexisting communications network that is (2) co-optable to the ideas of the new movement; (3) a series of crises that galvanize into action people involved in a co-optable network, and/or (4) subsequent organizing effort to weld the spontaneous groups together into a movement. Each of these elements needs to be examined in detail.

Communications Network

The four movements we have looked at developed out of already existing networks within their populations. The church and the black college were the primary institutions through which southern blacks communicated their concerns. In the North the church was much weaker and the black college nonexistent, perhaps explaining why the movement had greater difficulty developing and surviving there. The Movement, composed primarily of white youth, had its centers on the campus because this was where that constituency could readily be found. Nonetheless, campuses were too large and disconnected for incipient movement leaders to find each other. Instead they fruitfully used the national and regional conferences of the CIA-financed National Student Association to identify and reach those students who were socially conscious. Of course, once the Movement took hold, it developed its own conferences and networks, so the subsequent exposé of the NSA came too late to stifle its growth. The welfare rights movement, much more than the others, was created by the conscious efforts of one person. But that person had to find constituents somewhere, and he found them most readily in groups already organized by antipoverty agencies. Organizers for the national movement, in turn, were found among former civil rights activists looking for new directions for their political energies.

The women's liberation movement, even more than the previous ones, illustrates the importance of a network precisely because the conditions for a movement existed *before* a network came into being, but the movement didn't exist until afterward. Analysis of socioeconomic causes have concluded that the movement could have started anytime within a 20 year period. Strain for women was as great in 1955 as in 1965 (Ferriss 1971). What changed was the organizational situation. It was not until new networks emerged among women aware of inequities beyond local boundaries that a movement could grow past the point of occasional, spontaneous uprisings. The fact that two distinct movements, with two separate origins, developed from two networks unaware of each other is further evidence of the key role of preexisting communications networks as the fertile soil in which new movements can sprout.

References to the importance of a preexisting communications network appear frequently in case studies of social movements, though the theoretical writers were much slower to recognize their salience. According to Buck (1920, pp. 43–44), the Grange established a degree of organization among American farmers in the 19th century that greatly facilitated the spread of future farmers' protests. Lipset has reported that in Saskatchewan, "the rapid acceptance of new ideas and movements . . . can be attributed mainly to the high degree of organization. . . . The role of the social structure of the western wheat belt in facilitating the rise of new movements has never been sufficiently appreciated by historians and sociologists. Repeated challenges and crises forced the western farmers to create many more community institutions (especially co-operatives and economic pressure groups) than are necessary in a more stable

area. These groups in turn provided a structural basis for immediate action in critical situations. [Therefore] though it was a new radical party, the C.C.F. did not have to build up an organization from scratch" (1959, p. 206).

Similarly, Heberle (1951, p. 232) reports several findings that Nazism was most successful in small, well-integrated communities. As Lipset put it, these findings "sharply challenge the various interpretations of Nazism as the product of the growth of anomie and the general rootlessness of modern urban industrial society" (1959, p. 146).

Indirect evidence attesting to the essential role of formal and informal communications networks is found in diffusion theory, which emphasizes the importance of personal interaction rather than impersonal media communication in the spread of ideas (Rogers 1962, Lionberger 1960). This personal influence occurs through the organizational patterns of a community (Lionberger 1960, p. 73). It does not occur through the mass media. The mass media may be a source of information, but they are not a key source of influence.

Their lesser importance in relation to preexisting communications networks was examined in one study on "The Failure of an Incipient Social Movement" (Jackson, Peterson, Bull, Monsen, and Richmond 1960). In 1957 a potential tax protest movement in Los Angeles generated considerable interest and publicity for a little over a month but was dead within a year. According to the authors, this did not reflect a lack of public notice. They concluded that "mass communication alone is probably insufficient without a network of communication specifically linking those interested in the matter. . . . If a movement is to grow rapidly, it cannot rely upon its own network of communication, but must capitalize on networks already in existence" (p. 37).

A major reason it took social scientists so long to acknowledge the importance of communications networks was because the prevailing theories of the post-World War II era emphasized increasing social dislocation and anomie. Mass society theorists, as they were called, hypothesized that significant community institutions that linked individuals to governing elites were breaking down, that society was becoming a mass of isolated individuals. These individuals were seen as increasingly irresponsible and ungovernable, prone to irrational protests because they had no mediating institutions through which to pursue grievances (Kornhauser 1959).

In emphasizing disintegrating vertical connections, mass society theorists passed lightly over the role of horizontal ones, only occasionally acknowledging that "the combination of internal contact and external isolation facilitates the work of the mass agitator" (Kornhauser 1959, p. 218). This focus changed in the early seventies. Pinard's study of the Social Credit Party of Quebec (1971) severely criticized mass society theory, arguing instead that "when strains are severe and widespread a new movement is more likely to meet its early success among the more strongly integrated citizens" (Pinard 1971, p. 192).

This insight was expanded by Oberschall (1973), who created a six-cell table to predict both the occurrence and type of protest. As did the mass society theorists, Oberschall said that even when there are grievances, protest will not occur outside institutional channels by those who are connected, through their own leadership or patron/client relationships, with governing elites. Among those who are segmented from such elites, the type of protest will be determined by whether there is communal, associational, or little organization. In the latter case, discontent is expressed through riots or other short-lived violent uprisings. "It is under conditions of strong . . . ties and segmentation that the possibility of the rapid spread of opposition movements on a continuous basis exists" (p. 123).

The movements we have studied would confirm Oberschall's conclusions, but not as strongly as he makes them. In all these cases a preexisting communications network was a necessary but insufficient condition for movement formation. Yet the newly formed networks among student radicals, welfare recipients, and women can hardly compare with the long-standing ties provided by the southern black churches and colleges. Their ties were tenuous

and may not have survived the demise of their movements.

The importance of segmentation, or lack of connection with relevant elites, is less obvious in the sixties' movements. The higher socioeconomic status of incipient feminists and Movement leaders would imply greater access to elites than is true for blacks or welfare recipients. If Oberschall were correct, these closer connections should either have permitted easier and more rapid grievance solutions or more effective social control. They did neither. Indeed, it was the group most closely connected to decision-making elites—women of the Presidential and State Commission—who were among the earliest to see the need of a protest organization. Women of the younger branch of the movement did have their grievances against the men of the New Left effectively suppressed for several years, but even they eventually rejected this kind of elite control, even when it meant rejecting the men.

Conversely, Piven and Cloward show that the establishment of closer ties between leaders of local welfare rights groups and welfare workers through advisory councils and community coordinators led to a curtailment of militance and the institutionalization of grievances (1977, pp. 326–31). They also argue that the development of government-funded community programs effectively co-opted many local black movement leaders in the North and that federal channeling of black protest in the South into voter registration projects focused the movement there into traditional electoral politics (ibid., p. 253). In short, the evidence about the role of segmentation in movement formation is ambiguous. The effect may be varied considerably by the nature of the political system.

Co-optability

A recurrent theme in our studies is that not just any communications network will do. It must be one that is co-optable to the ideas of the new movement. The Business and Professional Women's (BPW) clubs were a network among women, but having rejected feminism, they could not overcome the ideological barrier to new political action until after feminism became established. Similarly, there were other communications networks among students than that of the NSA, for example fraternities and athletic associations. But these were not networks that politically conscious young people were likely to be involved in.

On the other hand, the women on the Presidential and State Commissions and the feminist coterie of the EEOC were co-optable largely because their immersion in the facts of female status and the details of sex discrimination cases made them very conscious of the need for change. Likewise, the young women of the "radical community" lived in an atmosphere of questioning, confrontation, and change. They absorbed an ideology of "freedom" and "liberation" far more potent than any latent "antifeminism" might have been.

NSA does not appear to have been as readily co-optable to the Movement as the new women's networks were to feminism. As an association of student governments, its participants had other concerns besides political ones. But while it didn't transform itself, it was a source of recruitment and a forum for discussion that gave the early SDS organizers contacts on many campuses.

While no data are available that would identify specific networks within the black churches and colleges that were co-optable to the emerging civil rights movement, we can reasonably assume there were some. Not all blacks initially supported the Montgomery boycott or agreed that the protests should be extended. The MIA and SCLC had to find like-minded people and then coordinate their actions.

Exactly what makes a network co-optable is harder to elucidate. Pinard (1971, p. 186) noted the necessity for groups to "*possess* or *develop* an ideology or simply subjective interests congruent with that of a new movement" for them to "act as mobilizing rather than restraining agents toward that movement," but did not further explore what affected the "primary group climate." More illumination is provided by the diffusion of innovation studies that point out the necessity for new ideas to fit in with already established norms for changes to happen easily.

Furthermore, a social system that has as a value "innovativeness" (as the radical community did) will more rapidly adopt ideas than one that looks upon the habitual performance of traditional practices as the ideal (as most organized women's groups did in the fifties). Usually, as Lionberger (1960, p. 91) points out, "people act in terms of past experience and knowledge." People who have had similar experiences are likely to share similar perceptions of a situation and to mutually reinforce those perceptions as well as their subsequent interpretation. A co-optable network, then, is one whose members have had common experiences that predispose them to be receptive to the particular new ideas of the incipient movement and who are not faced with structural or ideological barriers to action. If the new movement as an "innovation" can interpret these experiences and perceptions in ways that point out channels for social action, then participation in a social movement becomes the logical thing to do.

The Role of Crises

As our examples have illustrated, similar perceptions must be translated into action. This is often done by a crisis. For blacks in Montgomery, this was generated by Rosa Parks's refusal to give up her seat on a bus to a white man. For women who formed the older branch of the women's movement, the impetus to organize was the refusal of the EEOC to enforce the sex provision of Title VII, precipitated by the concomitant refusal of federal officials at the conference to allow a supportive resolution. For younger women there were a series of minor crises.

While not all movements are formed by such precipitating events, they are quite common as they serve to crystallize and focus discontent. From their own experiences, directly and concretely, people feel the need for change in a situation that allows for an exchange of feelings with others, mutual validation, and a subsequent reinforcement of innovative interpretation. Perception of an immediate need for change is a major factor in predisposing people to accept new ideas (Rogers 1962, p. 280). Nothing makes desire for change more acute than a crisis. Such a crisis need not be a major one; it need only embody collective discontent.

Organizing Efforts

A crisis will only catalyze a well-formed communications network. If such networks are embryonically developed or only partially co-optable, the potentially active individuals in them must be linked together by someone. This is essentially what George Wiley did for local recipient groups and what other SDS organizers did with the contacts they made in NSA and on campuses. As Jackson et al. (1960, p. 37) stated, "Some protest may persist where the source of trouble is constantly present. But interest ordinarily cannot be maintained unless there is a welding of spontaneous groups into some stable organization." In other words, people must be organized. Social movements do not simply occur.

The role of the organizer in movement formation is another neglected aspect of the theoretical literature. There has been great concern with leadership, but the two roles are distinct and not always performed by the same individual. In the early stages of a movement, it is the organizer much more than any leader who is important, and such an individual or cadre must often operate behind the scenes. The nature and function of these two roles was most clearly evident in the Townsend old-age movement of the thirties. Townsend was the "charismatic" leader, but the movement was organized by his partner, real estate promoter Robert Clements. Townsend himself acknowledges that without Clements' help, the movement would never have gone beyond the idea stage (Holzman 1963).

The importance of organizers is pervasive in the sixties' movements. Dr. King may have been the public spokesperson of the Montgomery Bus Boycott who caught the eye of the media, but it was E. D. Nixon who organized it. Certainly the "organizing cadre" that young women in the radical community came to be was key to the growth of that branch of the women's liberation movement, despite the fact that no

"leaders" were produced (and were actively discouraged). The existence of many leaders but no organizers in the older branch of the women's liberation movement readily explains its subsequent slow development. The crucial role of organizers in SDS and the National Welfare Rights Organization was described earlier.

The function of the organizer has been explored indirectly by other analysts. Rogers (1962) devotes many pages to the "change agent" who, while he does not necessarily weld a group together or "construct" a movement, does many of the same things for agricultural innovation that an organizer does for political change. Mass society theory makes frequent reference to the "agitator," though not in a truly informative way. Interest groups are often organized by single individuals and some of them evolve into social movements. Salisbury's study of farmers' organizations finds this a recurrent theme. He also discovered that "a considerable number of farm groups were subsidized by other, older, groups. . . . The Farm Bureau was organized and long sustained by subsidies, some from federal and state governments, and some by local businessmen" (Salisbury 1969, p. 13).

These patterns are similar to ones we have found in the formation of social movements. Other organizations, even the government, often serve as training centers for organizers and sources of material support to aid the formation of groups and/or movements. The civil rights movement was the training ground for many an organizer of other movements. The League for Industrial Democracy financed SDS in its early days, and the NSA provided indirect support by hiring many SDS organizers as NSA staff. The role of the government in the formation of the National Welfare Rights Organization was so significant that it would lead one to wonder if this association should be considered more of an interest group in the traditional sense than a movement "core" organization.

From all this it would appear that training as an organizer or at least as a proselytizer or entrepreneur of some kind is a necessary background for those individuals who act as movement innovators. Even in something as seemingly spontaneous as a social movement, the professional is more valuable than the amateur.

Notes

1. The only use of this significant word appears rather incidentally in Turner (1964, p. 123).

2. Data for this section are based on my observations while a founder and participant in the younger branch of the Chicago women's liberation movement from 1967 through 1969 and editor of the first (at that time, only) national newsletter. I was able, through extensive correspondence and interviews, to keep a record of how each group around the country started, where the organizers got the idea from, who they had talked to, what conferences were held and who attended, the political affiliations (or lack of them) of the first members, and so forth. Although I was a member of Chicago NOW, information on the origins of it and the other older branch organizations comes entirely through *ex post facto* interviews of the principals and examination of early papers in preparation for my dissertation on the women's liberation movement. Most of my informants requested that their contribution remain confidential.

References

Adorno, L. W., et al.
1950   *The Authoritarian Personality.* New York: Harper & Row.

Bird, Caroline
1968   *Born Female: The High Cost of Keeping Women Down.* New York: McKay.

Blumer, Herbert
1951   "Social Movements." In A. M. Lee, ed., *New Outline of the Principles of Sociology.* New York: Barnes and Noble.
1057   "Collective Behavior." In Joseph B Gittler, ed., *Review of Sociology: Analysis of a Decade.* New York: Wiley.

Brink, William, and Louis Harris
1964   *The Negro Revolution in America.* New York: Simon & Schuster.

Buck, Solon J.
1920   *The Agrarian Crusade.* New Haven: Yale University Press.

Cantril, Hadley
1941   *The Psychology of Social Movements.* New York: Wiley.

Clark, Kenneth B.
1966   "The Civil Rights Movement: Momentum and Organization." *Daedalus,* Winter.

Cloward, Richard
1966   "A Strategy to End Poverty." *Nation,* 2 May.

Coleman, James
1957   *Community Conflict.* Glencoe, Ill.: Free Press.

Currie, Elliott, and Jerome H. Skolnick
1970   "Critical Note on Conceptions of Collective Behavior." *Annals of the American Academy of Political and Social Science* 391 (September): 34–45.

Dahrendorf, Ralf
1959   *Class and Class Conflict in Industrial Society.* Palo Alto, Calif.: Stanford University Press.

Davis, James C.
1962   "Toward a Theory of Revolution." *American Sociological Review* 27, no. 1: 5–19.

Dawson, C. A., and W. E. Gettys
1929   *An Introduction to Sociology.* New York: Ronald Press.

Edelsberg, Herman
1965   "NYU 18th Conference on Labor." *Labor Relations Reporter* 61 (August): 253–55.

Ferriss, Abbott L.
1971   *Indicators of Trends in the Status of American Women.* New York: Russell Sage Foundation.

Firestone, Shulamith
1971   *The Dialectic of Sex.* New York: Morrow.

Flacks, Richard
1970   "The New Left and American Politics: After Ten Years." Paper presented at the American Political Science Association convention, September.

Frazier, E. Franklin
    1963   *The Negro Church in America.* New York: Schocken.
Freeman, Jo
    1975   *The Politics of Women's Liberation.* New York: Longman.
Friedan, Betty
    1963   *The Feminine Mystique.* New York: Dell.
    1967   "NOW: How It Began." *Women Speaking,* April.
Griffiths, Martha
    1966   Speech of 20 June, *Congressional Record.*
Gurr, Ted
    1970   *Why Men Rebel.* Princeton: Princeton University Press.
Haber, Robert A.
    1966   "From Protest to Radicalism: An Appraisal of the Student Movement: 1960." In Michael Cohen and Dennis Hale, eds., *The New Student Left.* Boston: Beacon Press.
Hayden, Casey, and Mary King
    1966   "A Kind of Memo." *Liberation,* April.
Heberle, Rudolph
    1951   *Social Movements.* New York: Appleton-Century-Crofts.
Hoffer, Eric
    1951   *The True Believer.* New York: Harper & Row.
Hole, Judith, and Ellen Levine
    1971   *Rebirth of Feminism.* New York: Quadrangle.
Holloway, Harry
    1969   *The Politics of the Southern Negro.* New York: Random House.
Holzman, Abraham
    1963   *The Townsend Movement: A Political Study.* New York: Bookman.
Jackson, Maurice, et al.
    1960   "The Failure of an Incipient Social Movement." *Pacific Sociological Review* 3, no. 1: 40.
Killian, Lewis M.
    1964   "Social Movements." In R. E. L. Faris, ed., *Handbook of Modern Sociology.* Chicago: Rand McNally.

King, C. Wendell
    1956   *Social Movements in the United States.* New York: Random House.
King, Martin Luther, Jr.
    1958   *Stride Toward Freedom.* New York: Harper & Row.
Kissinger, C. Clark, and Bob Ross
    1968   "Starting in '60: Or from SLID to Resistance." *New Left Notes,* 10 June.
Kornhauser, William
    1959   *The Politics of Mass Society.* Glencoe, Ill.: Free Press.
Lang, Kurt, and Gladys Engle Lang
    1961   *Collective Dynamics.* New York: Cromwell.
Lionberger, Herbert F.
    1960   *Adoption of New Ideas and Practices.* Ames: Iowa State University Press.
Lipset, Seymour M.
    1959   *Agrarian Socialism.* Berkeley: University of California Press.
Lowi, Theodore J.
    1971   *The Politics of Discord.* New York: Basic Books.
McCarthy, John, and Mayer N. Zald
    1973   *The Trend of Social Movements in America: Professionalization and Resource Mobilization.* Morristown, N.J.: General Learning Press.
Oberschall, Anthony
    1973   *Social Conflict and Social Movements.* Englewood Cliffs, N.J.: Prentice-Hall.
O'Brien, James
    1969   *A History of the New Left, 1960–68.* Cambridge, Mass.: New England Free Press.
Pinard, Maurice
    1968   "Mass Society and Political Movements: A New Formulation." *American Journal of Sociology* 73, no. 6 (May): 680–92.
    1971   *The Rise of a Third Party: A Study in Crisis Politics.* Englewood Cliffs, N.J.: Prentice-Hall.
Piven, Frances Fox, and Richard Cloward
    1971   *Regulating the Poor: The Functions of Public Welfare.* New York: Pantheon.

1977   *Poor People's Movements: Why They Succeed, How They Fail.* New York: Pantheon.

Rogers, Everett M.
1962   *Diffusion of Innovations.* New York: Free Press.

Rudwick, Elliott, and August Meier
1970   "Organizational Structure and Goal Succession: A Comparative Analysis of the NAACP and CORE, 1964–1968." *Social Science Quarterly* 51 (June).

Sale, Kirkpatrick
1973   *SDS.* New York: Random House.

Salisbury, Robert H.
1969   "An Exchange Theory of Interest Groups." *Midwest Journal of Political Science* 13, no. 1 (February).

Shils, Edward
1970   "Center and Periphery." In Center for Social Organization Studies, *Selected Essays.* Chicago: University of Chicago Press.

Smelser, Neil J.
1963   *Theory of Collective Behavior.* Glencoe, Ill.: Free Press.

Toch, Hans
1965   *The Social Psychology of Social Movements.* Indianapolis: Bobbs-Merrill.

Turner, Ralph H.
1964   "Collective Behavior and Conflict: New Theoretical Frameworks." *Sociological Quarterly.*

Turner, Ralph H., and Lewis M. Killian
1957   *Collective Behavior.* Englewood Cliffs, N.J.: Prentice-Hall.

Zinn, Howard
1964   *SNCC: The New Abolitionists.* Boston: Beacon Press.